# THE MAN WHO COULDN'T WAIT

V. J. Carroll worked as a journalist with Queensland Newspapers in Brisbane in the 1950s. He joined John Fairfax Ltd in 1960, became editor of the *Australian Financial Review* early in 1964, then managing editor of the *Financial Review* and the *National Times* from 1970 to 1975. For the next five years he was chief executive of Fairfax's magazine subsidiary, Sungravure. In 1980 he became editor of the *Sydney Morning Herald*, then editor-in chief until 1984 Before retiring from the company early in 1986 he was director of several Fairfax subsidiary companies, including Newcastle Newspapers and Illawarra Newspapers.

# THE MAN WHO COULDN'T WAIT

### V. J. CARROLL

William Heinemann Australia

*TO MY WIFE*
*VALERIE LAWSON*

This edition published 1991

First published 1990 by
William Heinemann Australia
22 Salmon Street, Port Melbourne, Victoria 3207

Edited by Norman Rowe
Typeset in 11/13 Garamond Light Condensed
by Southern Cross Typesetting, Keysborough, Victoria
Printed in Australia by Australian Print Group

National Library of Australia
  cataloguing-in-publication data:

Carroll, V. J. (Victor J.), 1924–
  The man who couldn't wait.

  Includes index.
  ISBN 0 85561 431 5.

  1. Fairfax, Warwick, 1960–    . 2. John Fairfax & Sons — Reorganisation.
  3. Consolidation and merger of corporations — Australia. 4. Corporate reorganisation
  — Australia. 5. Newspaper publishing — Australia. 6 Banks and banking — Australia.
  I. Title.

338.76107050994

# CONTENTS

# *Fairfax Family Tree*

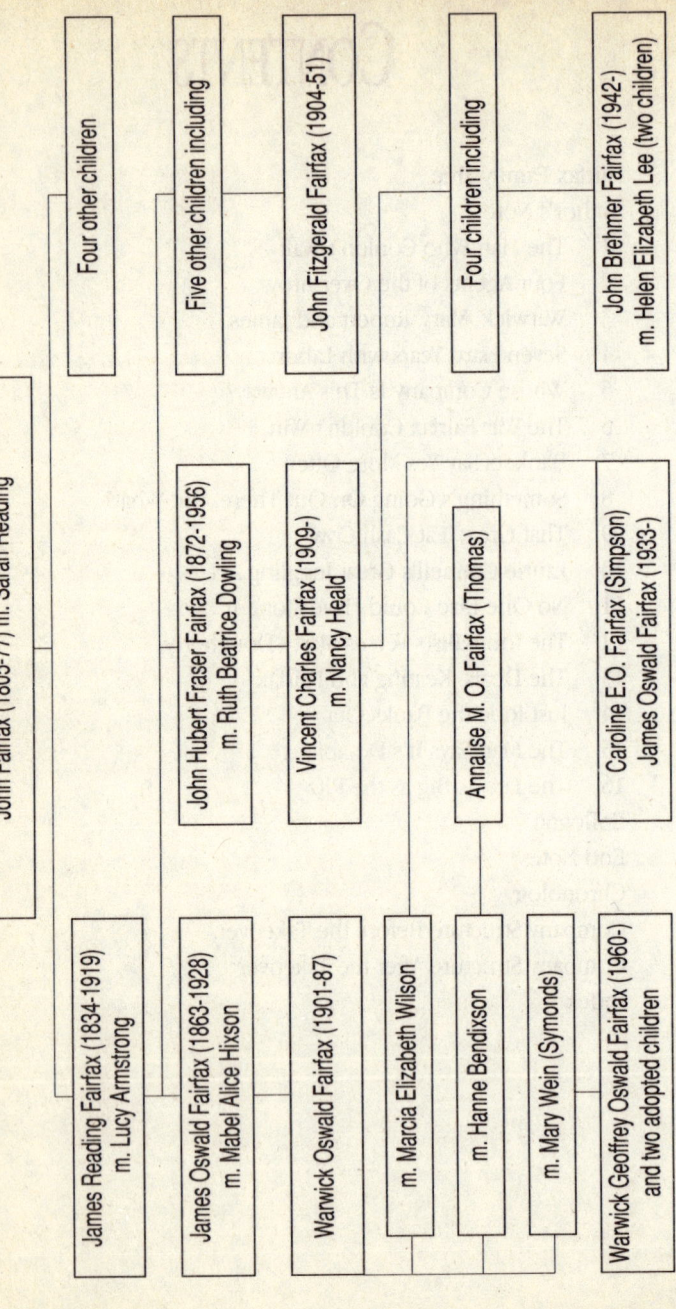

# AUTHOR'S NOTE

This book is about the John Fairfax Ltd takeover debacle. It began as a rich family saga of obsessions, bitterness and intrigue and became a case study of what happened when the banks were let loose in the 1980s. Both themes are spliced with the heady influence of the Fourth Estate factor — the factor governing the peculiar love-hate relationship that exists between the press and politicians and drives self-made men of property to pay outrageous prices to satisfy their desire to own newspapers and television networks. The Fourth Estate factor was very active in the 1980s. Combined with deregulation of the banks and foreign exchanges, it produced stockmarket explosions that left four major media groups — three television networks and the John Fairfax Group — over-loaded with debt. The clean-up of the resulting mess will continue well into the 1990s.

All four media groups were corporate follies, but the Fairfax folly was unique, and not only because it split the family that had owned and controlled one of Australia's leading newspapers for nearly 150 years. In the 1980s, as in all boom periods, a new generation of corporate adventurers appeared to make money-making look easy. The banks threw their corporate history books away and fell over themselves to help. There was no doubt about what the new takeover masters — Alan Bond, Christopher Skase, George Herscu, Abe Goldberg — wanted: they wanted more. They were real gamblers. As crises mounted in the corporate pyramids the banks had helped them build, they all went for one last big play to try and avoid disaster. Only the great survivor, Robert Holmes a Court, faced reality after October 1987 and sold down to the survival point.

Young Warwick Fairfax was different. He didn't want more. He was prepared to settle for less to achieve what he wanted. He saw himself as a crusader, coming home to save the company, in particular the *Sydney Morning Herald*, from a board of directors and senior managers who had helped make it one of the most desirable newspaper companies in the world. He was returning to recapture the Holy Land from the Turks. Warwick stood to inherit at least 30 per cent of the company. But he could not wait. Spurning the cautious advice of prudent merchant bankers, he put himself into the hands of assorted mercenaries, agreeing to pay them $100 million to do the takeover job. The ANZ Bank agreed to finance the raid. If the bankers were aware of the missionary nature of the enterprise, they appeared unconcerned. They had not met Warwick when they first made their loan commitment. Warwick was in the grip of his vision. His advisers were in the grip of their anticipated fees. If any party to the venture should have been expected to urge caution and restraint, it was the ANZ Bank. But when the stock-market fell in October 1987, and the takeover should have been called off, the bank charged on with Warwick, backing the crusade for $2 billion. Mission accomplished, at the cost of crippling the company with the debt he had borrowed to take it over, Warwick went off to live, modestly, in Chicago. He was more at home in North America than in Australia. Two years after the takeover he was working as a management trainee at the *Chicago Tribune*, learning the publishing business from the bottom up. A year later his equity in John Fairfax Group was probably worthless. The company's main hope for survival would be the introduction of new owners.

The takeover of John Fairfax Ltd was the apogee of the bank-financed takeover extravaganza in Australia in the 1980s. In the court case that followed Warwick's refusal to pay the $100 million fee to his advisers in 1988, expert witnesses were called to testify that a prudent merchant banker would, unlike Warwick's advisers, have urged him to call the whole thing off after October 1987. If a prudent merchant banker should have said, 'Don't do it, Warwick', what should a prudent commercial banker have said? This was not raised as an issue in the fee case, but it was the issue of the bank lending boom of the 1980s. The ANZ's $2 billion loan changed a very profitable, virtually debt-free company (sometimes wayward and indulgent, but a vigorous competitor and developer of new products) into a company dependent on a precarious and limited financial life-support system. On a generous assessment the bank's decision to go with Warwick after 19 October 1987 might have been described, paraphrasing Marshall Bosquet on the charge of the Light Brigade: It was magnificent, but was it banking?

Warwick Geoffrey Oswald Fairfax was conditioned to take a fairly elevated view of the world. His father, Warwick Oswald (later Sir Warwick) Fairfax, gave a snapshot of his view in his foreword to *Men, Parties and Politics*, a collection of articles published in the *Sydney Morning Herald* during the August 1943 Federal election campaign in which the newspaper's editorials, for the first time, did not oppose the Labor Party — though, it is worth remembering, neither did they support it. The paper hedged by advocating a vote for individual candidates. Labor won in a landslide:

> It is partly, I think, the very length of its history — now 112 years — which has given the last three generations of Fairfaxes controlling the *Herald* the peculiar sense of philosophic detachment from the world with which every day they deal, which is really one of the secrets of the *Herald*'s impartiality. This attitude is both incomprehensible and infuriating to some of those who live by politics, and to others, who think that the world is coming to an end because the wrong party gets in for three years and they lose a little money.

Impartiality? Neville Wran did not agree after 1976. But that essay in 1943 was a Fairfax view of the Fourth Estate factor — the special position the media have, or are assumed by the media and politicians to have, in the affairs of the nation. Before the 1980s the Fourth Estate factor was fairly predictable: the media were anti-Labor, with rare aberrations, like that of the *Sydney Morning Herald* in 1943, and when the paper positively supported Labor in 1961, and the *Age* and the *Australian* in 1972. This situation had changed, or was changing, when the Hawke Government set out to rectify it at the end of 1986 with new legislation that would break up the Herald and Weekly Times group and frustrate the growth of John Fairfax Ltd. The new laws triggered market reactions which changed the ownership and control of the Australian media in ways the Government could not have foreseen. In 1990 the Government was still changing the ownership rules to try and control the consequences of what happened in the market when they let the banks loose and changed the media rules in 1986.

This book is not structured as a straight chronological account of the events leading up to and following the Fairfax takeover. In the early chapters I have dealt separately with the four themes that came together in 1987: what was happening in the family, the company, Australian politics and world banking. In the final chapters I have again broken the narrative into themes: the continuing role of Government, particularly of the Federal Treasurer, Paul Keating, in shaping events; the roles of the ANZ Bank, Drexel Burnham Lambert and the company's advisers, particularly William E. Simon and his company WSGP; and finally how Rothwells's $100 million fee epitomised the way fees became the siren's call of banking, the professions and the property market in the 1980s.

If at times you need a fix on the main story line, refer to the Chronology at the end of the book: it gives a concise record of events from 1959 to 1990.

I have relied on many sources for information used in this book. These can be found in the End Notes, which also explain or expand on material used in each chapter.

Many of those involved in the events leading up to, during, and after the takeover, have been generous with their time and willingness to discuss what happened and why it happened. Two who would not talk to me for the purposes of this book were Mary Fairfax and Warwick Fairfax. Mary Fairfax referred all inquiries to Warwick who, once out of the witness box of the epic Supreme Court case following the takeover, was not talking publicly about anything. Nevertheless, in acknowledging those who helped me write this book, Warwick's contribution must come first. By refusing to pay the $100 million takeover fee he had agreed upon with Rothwells Ltd, he precipitated a court case which gave a rare, though limited, public insight into the business, professional and banking practices of the 1980s. This insight will, no doubt, be greatly illuminated by liquidators' examinations, special investigations and, possibly, prosecutions, in the 1990s. Journalists who reported the fee case were generous with their notes and documents, particularly John Hurst, Alan Deans, Catherine Armitage, Tony Stephens, Trevor Sykes and Gavin Souter.

During the 1980s Australian newspapers devoted more space to reporting events in their own industry than they had probably devoted in the previous 200 years. Living in Sydney I have relied mainly on reports in the *Sydney Morning Herald*, the *Australian* and the *Australian Financial Review* from 1979 to 1989, to refresh my memory and keep the record straight. The reports usually tried to interpret as well as record and were often written under the pressure of imminent deadlines. They stand up well to critical hindsight, which is more than can be said for many business and professional practices of that decade.

Apart from my obvious debt to these sources, and the Fairfax reference library which made them available, I am particularly grateful to the editor of the *Law Society Journal* for permission to use extracts from the Journal's profile of the Law practice of C. R. Fieldhouse, published in the *Law Society Journal*, vol. 21, 1983.

The Fairfax reference library does not show in the company's balance sheet and, as far as I know, has never been revalued. I am very grateful for continued access to its stores of information and for the help of the library staff, particularly of Franca Bopf. Sue Graham decoded my typed copy and transferred it, in much improved condition, to her word processor. Valerie Lawson supported me when I staggered and kept me going in this attempt to explain to myself what happened to a fine institution.

*V. J. Carroll*

# CHAPTER 1

# THE MAN WHO COULDN'T WAIT

At 10 a.m. on 7 December 1987, three Fairfax family directors of John Fairfax Ltd gathered for the last time in the boardroom of the company's grim concrete pile off Broadway, Sydney. They were there to hand over the company to its new owner, Warwick Geoffrey Oswald Fairfax, half-brother of the outgoing chairman, James Fairfax, cousin several times removed of Sir Vincent Fairfax, and of Sir Vincent's son, the deputy chairman, John B. Fairfax. The two non-Fairfax directors had already resigned. Sir Eric Neal had been a director for only 15 months. Sir David Griffin, who had been a director for 11 years, was at his country property near Mittagong. James had their resignations in his pocket. He had suggested to David Griffin that it was hardly worth driving to Sydney for the short, formal board proceedings that were to follow. Ten weeks previously, on the night of Sunday, 29 August, twenty-six-year-old Warwick (fifteen years younger than John, half the age of James and a third the age of Vincent), had called on James and John to tell them, 12 hours before he announced it to the world, that he was going to make a takeover bid for the company. The bid, through Tryart Pty Ltd, the shelf company acquired for the purpose, was now costing him over $2 billion, borrowed from the ANZ Bank. He was going to have to borrow a further $500 million before he started to reduce the debt.

It was the biggest takeover by one person in Australia's business history. Kerry Packer had paid $115 million for the outside interests in Consolidated Press Holdings Ltd four years previously. But he had bought out his brother Clyde in amicable circumstances some years before that. Whatever friendly intentions young Warwick may have had towards his half-brother and cousins, his bid had split the fifth generation of a family which had, wholly or substantially, owned and controlled the enterprise for 146 years — one of the longest continuous ownerships of any substantial enterprise in the world.

In the last 50 years the family and its managers and advisers had coped with the problem of maintaining the family's control while finding the funds for growth, a problem that had defeated most of the old Australian family enterprises many years previously. Now John Fairfax Ltd was staying in the family all right, in the hands of one man, the youngest, who would be the first sole proprietor since his great-great-grandfather, John Fairfax. His great-grandfather, James Reading Fairfax, had called himself senior proprietor and had run the business, building up its treasured property, the *Sydney Morning Herald,* for around 60 years. His grandfather had been a partner or director for 40 years. His father had been a director for 50 years, chairman for nearly 46 of them. On that family form young Warwick could have looked forward to 50 years at or near the helm, without borrowing $2 billion to buy out the rest of the family and the public. But he could not wait.

Warwick had planned his bid while ostensibly getting some work experience in the company's marketing department in the months after May 1987. His attendance had fallen away a bit in August, but who was going to question the movements of the late former chairman's son and heir who had, earlier in the year, a month after his father's death, while still at Harvard, borrowed and spent $30 million in one stockmarket hit to lift his stake in the company by 1.5 million shares? Warwick's increasing absences had been noted by his immediate minders in the company but their significance had been discounted by the top management. John Fairfax Ltd, like many Australian public companies in the first half of 1987, was deeply concerned with potential takeover threats. But its look-outs were focused on the world outside, particularly on the man from the West, Robert Holmes a Court, whom Fairfax newspapers had dubbed the Great Acquirer before October 1987, and the Great Divester after that.

With his capacity to send out confusing signals, disguise his aims, and manipulate the media, he might have been more accurately called the Great Bamboozler. In any case the Fairfax directors and executives felt fairly secure. The family, including young Warwick, and the company's retirement funds, controlled over 60 per cent of the company's shares.

A thought had been ticking away at the back of at least two minds among the company's top executives and advisers, that one day young Warwick might make a move for control of the company, but not yet, and certainly not on such a grand scale. Three days before springing a bid on his half-brother and cousins, he had attended a monthly board meeting with them, as he had done for several months, without revealing that he was anything other than what they assumed him to be: a formally well-educated tyro, there to learn his way around the business, one day to take his place on the board as they had done, eventually, if he wanted it, to become managing director and then chairman. No poker player ever played his cards so close to the chest as W. G. O. Fairfax did in the months leading up to 29 August. Now, ten weeks later, with the company as good as in his pocket, he was still giving nothing away.

As the deposed family members waited, with their legal adviser Rodney Halstead of Mallesons Stephen Jaques, and the company secretary, Ian Cumming, they were not sure who, or how many, Warwick was bringing with him to form his new board. During the planning of this meeting, Warwick's legal adviser, Aleco Vrisakis, had been asked that very question. He said he had been instructed not to reveal who would be on the new board. Perhaps Warwick himself was still not sure. When the agreement for the takeover exercise was being finalised and signed on 28 August between Warwick and his takeover adviser, Laurie Connell and their companies, Connell had pressed Warwick to agree to appoint Connell and his associate Bert Reuter to the Fairfax board when Warwick took control of the company. But Warwick would not commit himself. Six weeks previously James and John had said they would continue as directors of John Fairfax Ltd even though they were selling their shares. Time and events had shown their positions to be untenable. But they had not given Warwick formal notice of their intention to quit for good.

When Warwick finally came in it was with four men. One was Martin Dougherty, ex-journalist and public relations man, who had become close to Sir Warwick and Mary Fairfax during the 1980s. Dougherty had been in the Tryart enterprise from the start, had been the company's spokesman during the takeover offer, and had been widely assumed to be the new editorial director of John Fairfax Ltd. The others were Ronald John Cotton, former chief financial executive of John Fairfax, who was to be the new group managing director, operations; Alexander Emil (Aleco) Vrisakis, Tryart's legal adviser; and Lawrence Robert Connell, chairman of Rothwells Ltd, the merchant bank that had brought the takeover deal together for a $100 million fee that had set the high-fee merchant banking industry agog with shock, horror and envy.

Connell was the surprise. Rothwells had been badly holed in the 19 October share crash. A desperate rescue had been mounted for it with the help of his friend and fellow entrepreneur Alan Bond and the West Australian Government, but there were still doubts about its survival. Connell had at one stage been a prospective joint owner of Fairfax with young Warwick. He had indicated his intention to step down at Rothwells some months previously, but now it was thought, hoped, that Rothwells would need his undivided attention. After the October crash Reuter had grown apprehensive about Connell being on the Fairfax board. Reuter, who had become estranged from Connell in September, was concerned about the continuing confidence of the ANZ Bank and other banks financing the Fairfax takeover. Fairfax was going to need all the banking confidence it could get and Reuter thought Connell's presence would be negative. He had pressed this view on Cotton who had questioned Warwick Fairfax on the wisdom of having Connell on the board. But Warwick felt grateful to him.

Connell was not only to be a director, but deputy chairman. If James and John still had any doubts about leaving, this swept them away. Absent from the group was the man due to be the new chief executive: Peter King, an executive director of the Van Leer packaging company in Holland. King was a South African who had worked for Van Leer in Australia, a deeply committed Christian and believer in the universal skills of management. King had been asked by Warwick Fairfax before he made the bid on 31 August to take the job and later accepted. He was due in the office in February. Absent too was the person who had substantially conditioned Warwick for this purpose — his mother Mary, who had wanted to be a director herself but had been frustrated, partly by Martin Dougherty, who believed Warwick should be allowed to run the company as his own man, without his mother looking over his shoulder. She would have been looking over Dougherty's shoulder, too. That meant the end of a long friendship that had helped to start it all.

Mary Fairfax was a tireless booster of the two Fairfax men in her life. She boosted her husband back into the top executive position at Fairfax from 1969, when they returned from a couple of years in the UK, to 1976, urging him to take charge of the company as his birthright and unique talents entitled him to. Her frankness was sometimes stunning. On one occasion she received guests for a small dinner party at the family home 'Fairwater' telling them Sir Warwick would be a little late as he was taking a shower. Sir Warwick, then in his late seventies, appeared soon afterwards. Mary launched into a eulogy of his body, saying he was as irresistible as a young Greek god. Sir Warwick smiled, unperturbed, as though he heard this fairly often. She boosted the talents of her son, Warwick, his academic achievements and intellectual capacity to follow in his father's great publishing and journalistic footsteps. In fact, Sir Warwick had been a lucid writer, an occasional perceptive political columnist and an equally perceptive critic of the *Sydney Morning Herald*'s journalism, particularly during the 1940s. A memorandum he wrote on style and content in September 1940 was fresh and relevant 49 years later. Many would argue, however, that his biggest publishing achievement for John Fairfax Ltd was the appointment of R. A. G. Henderson as general manager in 1938.

All the boosting in the world could not provide two key elements of leadership which, at critical times, seemed to be missing in Sir Warwick Fairfax: energy and a willingness to stay in the kitchen when the heat was on. A succession of managing directors and general managers had provided those elements and more. In the months after August 1987, it became increasingly apparent that his younger son needed the same support. It was not until the dispute over payment of Rothwells's $100 million fee came to court, nearly a year after the takeover, that Warwick Fairfax revealed a tough inner core that surprised Fairfax watchers.

Mary had been a substantial backer of the Tryart enterprise. Sir Warwick Fairfax's shares, amounting to about 11.3 per cent of the company's capital, had been held since 1972 by his company, The Rockwood Pastoral Co. Pty Ltd. Rockwood shares were held for his core company, Tailer Investments Pty Ltd, as trustee for the Oriolo and Jones Trusts, set up in March 1972, with young Warwick and Mary Fairfax as beneficiaries. The trusts were named for the two settlors, Charles Lloyd Jones and Dr Enzo Oriolo. The settlors were nominal. The real power lay with the appointers of the trustees. The Jones and Fairfax families had been close since John Fairfax's *Herald* had carried David Jones's merchandise advertising in the 1840s. Dr Oriolo was an old family friend. The trust deeds were varied in 1984. The details remained confidential to those involved in the trusts, which together held the Warwick Fairfax family assets. The formal notice of the change in Rockwood's substantial shareholding following Warwick's purchase of 1.5 million shares on 17 February 1987, noted the existence of two separate trust deeds, one giving Warwick Fairfax power to appoint a new trustee, the other giving Mary power to appoint a new trustee. In effect, Warwick controlled the Oriolo Trust and Mary the Jones Trust. Those trusts, and the shares Mary held through her own company, Acrux Holdings Pty Ltd, were vital for the bid. She committed them to Warwick for the purpose. But after the stockmarket crash they caused crises in the bid's financing late in 1987 and re-financing late in 1988 when Mary questioned the wisdom of both moves and what she would get out of them.

Changes in the arrangements of both trusts could have been expected after Warwick married Gale Murphy of Canfield, Ohio, in May 1989. The Fairfaxes, like other very rich families, tended to arrange the disposition of their assets through trusts during their lifetimes, rather than rely exclusively on wills for the disposition after their deaths.

Sir Warwick Fairfax died on 14 January 1987. But the terms of his will remained unknown to other members of the family — James, his sister Caroline and his half-sister Annalise. This was of no great monetary consequence. Sir Warwick had made ample share settlements on his older children, James and Caroline and Annalise while he was alive, and Warwick's takeover had turned those shares into a lot of money. But their interests in the disposition of his estate went well beyond immediate financial concerns to intensely sentimental and practical ones, involving the family's and Sir Warwick's personal records (which included his unpublished book *Purpose*) and other possessions. Their father's final arrangements remained unknown to them. More than three years after his death his will had not been filed at the NSW Supreme Court. It may well have been that he had no substantial assets when he died. But it was believed that, over the years, Mary had thrown the full array of her considerable persuasive powers into convincing her husband that she should have sufficient power to protect young Warwick from the scheming world of predators, male and female, which awaited him. Now the shares she, or the appointed trustees, had been holding safe for Warwick, were committed to the Tryart takeover.

Warwick and his team arrived for the 7 December meeting half an hour late. They had intended bringing the cheques paying off the outgoing Fairfaxes: in round figures $163 million for James, $306 million for the family companies of Vincent and John. But their intentions were based on a misunderstanding. There were fine but important legal points involved in this handover operation. Warwick Fairfax's company, Tryart, had sent out the formal documents offering $8.50 a share to John Fairfax Ltd shareholders late in October, followed quickly by documents from the John Fairfax board and an independent report from Macquarie Hill Samuel recommending that shareholders accept the offer. By 5 November Tryart had acceptances for 84 per cent of the shares (including those of James, John and Vincent and their family companies) and declared the offer unconditional. By 10 November Tryart had 90 per cent and the next day notified the stock exchange that it would move to acquire the remainder compulsorily if necessary. Warwick Geoffrey Oswald Fairfax hoped the company would be his by his twenty-seventh birthday on 2 December. But the company could not become Warwick's, the existing board would not hand over, until the shareholders had been paid for their shares.

Tryart and the ANZ Bank (which was providing the $2.1 billion to pay the shareholders and other costs) wanted the new board to take over as quickly as possible. Only then could the necessary resolutions be passed giving the bank security over John Fairfax's assets and cash flows. The importance of this became dramatically apparent six weeks later when Westpac and the National Australia Bank took legal action to enforce their claim for repayment of the loans they had made for the purchase of HSV7 in February 1987. After an exchange of views in November it was agreed between the John Fairfax and Tryart legal advisers and the ANZ Bank, that payment would be made by or on 7 December to all those shareholders who had accepted up to 5 November when the offer was declared unconditional. Then the old board would hand over and the new board move in. The new board assumed that meant they should bring the cheques with them from Rothwells, Laurie Connell's merchant bank handling the matter, pay out the old board and wave them goodbye. But with amounts like that involved, nothing is left to chance. Mallesons Stephen Jaques had already arranged to pick up the cheques for their Fairfax clients, James, John and family. They were, after all, only 20 floors above Rothwells in the AMP Society's big building at 50 Bridge Street. The AMP picked up the cheques for its own Fairfax shares the same day. So the outgoing Fairfaxes had waited as the clock ticked on and the matter of the cheques sorted itself out.

Newspapers are run on deadlines. Clocks dominate the walls and many of the ceilings of the Fairfax building. The clock in the boardroom shared the panelled walls with portraits of Fairfaxes: the first John Fairfax; his sons Charles John Fairfax and James Reading Fairfax (JR); JR's sons Geoffrey Evan Fairfax and James Oswald Fairfax (JO); JO's son Warwick Oswald Fairfax; and the latter's cousin Vincent Charles Fairfax, whose father John Hubert Fraser Fairfax, although a director of the company, had been mainly interested in his pastoral properties. Hubert did not rate a portrait on the boardroom walls.

The portraits reflected the generational changes in appearance and style of a wealthy middle-class Australian family whose fortunes had been founded by a migrant English printer in the mid-nineteenth century. John Fairfax had the big and bushy mid-century beard of a sturdy, devout Congregationalist committed to his family, business and good works. His son, James Reading Fairfax, wore a beard more elegantly pointed, in the style of Edward VII. With the firm's increasing wealth James was able to widen his interests in the theatre and arts while maintaining the good works and being very much in charge of the business. James Reading was the first Fairfax to appoint a manager. He went for the best: Hugh George, manager of the *Argus* and *Australasian* in Melbourne. James Reading was also the last male Fairfax Congregationalist. His sons switched to the established church, the Church of England, much to the benefit of St Mark's Church in Darling Point.

The Fairfaxes always lived in Sydney's oldest and best eastern suburbs: Bellevue Hill, Woollahra and Double Bay. Money tended to be newer and more ostentatious in suburbs further east along the Harbour. St Mark's was their parish church. Young Warwick took his early Christian instruction there and at Cranbrook School, opposite 'Fairwater', his family home. The family had a continuing commitment to the Church. Sir Warwick's interest had been intellectual; Vincent's was practical and benefactory. Young Warwick's, however, was spiritual.

As they became Anglican the Fairfaxes seemed to become more aquiline. The breadth of James Reading's character and interests seemed to be divided vertically between his two sons, James Oswald and John Hubert and their heirs. James Oswald's son Warwick Oswald (later Sir Warwick) was so interested in ballet that, as an adult, he took lessons; he wrote plays and books about religion, philosophy and metaphysics. His son, James Oswald, young Warwick's older half-brother, was an erudite and shrewd collector of works of art. John Hubert's son, Vincent, was a pastoralist and businessman like his father, a director of the Bank of NSW and the AMP Society like his grandfather, a practical man of affairs who maintained the commitment to good works at St Mark's Church, the Boy Scouts and the Boys Brigade. Vincent's son John carried on this line. He worked as a journalist, in the advertising department of John Fairfax Ltd and then as general manager of the *Canberra Times*, before becoming a director and deputy chairman of the company, with particular responsibilities for the broadcasting and magazine subsidiaries. Thinkers on one side, doers on the other. But the real energy of the company since James Reading Fairfax had come from the managers.

James and John, like their fathers, had little in common apart from their holdings in John Fairfax Ltd. Warwick and Vincent lived next door to each other in two great houses on Sydney Harbour at Double Bay: 'Fairwater' (Warwick) and 'Elaine' (Vincent). The properties, together occupying over 1.5 hectares, ran down to the high water mark of Seven Shillings Beach. Within five kilometres of Martin Place, the centre of the central business district, they were probably the best residential properties in Sydney. A high brick wall separated them from the little sandy beach, doubly ensuring privacy. The beach was secured from public access by barriers at each end. They were neighbours without being neighbourly for years before a gate was put in their dividing fence, which allowed Vincent and his wife Nancy access to Warwick's swimming pool. But the common interest in John Fairfax Ltd had always, or nearly always, prevailed. The paintings on the board-room walls included two recent portraits of Sir Warwick and Sir Vincent. The portrait of Sir Warwick Oswald Fairfax had particular significance. That portrait, commissioned late in 1980 had effected a kind of reconciliation with his son James after an estrangement of four years during which they had spoken to each other only at board meetings.

Young Warwick's bid had already survived the biggest stockmarket crash on record. On 19 October and the week following, after a fast-moving September during which the whole Fairfax takeover deal seemed to come together for Tryart, stockmarkets throughout the world, led by Wall Street, had fallen through the floor. In the manner of markets they had only just been through the roof. The Australian market had been devastated. Committed in late

September to outlay about $2 billion for the Fairfax shares he
didn't already own or control, Warwick might have got them for
less than two-thirds of that if he had made his bid in late October.
The crash had also killed off the grand plan to recoup at least
$275 million of the $2 billion by floating off 55 per cent of an
augmented Fairfax subsidiary, David Syme, which owned the *Age*
and other assets in Melbourne. This may have been a blessing
in disguise. That plan always seemed to carry with it the danger
that the *Age* would be raided by Robert Holmes a Court, Kerry
Packer or others. And in any event the *Age*'s revenues were so
buoyant that Tryart might be better off keeping all of Syme if
it could.

Through this period, when the newspapers he was about to
own were full of forebodings about what the October crash meant,
young Warwick's commitment to the bid never wavered. As a
young man of strong Christian convictions, who lived and shared
retreats with a small group of young Christians, he may have
welcomed this test of his resolve. At meetings before the adventure
started, both Laurie Connell, chief negotiator and dominant
member of the Tryart team, and Bert Reuter, the financial architect,
had put bluntly to Warwick the testing times ahead. Where, asked
Connell, do we call it off? Where is the break point? 'There is
no break point,' said Warwick. That resolution did not appear to
waver after 19 October. It was no time for the weary, languid or
sore distressed. In fact, Warwick thought the crash favoured him.
It frightened off any potential counter-bidders and made his bid
look more attractive; 19 October made the bid unbeatable. Later,
when his mother Mary Fairfax was asked what made Warwick run,
what deep convictions had moved him to this astonishing coup,
she replied, 'Warwick is interested in two things: Jesus Christ and
journalism.' Armed with these, an MBA from Harvard's Business
School and the ANZ Bank loan, he was about to assume the
responsibilities he had been preparing for all his life.

The first thing the company secretary Ian Cumming did in
preparing for this 7 December meeting, as he did before every
board meeting, was to turn on the boardroom air conditioner.
The building had not been air conditioned when it had been

rushed up 30 years previously. But the boardroom had its own unit. It wasn't always used. Years before, when the printers had complained about extraordinarily hot working conditions in summer, when temperatures were elevated by the 40 tonnes of molten lead and antimony being constantly recycled through the composing, stereotyping and machine rooms, the managing director, R. A. G. Henderson, met their delegates in the boardroom. The air conditioner was turned off. Henderson sat there, a gnome in a dark three-piece suit, as the temperature and tempers rose. If he ever sweated, nobody saw it. Frustrated, the printers went back down to the production floors to cool off.

Later, of course, Henderson gave in and the building was gradually cooled and air conditioned, production departments first, but the boardroom retained its own unit. Years later, in 1976, when 1400 production and maintenance workers went on strike for 60 days over issues related to the introduction of new labour-saving equipment, the secretary of the NSW Labour Council, John Ducker, led union delegates to the same room to try to resolve the issues with management. The air conditioner was left off then too.

The 7 December meeting, however, was a board matter. It was summer. The new owner was coming. The air conditioner was on.

Usually when important visitors were expected at John Fairfax Ltd, arrangements were made for their reception — precious space in the carpark for their cars, since legal parking was virtually impossible in the street outside (particularly at mid-morning when Jones Street belonged to the trucks rushing first editions of the *Sun* to newsstands and newsagencies throughout the city). Once, if the visitors were important enough, a senior executive met them in the foyer and took them up in the executive lift — special key only. But the executive lift was done away with when a new, more egalitarian generation of executives took over in 1980. Warwick and his team did not ask for special treatment and got none. They met at the Rothwells offices in Bridge Street and waited while the misunderstanding about the cheques was sorted out. Then they drove to Jones Street in taxis or private cars. They had decided, against the natural instincts of some, that this was not an occasion for stretched limos and formal reception at the door. The move into the Fairfax building, the final stage of the takeover, should be kept low key.

The transition in ownership and control would not be easy and nobody knew this better than Ron Cotton, the new managing director, operations. Cotton had worked for John Fairfax Ltd from 1981 to 1985. He knew the prejudices and prickly sensitivities that would need to be soothed, the allegiances that had to be won, if the transfer of power was to take place quickly and effectively. This was no time for pomp and circumstance. The previous Friday he had arranged for a buffet luncheon in the directors' lounge-dining room on the thirteenth floor to be held after the 7 December board meeting so that the editors and managers could meet the new owner and executives and at least be able to put a face and presence to the names they had been publishing, reading and writing about, not always in flattering terms, over the previous ten weeks.

Cotton came from Ampol Petroleum to the chief financial executive's job at Fairfax in January 1981. He left in May 1985. His four years with the company led to fundamental differences with the group general manager, Gregory John Gardiner, about the way the group should be run. Cotton was not the first, or the last, to see the Fairfax group as a number of separate and absurdly independent empires, often competing against each other rather than competing as a unified force among the other big media groups. And it was true that, since Angus McLachlan retired as managing director in 1968, there was nobody of sufficient experience, natural authority and will to exercise, even if he wanted to, the monolithic control that Kerry Packer had over his privatised Consolidated Press or Rupert Murdoch over News Corporation. Rupert Albert Geary Henderson, managing director from 1949 to 1964 and general manager before that, and Angus McLachlan, his general manager and briefly his successor, built the Fairfax group, knew every page size and column width and programme schedule of it. They had the authority, which only the respect of its editors and producers and managers could give, over every part of it. That authority decentralised in the 1970s as the company grew and the editors and managers became more independent. That coincided with a difficult period economically and great tensions at the top of the company.

Certainly the company and its profits seemed to have a new lease of life in the 1980s, even after television ceased to be a licence to print money. But there was still the vital question of balance: how far could a company let loose the energies and initiatives of its creative executives, yet maintain a unity of purpose and character? At one extreme was Kerry Packer, running his privatised television-magazine-investment empire, often with a seemingly capricious but well-developed instinct about when and what to buy and sell. At the other was the Herald & Weekly Times (HWT), before it was taken over by Rupert Murdoch's News Corporation earlier in 1987, a company whose main initiatives in the previous 30 years had been the development of interlocking shareholdings between its member companies and a fortress mentality that stifled vigour and creativity. During the 1980s the Fairfax group appeared to be taking a middle course between these two. Its family-dominated ownership seemed to make it secure from raiders and at the same time allowed a flowering of its products, particularly the *Age* and the *Sydney Morning Herald* and the *Australian Financial Review*. This alternately amused and outraged its critics at Consolidated Press and News Corporation, who scorned its lack of discipline but envied its products. The dangers of the Fairfax model became evident in the mid-1980s as the *National Times*, which had been both swan and ugly duckling of an indulgent board and general manager for 15 years, lost its humour and sense of proportion and became obsessed with its own missions. As it happened, both structures, the HWT, the former fortress of Flinders Street, and John Fairfax Ltd, the seemingly impregnable loose-limbed beauty of Broadway, fell to raiders in 1987.

Cotton had left Fairfax in May 1985 and gone to work for United Permanent Building Society, which merged into one of the new banking licences, the National Mutual Royal Bank. But he maintained contact with Sir Warwick Fairfax, who had been on the board when Cotton worked for the company. Cotton had attended the Advanced Management course at Harvard in 1974 and was familiar with other management schools at Wharton,

Hawaii and Stanford. He was consulted when young Warwick was considering his further education in the mid-1980s. Cotton was a joiner, an organisation man, who put store in office and titles and contacts. He had been national president of the Australian Society of Accountants and active in other professional accounting and management bodies. He was approached by young Warwick to join the new ship Tryart in September, decided to go aboard in November and took office on 20 November. All the deals had then been done. He had to make them work. Some former Fairfax executives, who had worked with him, doubted his capacity to do so.

The script for the 7 December board proceedings had been virtually agreed in outline between Rod Halstead for Fairfax and Aleco Vrisakis for Tryart. It was strictly formal. First, Sir Vincent was introduced to the new team. Of all the Fairfaxes he had taken Warwick's bid the hardest. He had been shell-shocked and initially wanted the board to make a public statement condemning Warwick. Vincent had made a public career out of probity and integrity — chairman of the Bank of NSW and the AMP Society, of the Boy Scouts and the Boys Brigade his grandfather had founded. Vincent had had little in common with his late cousin Warwick, except for their shareholdings in John Fairfax Ltd, but when the chips were down family unity had always prevailed. Now it was being blown apart by Warwick's son who had sat as an invited guest at board meetings while plotting his coup.

The company's Articles of Association allowed for seven directors. There were currently five, leaving two vacancies. At 10.30 a.m. James, John and Vincent, sitting as the current board, at Warwick's request, elected Warwick and Laurie Connell to the two vacancies on the board. The three older Fairfaxes then resigned, James also lodging the resignations of Sir Eric Neal and Sir David Griffin. Warwick and Connell then, as the new board, appointed Cotton, Dougherty and King as directors. James Fairfax made a short, gracious and generous speech wishing the new board well. As spokesman for the new board and out of a sense of the fitness of things, Martin Dougherty thanked him. Warwick grunted, and that was that. James had asked for a few days to clear his office and continued use of his space in the car park for that period. John was already packed and ready to go. Vincent did not have an office in the building. The new board went on with other business. High on Connell's agenda was the appointment of Tryart people to the boards of the subsidiary companies and the trustees of the superannuation funds.

The John Fairfax pile was no architectural masterpiece. It was, on a most generous assessment, a no-frills building, a near-rectangular box built strictly for newspaper production. It occupied most of the near-city block with some extra floors on top at the front to house administration departments, the board and senior executive offices being on the uppermost fourteenth floor.

Looked at from the entrance at Jones Street, the fourteenth floor was shaped like a reversed L. As chairman, James Fairfax had occupied the big room at the lower right hand (north-east) corner, with windows looking over Ultimo and Pyrmont to the Sydney Harbour Bridge. The boardroom was next to it going up the upright, followed by a row of executive offices. James had taken this room when his father, Sir Warwick, had been deposed as chairman in 1976. Apart from the occupant, the room was distinguished by the spare elegance of its furnishings. John, deputy chairman and an active director and chairman of some of the company's key subsidiaries, occupied the smaller room next to James. James had used that room before he became chairman. The next office along this eastern front of the fourteenth floor was the real control room of the Fairfax group, the office first occupied by Rupert Albert Geary Henderson, the company's managing director, who had schemed and built the defensive network of media products around the flagship, the *Sydney Morning Herald*, a network that was about to be substantially dismantled. Many thought they still smelled volcanic action from that room for years after Henderson retired as managing director in 1964. He remained on the board and a major force in company strategies until 1978. He was followed for three years by his general manager Angus McLachlan, who retired after a heart attack in 1968. McLachlan was the last managing director until 7 December 1987. Then there were two.

Sir Warwick Fairfax, chairman of the company, public and private, for all but six weeks of the 46 years before he was deposed in 1976, insisted it was company policy (it may have been Rupert Henderson's policy) that only a journalist could be managing director of a company so committed to journalism as John Fairfax Ltd. Henderson had been a vigorous reporter on the *Sydney Morning Herald*, McLachlan a distinguished news editor. There was no clear successor in sight in 1968. There followed a unique period in the history of the company, perhaps of any public company. Sir Warwick Fairfax ruled as chairman and chief executive as a committee of one appointed by the board. Robert Percy Falkingham, a stern moralist, forceful accountant and confident executive pushed his way through and occupied the managing director's office as general manager for 10 years until he was succeeded by Greg Gardiner as group chief executive. Gardiner wasn't a journalist either. He had left the Friday before this 7 December board meeting at which the company was changing hands.

Further along, past the secretaries' common room, fairly empty now that the secretaries had left or were leaving with the executives they had worked for, was a large room first occupied by Angus McLachlan as general manager and more recently by Fred Brenchley, general manager of Broadway operations. Brenchley, as much as anyone, had transformed the economy of the *Sydney Morning Herald*, lifting its revenues and cutting its direct production costs, so that, when television profits ran out of steam in the mid-1980s, the *Herald* could make up for the lost momentum in television, which had provided much of the profit growth in the previous decade. Brenchley had left the previous Friday too.

A smaller office at the south-east corner of the building had been occuped by Allen Cragg, another former *Sydney Morning Herald* news editor who, as an administrative assistant, knew how that Broadway building worked. Cragg had left in the middle of November. Next to that room, on the small return perpendicular of the L, balancing the boardroom on the northern side of the building, was a conference room. This room overlooked Broadway and the walled city of the Carlton-Tooth brewery. To long-term inmates it was the Kremlin overlooking the Vatican.

Max Suich, the chief editorial executive, who, with Greg Gardiner and James Fairfax, had formed the triumvirate that had run the company for the past seven years, worked on the fifth floor among the editors and journalists. He had left the previous Friday too.

After the old board had gone, the new executives moved in: Cotton into the former control (Henderson, McLachlan, Falkingham, Gardiner) room, Dougherty into the former general manager's (McLachlan, Brenchley) room. Marty brought his brother Paul, a journalist who had also worked for John Fairfax Ltd at times in the past and for Rupert Murdoch's News Corporation. Paul occupied the small corner office next to Marty. The spacious chairman's office on the north-east corner was reserved for Peter King, who would move in in February. When Warwick was in the building he would use the smaller office next door, between King and Cotton. As sole proprietor he was removed from the management hierarchy. Seemingly unimpressed by the trappings and perquisites of wealth and power, Warwick drove a red Toyota car to work and around the city. His executives drove Jaguars and Mercedes Benz. Some of the new hands were at the controls. But only Cotton, as a former executive, had any idea of what the controls were, or how they worked. Their secretaries moved in and started to feel their way into the secretarial network essential to the smooth workings of large organisations.

Although young Warwick and his advisers had been increasingly critical of the executives and the board they had replaced, the capacities of the new team to run a large media organisation were, with the exception of Cotton's, unknown. The company they had taken over had never been so profitable. Its two main newspaper properties, the *Age* and the *Sydney Morning Herald*, were regarded as rivers of gold. Rupert Murdoch regarded the *Age* and the *Sydney Morning Herald* as among the 10 best newspaper properties in the world. Their earning capacities had flowered under group general manager Greg Gardiner, Greg Taylor at David Syme in Melbourne, and Max Suich and Fred Brenchley at Broadway. Taylor, managing director of David Syme Ltd and a former editor of the *Age*, was the only one of these four who had been pressed to stay. Taylor looked at one stage as though he was going to be demoted under Bert Reuter, early architect of the Tryart bid. But Reuter seemed to fade from the scene during September and October as Connell's deal-making talents came to the fore. In any event, the 19–20 October stockmarket crash eliminated the Warwick team's grand plan to make Syme the publicly listed vehicle for growth. The old John Fairfax board and management had generally been very careful to respect the Melbourne sensitivities of David Syme Ltd, and perhaps young Warwick saw the wisdom of continuing the policy.

The takeover was complex and costly, and as the weeks passed, became increasingly controversial. A board and management with a good, though not unblemished, track record, seemingly securely in control, was displaced. Concern for the capacity of their successors to run a business as big as John Fairfax Ltd rose as details of the deals they had done during September became known.

The departing board and executives were not error free. There had been increasing criticism of how the company had come out of the takeover battle with Rupert Murdoch for the HWT early in 1987 and particularly of its purchase of the Melbourne television station HSV7, which had been followed by some clumsy attempts at staff reductions. The group's profits in recent years had been substantially boosted by windfall gains from its investment in the news service AAP and, through that, in Reuters, which had made a bonanza out of the worldwide boom in the financial information market. Nevertheless, the trading profits were at or near record levels and after the sale of HSV7 to Christopher Skase's Universal Telecasters, Fairfax would have been virtually debt-free by the end of 1987. Now it was being saddled with the $2 billion debt Warwick had used to buy it.

Gardiner, the group general manager, was being replaced with Ron Cotton, the treasurer he had let go in 1985 and not bothered to replace. Max Suich, a journalist and effective corporate executive and strategist, was being replaced by Martin Dougherty, a journalist and former short-term editor of Murdoch's *Truth* and *Daily Mirror*. Dougherty had in recent years run a public relations company. He claimed a long client list: Murdoch; Packer; Donald

Trump, the New York hotel owner; West Australian Development Corporation; Australian Gold Mining Industry Corporation; Australian Hotels Association; the Newspaper Advertising Bureau; Ron Brierley; Kevin Parry; and others. The Gold Industry paid the highest retainer fee of $12 000 a month. It was a profitable business. But to many newspapermen this was the very antithesis of journalism.

A PR man's job is to get in to the papers what is good for his client, while the journalist's job is to get in what important people, including the PR man's clients, want to keep out. This led to Dougherty's undoing at Fairfax. Fred Brenchley, another strong journalist who, as an executive, had done some of the toughest management jobs for Fairfax in the preceding ten years, particularly in lifting the Broadway factory's productivity, was being partly replaced by Peter Gaunt whom Brenchley had brought in as a marketing man to help boost the *Sydney Morning Herald*'s revenues. Gaunt was a good salesman. His management capacities and staying power were unknown.

Whatever their faults, the managers and directors who had just left had proven track records as stayers. They had seen the company through crises, through bad times and good. How strong were the long-term commitments of the incoming team? The combined strategic functions of the board and top management were apparently to be borne mainly by Peter King, with young Warwick Fairfax as last man down. There were inevitable doubts and concerns about the dramatic changes at Fairfax. As the months passed they were fully justified. Within two months Marty Dougherty had gone, his brother with him. Two months later Laurie Connell had gone. Sixteen months later Ron Cotton had gone. The assets sales arranged in September, which were to reduce the company's debt by the end of December, were substantially amended or abandoned and others arranged to take their place. Warwick Fairfax was virtually invisible. Sixteen months later he went to live in the USA where he felt much more at home.

The endemic problems of how to ensure the Fairfax inheritance, retain control while financing growth, maintain the mission of principle before, or at least with, profit, and cope with managers who were stronger than the owners, had recurred at John Fairfax Ltd during the twentieth century. In general they were successfully overcome. Then young Warwick came home with his own solution: buy the company back. Instead of expanding, shrink. That seemed to solve the first problem. It preserved the ownership, though of a much diminished company, for the 'Fairwater' side of the family. But in doing so it risked exacerbating the others. Warwick carried an enormous debt. To reduce it he had to sell key parts of the empire. If his earnings slipped, his creditors would be much more demanding than any outside shareholders. On 7 December 1987, and increasingly as events unfolded thereafter, he was leaning heavily on the high revenues of the two rivers of gold, the *Sydney Morning Herald* and the *Age*. They still looked very good after the 19 October crash, due largely to the success of the world's central bankers and political leaders in insulating the real economies from the crash, and to the efforts and planning of the people Warwick had deposed. But they fell well short of servicing Warwick's debt.

How had this come about?

# CHAPTER 2

# FOUR AGENTS OF THE OVERTHROW

During the 1980s four separate forces gathered momentum, came together and finally erupted in the third quarter of 1987 to overthrow the ownership and control of John Fairfax Ltd: the balance of power in the family was changing; the management style had changed in 1980 and its effects were disturbing to one important branch of the family; the Australian Labor Party (ALP) came to power in Canberra; and rising world liquidity and deregulation of money markets opened the way for financial deals based on debt of a size and shape previously undreamed of.

Many companies were taken over or threatened with takeover during that period, including Australia's biggest, The BHP Co. Ltd. But John Fairfax Ltd was unique: the enterprise had been substantially owned and controlled by one family for 146 years. While most companies, including John Fairfax Ltd, had their antennae out sweeping the stockmarket for early warning signs of market raiders coming in their direction, the Fairfax raid came from within from a member of the family itself.

By the 1980s control of the company was firmly established in the hands of the fifth generation of Fairfaxes in Australia. Sir Warwick Fairfax's son by his first marriage, James Oswald Fairfax, was 44 when he became chairman in 1976. James held about 18 per cent of the company's shares. His distant cousin, John Brehmer Fairfax, deputy chairman since 1985, was nine years younger than James. He and his family companies held about 14 per cent of the shares. John's father, Sir Vincent Fairfax, a director since John Fairfax Ltd floated as a public company in

1956, and at times before that, was still on the board. Sir Warwick Fairfax, who had been deposed as chairman in 1976, was also still on the board. He, his third wife Mary, and their son, Warwick, had about 13 per cent of the share capital. Other family interests made up about four per cent. Before the company floated in 1956, Sir Warwick had owned or controlled over 70 per cent of the shares. The public share issue halved his equity in the company. He had been deposed as chairman six weeks early in 1961 in the wake of his third marriage. That was while he settled a damages claim brought by his new wife's former husband, Cedric Symonds. When he was re-elected he accepted that 'any powers that he might exercise as chairman could come only from the board of directors'. Nine years later this condition rebounded on other directors.

In 1970 the company wrestled with the problem of who to appoint as chief executive. The previous managing director, Angus McLachlan, who had not fully recovered from a heart attack, had retired in 1968. There was no obvious successor to McLachlan. Sir Warwick was chairman and while the other directors argued that he could naturally assume increased responsibilities from that position, he insisted on being appointed executive chairman by the board. A solution was found within the company's Articles of Association. Sir Warwick retained his position as chairman and was appointed an executive committee of one. He had a strong general manager in R. P. Falkingham, who had joined the company as treasurer in 1957.

As the company entered the storms of the 1970s — inflation, government price restraints, high interest rates, political upheaval, recession — it became obvious that Falkingham was the man the board looked to for the determined helmsmanship the company needed to come through intact. But Sir Warwick continued to act as chief executive, issuing orders to senior executives without consulting Falkingham. Editorial direction was also a problem. Falkingham had no authority there. In the Fairfaxes' eyes, he was wont to say later, he was 'just a good clerk'.

Some board members felt Sir Warwick was not allowing enough board discussion of the newspapers' editorial directions in those trying years. The position became intolerable. Sir Warwick was told by the other directors that he should stand aside for a younger man. He resigned as chairman in 1976 and his son James was appointed to head the board.

James and his father did not speak with each other, except on the formal occasion of board meetings, for the next four years. The ice was finally broken in 1980 when it was considered time for portraits of Sir Warwick and Sir Vincent to join those of their forebears on the walls of the company's boardroom. Who was to paint Sir Warwick? He had always admired the portrait of Sir Alastair Stephen, painted by Bryan Westwood, which hung at the offices of Stephen Jaques and Stephen, the family's and company's lawyers for many years. James, who had made art one of his major interests, organised the portrait of Sir Warwick by Westwood, commissioned through the Robin Gibson Galleries on 9 December 1980. Two weeks later Sir Vincent's portrait was commissioned through the same gallery, also to be painted by Westwood.

Sir Warwick's portrait hangs over the boardroom fireplace, the subject facing and dominating the room, right hand on hip, the left holding a tightly-rolled copy of the *Sydney Morning Herald*. He wears his clothes with a comfortable elegance. He is aloof, confident, challenging. It could be a modern version of an eighteenth century Court portrait by Van Dyck, or of a Gainsborough gentleman, born to authority. This was Sir Warwick Fairfax, leader of a proud company. It contrasted with the portrait painted by Judy Cassab 26 years previously. The Cassab portrait — hung in the library at 'Fairwater' — was of Warwick Fairfax, playwright and philosopher. That was when Rupert Henderson was running the company, before Sir Warwick's third marriage. Sir Vincent's portrait hangs slightly below Sir Warwick's to the right. He is in profile, facing his right, a practical man of affairs, a flatter — a more prosaic portrait than Sir Warwick's. If Westwood had doubts about it, Vincent was not concerned. He was tired of sitting.

The commissioning of Sir Warwick's portrait led to a timely, though still guarded, reconciliation with James for there were other important matters to be discussed over the next few years relating to the disposition of shares James had bought from his father 20 years previously. The Kinghaven shares, as they were known, played an important part in young Warwick's bid for control in 1987. The board moves against Warwick Oswald Fairfax in 1961 and 1976 had left an inevitable undercurrent of bitterness and tension but, for the time being at least, the board looked reasonably stable in the 1980s. There loomed, however, the problem of accommodating young Warwick Geoffrey Oswald Fairfax, child of Sir Warwick's third marriage. At first this did not seem to be a big problem. But young Warwick was an enigma. His education had been different from that of any previous Fairfax. He had gone to Balliol like his half-brother James, his father and his grandfather, but then worked at the Chase Manhattan Bank and briefly in the marketing department of the *Los Angeles Times*. He had gone to the Harvard Business School. He had been carefully nurtured and conditioned by his father and mother to take over his inheritance. His father, as he entered his eighties, was concerned that young Warwick should get the full benefit of his shares when he died and, eventually, those of his half-brother James, who was unmarried and childless. Together they would make young Warwick, in due course, by far the biggest shareholder in the company.

Thus the balance of power in the company was changing, and after 1985, when James Fairfax established a new trust for the Kinghaven shares in favour of Warwick, would change rapidly. In addition to this, after 1984, tensions developed within the family about the way the company was being run. The Warwick Fairfax side, the 'Fairwater' Fairfaxes, became increasingly critical of the management on business and editorial grounds. When young Warwick made his bid for control in August 1987 it was widely thought that he was privatising the company to secure it against raiders. That may have helped precipitate his actions. But primarily he was rescuing the company from the hands of people he and his advisers thought were incapable of taking it, in good order and condition, into the twenty-first century.

In 1980, when Falkingham retired as general manager, the company skipped a generation of managers. It appointed Gregory John Gardiner, the 37-year-old administration manager, as general manager of the group. The company also solved the problem that had plagued it during the 1970s of who should, or rather could, control the editors by appointing Maxwell Victor Suich as chief editorial executive. Both appointments were debated at length by the directors. Sir Warwick Fairfax opposed Gardiner but had no acceptable alternative. Max Suich had been a prickly innovator as editor of the *National Times* and managing editor of the *Sun-Herald*, sometimes upsetting the conservative directors. But his ability was unchallenged. Eventually the new executives were appointed. They were answerable individually to the board. In certain circumstances, perhaps in most circumstances, one or the other would have emerged absolutely on top of all departments, usually the one who controlled the money. But this was not what the board wanted and it was not what happened. Gardiner and Suich worked closely together, with mutual respect for each other's capacities. Gardiner ran the business, Suich ran the journalism in Sydney with a policy of appointing 'a coterie of independent editors'. With James Fairfax as chairman, they formed a closer, less formal but more united executive team than had existed at Fairfax since the Henderson-McLachlan-Falkingham regime 20 years previously.

There had often been tensions between the Fairfaxes and their managers, ever since James Reading Fairfax appointed the first outside manager in 1878, the year after his father, the first John Fairfax, died, particularly as the later managers coped with the double problem of looking after the family's interest and looking after the business. But the tensions that developed in the 1980s were of a different order.

As Gardiner and Suich pursued policies of letting the talents flower and the profits flow, their critics saw the company falling out of control. The Fairfaxes had always proclaimed principles before profits, though occasionally this commitment looked pretty thin. At the same time the company's newspapers seemed, to their critics within the family, to be straying from their traditional commitment to the four pillars of Fairfax editorial policy: Christianity, the Monarchy, policies before parties, and middle-class values, including free enterprise. There was plenty of room for argument about this. But there was no doubt that in the 1980s profits were pursued with more vigour than in the past. Gardiner had worked at J. Walter Thompson and Bowater Paper, which had helped him develop a feel for the publishing industry, but the dominant influence in his pre-Fairfax business life had been his years at the merchant bank Development Finance Corporation Ltd. He was well aware that strong profits meant high share prices and high share prices meant security against attack and a commanding position for growth.

Most of the growth in the previous decades had been defensive or reactive, aimed at keeping the enemies out. The main enemy had changed from Frank Packer to Rupert Murdoch, but the strategy had not. The company had expanded when it was forced to expand. In the 1980s, however, the company's new generation of managers showed signs of wanting growth that was not directly connected with defence. This not only involved increasing investments in expanding companies like Rural Press, and new products like the magazine group centred on *Business Review Weekly*, but the first small steps overseas: purchase of the *Spectator* in London and half of Fourth Estate Holdings Ltd, owners of the *National Business Review* in New Zealand. The company bought a half-share in *Time* magazine in Australia and New Zealand and took management control of it. It became recognised as a potential buyer of publishing properties in the United Kingdom, North America and Asia. But if it was to have the funds to take advantage of opportunities to grow, it was felt the company's capital should be expanded. To get around the problem of doing this while maintaining the family's controlling position, an ingenious preference share issue was proposed in 1984. Known as the PIPs issue (of Participating Irredeemable Preference shares), it was designed to raise new capital and return some money to the family without watering down their voting power. This was opposed by the 'Fairwater' Fairfaxes and was finally defeated by the Australian Stock Exchange's refusal to list the preference shares if they were issued. To the 'Fairwater' side of the family, the proposed issue confirmed the suspicion that the management, no longer the family as a whole, had control of the company. Later, when young Warwick made his bid, some of those he displaced wondered whether the preference share issue had been opposed so strongly because it would have increased the eventual cost of buying the company. They were partly right. The impact on a possible future privatisation was a factor in the 'Fairwater' Fairfaxes' attitude to the issue. Others thought that the further substantial growth envisaged would have made it more difficult for young Warwick to take over as managing director, though that seemed to have underestimated his self-confidence at that time.

Certainly the proposed preference share issue was a decisive factor in the hardening criticism by the 'Fairwater' Fairfaxes of the James Fairfax-Gardiner regime. They felt their criticisms were overwhelmingly reinforced when the company bought HSV7 Melbourne in 1987 following the company's failure to block Murdoch's takeover of the Herald & Weekly Times (HWT), and then made some damaging tactical errors in attempted staff retrenchments. The Stock Exchange was an eventual loser. The share issue it had refused to list was one factor leading to the eventual removal of all John Fairfax shares from the Stock Exchange lists. But the exchanges had acted on a principle that coincided with self-interest: if Fairfax had been allowed to protect the family interest in this way, the open market on which takeovers and stockbrokers had thrived could have been endangered.

The third destabilising force overlapped the second, just as the second overlapped the first. The ALP, which had won government under Neville Wran in NSW in 1976, won government in Canberra under R. J. Hawke in 1983. State Governments had no direct powers over the media, but the Federal Government controlled radio and television broadcasting. After 1983 a Labor Government was thus able to create conditions for the break up of the two media groups it saw as its traditional enemies: the HWT group in Melbourne, Brisbane, Adelaide and Perth, and the John Fairfax group in Sydney and Melbourne. The Melbourne *Herald* and its satellites had always been anti-Labor. The Fairfax papers were different. The *Sydney Morning Herald* had traditionally been strongly against ALP policies, but it had twice, in 1942 and 1961, refused to endorse the policies of the conservative parties under R. G. Menzies. In the 1980s it was much less predictable. The *Sydney Morning Herald*, the *Age*, the *Australian Financial Review*, the *National Times*, the Newcastle *Herald*, the Illawarra *Mercury* and the *Canberra Times* could differ substantially on Government and Opposition policies. These differences, at first resisted by the Fairfax board under Sir Warwick Fairfax, were gradually accommodated. The company grew to make a virtue of diversity. The papers often took the same line on issues. But this was due to a coincidence of editorial views rather than to any consultation. There was no handing down of editorial policy that had to be, or was expected to be, followed by all papers. Editors might be criticised afterwards. But they did not feel 'This is what the board would like to say about this issue, therefore we say it'. It was a policy of responsible independence. It still sometimes shook the board but not nearly as much as it shook the ALP. The Liberal and National Parties, which had been confident of Fairfax editorial support, often felt they had been betrayed. In a sense the ALP felt betrayed too. The *Sydney Morning Herald* editorials, particularly before elections, had traditionally been anti-Labor but the news columns had usually bent over backwards to appear balanced. In the 1980s the editorials started to favour many Labor policies and even the Party at elections, but the news columns pursued vigorously Government corruption and abuse of power, and editorials backed them up.

There was another problem. The ALP lived on monolithic discipline, particularly when the NSW Right Wing assumed command after Neville Wran's decisive win in 1976 and R. J Hawke's in 1983. The men who ran the Party in Sydney found it hard to accommodate the idea that a board like John Fairfax's could be in a position to wield such power and not use it. So whenever the Fairfax papers came out with the same line critical of some aspect of Labor's policies or administration, it was deemed a Fairfax plot. At least the *Sydney Morning Herald* of the previous three decades had been predictable. The ALP thought it could deal with the other two big Sydney-based media owners, Kerry Packer and Rupert Murdoch. They were pragmatic, knew their own interests. At least there was no doubt about who was boss and who set the editorial tone of their media empires. But who could Labor politicians deal with on those terms at Fairfax? The HWT was beyond redemption. New technologies and market pressures were forcing changes in the ownership rules for radio and television stations. They opened up the opportunity for company raiders to break up both groups.

None of these three forces would have been effective without the revolution in world banking and money markets, which gathered pace during the 1980s. In the space of half a generation, bankers who had once seemed reluctant to say 'yes' to borrowers suddenly became reluctant to say 'no'. Deregulation in a world awash with money broke down traditional constraints for banks and borrowers. The first three forces provided motives and opportunities for the ownership revolution at Fairfax in 1987. The fourth provided the means.

## CHAPTER 3

# WARWICK, MARY, RUPERT AND JAMES

Two months before he married Mary Symonds in July 1959, Warwick Oswald Fairfax, on the advice of his managing director, R. A. G. Henderson, and his solicitor, Alastair Stephen, transferred half of his shares in John Fairfax Ltd to his son James, on a long-term payment plan. The transfer was nominally made to minimise death duties. But the effect was to remove half of Warwick's shares from the influence of his third and most ambitious wife on the eve of their marriage. It was a declaration of hostilities between Henderson and Mary Fairfax, the start of a 28-year siege between 'Fairwater' (the home of Warwick and Mary) and the company's top executives, including James Fairfax, which culminated in young Warwick's takeover of the company in 1987. That transfer in 1959 came to be bitterly regretted at 'Fairwater'. Soon after his marriage to Mary, Warwick Oswald Fairfax severed his professional association with Alastair Stephen, a man he had known all his life. They had shared a tutor as small boys.

When young Warwick Geoffrey Oswald Fairfax made his bid for total ownership and control of John Fairfax Ltd in August 1987, the shockwaves obliterated the fact that, whether he knew it or not, he was continuing and bringing to a conclusion a fundamental company policy that had been interrupted when John Fairfax & Sons Pty Ltd floated as a public company in 1956. That policy was dictated by the need to avoid at least two of the three factors that traditionally undermined family control of big enterprises: inheritance taxes, the spread of family holdings among an ever-increasing number of heirs with weakening commitments to the enterprise, and wayward genes. That they were able to avoid fulfilment of the Australian version of the general rule about the rise and fall of family fortunes — 'bowyangs to bowyangs in three generations' — was substantially due to the efforts of Rupert Albert Geary Henderson. For years before going to the public for capital in 1956, he had orchestrated a policy of concentrating the ownership of the company into fewer and fewer hands, mainly into the hands of Warwick Oswald Fairfax (and, at least until Mary Fairfax came along, power into the hands of R. A. G. Henderson). The policy and the inevitable concern about the dangers of death duties breaking up those concentrated family holdings, had a remarkable fallout when young Warwick made his bid for the company in 1987.

A letter from the company to the Federal Treasurer, J. B. Chifley, in 1944, recorded in Gavin Souter's *Company of Heralds*, reflected the concern about death duties and the family's assumptions about the special position of the *Sydney Morning Herald*:

> We believe it would be inimical to the national interest for the paper to become a public company, and it would be equally dangerous were it to come under the control of any individual interest not concerned primarily with the national weal. A public company owes its first duty to its shareholders and the making of profits. That has always been a secondary consideration in the conduct of the *Herald*.

The problem of financing expansion and providing for death duties while maintaining a family's or individual's control was not unique to newspaper companies. But the newspaper industry felt it more than most. Newspapers had unique properties not only for families like the Fairfaxes, who believed they had special responsibilities for looking after a national treasure like the *Sydney Morning Herald*, but for strong individuals who wanted to use newspapers to extend their power, who were attracted by their influence on people and policies, by what might be called their extraordinary prestige yield, power return or the Fourth Estate factor.

Outside shareholders could provide the capital for growth but, if they had votes, they also eroded control. In England the great newspaper empires of the Berry brothers, Lords Camrose and Kemsley, and of Lord Beaverbrook, had been built substantially on capital raised by issuing non-voting shares to the public, while keeping the voting shares in the family. Camrose took the added precaution of building into his company's Articles of Association a provision that he would be chairman and editor-in-chief for life if he wanted. The greatest of them all, Alfred Harmsworth, Lord Northcliffe, had been so successful from the start with his magazines and the *Daily Mail* that he could fund his later ventures, including resuscitation of the *Times*, from his accumulated wealth. His brother, Lord Rothermere, devised protective capital structures as the group grew more diverse. Nobody was in any doubt about who controlled Northcliffe newspapers.

In North America families held on to control of great newspapers like the *New York Times*, the *Washington Post* and the *Wall Street Journal* and of widely based publishing empires like Thomson Newspapers and Hearst Corporation. But family tensions divided the ownership of others. In Louisville, the Bingham family's differences seemed so irreconcilable that their parents decided to sell their inheritance, the *Courier-Journal* and the *Louisville Times*. At the *St Louis Post Dispatch*, the Pulitzer family split under hostile takeover pressure in 1986 and three grandsons of the founder bought out the dissident family members who had wanted to sell to an outsider. The Pulitzer split had some similarities with subsequent events at Fairfax. But in none of these newspaper companies in the UK, or North America had family control gone back more than three generations. In 1987 the Fairfax company was in the hands of the fifth generation. Non-voting ordinary shares, which substantially financed companies like Beaverbrook's Daily Express Newspapers Ltd and the Graham family's *Washington Post*, while the family held the much smaller voting stock, were frowned upon in Australia. Ezra Norton at Truth and Sportsman Ltd had followed the British pattern and relied on public issues of preference shares in which shareholders surrendered voting power in exchange for a fixed dividend taken from the profits before any ordinary dividend.

Frank Packer had relied on a complex company structure that included preference shares. The Fairfaxes toyed with a plan for a public preference share issue in the 1940s but dropped it. Later they let the public in with full-voting ordinary shares, which made the problem of maintaining the family's control increasingly acute. A proposal for a much more complex preference share issue in 1984 divided the family and played a part in precipitating young Warwick's bid for control in 1987. For less conservative companies the problem of financing growth while retaining ownership and control was substantially solved in the 1970s and 1980s by the great liquidity of the banking and financial systems. Rupert Murdoch was able to finance the growth of News Corporation Ltd, from being a small Adelaide owner of one and a half newspapers to one of the biggest media groups in the world, largely on borrowed money while maintaining his family's equity in the company. Warwick Fairfax was able to buy back John Fairfax Ltd with borrowings that would have been unthinkable 30 years previously.

If the ANZ Banking Group could have loaned money in 1956 in the way it was lending in 1987, the company would never have needed to go public. Soon after John Fairfax Ltd floated, the ANZ was unable to advance money for expansion, but also partly to help the company pay its Christmas wages bill in December 1956. It was a decision taken by the London board, much to the embarrassment of the Australian head office in Melbourne. Ian Potter, the Melbourne broker who underwrote the public share issue, scraped some funds together and the company quickly corrected its stretched finances. The ANZ shifted its headquarters and board to Australia in 1976.

Basically, if a family wanted to keep control of an expanding company, without going very deeply into debt to maintain its equity, or by issuing non-voting shares, it had to keep re-concentrating the ownership, to keep drawing in the naturally expanding but weakening perimeters caused by growing family numbers. Henderson achieved this while Fairfax remained a small company, but later lost control. One way of doing it in North America was not available in Australia in the 1980s. In North America a company could buy back its own shares. In January 1989, the *New York Times* sold its cable TV network for US$488 million. This was done partly for tax advantages. Some of the funds could be used to repay debt. But the company also said the funds could be used to buy back some of its own stock. In this way a company could mop up outside or wayward family shareholdings while maintaining, even enhancing, the core family ownership. It was not an option available to John Fairfax Ltd when it sold its TV interests in 1987.

Balancing principle, or mission, against profit was another continuing problem for newspaper owners. At the UK Royal Commission into the Press in 1947 Lord Beaverbrook claimed, with typical hyperbole, that he ran newspapers for propaganda not profit. But even he, who had already made several fortunes in other industries, was careful to add, 'No paper is any good at all for propaganda unless it has a thoroughly good financial position.' Even the great C. P. Scott, editor and, for a while, owner of the *Manchester Guardian*, who fought for a principle in a way the Fairfaxes never did, by opposing the UK Government's aims and methods in the Boer War, emphasised that a newspaper 'is a business like any other business, carried on for profit and depending on profit for prosperity and existence'. Principle survived on profits. Sometimes it appeared better for the directors to look after the principles and the management to look after the profits. In the mid-1970s, when revenues were being squeezed by price and credit restraints while costs soared, the Fairfax directors came up from one of their pre-board meeting lunches and told the general manager, R. P. Falkingham, that all costs, including wages and salaries, had to be cut by 10 per cent. Falkingham told them they would have to get someone else to do it. He thought for a while he had lost his job but the board let the 10 per cent order fade. Falkingham imposed his own economy campaign.

By the late 1940s the third generation of Fairfaxes had died or retired and the board consisted of three cousins, Warwick, Vincent and John Fitzgerald Fairfax, a journalist on the *Herald*. Warwick was the biggest shareholder. Henderson persuaded John F. to resign and sell his shares, three-quarters to Warwick and one-quarter to Vincent. By 1950 the ownership of the company's 38 998 £10 shares was concentrated in Warwick with 28 003 and Vincent with 10 995. Warwick Fairfax and Henderson then went to work on Vincent, who had recently become a director of the Bank of NSW. Warwick and Henderson claimed it was against company policy to have working partners holding positions that might prejudice the *Sydney Morning Herald*'s editorial policy. This would have meant, of course, that no working director could hold a position in any outside institution or enterprise — not a bad principle for any newspaper to observe but certainly not one observed at John Fairfax Ltd. In any event, Vincent was no longer a working director. But he was asked to resign and pass in his shares. He left the board but kept the shares. When the company floated with a public issue and joined the Stock Exchange lists in 1956, Vincent rejoined the board. The public funds were needed to pay for Associated Newspapers Ltd, Sydney, owners of the *Sun*, the *Sunday Sun* and the *Sungravure* magazine group. Frank Packer at Consolidated Press had bid for Associated Newspapers first, then Associated had looked to its old friends at the Melbourne Herald & Weekly Times (HWT) for rescue, but Henderson intercepted all the plays and won. The cost, however, was the end, or at least a 30-year suspension, of the concentrated ownership strategy. That had to give way to a much grander strategy of protecting the crown jewels, the *Sydney Morning Herald*, by maintaining the balance of power in the publishing industry in Sydney and ultimately in Australia. Packer would not be allowed to grow, or the HWT or anyone else come to Sydney, or even to NSW, by buying any existing publisher.

Eight years later Henderson did it again. Arthur Shakespeare, owner of the *Canberra Times*, was approached by Packer and the HWT to sell his paper. Henderson had been there before them. Shakespeare had agreed that, if he sold, it would be to John Fairfax. The defensive perimeter continued to grow in the 1960s. Fairfax had already bought an uneasy partnership with the Wansey family in the *Newcastle Herald* — again upstaging Consolidated Press, which had recently approached the Wanseys.

Henderson had been the *Sydney Morning Herald*'s reporter in Newcastle 50 years previously. Fairfax also bought the *Illawarra Mercury* at Wollongong, from Henderson himself. The *Canberra Times* became another river of gold until some advertisers rebelled against its rising advertising rates. The *Newcastle Herald* and *Illawarra Mercury* became rich but smaller rivers until recession hit the steel and coal mining industries and unemployment made big holes in their advertising revenues in the 1980s. But they would recover. The Fairfaxes had invited the public in as shareholders to help pay for protection. But public ownership could make the family's control vulnerable. Henderson made one major error. He dropped the company's guard in 1961 and let in Rupert Murdoch. The defensive pattern was already well established when Ezra Norton wanted to sell out of Truth and Sportsman Ltd in 1958. To head off the HWT, Frank Packer's Consolidated Press or any other major publisher from using this opportunity to move into Sydney, Fairfax loaned O'Connell Pty Ltd, a company its solicitors Stephen Jaques and Stephen had on a shelf, the money to buy Norton's shares in Truth and Sportsman Ltd, sent in a Fairfax trio to run it and changed its name to Mirror Newspapers Ltd. Rupert Murdoch was then 29 years old with a controlling interest in News Ltd, Adelaide, inherited from his father Sir Keith Murdoch. He already had a small toehold in Sydney. A year previously he had bought Cumberland Newspapers, a suburban newspaper chain based mainly on the Parramatta *Advertiser.* Cumberland had been offered to Mirror Newspapers for £1 million, but Henderson knocked it back. Murdoch snapped it up early in 1960 and started the *North Shore Times.* When he offered to buy Mirror Newspapers, Henderson sold it to him for £500 000 profit to Fairfax. Gavin Souter records in *Company of Heralds* that the first Warwick Fairfax knew of this was when he read it in the radio news sheet of the ship he was travelling in between Suva and New Zealand. The sale gave Murdoch his start in Sydney, and Fairfax strategy became increasingly concerned thereafter to stop his further growth in Australia. In the end Murdoch won.

It may be that Henderson thought he was selling young Murdoch a dump, while taking a handsome and much needed profit for Fairfax. Such an explanation ignores the regard Henderson must already have had for Murdoch and the complex relationships between proprietor and manager at John Fairfax Ltd. Warwick Fairfax could not do without Henderson, whose stewardship of the company and the family's interests had been peerless. That was why Henderson, as managing director, was able to do the deal with Murdoch without consulting Warwick Fairfax, even though, a year previously, Warwick had expressed his opposition to selling the *Mirror* to Murdoch. Henderson was interested in Murdoch. He had qualities Henderson admired and searched for among his own editors and managers: ability, energy, daring tempered with judgement. In his first five years as publisher of the Adelaide *News* Murdoch had already shown the hallmarks of a potentially great entrepreneur: an ability to break conventions and make his own rules. He had shocked the Adelaide establishment by making a takeover bid for the much bigger Adelaide *Advertiser*, with funds to be borrowed from the Commonwealth Bank. Valued at £14 million, it would have been the biggest takeover bid ever made in Australia. The bid failed but was a portent for the future. Henderson continued to enjoy Murdoch's company for years afterwards. Although there were financial arguments for the sale of the *Mirror*, Falkingham, the Fairfax treasurer, found them unpersuasive and argued against it on strategic grounds.

Years later Henderson would speak bitterly of the Fairfaxes, particularly of Warwick Fairfax, who continued to remind him of the error of that sale to Murdoch. Much of that bitterness though, came from Warwick's marriage to Mary Symonds a year before the *Mirror* was sold. That started a rare and tense triangular relationship, a struggle between a powerful and determined manager and an ambitious and determined wife for control of a complex, intellectual, self-centred man, Warwick Oswald Fairfax. It was a struggle Henderson could not win. He had run Warwick Fairfax for most of the past 30 years. Then Mary took over. Mary Fairfax later claimed that, in the end, Henderson hated her husband. He certainly was not warmly disposed to Mary Fairfax.

It is hard to believe that Henderson sold Mirror Newspapers to Murdoch without considering the possibility that here was the man who one day might challenge the Fairfax publishing company in a much more vigorous and direct way than Frank Packer or any other potential newspaper competitor. But Henderson had achieved his immediate aim. He had stopped Packer from buying Norton's newspapers. That would have added the afternoon

*Daily Mirror* to Packer's morning *Daily Telegraph* and achieving economies of production and marketing that would make him a more formidable competitor for Fairfax. Henderson could not have foreseen that 15 years later the threat would occur in reverse when Packer sold Murdoch the *Daily* and *Sunday Telegraph*. By that time Murdoch's big break had come from London, when he heard that the Carr family might sell out their interest in the *News of the World* to someone other than Robert Maxwell. Murdoch used his most valuable Australian assets, particularly Southdown Press (*New Idea* and *TV Week*) to lever himself into London. Those assets did not include Mirror Newspapers. It was not until 1987, when he took over the HWT, that Murdoch felt strong in Australian newspaper publishing.

Did Fairfax really need to go public? As the capital cost of the defensive perimeter grew in the early 1950s, the Fairfax company had sought other funds. Its financial adviser, F. E. Trigg, a Price Waterhouse partner, had canvassed a £2 million loan from the MLC life assurance company. The MLC board seemed to favour the loan but it was unexpectedly knocked back when it was argued there might be adverse repercussions 'from a capitalist institution lending to another capitalist institution when it might be said that the money should be invested in housing loans'. Those were the days when people shifted their money away from banks that became involved in hire purchase finance. They soon ran out of banks. After the MLC loan failed, Trigg became a strong advocate of public flotation and won Henderson's support. The float was underwritten by Ian Potter & Co. and raised £2 million, of which £100 000 went to the family who had already received a special dividend of £100 000. So the net cash gain was about £1.8 million, less Potter's fee. The new share issues in the next few years raised a further £3.7 million. There were no calls on shareholders for capital after 1964. With better financial management in the first half of the 1950s the company might have avoided the public flotation. But the rate of expansion outstripped the company's financial management resources until R. P. Falkingham joined in 1957. By then the company was public.

In any event the whole trend of corporate finance in the 1950s and 1960s was towards stock exchange listing of a company's shares. Stockbrokers measured their success by the number of new company flotations they handled. The era of takeovers, privatisation and the substitution of debt for equity capital was three decades away. James Oswald Fairfax joined his father Warwick, his father's cousin Vincent, and R. A. G. Henderson on the board of the new public company in May 1957. He had just returned from the UK where he had taken a masters degree at Oxford and worked on the Glasgow *Herald* as a reporter and sub-editor. He was 24. James had 13 096 shares, about 0.3 per cent of the capital, mostly transferred to him by his father when he became a director. Two years later he acquired a further 112 781 shares transferred from two family trust accounts held in the names of his father and his father jointly with the family solicitor Alastair Stephen. But most significantly, in June 1959, on the eve of his marriage to Mary Symonds, Warwick Fairfax sold James an additional 595 760 £1 shares, very nearly 15 per cent of the capital, about half of Warwick's remaining holding, on a most liberal time payment system. Those shares were initially transferred to an account held jointly by Warwick and James's company, Kinghaven Pty Ltd. As they were paid for they were transferred to Kinghaven alone. The agreement allowed James to acquire at least 11 200 of those original £1 shares (44 800 of the 5/- shares after the share split in 1960) a year at a price fixed in 1959 — a total cost of about £50 000 a year.

The sale obviously had three purposes: it had the long-term purpose of keeping ownership in the family in as few hands as possible at a time when Warwick was entering into a new relationship, the consequences of which were unforeseeable, but of great concern to his advisers; by transferring the shares in direct line it minimised the impact of death duties; and it avoided gift duty by making the transfer a sale and purchase. The final payment for those shares was not made until after Warwick Fairfax died in 1987. But they had a great windfall for James long before that. He gradually bought the original shares, but received all the bonus shares issued on the total original holding. In June 1960, the company decided to split the £1 shares into four 5/- shares and make a one-for-four bonus issue. By then James had bought 21 200 shares, which had been transferred from the joint account to

Kinghaven. The share split and bonus turned them into 106 000 5/- shares. In addition Kinghaven received 478 000 bonus shares from the joint account. Kinghaven continued to receive this benefit throughout the life of the joint account. It played a critical part in future events in the family and in the company.

The Kinghaven agreement could not have been easy for Warwick Fairfax. He was 58 and about to be rejuvenated by a third marriage. That year, 1959, was one of the more eventful in his life. In February he had been sued by the Sydney solicitor Cedric Symonds, who alleged Fairfax had induced Mary Symonds to leave her husband and claimed £100 000 compensation. In March he had been divorced by his second wife, Hanne Fairfax, for failing to comply with an order for the restitution of conjugal rights. Seven months previously Cedric Symonds had divorced Mary on the same grounds. In June Warwick transferred all those shares to the joint account with James. At midnight on 3–4 July 1959, when his second wife's divorce became absolute, he married Mary Symonds at 'Barford', the Bellevue Hill home he had built for his first marriage. Warwick Geoffrey Oswald Fairfax was born on 2 December 1960. The family moved down to 'Fairwater', Double Bay, in 1969. Sir Warwick had grown up there. His mother had died there in 1965. Warwick Fairfax's energy levels, as far as the company was concerned, seemed to vary a good deal over the years. Mary Fairfax gave him a new charge. After leaving the running of the company to R. A. G. Henderson in the 1950s and mid-1960s, he returned after a long sojourn in London and immersed himself once again in John Fairfax Ltd affairs. This also led to increasingly strained relationships with Henderson and his general manager McLachlan, a tension that continued with their successors Falkingham and Gardiner.

Relations between Warwick Fairfax and his chief managers never recovered to the close rapport he and Henderson had enjoyed in the years before 1959. Although he was pressed to stand down from the chairmanship in anticipation that, if Cedric Symonds's suit went to court he would bring evidence that might embarrass the Fairfaxes and the company, Warwick Fairfax always maintained that the matter would be settled out of court. He was in a unique position to know this since he would be paying for whatever the settlement was. In fact, it was settled soon after he was deposed on 13 January and he was returned to the chair on 9 March. James played an important part in the unseating and reseating of his father. By January 1961 the 0.3 per cent of the capital he had had in 1957 had built up to over nine per cent. In addition to his own and the Kinghaven shares, James was acquiring another block of shares from his father's mother, Mabel Fairfax, in an arrangement similar to the Kinghaven purchase. These shares went into another of his companies, Bridgestar Pty Ltd, as they were bought out of the joint account of his grandmother and Bridgestar. Again, Bridgestar received the bonus shares due to the joint account and by January 1961 that holding was up to 113 083 shares. By early 1961 James and Vincent Fairfax together spoke with more votes than Warwick did.

The unseating of Warwick Fairfax was a traumatic event for everyone and Henderson sought to minimise the damage with two commitments. On the day before the 13 January board meeting James wrote to his father undertaking to arrange that, in the event of him (James) dying without legitimate male issue, the Kinghaven shares should pass to a trust to be held for the newborn son of Warwick and Mary, Warwick Geoffrey Oswald Fairfax, who was then 41 days old. The terms of the letter revealed a lot about the Fairfaxes' conservative views of succession. Daughters ranked with illegitimate sons outside the line of succession. Warwick Fairfax had two daughters Caroline, from his first marriage to Marcie Elizabeth (Betty), and Annalise, from his second marriage to Hanne. He was closer to Annalise than to Caroline. But neither was considered a possible director, let alone major shareholder and possible chairperson of the company. The limitations of this tradition were shown by the women who successfully took control of the *Wall Street Journal* and the *Washington Post* and exercised great influence at the *New York Times*. At Warwick Fairfax's request, Henderson also wrote to him on the same day as James, promising to help in Warwick's reinstatement as chairman.

Warwick Fairfax's legal adviser, Alastair Stephen, had given his client some hard-nosed advice on the protection of his interests during this period. Warwick found this advice unpalatable and severed his personal connection with Stephen Jaques and Stephen. Warwick and Mary went through a number of advisers in the following years. In the early 1970s they had been advised by Melbourne lawyer Philip Munz, Sydney solicitor John Gaden and Sydney business consultant William Perndt. That was when the basic Rockwood-Tailer Investments-Jones and Oriolo trust structure was established. The Rockwood Pastoral Co. Ltd had been an inactive subsidiary of the Scottish Australian Co. Ltd. In 1972 it was acquired principally to hold Warwick Fairfax's shares in John Fairfax Ltd and converted to a private company. Tailer Investments Pty Ltd was set up in Canberra, mainly to act as a trustee, and the Charles Lloyd Jones and Enzo Oriolo trusts were established. Rockwood's capital was expanded with large and complex preference share issues in the 1970s to accommodate trusts and taxation schemes but the basic Rockwood-Tailer-Jones and Oriolo structure remained. The boards of directors changed as advisers changed. Munz left the boards in the early 1970s, Gaden retired in 1976, Perndt resigned at the end of 1977.

By 1978 Gaden and Perndt had been replaced by Sydney solicitor Adrian Lane and J. C. Fletcher, former president of the Rural Bank of NSW. Sir Rupert Clarke and Wilfred Brookes of Melbourne joined the board.

A strange aberration occurred in the NSW Corporate Affairs Commission records in 1980–81. A company return dated 30 June 1980 showed that John Walker Wynyard of 29 George Street, Sydney, resigned as a director that day. John Patrick Connell and Dirce Pty Ltd, were appointed directors. Stoici Pty Ltd of 142 Cathedral Street, Woolloomooloo, continued as a director. Notice of Wynyard's and Stoici's appointments was not among the official Corporate Affairs Commission files. On 19 February 1981 Connell, Stoici and Dirce resigned and Otto Herbert Matthew Noe and Mewate Pty Ltd were appointed directors. There was no indication that any of the existing Fairfax directors had ever resigned. The company filed its normal annual return for the year to 30 June 1980 and normal returns continued after that.

John Wynyard was one of the biggest organisers in the tax avoidance industry that flourished and reached its peak in 1980 before its excesses provoked anti-avoidance legislation by the

Fraser Government, later strengthened by the Hawke Government. On 30 June 1980 Wynyard and his associates had processed about 2000 companies to relieve them of paying taxation in that year. Wynyard died in August 1985 while facing charges of conspiring to defraud the Commonwealth of $126 million in income tax. He had earlier estimated that his activities had cost Commonwealth revenues about $200 million. He maintained that what he had done was always 'on the advice of at least two QCs', was legal at the time, and that he was not substantially involved in the notorious 'bottom of the harbour' schemes in which records of stripped companies were destroyed. The shells of the companies Wynyard treated generally remained as subsidiaries of his operating companies. Retrospective legislation enabled the Hawke Government to recover much of the taxes avoided by these methods. John Patrick Connell, Wynyard's associate, was extradited from Boston, USA, to face charges relating to tax avoidance. Otto Herman Matthew Noe was a Sydney taxi driver who appeared as a director on at least 1000 companies Wynyard had processed. Dirce and Stoici were companies Wynyard commonly used for the same purpose. Tax avoidance was rife throughout Australia.

The NSW Corporate Affairs Commission claimed in 1982 to have identified 4000 companies that had apparently been involved in Wynyard-type schemes and 1000 directly identified with Wynyard. The names were never publicly revealed. The Fairfax newspapers actively attacked the tax avoidance industry during this period, the *Australian Financial Review* and the *National Times* having started the attack in the late 1970s. One of Wynyard's companies filed a return with the Corporate Affairs (Companies) Office on 15 December 1980, advising that Rockwood's address had been changed to 142 Cathedral Street, East Sydney. That address (in Woolloomooloo, not East Sydney), an old, small and worn terrace house fronting directly on to the footpath, was meant to be a last resting place for many of Wynyard's stripped companies. But Rockwood's annual returns continued to come from another registered office at Deloitte Haskins and Sells, 15–19 Bent Street and later 255 George Street, until 1988 when it was transferred to Peat, Marwick, Hungerfords on the 29th floor of the Tower Building, Australia Square. The phantom at Woolloomooloo would not go away. In December 1987 a return registering the share mortgage between the ANZ Bank and Rockwood covering a credit facility the ANZ had taken over from Midland Australia showed Rockwood's registered office at 142 Cathedral Street, Sydney. Another ANZ mortgage document dated 10 November 1987 referred to Rockwood as a company 'incorporated under the laws of the State of NSW having its registered office in the Australian Capital Territory at 142 Cathedral Street, East Sydney, in the said State'. Some confusion was understandable. Laurie Connell's company, Rothwells Ltd, also had a mortgage over some of Rockwood's shares at that time. That document showed Rockwood's address at 235 Jones Street, crossed out to third floor, 19 Hamilton Street Sydney. They were both John Fairfax Ltd properties.

Whatever its official residence, The Rockwood Pastoral Co. Pty Ltd was a company on which ownership and control of the John Fairfax group turned quite dramatically in 1987 and 1988. On 28 October 1988 the solicitors Freehill, Hollingdale and Page lodged a notice dated 30 September 1988 stating that the registered office of The Rockwood Pastoral Co. Pty Ltd had changed from 142 Cathedral Street to 235 Jones Street, Broadway. It was signed by W. G. O. Fairfax. Early on 1 October Mary Fairfax finally signed away her interest in Rockwood.

John Wynyard and his cohorts had filed those returns without the authority of Rockwood's directors and, probably, without their knowledge. But it seems unlikely that he filed company returns at random. Rockwood was merely a conduit for dividends that disappeared into a maze of companies downstream and his contact may have been somewhere in that maze. The NSW Corporate Affairs Commission was unable to throw any light on these curious entries in the record. The Commission's investigators had been interested in Wynyard in the early 1980s, but they had become demoralised and starved for funds by the Greiner Government as Australia developed into a corporate crooks' paradise. It was unable to say how many companies might have had similar phantom returns in their files.

The 'Fairwater' Fairfaxes used a succession of accountants as they had lawyers. In the early 1970s Price Waterhouse handled

Rockwood's returns. They were succeeded by Irish Young and Outhwaite, who merged into Deloitte Haskins and Sells about the time Wynyard and Connell appeared in those odd returns. Deloitte's was succeeded by Peat Marwick in the late 1980s. The board continued to change. Adrian Lane left in February 1983. He was replaced by Max Sandow, former NSW manager of the ANZ Bank, who was also a director of Kerry Packer's Consolidated Press. Young Warwick Fairfax (described as 'banker') joined the board in April 1985. J. C. Fletcher resigned in March 1988 and was replaced by Peter Done of Peat Marwick. Sir Rupert Clarke resigned three months later.

The Jones and Oriolo discretionary trust arrangements made in the early 1970s so impressed Sir Warwick that he pressed James to make a similar arrangement for the Kinghaven shares. As a result, James established a discretionary arrangement known as the Lorimer Dods trust (Sir Lorimer Dods was chairman of the Children's Hospital, of which James was a director and major benefactor) to handle the Kinghaven shares in his estate. There was still no irrevocable commitment of those shares to young Warwick since the trustee still had discretion to vary the terms of the trust. Warwick was still a minor. The discretionary trust also avoided complications about changes in ownership under the Broadcasting and Television Act. Later Sir Warwick retained Carnegie Fieldhouse as an adviser. Fieldhouse, who liked to describe himself as a quiet family solicitor, had a Sydney practice specialising in personal advice to very rich clients. Some lawyers described it as a boutique practice.

As adviser to Warwick Fairfax, Fieldhouse soon asked what had been done to fulfil the intent of the 1961 letter that the Kinghaven shares should eventually be held in a trust for young Warwick Fairfax. A trust had been established all right, but it was discretionary. This resulted in protracted negotiations between Fieldhouse and James's lawyers, facilitated by the reconciliation between James and his father in August 1980 as young Warwick approached his majority. Finally, in August 1985, this led to the Guilford Bell Settlement. The Lorimer Dods trust was in effect transformed into Guilford Bell which became a fixed trust with young Warwick a primary beneficiary. By that time the original

595 760 £1 shares Warwick senior had committed to James in 1959 had, as a result of a share split, two cash and six bonus issues, grown to 7 931 961 ordinary 50c shares held by Kinghaven in John Fairfax Ltd.

Under the Guilford Bell Settlement James retained control of the shares during his lifetime. When James died, control was to pass to young Warwick. James retained the income and the shares could not be sold or dealt with without the written consent of both James and Warwick. James had in effect settled the shares on Warwick but kept control of them and their voting rights and the income they produced until he died. By the time Warwick launched his takeover bid for the company at the end of August 1987, further bonus share issues had lifted this Kinghaven parcel to 33 994 116 shares. James sold his interest in the shares to Warwick for the estimated discounted future value of the income he would have received if he had held them until his death: $22.7 million. If the Guilford Bell Settlement had not taken place two years previously, those shares could have cost young Warwick $289 million. As it was James had not charged a premium for handing over control of those shares as well as the future income. It was a generous settlement, more than fulfilling the spirit of the 1961 letter. Counsel for Laurie Connell of Rothwells, who was Warwick's chief adviser in the 1987 takeover, later claimed his role in the arrangement helped to justify his $100 million fee.

Although the fate of the Kinghaven shares had been settled in 1985, Sir Warwick continued to press James about the disposition of the other shares he held, in his own name and those in Bridgestar. This was resolved late in 1986. After James died young Warwick would control the voting rights of the shares, although the income from them would go to other beneficiaries. Thus on James's death young Warwick would, with shares inherited from his father and mother, have control of well over 30 per cent of the votes in the company.

Sir Warwick Fairfax died on 14 January 1987. He had outlived the need to make complex arrangements for the minimisation of gift and death duties. In 1970 a Western Australian, Sydney Ambrose Negus, won a seat in the Australian Senate by campaigning on the single issue of abolishing death duties. He served only one term of three years but it was a pointer to the electoral appeal of his cause. In January 1977 the Bjelke-Petersen Government of ageing landowners in Queensland abolished death duties in that State. The political tide became irresistible. The Wran Labor Government in NSW followed suit in 1981.

The transfer of the Kinghaven shares to James, which helped depose his father twice from the chairmanship of John Fairfax Ltd, and helped build all that resentment and bitterness at 'Fairwater', need never have been made if the main purpose had been to avoid death and gift duties. The timing of the Kinghaven arrangement was much more significant. The effect was to secure half of Warwick's shareholding in James's hands, on terms very favourable to James, before Warwick entered his third marriage. It was his longest and apparently most satisfying marriage. But that 1959 arrangement, and the marriage to Mary, set in train the turbulent events in the Fairfax family and company over the next 30 years.

The accumulated bitterness of those years did not die with Sir Warwick Fairfax. It was securely in the custody of his widow, Mary, and had played a big part in the conditioning of her son, Warwick Geoffrey Oswald Fairfax. Politics were helping to create conditions that would turn that bitterness into action.

## CHAPTER 4

# SEVEN HARD YEARS
# WITH LABOR

Sir Robert Askin, Liberal Premier of NSW, died on 9 September 1981. On the day before his State funeral the *National Times* published a major article headed: 'Askin: Friend to Organised Crime'. It was written by David Hickie, a reporter who had, nine months previously, written a profile of Perc Galea, the Prince of Punters, a favourite racing identity with the Sydney media. Galea also controlled much of the flourishing illegal gambling industry in the city. This was well known but less well reported. The September article linked Askin and two police commissioners with Galea, casinos and starting price betting. It alleged that Askin and the policemen received substantial sums of money to protect these illegal gambling institutions and their owners from prosecution.

In the uproar that followed, some of the criticism levelled at the *National Times* was focused on the accuracy of, and evidence for, Hickie's charges. But the paper was mainly criticised for its 'lack of taste', for publishing the article on the day before the funeral. The critics included the board of John Fairfax Ltd. Max Suich, as chief editorial executive, was responsible for the editorial contents of all the Sydney newspapers. Hickie had pointed out in the article that it could only be published after Askin's death. The defamation laws prohibited publication while he was alive. But so soon after his death? What about the feelings of Lady Askin and of Askin's many friends? It was remarkable that this criticism was focused on the timing rather than the substance of the allegations. (Askin, a bank clerk before he became a politician, left an estate worth nearly $2 million mainly to his wife, who died three years later. Her estate, which included what Askin had left her, was valued at $3.7 million.)

Suich had been chief editorial executive for only a year. This was a critical test. He took full responsibility, apologised for the error of judgement in timing, and prepared the way for a board decision that was to have a major impact on the company's relations with the NSW and Federal Labor Party Governments and their friends over the next six years, and ultimately on the company itself. The board recommended, as a matter of company policy, that all Fairfax newspapers, particularly the *Sydney Morning Herald*, be more serious and vigorous in the investigation of organised crime in Sydney. There followed six of the most abrasive years in the long history of strained relations between press and politicians. Hickie's article had pointed at Askin, a Liberal Party leader. But Labor copped the fallout. And Fairfax then copped the fallout of Labor's resentments, some of which were real, some of which — such as allegations of a Fairfax conspiracy against Labor — were manufactured to divert attention from Labor's bad apples. The conspiracy allegations developed a life of their own and ultimately infected the Hawke Labor Government's judgement on media policy.

Organised crime, that is, crime that connected criminals with police and politicians and corrupted the whole system of justice, had thrived in Sydney for years but had become much more institutionalised in the Askin years of 1965–1975. In 1981 the politicians in power were those of the Right Wing of the Labor Party in NSW. Their best and brightest, Neville Wran, a lawyer, had led the Party to victory in 1976 when the Party's fortunes and morale in Australia as a whole were very low. Wran's election began a great renaissance in Labor's electoral fortunes throughout Australia. It also began a radical change in Labor's political style and in its attitude towards business and the media. The new Labor leaders sought co-operation rather than confrontation with their traditional enemies. But the Fairfax group was difficult to handle, particularly after 1981, when the Wran Government, since it was in power, took the brunt of the Fairfax resolve to go after corruption. Sir Warwick Fairfax had been chairman and executive head of the company during Askin's years. He had been friendly with Askin, who had cultivated him while running an increasingly corrupt state. That should not happen again.

By coincidence, Federal Police surveillance, including the use of telephone taps, was then revealing a network of corruption involving NSW police and politicians, which the State Government could no longer side-step. The Liberal-National Party Government in Canberra felt no protective obligations to the Labor Government in NSW. The Liberal Prime Minister, Malcolm Fraser, told Max Suich at dinner in Canberra late in 1981 of Federal Police investigations into the NSW Deputy Police Commissioner, Bill Allen, who was suspected of corruption. The *National Times* and the *Sydney Morning Herald* followed up the story. Seven months later Allen was allowed to retire, disgraced by a Police Tribunal inquiry. Canberra continued to be a source of information on corruption in state politics.

During the Fitzgerald Inquiry into corruption in the Queensland police force in 1988 it was revealed that Fraser had warned Queensland's Deputy Premier and Treasurer, Sir Llew Edwards, in 1982, of a possible attempt to whitewash the awarding of casino licences in that State. One of the applicants was a Gold Coast property developer, Eddie Kornhauser, who was an old friend of R. J. L. Hawke. Fraser recognised that the Labor Party with Hawke as leader would be a big threat to his own Government. It was in his interests to hit Hawke and the Party's power centre in NSW with whatever he could. Milton Cockburn and Mike Steketee reported in their *Unauthorised Biography of Wran*: 'It [the Allen Affair] was ... the beginning of a series of scandals which were to break over the Government in the coming years. The common thread running through most of them was information obtained from the Federal Police.'

The *National Times* continued to be the main news breaker on the corruption front. But the rising prosperity of the *Sydney Morning Herald*, as the new management team solved production problems at Jones Street and opened the way for increasing advertising volumes, enabled that paper to devote more of its broadsheet pages to the coverage of corruption, which in turn helped make it the major State political issue of the 1980s. In the mid-1980s the *Herald* produced an annual four-page progress report on the fight against corruption, which was also an annual reminder of the scale on which it had been allowed to develop.

The increasingly bitter relations this caused with the Wran Government flowed through to Canberra after R. J. L. Hawke led Labor to victory in the 1983 Federal election. Hawke had overthrown W. G. Hayden for the leadership of the Party just before the election. He had done so with the strong backing of the NSW Right Wing of the Party.

The Fairfax company, typically, did not have a collective attitude to Hawke. The *Sydney Morning Herald* had been fairly uniformly critical of the ALP and of Hawke during the 1970s when he had been leader of the Australian Council of Trade Unions (ACTU). Sir Warwick Fairfax, however, had a cautious regard for Hawke and saw him as a possible future constructive leader of the ALP. Early in 1977 an incident occurred that revealed a good deal about both men. At an official dinner in Canberra, Warwick Fairfax and R. J. L. Hawke and their wives sat (with others) at the same table at Hawke's request. Hawke came on loudly and strongly at Fairfax, baiting him, criticising the media in general, the *Sydney Morning Herald* in particular. Fairfax gave it back to him, less loudly but just as strongly, suggesting that such behaviour did him no good at all. Conversation lapsed at surrounding tables. Mary Fairfax tried to intervene and keep the peace. The two men eventually went to a table by themselves where Hawke expressed a personal regard for Warwick Fairfax and some regard for the *Financial Review*. Then he revealed his purpose in seeking Warwick Fairfax out that night: he thought Australia was divided, parties and organisations destructively pitted against each other, that the nation lacked a common purpose. It was a preview of the message of consensus he took to the people as leader of the ALP to win the Federal election later in 1983. In 1977 it had a sympathetic hearing from Warwick Fairfax. But it was the very public barney before the private talk that captured attention. Observers on the night, and those who reported the event, assumed, naturally enough, that Warwick Fairfax had been deeply offended and that the slanging match was bitter. That was a misreading of Fairfax. It was as natural for him to treat the slanging match as neither here nor there as it was for Hawke to start it. Relations between the two became relatively warm.

But Hawke had his own reasons for resenting the Fairfax press, particularly the *National Times*. As president of the ACTU in the late 1960s and early 1970s he had been befriended by Peter Abeles, head of the rapidly growing transport group, Thomas Nationwide Transport (TNT). Abeles, like other Austro-Hungarian migrants who had become very successful businessmen in Australia, was unencumbered by political prejudices. To Abeles, Labor governments and trade unions were not the natural enemies most Australian and English businessmen assumed them to be, but parts of the business structure, potential allies in pursuing profits and growth. Abeles was close to Hawke and Askin. After Askin retired from politics in 1975 he became a director of TNT. When TNT expanded to North America, it had to deal with the Teamsters Union and used people as go-betweens who had strong Mafia connections. The *National Times* pursued these connections. It also pursued possible patronage of key officials of the Australian Transport Workers Union by TNT executives. In 1984 Hawke appointed Abeles to the Reserve Bank board. Abeles was also a business confidant of Rupert Murdoch. Both were businessmen of the world. Their companies jointly owned Ansett Transport Industries, of which they were joint managing directors. They worked in industries that were politically highly sensitive. They were skilled in dealing with governments, including the Hawke and Wran Governments. But the Abeles-Hawke relationship was personal as well as political and Hawke resented the way the *National Times* pursued his old friend and their relationship.

The Fairfax group chose not to belong to these political power networks and remained outsiders as the new Labor leaders expanded their business connections. It resisted seduction. The Wran Government in 1979 awarded the licence to run Lotto in NSW to a consortium of Kerry Packer's Consolidated Press, Rupert Murdoch's News Corporation and Robert Sangster's Vernons Ltd. No tenders were called. The *Australian Financial Review*, then under Max Walsh, managing editor, and Fred Brenchley, editor, vigorously attacked this arrangement as a blatant exercise in political patronage. Walsh and Brenchley did not know that

Fairfax had been approached by Franco Belgiorno-Nettis, a very successful Sydney businessman, whose company, Transfield, was a major engineering contractor with close links to the NSW Government. Belgiorno-Nettis was also a patron of the arts. He said he thought he could arrange for Fairfax an interest in the Lotto licence. He would take an equity if Fairfax wanted him to, but his own interest was that of a benevolent go-between, an ambassador, only. The offer was rejected on principle. Fairfax had a long-standing policy of staying within the media industry. However, the company objected to the State giving new sources of cash to its competitors, and the chairman, James Fairfax, let Premier Neville Wran know it.

Thus all three major media groups in Sydney were approached to share in Lotto's future profit flows. There were legitimate business reasons for this. The television stations, radio and newspapers could give valuable publicity to Lotto draws and prize moneys and this would build Lotto sales. But the public would have been interested in Lotto draws anyway, as lively news items, just as they had been in the State Lottery draws and in the publicity given to winners before the kidnapping and murder of one winner's child in the early 1960s gave ticket buyers the option of anonymity. In addition, Murdoch and Sangster owned Soccer Pools in Australia. By bringing them into Lotto the Government neutralised a big potential competitor for the small gambler's money. There were also very convincing political reasons for passing profitable business opportunities to the media. Favours granted could mean favours returned at a critical time. But primarily it was an investment in mutual understanding. The Lotto franchise became modestly profitable for the owners, extremely profitable for the Government. Fairfax's immediate rejection of the Lotto opportunity confirmed its position as an outsider. In the NSW Labor lexicon it remained a baddy, while Murdoch and Packer had become, if not totally committed goodies, at least not-so-baddies, who knew where their commercial advantages lay.

Wran had won the 1976 NSW State election with a useful portfolio of resentments against Fairfax. The *Sydney Morning Herald* had pulled out all stops in its editorial campaign against Labor. A barrage of leaders in the *Herald* before the election dismissed Wran as 'Whitlam writ small' and 'a reassuring front man with his lawyer's plausible tongue and his Darling Point address'. The *Herald* harped on Wran's socialist commitments as a Labor Party member and emphasised the dire consequences if he became Premier. The final front page leader referred to the Liberal Party as 'a Party with a long record of honest government'. This was not a normal anti-Labor campaign. The *Herald* editors, strongly supported by Sir Warwick Fairfax, seemed to sense that the Liberal-Country Parties' time was running out. They were right. Wran won and never forgot the moral advantage those leaders gave him. Brian Dale, who had been Wran's press secretary, later wrote in his book *Ascent to Power* about those years:

> Whereas none of the other editorials advocated direct support for Wran they were not, in his eyes, as vicious as that in the *Sydney Morning Herald.*
>
> In the ten days between polling day and the night Willis (the Liberal leader) conceded, Wran referred frequently to the *Sydney Morning Herald*'s editorials. 'The others weren't for us but they were never totally against us. If we win we should try and defuse their hatred of us. It may be a vain attempt but we'll try it.'

Although he greatly enhanced Labor's standing with the NSW middle classes by running a government comfortable with finance, business and the professions, and by his own sharp mind and attractive mix of urbanity and earthiness, Wran came from a hard political school. The NSW Right Wing of the Labor Party was committed to one thing: winning. It was not diverted by ideologies, like the Left Wing of the Party. It did not believe in giving the enemy — and any critic was an enemy — room to move at all. Critical allegations were automatically denied and the people who made them denigrated. If there was substance to the allegations, that would be dealt with privately, but never admitted. If public pressure forced some sort of acknowledgement of, and action on, a potentially damaging issue, the response must be carefully controlled to minimise the damage. They were in fact basic rules of *Realpolitik* for gaining, and staying in, power for any political party, but they were more ruthlessly and systematically applied in NSW than in most States.

As the accusations of corruption increased, Wran's instinctive and calculated reaction was to defend the accused and berate the accusers, rather than accommodate the matter by suggesting an official inquiry. Admirable though this may have been from the principle that anyone is presumed innocent until proved guilty, the Wran position appeared not to admit the possibility of guilt. The case of the Chief Stipendiary Magistrate, Murray Farquhar, was critical for the Wran Government as Evan Whitton pointed out in his book *Can of Worms*. Farquhar's conduct of a case in 1977 involving senior members of the ALP had been criticised by the Court of Appeal. But Wran refused to suspend him and refused to acknowledge growing evidence against Farquhar, who, when he retired from the magistrates' bench, was appointed full-time chief adviser to the Government on drugs and alcohol. Farquhar was later found guilty of perverting the course of justice in another 1977 case involving Kevin Humphreys, secretary of the NSW Rugby League, and was sentenced to four years in prison. As Whitton pointed out, if Wran had suspended Farquhar after the earlier 1977 case, he would have saved himself a lot of trouble later on.

Government efforts at damage control eventually had to give way to the pressure of public concern about the mounting evidence of police and political corruption, fanned by media reporting, mainly in the Fairfax press and the Australian Broadcasting Corporation. Wran instituted a number of inquiries and Royal Commissions, one of which involved himself. As a result, reforms started in the police force and the courts, which began to turn back the tide of corruption that had risen so strongly in the 1960s and 1970s. By the time Wran retired from politics in 1986, clean-up action was underway on many fronts. But corruption as an issue still dominated New South Wales politics, particularly after the former NSW Minister for Corrective Services, Rex Jackson, was convicted of conspiracy over the early release of prisoners and jailed.

The damage to the Labor Party in NSW had been done. Wran's successor, Barrie Unsworth, continued Wran's policy of lambasting the *Herald* wherever and whenever he could, but the voters were deserting Labor and Unsworth led the party out of government in 1988. Wran was an actor manqué. His exit was beautifully timed. Labor's Right Wing considered the Fairfax group largely responsible for Labor's reversals in NSW. That was flattering. Fairfax rejected overtures. It was not amenable. But if it could not be wooed and not intimidated by public denigration there were other ways in which a politician in power could screw a company like John Fairfax Ltd. In addition to the 1976 election editorials and the 1979 *Australian Financial Review* Lotto editorials, Wran had a mounting accumulation of hurts. In 1981, the *Australian Financial Review*, then under a new editor-in-chief, P. P. McGuinness, criticised the state of NSW finances in an article headed 'How Wran has Squeezed NSW Dry'. Wran responded in the Parliament, claiming the *Australian Financial Review* was a 'paper without principle' and that it was taking over the role of NSW Opposition on instructions from the 'hierarchy' of John Fairfax Ltd. The *Financial Review* replied with a leader headed 'A Premier without Principle'. The frailty of the Fairfax 'hierarchy' argument was obvious. The *Sydney Morning Herald* took an opposing view of the state of NSW finances. It was running its own campaign about the state of the electricity industry of NSW. That was one more to add to Wran's tally of grievances.

The afternoon newspaper, the *Sun*, gave Wran his chance. On 23 February 1982 the paper published a photograph of the Premier taken from an unusual angle in which he bore some sort of likeness to Adolf Hitler. The accompanying text referred to him as Hitler and Adolf Wran. It was meant to be a joke. Some joke. Wran sued and the matter was finally settled out of court on terms not to be revealed. The settlement was handsome though not in the league of the $400 000 Alan Bond later paid the Queensland Premier, Sir Joh Bjelke-Petersen, to settle an alleged libel committed by the television station he had recently bought, QTQ9. But Bond later said he regarded the payment as part of the price of doing business in Queensland. This was certainly not a factor in the Wran settlement. Fairfax wanted to settle the matter as cheaply as possible. Wran's suit had emphasised a particular leverage politicians had in using the laws of libel. Wran had many opportunities, and used them, to claim that the Fairfax press was conducting a vendetta against him and the Labor Party. The newspapers were bound to report these claims. Cumulatively, they could gain some public credence. The politician could thus, in effect, argue his case and condition the public, from whom a jury would be drawn, to accepting his eventual claim to cumulative damages.

Wran continued to sue or threaten to sue the Fairfax papers and the company's Sydney radio station 2GB, whose morning announcer, Mike Carlton, was a mordant satirist. When the 2GB case came to court, the jury could not agree and nothing happened except that both sides accumulated big legal bills. At a NSW Labor Party Conference in 1983, Wran attacked 'the flagship of the Liberal Party of NSW, the *Sydney Morning Herald* and its subsidiary publications' which, he claimed, would stick to the Liberal Party 'through thick and thin in an endeavour to embarrass us and help our Conservative opponents'. The party faithful lapped it up. The *Herald*'s Milton Cockburn pointed out that an attack on the Murdoch press would have got just as enthusiastic a reception but for some reason or other it was spared. In fact, it was not until 1988, after Wran had retired, that the *Herald* again supported the election of a Liberal Government led by the relatively young Nick Greiner. Wran continued to talk about the Fairfax organisation being engaged in a vendetta against the Government, repeating the phrase in an interview with the *Australian* in 1984. 'The Fairfaxes are engaged in what's almost a vendetta against the Government; they have locked themselves into a conspiracy syndrome. They don't like us.' 'Why?' asked the interviewer. '…a whole variety of reasons, one of which is that I don't like them'. In that month he took a final retribution against the company by withdrawing all NSW Government classified advertising from the *Sydney Morning Herald*, transferring the business to the *Daily Telegraph*, owned by Murdoch's News Ltd. This was done by an instruction to all ministers on 7 September. Fairfax was advised on 12 September and the order took effect from 17 September. In the uproar that followed, Wran returned to the Lotto contract: 'A lot of the disenchantment the Fairfax organisation feels is that it sought to get the Lotto contract by the back door, unlike those who came by the front door, and they have been disenchanted ever since.' In fact, Fairfax had been approached and closed the door, politely but firmly. But that was the way the game was played, and Fairfax stuck to the task of getting the advertising back.

Although Wran maintained that cancellation of the advertisements was done for sound commercial reasons, the real reasons were as blatantly political as those of the NSW Labor premier Jack Lang in 1931, when he withdrew classified advertisements from the *Herald* and placed them with the *Telegraph*. As he later wrote: 'My attitude was that I was not going to subsidise them to attack a Labor Government.' Lang had a precedent: the previous NSW Conservative Government had withdrawn government advertisements from the *Labor Daily*. Wran's actions meant a loss of revenue of about $1.5 million a year to Fairfax. The advertising was restored to the *Herald* on 1 January 1986. Wran resigned on 4 July 1986 and retired from politics. He entered private business, was retained by Kerry Packer's Consolidated Press and became chairman of Whitlam Turnbull & Co., a private investment bank substantially financed by Packer. Whitlam Turnbull later became an adviser to John Fairfax Ltd after the Tryart takeover and Wran became a confidant of Mary Fairfax.

By the time Wran left politics, the matter of what to do about Fairfax and the apparently incorrigible Melbourne-based media group the HWT was in the hands of the Hawke Government in Canberra. Fairfax had a much more ambivalent relationship with Labor in Canberra than it had with the State Government in Sydney. The *Sydney Morning Herald* and the *Australian Financial Review* and, less enthusiastically, the *Age*, generally supported the Hawke Government's economic policies, but all the Fairfax papers, particularly the *National Times*, maintained their big interest in corruption at all levels of government. This was a continuing danger to Labor. Corruption exposures threatened the sacred old-mates networks, which were often more important to sections of the Party than sound economic policy. That had been shown in one of the most dramatic developments leading from publication in the *National Times* and the *Age* in 1984 of previously secret NSW police tapes of illegally tapped telephone conversations of suspected criminals. Those tapes threw a lot of light on old networks and led to the prosecution of High Court judge, Lionel Murphy, one of the NSW Party's favourite sons. Murphy had been a friend of Wran's for many years and was best man at Wran's wedding in 1976. Publication of those tapped telephone tapes added greatly to Wran's dislike of the Fairfax press.

The *National Times* in particular became concerned about the way the Hawke Government seemed to be cutting off the Costigan Royal Commission's inquiries. The Costigan Commission had been appointed by the Fraser Government in 1980 following disclosures in Kerry Packer's *Bulletin* magazine of corruption in the Painters and Dockers Union. The Commission's inquiries had taken it deep into the tax avoidance industry and then into the drug trade. The Costigan Commission had a number of case summaries on people and activities, which were certainly not evidence. On 14 September 1984 the *National Times* published the substance of one, containing allegations and innuendos against a well-known businessman, code-named by the *National Times* as 'Goanna'. Initial public reaction was relatively mild but it was quickly taken up in Federal Parliament by the Liberal Party leader, Andrew Peacock. The story became the focus of national politics. A Federal election loomed. As leader of the Liberal Party, Andrew Peacock was under pressure from his Party and from his deputy, John Howard, to perform or step down. Corruption was the issue on which he might survive. In Federal Parliament he took up Costigan's cause, accused the Prime Minister, Hawke, of being soft on organised crime, and called him 'a little crook'. He withdrew the last charge but in the following days continued to say outside the parliament that he was not afraid of naming the criminals to whom he had referred. Speculation about the identity of Goanna became a national sport. In the middle of it all the *National Times* reported a brush Hawke's daughter, Rosslyn, had had with the law on drug charges, of which she was acquitted on appeal. Hawke appeared on television and wept. At the State level, Wran had just imposed his bans on advertising in the *Sydney Morning Herald*, and Judge Foord of the District Court had been forced to step down as he faced conspiracy charges. The last two weeks of September 1984 were possibly the most dramatic of the stormy 1980s.

Gossip quickly identified Goanna as Kerry Packer and it was only a matter of time before he would be identified in Parliament. On the last Friday in September Packer took the initiative, identified himself as Goanna, denied all the Costigan allegations, referred to a campaign of innuendo and slur allegedly conducted aginst him by Fairfax newspapers, claimed Fairfax was seeking commercial advantage in publishing the material and demanded damages, which would be donated to a charity of Packer's choice. The Fairfax papers apologised at length in 1985. No damages were paid. Two years later, in March 1987, Packer was exonerated of Costigan allegations after investigations by the Office of the Director of Public Prosecutions, Ian Temby, and the Commissioner for Federal Police, General Gray. By that time he had sold his two television stations and other television and radio interests to Alan Bond for $1 billion. After years in the headlines, Packer became a very private man for a while.

The Goanna affair had important political consequences. It reinforced a campaign of denigration of the Costigan Commission and its methods. Costigan had been most effective in pointing to the way in which most forms of criminal activity overlapped, particularly by following the money trails from the tax avoidance and illegal drug industries. Those industries flourished with the advice and co-operation of bankers, accountants and lawyers. It also confirmed Labor's view that Fairfax was out of control and dangerous.

Fairfax was becoming increasingly isolated from the other Sydney media owners and the key political networks. And its newspapers, except the *National Times* and the *Sun*, were becoming increasingly prosperous. Max Suich summed it up at a lunch held at the Imperial Peking Harbourside restaurant in Sydney just after he left the company in December, 1987:

From the early 1980s there were frequent claims from other media proprietors that the journalists were out of control. The attention that Max Walsh had given to News Ltd did not disappear with his departure. [Walsh had left to join Kerry Packer's Consolidated Press.] Kerry Packer also came under scrutiny. State and Federal Governments, enlivened by guilt, fear of exposure, and the healthy paranoia this excites, put in the boot. Threats to individuals and against the company were made and resisted and usually neither editors nor journalists knew — a necessary ignorance because if threats are acknowledged, it has the desired effect of spreading fear and loathing.

Suich's speech was later printed as an article in the *Bulletin* of 23 February 1988. The paranoia was cross-infectious. To Labor, particularly to Hawke, the Fairfax papers seemed to be conspiring to single out Labor's mates for attack (particularly Hawke's mates — Packer and Abeles). To Fairfax, Labor seemed unduly protective and solicitous of those mates' interests.

These issues came to a head in September-October 1986 as the Hawke Government was considering radical changes to television ownership policy. Australia's first satellite, first proposed by Kerry Packer in 1978 and launched in August 1985, revolutionised the potential economics of the television industry, putting the whole Australian consumer market within reach of one telecaster without the great expense of laying special coaxial cable networks into the country regional stations. National networking and the offer of a greater range of programmes in provincial areas became much more possible than in the past, when programme networking had been virtually confined to the major capital cities. Until late 1986 any owner was limited to owning two television stations, whether they were in Sydney and Melbourne, as Packer's and Murdoch's were, reaching 43 per cent of the total Australian market, or in Cairns and Rockhampton, reaching only two per cent. Fairfax's Sydney and Brisbane stations reached 31 per cent. The HWT's stations in Melbourne and Adelaide reached 27.5 per cent. It was sound commercial logic to scrap the old two-station rule.

Whether it was sound commercial logic for a two-station owner then to buy five or six was another matter. The big question was: how to do this to Labor's best advantage? Hawke sought to take personal charge of making this policy. His chief political adviser was Peter Barron who had been Wran's political adviser. Barron was a committed advocate and practitioner of NSW Right Wing *Realpolitik*. Hawke originally wanted Packer and Murdoch to be allowed to keep their 43 per cent (and be allowed to sell that advantage on, instead of being subject to the normal grandfather provisions, which would have limited the advantage to the existing owners), while limiting other owners to 33 per cent. This was opposed by his Communications Minister, Michael Duffy, who wanted a limit of 43 per cent for all. That led to a long-running struggle between the two for variations on these original proposals, none of which was a really satisfactory long-term policy for the industry. Barron left Hawke in September and joined Kerry Packer's company. The Hawke-Duffy deadlock was broken soon afterwards by the Federal Treasurer, Paul Keating, who drove home the fact that a new television ownership policy could be turned into a total media policy by virtually abolishing, or at least greatly enlarging, the limits on television ownership, and at the same time applying limits to cross-ownership of television, radio and newspapers in any one market.

Paul Keating, like R. J. Hawke, had his own personal reasons for resenting elements of the Fairfax press. Hawke's were largely related to his friend Peter Abeles, Keating's to his friend Warren Anderson, a very successful shopping centre developer. The *Sydney Morning Herald*, in September 1984, had given splash page one treatment to charges by the then leader of the NSW Opposition, Rosemary Foot, that Keating, a former NSW Minister for Planning and the Environment, Eric Bedford, and a former Minister for Corrective Services, Rex Jackson, were part of a 'network' of favouritism that benefited land owners in the rich eastern harbourside suburb of Vaucluse. The State Government had agreed to sell Anderson parts of a reserve next to his property for what Rosemary Foot said was a price 'amounting to a gift'. The Premier, Neville Wran, had stopped the sale in January. Keating had stayed at Anderson's house in December. Rosemary Foot also alleged that Anderson had paid Tom Domican $20000 a year to work for Graham Richardson, one of the leaders of the NSW Labor machine. Domican was a strong arm man with a criminal record from London, who had faced conspiracy charges concerning the Enmore branch of the Labor Party. The charges were dismissed, but the Enmore conspiracy allegations continued to be a festering sore for Labor.

Foot's allegations were very embarrassing for the NSW Labor Party. Wran had not revealed that he was planning an early election. Reactions to the charges were quick and heavy. Suich and Gardiner saw Keating at Gardiner's house to reassure him that this was not part of a personal campaign, apparently with some success. But the *National Times* became obsessed with the Keating-Anderson connection and devoted a lot of resources to exploring it in the next two years. Keating was privately furious about the *National Times* investigations aimed at finding some corrupt, or corrupting, link between him and Anderson. But he refused publicly to acknowledge them or do anything about them, which only encouraged the investigators. In the event, the investigations proved to be more upsetting for Keating than the resulting article that was published in September 1986.

Keating's man was waiting in Sydney for the paper to come off the presses. He quickly scanned the article they had been waiting for. He rang Keating in Canberra: it was a fizzer. The *National Times* claimed that some of Anderson's companies had been involved in large-scale tax avoidance, that the Taxation Department was trying to recover those taxes, and, by innuendo, that the Treasurer's association with Anderson could carry dangers of patronage and exchanges of favours, particularly since they were both interested in French antiques. The story was more damaging to Fairfax than to Keating. It had no effect on the favourable treatment Keating was getting for his economic management from the media, and became subsumed into Hawke's own mounting criticism of the Fairfax press.

Hawke was particularly incensed by two articles in the *National Times* and one in the *Sydney Morning Herald* about what the Herald's chief Canberra political writer, Mike Steketee, called 'his [Hawke's] least favourite Labor Party issue — uranium'. In an outburst to a Labor Caucus meeting on 15 September Hawke gave vent to Labor's conspiracy theory about the Fairfax group. 'We should set our own agenda and not have it set by the Fairfax press, which is clearly committed against us,' he said. To most editors and proprietors nothing could be more flattering than to be told they were setting the political agenda. In an interview with Paul Kelly of the *Australian*, Hawke said:

It's no accident that the targets of their [the Fairfax group's] attack have either been leading figures of the Labor Party or friends of leading figures of the Labor Party. Therefore it's a political question as well. If I find them engaged in something which is inimical to the interests of the Labor Party, then they'll find me there as a tough opponent.

With a recommendation on the new television ownership policy due in the next few weeks, Labor's relations with Fairfax dominated political news and comment. In such a climate it was natural to assume that Labor would come down with a policy most damaging to Fairfax. Yet it did not. Hawke had initially, with Barron at his side, wanted a policy favouring his new mates, Packer and Murdoch. But that was politically unacceptable to the body of the Party. Duffy and Hawke (Barron) became locked in a struggle for policy. A ministerial committee of Hawke, Keating, Industry Minister John Button, who had been the Government's original deep thinker about media policy, and Michael Duffy, had been formed to consider the issue. Keating had been interested in media policy for a long time, an interest possibly inherited from his early mentor, Jack Lang. Ten years previously, when Labor was in opposition, and he was a spokesman on resources policy, he had introduced a private member's bill advocating limits to cross-media ownership. He continued to be a strong advocate of using the Government's direct powers over television and radio to devise a total media ownership policy. Once the Federal Budget was out of the way in August he directed his energies to selling his media policy to the ministerial committee. This policy would allow any one TV station owner to reach 75 per cent or even 100 per cent of the Australian market, thus creating in effect a six-station rather than a two-station ownership policy. But one owner would not be able to own a newspaper and a television station in any one market, except for those that already existed. This would freeze existing cross-media ownerships. The policy would have three effects: it would break up the two-station ownership, which would benefit Packer; it would help break up the HWT; and the cross-media limitations would prevent John Fairfax Ltd from benefiting from the HWT break-up.

The initial Hawke policy would have blatantly favoured Packer and Murdoch. It could be argued that Keating's proposal was more even-handed. Ground rules would be set for the future. Existing cross-media holdings would be protected while they were held by existing owners. Keating worked on Peter Westerway, who ran a long-term policy unit in Duffy's department, and on Button and Duffy on the ministerial committee. Hawke was won to a 75 per cent reach, in effect a six-station reach — one station in each mainland capital and one regional. Paul Kelly in the *Australian* reported that Hawke told some senior ministers in the week before the key Cabinet meeting on the issue, that if Cabinet approved the new 75 per cent ownership rule for the Packer and Murdoch groups, then his Government would win the next election.

Labor did win the next election seven months later. But it was due largely to the disarray in the Opposition Parties caused by the Federal political ambitions of the Queensland Premier, Sir Joh Bjelke-Petersen, who had been supported for years by Murdoch's flagship paper, the *Australian*, and to the attack on Opposition Leader John Howard's economic policies led by the Fairfax newspapers. Packer had sold out of television to Alan Bond. His magazine, the *Bulletin*, was no longer a force in national affairs. Kelly reported that Keating had won the policy battle when he won Button and then, at the key Cabinet meeting, won Bill Hayden, the man Hawke had displaced, who did not believe in any form of mateship with any media proprietor (and therefore had a sentimental core of supporters among Fairfax journalists). Hayden, according to Paul Kelly, conceded the intellectual respectability of the Keating proposition.

The new policy was announced on 25 November, effective from that day, although the legislation would take months to prepare and pass through Parliament by Minister Michael Duffy, who had never supported it. The need for the policy to be set and announced had become urgent. Speculation on a coming takeover play for the HWT was mounting and the new rules should be set before that happened. Murdoch, who was aware of the Keating proposals, and of their strategic consequences for his future in print or television in Australia, had virtually committed himself to bid for the HWT. Packer, shaken by the Goanna affair, and probably already conditioned to get out of television's very public arena, knew that he would either have to spend many millions to expand, or sell out. He had already been talking to Bond, owner of Channel 9, Perth, about who would buy out whom. Fairfax had been preoccupied with the war of words with Labor and with the consequent speculation about how Labor would favour its mates in the new television policy. But, being estranged from Labor, Fairfax had played no part in setting the new policy. Keating said he had told Fairfax's television chief, Ted Thomas, about his proposals late in 1985 but Thomas regarded this brief, casual, conversation as kite flying and did not report it formally to the Fairfax board. Keating and Gardiner had met casually at the Melbourne airport in September when the Hawke-Duffy debate was at its height. Gardiner seized the opportunity to protest at the unfairness of Hawke's proposal, which would have trapped Fairfax with 31 per cent of the market. Keating said that would not happen, that the new rules when they came would apply evenly to all.

But Fairfax appeared not to have planned fully for the strategic consequences of the 25 November announcement before Murdoch bid for the HWT on 3 December and Fairfax was forced into a battle without having a clear, long-term strategic goal accommodating the 25 November statement. But then it never did have long-term strategic plans, other than to limit Murdoch's growth in Australia. Fairfax had always been a strategic counter-puncher.

Keating's role showed what a pile driver of a politician he was. He had laid out the new ground rules for media ownership. By deregulating the banking system in the preceding two years, he had provided the participants with the market ammunition in the form of huge lines of bank credit for the takeovers that were to ensue. But he could not have foreseen or determined the outcome. That was left to the market. Nevertheless, Keating had to be concerned with the outcome. His policies were being tested. And although he had been critical of Fairfax's media spread and wrought about the *National Times* investigations of his relationship with Warren Anderson, the Fairfax papers had been the strongest supporters of his performance as Federal Treasurer and would be important when he eventually made his bid for Labor Party leadership and the Prime Ministership. Keating, as the probable next leader of the Party, knew very well that Labor, if it was to stay in government by commanding the middle ground of Australian politics, needed the continuing critical approval of uncommitted newspapers like the *Sydney Morning Herald*, the *Age*, and the *Australian Financial Review*.

Keating had been one of the key Labor Ministers Sir Warwick Fairfax had taken young Warwick to meet on the assumption that the 'Fairwater' heir would take the same interest in political affairs as his father had for over 50 years. That may have been a vain assumption, but the visit was not that of an intransigent class enemy as the Labor Party had liked to portray the Fairfaxes in the past. Keating was an occasional visitor at Fairwater, as guest of Mary Fairfax. He had been to dinner there on one occasion with, among others, two shooting stars of the 1980s, Bruce Judge of Ariadne Holdings and Kevin Parry of Parry Corporation. Both companies crashed spectacularly after October 1987 and their founders were removed as directors. But for a while they, particularly Parry, were on the fringe of Fairfax affairs. Mary Fairfax admired the share trading adventurers and was a director of Sir Ronald Brierley's Industrial Equity Corporation and Industrial Equity (Pacific), which survived 1987 in better condition than Ariadne or Parry. She cultivated a salon of those she regarded as the movers and shakers of business and politics, including trade union leaders.

In the aftermath of the HWT takeover and the subsequent Tryart takeover of John Fairfax Ltd, Keating was inclined to be critical of Fairfax's failure to come out of the HWT battle much better than it did. He thought that if Fairfax had clearly defined Queensland Press as its strategic objective (which it initially had) and played its cards correctly, Murdoch could have been persuaded to part with that company out of the HWT group. The emphasis was on playing its cards correctly — not only in the stockmarket, but in Canberra. Perhaps, after the events, Keating would have felt more comfortable with the more balanced print media ownership in Australia, which would have occurred if Fairfax had won Queensland Press. That would have made it more evenly matched with Murdoch's News Ltd and the HWT. But Fairfax lost the stockmarket battle. Keating continued to be influential in the events at Fairfax flowing from the Tryart takeover. But he could not control what happened in the market place.

Superficially, the beneficiaries of Labor's new media ownership policy appeared to rank in direct order of mateship. Packer had the most spectacular result. He was unaffected by the cross-media ownership rules but, since he had no metropolitan newspapers, if he chose to sell, greatly benefited by the new television reach rules. He chose to sell to Alan Bond for $1 billion. Murdoch, with a head start, acquired dominance of the Australian newspaper market in which he had been running a poor third, at a cost greatly reduced by the high prices he got for his television stations at values established by Packer's sale to Alan Bond. Strategically, Murdoch did best by far. But only the most starry-eyed Labor politician would call him a mate of the Party, whatever special relationship he may have had with Hawke, or Hawke thought he had. Fairfax ran third in this three-horse race. The HWT disappeared, possibly because it no longer had a will to do otherwise. The only matter to be resolved before it went was its price. Holmes a Court, who beat them all and emerged with a newspaper for nothing, was in a class of his own. Tactically, he did best. But he was no Labor mate. The immediate consequences of the 25 November media policy were determined in the market, not by any real or imagined concepts of Labor mateship.

Whether Alan Bond, whom Hawke also claimed as a mate, and the other new television proprietors would turn out to be winners or losers remained to be seen. They were burdened with debt, which could make their long-term tenures unstable. Packer's sale to Bond established an astronomical price level for television stations, which played a substantial part in the outcome of the takeover struggle for the HWT and subsequent events at Fairfax. Labor sought to maximise political advantage from its 25 November media policy. But its motives were confused between the destructive one of paying off old scores and the constructive one of spreading media ownership. In the long run all it may have achieved was a new concentration of ownership, on balance, to its own disadvantage. Murdoch owned major metropolitan newspapers in all states except Western Australia. In the March 1990 Federal elections, some favoured Labor, some the Liberal-National Parties, and some sat on the fence. In general, they followed the Murdoch precept of reflecting the political sentiment of their constituencies. If any party wanted Murdoch's support, the best way to get it was to be well in front in the opinion polls. His national paper, the *Australian*, aimed at the top end of the market reflected and stroked what it saw as Conservative opinion and prejudices. There were no signs of it favouring Labor in an election.

In the seven-year war of words with the Labor Party, Fairfax was by no means the loser. Its main newspapers had come through stronger than ever. But it lost the subsequent war in the stockmarket, partly because it was not prepared, partly because its energies had been concentrated on journalism and the political publishing battles, which strained its relations with the Hawke Government at a time when the Government was remaking media policy, and partly because it was inhibited by an unaggressive strategic tradition. It had never made a hostile takeover bid. It had always reacted to offers, as it did to Murdoch's bid for the HWT. But the new ownership rules required quick, aggressive takeover action if substantial positions were to be quickly secured in either network television or in newspapers in Brisbane, Adelaide and Perth. Alternatively, it could have done nothing and waited for the market stampede to end. That would have taken the most nerve. It had fumbled but then rapidly quit television at a handsome price. It had national publishing products to develop.

The company's actions in the months following the 25 November new media policy announcement convinced young Warwick and his mother that the time had come to move against the existing management and control of the company. That decision was the climax of many years of tense relations between the 'Fairwater' Fairfaxes and Jones Street management, going back to 1959 when Warwick Oswald Fairfax married Mary Symonds.

Those relations had deteriorated with increasing momentum after 1980 but were hardly related to serious criticism of the company's stategies. The criticisms were more directly related to one woman's ambitions, expressed first through her husband, then through their son. Controversy over the company's moves, after 25 November 1987 gave the 'Fairwater' Fairfaxes a sustainable reason to move. The death of Sir Warwick Fairfax on 14 January 1987 gave them the freedom to do so.

# CHAPTER 5

# WHOSE COMPANY IS THIS ANYWAY?

Shortly after Greg Gardiner took over as general manager of John Fairfax Ltd in 1980 he put a fundamental question to the board: do you want to remain a public company or do you want to become a private company again? He produced a statement of costs and benefits. The answer was quick and unequivocal: John Fairfax Ltd would continue as a public company. The question was raised at times over the next six years, particularly after Kerry Packer privatised Consolidated Press Holdings Ltd (CPH) in 1984. There was no boardroom support for privatising Fairfax. In fact, the pressures within the family, particularly from Sir Warwick Fairfax, were the very opposite to those involved with privatisation. The family showed little desire to go into debt to increase their equity in the company, or even to maintain their equity in the event of a new share issue. Sir Warwick, when chairman in the mid-1970s, had suggested a plan to convert equity capital into debt: he had brought to the board a scheme for restructuring the capital, borrowing a lot of money and increasing the company's long-term debt in order to give a substantial capital return in cash to shareholders. In this way debt would replace equity. The equity capital could then be rebuilt with bonus issues made from asset revaluations.

This was an early version of what became commonplace in the 1980s, particularly in North America, as takeover raiders and greenmailers, fed with funds and ideas originated partly by the US investment house, Drexel Burnham Lambert, but hungrily absorbed by bankers and brokers everywhere, revolutionised conventional ideas about debt and its relationship to equity. In effect, Sir Warwick's proposal in the mid-1970s was a conservative forerunner of the later trend towards replacing equity with debt. But it was not a privatisation proposal. It was dismissed by the board. Debt was not then as fashionable as it became in the next 10 years. But it showed that Sir Warwick Fairfax wanted cash before he wanted more shares. That was why he had started plans to have most of 'Harrington Park' (his country property) re-zoned for housing as part of a long-term mini-city development. He wanted to sell the land for cash rather than borrow and carry the development costs. The 'Fairwater' Fairfaxes lived well.

Kerry Packer had his own good reasons for privatising CPH. He was not a natural public company operator. Packer wanted to buy, sell, and use assets in his own way, without reference to, or responsibility for, other shareholders. His way might result in big fluctuations in profits from year to year and daring switches in direction, rather than the steady growth expected of a public company. In addition, he had one big advantage in buying back the company: CPH already owned 48 per cent of itself. Packer borrowed $300 million for the buy-back and got a bargain, which he then exploited in his own way. The big test for Packer's privatisation would come when his children and their children inherited the company. Then they might feel the need for cash rather than assets and CPH would be back on the stock exchange lists. By that time the brokers and merchant bankers would be arguing the case for refloating the leveraged buyouts they had advocated so strongly in the 1980s, just as the conglomerates built in the 1960s were being dismantled in the 1980s.

At Fairfax, Gardiner had raised the privatisation issue because he was well aware of the tensions that had arisen over the years when Fairfax, a public company, continued to be run as a private one. He had watched the way his predecessor, R. P. Falkingham, had imposed some public company disciplines, while maintaining a faithful stewardship for the family. The tensions were probably irreconcilable, but they became easier to manage after Sir Warwick Fairfax was succeeded as chairman by his son James in 1976, and two outside directors, Sir David Griffin and Arthur Lissenden, joined the board. David Griffin had known Warwick Fairfax since the 1920s when their families had holiday homes in the Blue Mountains. Griffin was a Sydney solicitor, a Singapore prisoner-of-war in the Second World War, a former Sydney Lord Mayor and a company director, whose major achievement had been as chairman of Gove Alumina.

Arthur Lissenden was a former chairman of Bowater Corporation of Australia Ltd, who had supplied the company with newsprint for many years, knew the paper business backwards and had a rigid regard for public company duties and responsibilities. With James Fairfax as chairman, John Fairfax as deputy chairman and two new directors on the board, the company became more comfortable with its public status. But tensions with the 'Fairwater' Fairfaxes and the fundamental problem of reconciling family and company interests, though submerged, remained.

With a unanimous commitment to remaining as a public company, Gardiner's immediate strategy as chief executive was to unleash the earning capacity of the great assets the company had, particularly the *Sydney Morning Herald* and the still partly-owned *Age*. Reflecting its private-company mentality, profit maximisation had not been an over-riding priority of the company in the 1960s and 1970s. Falkingham had been criticised by some board members for pushing too hard for profits. The official explanation for this attitude was a lofty concern for principle and quality, but a more telling commercial concern was to preserve the *Sydney Morning Herald*'s position in the market by keeping the cover price and advertising rates down and thus keeping competitors at bay. The company had made an awful error in 1976 when it had raised the cover price of the *Sun* to 12 cents, expecting Murdoch to follow with his competing paper, the *Mirror*. Instead Murdoch kept the *Mirror* at 10 cents and did irreparable damage to the *Sun*'s competitive position. The *Sydney Morning Herald* had broken its competitors in the nineteenth century by cutting its price.

The policy of profit restraint was essentially defensive and negative and by the end of the 1970s Falkingham was winning his argument for a more aggressive attitude towards profits. During the 1960s and 1970s the family could wear some restraint, even make a virtue of it, but by the 1980s the family was growing, and the ownership was no longer being concentrated on the Henderson principle, as it had been a generation previously. Vincent Fairfax had had four children, all of whom now had children of their own. Vincent's son, John, was deeply committed to the company and it anticipated that his son should work there eventually. John's brother Timothy ran a cattle property in Central Queensland and had a young family. His two sisters were married with children. Inevitably the dividend cheques for the family companies and trusts would have to become substantially bigger or they would have to be spread increasingly thin. In the year to 30 June 1980 the company had made an operating profit of $9.7 million after tax. The dividend took a little less than half: $4.6 million. Seven years later the profit had grown to $42.2 million. The dividend took $16.7 million. Although the total dividend had risen substantially, the ratio to profits had actually fallen.

To the 'Fairwater' Fairfaxes this looked like yet another triumph of the managers over the owners, one of an increasing number of black marks against the Gardiner regime. All of this profit growth had taken place in the five years to 1985. For the next two years operating profits had been flat due largely to lack of growth in television earnings, and the absorption of the costs of developing new publications and new printing equipment. Gardiner was a firm believer in financing the development of new products out of current revenue, thus making their costs tax deductible, rather than relying exclusively on growth by acquisition. His spending had been generous, perhaps too generous. But the company had firmly established its leadership in the burgeoning field of business publications, with strong profit prospects for the future, and the *Age* and the *Sydney Morning Herald* had greatly expanded and strengthened their readership and revenue bases.

One of Gardiner's high priorities in 1980 had been the smooth functioning of the Jones Street plant. The company had introduced new technology, fought an eight-week printers' strike in 1976 and then a 31-day journalists' strike in 1980 to make way for it, but it didn't work. The new, complex, specially-designed computerised system was aimed at great economies in typesetting and page makeup, editorially and in classified advertising, but it was far too ambitious. At peak work hours at night the system would fail and work on the night's papers would stop. The stoppages played havoc with work flows and the company paid penalties to ease the journalists' frustrations. The newspapers would fail to meet printing deadlines and the resulting delays in delivery to newsagents were damaging sales. A drastic solution was needed, a solution that could probably only be undertaken by a new generation of managers. Gardiner called on Fred Brenchley, who had been running the company's magazine division, to take over the Jones Street operation. Brenchley installed new and well-tried equipment, which achieved the cost savings the others had promised, and scrapped the failed system. The turnaround in morale and efficiency was remarkable. This allowed the company to exploit the classified advertising market much more aggressively than it had ever done in the past. The *Age* was already showing the way. Saturday's *Sydney Morning Herald*, which had never run more than 156 pages, and which had fallen to under 120 pages during the 1982 recession, was running at 204 pages at the end of 1987, over 220 pages in 1988, with a free, advertising-rich colour magazine inside it. Rises in advertising rates and cover prices showed what the market could bear for these newspapers and for the *Australian Financial Review*, which had also become very profitable.

In addition to the growth in publishing profits the company had a great windfall from its indirect investment in Reuters, through its holding in Australian Associated Press (AAP). The shareholders of AAP, mainly Fairfax, the Herald & Weekly Times (HWT) group and Australian Provincial Newspapers, were, like any other family, eager to get their hands on the cash available when Reuter shares were listed in London and New York stock exchanges in 1984. Between 1984 and 1987 Fairfax received over $123 million in capital dividends from the sale of AAP's Reuter shares. This and retained profits had helped finance Fairfax's expansion. With Gardiner as chief executive it had completed the purchase of David Syme Ltd, bought the highly profitable BTQ7 in Brisbane, increased its stake in Rural Press and made a number of smaller acquisitions in the UK and New Zealand. It had produced a successful colour magazine for insertion in the *Age* and the *Sydney Morning Herald* and started to put a premium price on Saturday's *Sydney Morning Herald.* The company was expanding its national publishing base. The biggest gains in circulation and display advertising volumes in the 1980s had been made by the *Australian Financial Review,* by Murdoch's *Australian* and by the new business magazines. The *National Times* had lost its way, but with new and firmly set directions, although it had been re-named the *Times on Sunday,* it could share in this continuing growth in the 1990s. These developments would ultimately require more secure access to printing and distribution facilities in all States. Its radio subsidiary, Macquarie Broadcasting, was at or near the top of the ratings in its major markets with funny, sharp, aggressive, thoughtful news-talk programming. The Sydney television station, Channel 7, was not as profitable as it had been but that was largely an industry-wide malaise.

There were flaws in the company's operations. Some of its spending on expansion appeared extravagant, lacking discipline. This could be explained by the buoyant profits and the confidence the company's top executives had in each other. It appeared that nobody was saying 'No' often and firmly enough. There was also the continuing problem of the Sydney afternoon paper, the *Sun.* For years the *Sun* and Murdoch's *Daily Mirror* had slugged it out with increasing losses. It was a war of attrition that would have to end sooner or later. It was in neither company's interests for the war to continue but each waited for the other to wave the white flag. Eventually truce was sought in the aftermath of the February 1987 purchase of HSV7, but peace terms were not settled before young Warwick made his takeover bid on 31 August. Then, it wasn't peace but total surrender, with John Fairfax Ltd, laden with debt, in no condition to bargain.

In 1986, before all this happened, the company's critics, particularly its competitors and political adversaries, claimed it had lost control of its costs as well as its editors. But they lusted after its products. Fairfax was in front where it mattered — in the market place. Those who had the chance were not averse to fostering discontent at 'Fairwater'.

It was not on his record as a developing publisher that Gardiner was most vulnerable to criticism. It was as a corporate strategist and stockmarket tactician, concerned not so much with the consumer markets its products served as with the buying and selling of large blocks of assets, the arrangement of capital finance, the design of the company's base and directions for the future that Gardiner's role was, inevitably, more controversial. Fairfax strategies had generally been defensive. The company had usually been forced into growth for its own self-defence. The purchase of a stake in the *Age* in the 1960s was an exception. It kept the great Melbourne paper, with all its similarities to the *Sydney Morning Herald*, out of the hands of the HWT or any other rival. But basically it was too good an opportunity to be missed.

A crunch came in 1979 when Fairfax determined to block Rupert Murdoch's bid for the HWT, which valued that company at $252 million. All the action in that first bid took place in the week ended 23 November 1979. Murdoch bid on Tuesday morning, stopped buying in the market on Wednesday under pressure from the Trade Practices Commission, sold out on Thursday to Potter Partners, who had come into the market on Wednesday (allegedly on behalf of unidentified friends of the HWT, but in fact on instructions from that company itself), and on Friday the friends — Queensland Press and John Fairfax — agreed to divide the Potter-bought shares between them so that they each ended up with 14.9 per cent of the *Herald*.

In statements announcing these acquisitions Queensland Press said it had increased its holding in the HWT from 8.4 per cent (which it had gradually accumulated over the years) to slightly under 15 per cent 'as a result of purchases on the market'. The Fairfax statement said only that the company had bought slightly under 15 per cent at a cost of $50 million — there was no mention of 'on the market'. That both companies ended up with slightly under 15 per cent, the limit that either could hold under the Broadcasting and Television Act without selling some of their other television interests, seemed more like a fortuitous accident than an outcome carefully planned from the moment the HWT 'friends' started buying in the market. The cost to Fairfax of over $50 million was five times the standby facility Falkingham, the general manager, had arranged with the ANZ Bank. Falkingham asked Gardiner, then effectively treasurer of Fairfax, whether he could raise the money. They were in Melbourne, at the HWT offices. Gardiner was sure he could. At 12.45 p.m. he picked up the phone and started, first call to the ANZ, the company's bankers. They could not handle such an amount at short notice. By 2 p.m. Gardiner had organised $80 million, unsecured. Murdoch had sold out with a $2 million profit.

The market was agog at Murdoch's opportunism. In three days he had made a $2 million profit at the expense of his enemies. Tactically it was dazzling. Strategically it was something else. He had accidentally delivered to Fairfax, at considerable cost to them, the means of blocking any further raid he might make on the HWT. Fairfax had a permanent block on Murdoch through an arrangement with Queensland Press that gave each first offer on the other's shares, which together made up nearly 30 per cent of the HWT capital.

In the 1980s the spirit of the company, under younger directors and managers, turned from defence to offence. At the Australian Broadcasting Tribunal's inquiry in 1981 into Fairfax's purchase of 14.9 per cent of the HWT, Gardiner was asked why it had bought the 14.9 per cent when it was clear Murdoch's bid had been aborted by the Trade Practices Commission. Gardiner explained that the fact that the bid had happened had steeled Fairfax's resolve and confirmed the need to make sure it did not happen again.

The costs of carrying that 14.9 per cent irked Gardiner, however. In July 1982, the company unwound that defensive stake by selling most of it (12 per cent) to Queensland Press. The HWT had again been under attack from Robert Holmes a Court, who had made a tentative bid for 50.1 per cent of the company in December 1981. The bid seemed to be getting nowhere but it must have helped HWT chief, Sir Keith Macpherson, bow to pressure from Fairfax and undertake a costly reorganisation of his group's defences. Another reason for doing so was that an alternate buyer for Fairfax's HWT shares was Robert Holmes a Court. That was a fate to be avoided at all costs. The costs fell on Queensland Press which, in two and a half years, had increased its holding in HWT from 8.4 per cent to 26.9 per cent of that company's capital. Australia was entering a new high interest rate regime and Queensland Press was supporting the HWT family in a very big way, at a considerable strain on its own economy. Murdoch chose that time of August 1982 to launch the *Sun*, a tabloid competitor in Queensland for Queensland Press's flagship, the *Courier-Mail.*

The sale to Queensland Press was a financial gain for Fairfax but a strategic loss. It meant that Fairfax gave up its right to first refusal on Queensland Press's 14.9 per cent of HWT. It had given up the potential block on another bid for the HWT by Rupert Murdoch. The deal, however, seemed to strengthen HWT's own internal defences by increasing the cross-holdings with Queensland Press. QP now owned over 26 per cent of HWT, which held 39 per cent of QP. The centre of gravity of the HWT group, instead of being fixed firmly in Melbourne, was starting to be divided between Melbourne and Brisbane. Murdoch showed no particular interest in these developments for his own takeover strategies. There was a big bonus for Fairfax in the deal. Because QP's equity in the HWT had increased, it had to shed the 19.9 per cent interest it had held in BTQ7 since it had formed the company 15 years previously. Fairfax bought that interest at fourteen dollars a share — well above the then market price of ten dollars, but a bargain in the light of BTQ's future performance.

After these decisive, though controversial moves, Fairfax seemed tentative. Having bought QP's equity in BTQ, it failed to go ahead with a full takeover offer for that company. It did not move on the remaining 80.1 per cent of BTQ for 16 months and then only when forced to by the independent television operator, Television Wollongong (TWT). This maverick had built up an equity of 16 per cent in BTQ when it offered $18.50 a share for the remainder. BTQ's board, which included Fairfax representatives, rejected the offer. Fairfax then offered twenty dollars and became locked in a market battle with TWT, the price rising in small steps until Fairfax won with a bid of $27.50 a share, nearly double the price it had paid 16 months previously. It was still a good buy.

While this action was going on in Brisbane, the company had a great break in Melbourne. The Syme family, led by Ranald

Macdonald, managing director of David Syme & Co. Ltd, publishers of the *Age*, agreed to sell their remaining holdings to Fairfax in September 1983 for $3.80 a share. Macdonald had been highly critical of the 1979 deal in which Fairfax had bought 14.9 per cent of the HWT. He had never been consulted, he regarded it as a conflict of interest for Fairfax, and therefore a threat to the *Age*, and he had been outspoken about this at any public forum available.

The Fairfax board and chief executive were not unhappy to pay him out and appoint a new managing director. Macdonald had presided over a great revival of the *Age* in the late 1960s and 1970s, but his business judgement was erratic. He was a turbulent priest in a parish easily stirred up about real or imagined threats to one of its icons, the *Age*.

Purchase of these family holdings built JFL's stake in Syme to over 70 per cent. JFL then offered $3.80 for the rest of the shares. The biggest outstanding holding was in the hands of the HWT with 14.08 per cent. Robert Holmes a Court saw the opportunity for a squeeze play and offered five dollars for the HWT shares. Fairfax's $3.80 continued to be accepted by small share holders and by the time the offer closed, the company had 83.77 per cent of Syme. The HWT had 14.1 per cent and Holmes a Court most of the balance. To keep the shares listed, Fairfax had to resell some of its holdings into safe hands, mostly senior employees of the two companies. The outside holdings in Syme were not cleaned up until May 1985 when Fairfax offered $10.20 and beat Holmes a Court on the floor of the Melbourne stock exchange at that price. The HWT accepted $10.20 and, although Holmes a Court made a last minute bid to embarrass the company by offering $12, he too sold out. A month later Fairfax sold the remaining 2.9 per cent in the HWT it had held since 1979 for $15.57 million.

The acquisitions of the outside interests in BTQ and David Syme had developed into long stockmarket battles of attrition, in BTQ's case probably unnecessarily so. But under full Fairfax ownership and control and under the new management of Greg Taylor, a former *Age* editor, David Syme became the major profit generator for the group. BTQ was highly profitable. But one of the strategic consequences was a sleeper.

The close relations Fairfax and the HWT had formed over many years, as joint sponsors and owners of AAP and Australian Newsprint Mills and then combining in the HWT's defence against Murdoch, had been loosened. Macpherson's days of power at the HWT were numbered. John D'Arcy, the managing director at Queensland Press, was the up-and-coming man in the group. Gardiner was a strong believer in the importance of personal relationships. He cultivated D'Arcy and believed he had what he liked to call a 'good understanding' with him. It was easy to do this with D'Arcy, a big, gregarious, outgoing Queenslander, who was by far the most visible executive of Queensland Press. But he was also a calculator, who had never been happy with the Fairfax-HWT-BTQ share deals, which Queensland Press had accepted in the early 1980s. Nevertheless, the relationship appeared to become even more important when D'Arcy finally, with some reluctance, moved to Melbourne to take over from Macpherson as chief executive of HWT. Nobody at Fairfax had bothered to understand the much more reserved chairman of QP, Keith McDonald. When Murdoch launched his second bid for the HWT late in 1986, there was no turning to Fairfax for help or comfort as there had been in 1979.

Although the final phases of the market struggle for David Syme and BTQ were drawn out, the main objectives had been quickly achieved. By the end of 1983 Fairfax had over 80 per cent of each company, Jones Street was working well at last and Australia was pulling out of the 1982-83 recession. The impact on profits was dramatic. Profits after tax for the year to 30 June 1984 more than doubled to $30.7 million. The buoyancy of that year, which was not a particularly good one for Australian companies generally, and the opportunities that seemed to be opening up for further expansion in Australia and overseas, had revived the old problem of how to enlarge the company's capital base without diluting the family's equity. In Gardiner's opinion — an opinion widely shared in the company — Fairfax did not have the capital base for a major acquisition, a really big leap forward, if the opportunity occurred.

The company was thinking bigger. The chief editorial executive, Max Suich, had been greatly stimulated by the views of the world he was getting as a director of AAP and, through AAP, of Reuters. Gardiner had a good relationship with the senior partners of Dominguez Barry, one of the coming brokerage firms in Sydney. It had made a name for itself in the fixed interest market and linked with Samuel Montague, the London brokers. Stephen Higgs from DBSM came up with what seemed to be an attractive solution to Fairfax's problem: an issue of participating irredeemable preference shares (PIPs) to raise $96 million. The concept was attractive: the new funds would ease the company's debt; expand its capital base (from which it could greatly increase its borrowing capacity for a big acquisition); give the family immediately about $6 million from the underwritten sale of their rights to the new shares; and the new shares carried no votes, except in exceptional circumstances, as was usual with preference shares. The issue was approved by the board. Sir Warwick Fairfax at first dissented but then agreed to take part in the issue. It was underwritten and enthusiastically received by institutions, which would be the main holders of the new shares; and it appeared to have the support of Sydney stock exchange officials, subject to approval by the stock exchange listing committee. Apart from natural reservations about the value of the share issue, and its possible consequences, it became a focal point for Mary Fairfax's suspicions about relations between Gardiner and Holmes a Court.

The 'Fairwater' Fairfaxes rebelled. Sir Warwick Fairfax raised legal objections to the issue and indicated he had changed his mind and would not take part in it. If profits fell and failed to cover the preference dividend, then these new shares could vote and threaten Fairfax family control. This was a remote prospect, but possible. The big house at Double Bay became an anti-PIPs campaign headquarters. One key objection was that the PIPs issue could block permanently any attempt to privatise John Fairfax Ltd.

Sir Warwick Fairfax had written in a memo, refuting arguments for the issue: 'By issuing PIPs shares we are tying up the company for ever. We eliminate our ability to go private and we are giving away something to non-family shareholders, something which we do not need to give away.' He was projecting a possible privatisation by the whole family, rather than by one member of it.

Whose company was this, anyway? Advice was sought from senior counsel and from the merchant bankers, Lloyds. John B. Fairfax had a high opinion of the work Lloyds had done for him. Arthur Charles, a Lloyds director, was married to a Fairfax and one of John's close friends. John had mentioned Lloyds favourably one night at 'Fairwater' and this was apparently remembered when advice was sought about the PIPs issue. The Lloyds advice to the 'Fairwater' Fairfaxes was far from enthusiastic about the issue. It was an interesting, innovative concept in itself, but the company showed no compelling need for new capital. World markets were buoyant and looked like staying that way. There were no indications that money was about to dry up. The world was awash with funds. The company could borrow or look at ways of raising new capital if and when it needed to. The PIPs issue would prove expensive over the years and could, under exceptional circumstances, make the company marginally more vulnerable to outsiders.

This was cool, dispassionate advice. It was music to 'Fairwater' ears but bitterly disappointing to John B. Fairfax, who continued to support the issue. So impressed was 'Fairwater' that Arthur Charles was briefly considered as a possible candidate for the Fairfax board, a merchant banking presence as a counterweight to Gardiner. This idea died before it got off the ground, perhaps helped on its way by Lloyds' concluding advice that, no matter what the merits or demerits of the issue itself, it was a matter for the Fairfax board to decide, and that, if the directors decided for it, Sir Warwick should go along with it. That over-riding advice ran counter to his actions since the first board meeting at which the issue had been considered. It was unwelcome at the time but seemed to be accepted when various capital issue proposals were considered in the next two years.

Why did the company need the new capital? Gardiner had made the usual amorphous statement companies make when raising new capital, that is, it was needed for expansion. If a definite takeover target was in sight no company was going to let everyone know about it. That would only raise the takeover price. But to the PIPs issue's critics this was a major concern. And to 'Fairwater' it reinforced the conviction that the managers had taken control of the company and were running it to build their own empires rather than to enrich the shareholders. Mary Fairfax thought Gardiner was lining up some sort of option deal for himself. She was apprehensive that he would do a deal with the Perth raider, Robert Holmes a Court, to erode the family's position. Gardiner was also a trustee of the long service and retirement funds and could influence the votes their shares carried. There were no Fairfaxes among those trustees. The retirement funds held the balance between the Fairfax family voting power and that of the public at large. Although it was unlikely that the public would ever vote as one, the problem of how the retirement funds would vote in certain circumstances was worrying and persistent.

Suspicions about each other flourished in Jones Street and 'Fairwater'. Apart from Sir Warwick Fairfax, the other Fairfax family board members continued to be enthusiastic about the PIPs issue. Worse followed. The stock exchange's joint listing committee, headed by Hattersley and Maxwell (later Kleinwort Hattersley) partner, Reg Keene, ruled that the PIPs shares, if issued, would not be listed on the Australian exchanges. The matter went to the full stock exchange committee headed by a progressive chairman, Jim Bain, who was reluctant to turn down the listing of a new security and suggested that the company and its brokers look at ways of making it more acceptable. To the exchanges the PIPs shares were very thinly disguised non-voting ordinary shares. Such shares were no longer listed on the Australian exchanges. They were considered undemocratic.

The PIPs issue became the subject of vigorous lobbying from both sides. Gardiner, accompanied by his chief financial executive, Ron Cotton, and Stephen Higgs and Jim Dominguez of Dominguez, Barry, Samuel, Montague Ltd, addressed the stock exchange committees. There was an equally vigorous counter-lobby from 'Fairwater' in Sydney's financial district against the issue as it passed back and forth between the exchange's listing committee and the full committee under Jim Bain. The *Bulletin*, Kerry Packer's news weekly, published an article at the beginning of October headed 'Fairfax Fund Raising — the Mystery and the Drama'. The article canvassed the 'Fairwater' objections, raised the spectre of the preference shares being given full voting rights (thus reducing the family's equity to 35 per cent), and used figures and information that could be sourced to confidential board papers. The article, by the *Bulletin*'s editor-in-chief, Trevor Kennedy, referred to ambitious management leading 'a fairly dozey board' into major expansion. This was followed by a big spread in the Melbourne *Herald* with more inside information, including reference to one opinion paper pointing out that non-voting shares were Robert Holmes a Court's springboard for taking over Sir Lew Grade's Associated Communications Corporation in London.

For the past five years Mary Fairfax had been preoccupied by the threat of Holmes a Court to her husband's company. Normally these articles would not have caused much anguish at Jones Street. The Fairfax papers in recent years had pulled no punches in reporting and commenting on their competitors' affairs. But to Jones Street these pieces, containing confidential board information, were deliberately inspired from 'Fairwater', one of whose advisers was Mary's and Warwick's confidant, Marty Dougherty. Marty was handling the public relations campaign against the PIPs issue and later, in the fee case, claimed credit for its defeat. During the court case over the payment of Rothwells's $100 million fee, T. E. F. Hughes, QC, questioned young Warwick's integrity over passing confidential board papers to Bert Reuter before the takeover bid in August 1987. Warwick pointed out that his father had used board papers to seek outside advice over the capital raising proposals in 1984.

All these lobbying and public relations campaigns were, however, irrelevant. The PIPs issue perished on the position Reg Keene had taken from the outset: if Fairfax was allowed to do this the way would be open for any company to do it. In the developing takeover climate the Australian exchanges had stuck to a level playing field policy aimed at keeping the markets free and open, so that neither takeover bidder nor defender could take an unfair advantage. The playing field still had some very rough patches, such as a sliding scale of voting, which some older companies, like Amalgamated Wireless (Australasia) Ltd (AWA), could use to entrench existing directors and managers at great cost to shareholders. But, overall, this policy of enlightened self-interest had worked so well in the booming mid-1980s that many, if not most, shares had a takeover premium superimposed on what might have been considered their normal price. Higher prices were good for stock exchange business. If the Fairfax PIPs issue went through, other companies would follow and raise capital in this way, while preserving control with existing managers and directors. The new rough patch in the playing field would spread and threaten the takeover buoyancy the exchanges' policy had so well nurtured. The stock exchange listing committee would not budge. In October 1984, two months after the PIPs issue was taken to the Sydney stock exchange and appeared to be assured of official blessing, the issue was abandoned.

The PIPs issue had been condemned by 'Fairwater' because it threatened the family's control of the company. It was knocked on the head by the stock exchange because it would entrench family control of the company. In the meantime Rupert Murdoch, Alan Bond and Robert Holmes a Court continued to expand rapidly, while continuing to control their listed companies, by borrowing and borrowing and borrowing.

In 1988, when Warwick came to refinance the takeover debt he had incurred, important elements of the new finance organised by the US investment house, Drexel Burnham Lambert, were the equity appreciation rights issued to enhance the attractions of the low-ranking debentures. These were, in effect, rights to non-voting equity shares in John Fairfax Ltd. Gardiner's attempt to adapt such shares for the Australian market through the ill-fated PIPs issue was an important part of the case Warwick made for taking over Fairfax and getting rid of Gardiner.

Mary Fairfax gave Marty Dougherty a painting and about $20 000 for his work on the PIPs issue. Marty had enabled the *Bulletin* and the Melbourne *Herald* to have some fun at Fairfax's expense. But that was irrelevant to the outcome. Reg Keene and the stock exchange's listing committee blocked the PIPs issue. Keene had never heard of Marty Dougherty.

# CHAPTER 6

# THE WAR FAIRFAX COULDN'T WIN

The PIPs affair widened and deepened the gap between 'Fairwater' and Jones Street. Suspicions of each other were fed by rumours and second- and third-hand reports. While the PIPs issue was still burning, James Fairfax had a call from his father saying that he had received information that James should have. James went to see Sir Warwick at a lawyer's office in the city. The old man reported that he had been told by a very reliable source that Gardiner was in league with Holmes a Court. Who had told him? Someone who had just returned from North America who had been told by a leading East Coast businessman. Any evidence? No. James dismissed the charges. But the conspiracy seen from 'Fairwater' provoked a counter-conspiracy theory at Jones Street: Murdoch, a leading East Coast businessman, had been playing host at the Olympic Games in Los Angeles to selected friends, retainers and clients of the 10 TV Network, which was televising the Games to Australia. One of them had been fed the Gardiner-Holmes a Court story and had relayed it, as Murdoch intended, to Mary Fairfax who in turn told Sir Warwick, using the story as evidence to support her long-standing conviction about the existence of a Gardiner-Holmes a Court plot to take over John Fairfax Ltd. Under the influence of such conspiracy theories, the 'Fairwater' and Jones Street forces became increasingly estranged. The PIPs issue had failed but the fuses it lit burned strongly for the next three years. Murdoch helped keep them burning. In the fee case, in October 1988, a document was produced in court, which appeared to have been written by

Sir Warwick Fairfax on Monday, 10 September 1984. The document referred to a meeting that occurred at the Rugby League semi-final football match in Sydney the previous day between Sir Warwick's informant and Ken Cowley from News Ltd. Cowley had told the informant (who had approached Cowley) that he knew about the proposed PIPs issue and indicated that Rupert Murdoch wanted to take a position in the shares. Cowley said that if Fairfax went ahead with the issue, the company would be taken over within two years. Murdoch was driving a wedge between 'Fairwater' and Jones Street. Cowley said Murdoch had not gone ahead with his bid for St Regis Paper Co. in North America because he would have had to raise more capital, and that would have diluted his own equity. (Murdoch had bought 5.6 per cent of St Regis and, in August 1984, said he would bid for 50.1 per cent of the company. This would have cost him $900 million. St Regis had only just been greenmailed for $51 million by Sir James Goldsmith in March and $141 million by Loews Corporation in April. Now Murdoch was trying them on in June. St Regis had had enough and merged with the Champion Paper Company. Murdoch sold his 5.6 per cent stake for a profit of $37 million. The reader can decide why Murdoch didn't go ahead with the St Regis bid. A year later he bid $1.6 billion for the US television network, Metromedia, and became a US citizen on 5 September 1985 to consummate that takeover.)

The PIPs issue was announced publicly the next day, 11 September. However, it had been broached with five institutions, which had been supportive, and with the Sydney stock exchange, some days before that and could easily have been picked up by Murdoch's intelligence network. Sir Warwick used that 9 September information to strengthen his argument against the PIPs issue. Murdoch continued to be solicitous of the problems of the 'Fairwaters' with the Jones Street management. He offered to help Sir Warwick to privatise John Fairfax Ltd. Sir Warwick would keep the *Sydney Morning Herald* as a core asset. Murdoch's price would be some of the other assets of the group. The 10 September 1984 document reported that Cowley had said that Gardiner was very clever and would build the company up to a colossus but at the cost of the family's control. He was stroking very responsive nerve endings at 'Fairwater'. Sir Warwick Fairfax was bitter and nearing the end of his life, in some ways a Lear-like figure in his final years, worried about his heirs and the distribution of his estate, sometimes petty and petulant in his impatience with small matters. But in supping with Murdoch he continued to use a very long spoon.

The PIPs issue had brought young Warwick Fairfax more directly into the 'Fairwater' councils. He was working at the Chase Manhattan Bank in New York. If you wanted funds, he suggested, what about the Euro-dollar market? He was already being conditioned to concepts of the use of debt, which would have horrified business in the 1950s (they certainly would have horrified the cautious, conservative Fairfaxes), but which became a way of life in the 1980s. The PIPs issue also introduced to Fairfax family affairs John Barber of Morgan Stanley, a friend of Warwick from New York. Barber was in Australia at the time. A guest at 'Fairwater' and 'Harrington Park', he wrote a paper criticising the PIPs issue and became influential in the family's thinking about privatisation plans for John Fairfax Ltd from 1985 onwards. Barber later worked for William E. Simon's company, WSGP, which became an adviser to Fairfax after the takeover. He became a director of John Fairfax Group (USA). Fairfax parted company with William E. Simon and WSGP late in 1989.

The loss of the PIPs issue did not seem to inhibit Fairfax's growth or ambitions. This appeared to justify the 'Fairwater' stand on PIPs. It certainly did nothing to allay suspicions about what the managers were up to or their competence to do it. Fairfax continued to expand at Broadway with new publications and in 1985 bought the *Spectator* in the UK and half of Fourth Estate Holdings Ltd, publisher of *National Business Review*, a prosperous weekly in New Zealand. They were relatively small acquisitions but potentially important springboards for the future. One big opportunity for overseas growth presented itself in 1985: the *Daily Telegraph* in London was in danger of sinking underneath the debts incurred in its modernisation programme. Fairfax executives talked with the *Daily Telegraph* about establishing a relationship and a possible injection of equity capital to replace some of the debt. But the talks, with the chairman's son Nicky Berry and the company's advisers Rothschilds, were tentative and Fairfax was beaten to the punch by a Canadian, Conrad Black, who had been able to establish a much more telling relationship with the chairman, Lord Hartwell. Black put in £20 million and a new managing director as part of a longer term plan to acquire up to 51 per cent of the company. The *Daily Telegraph* would have been a big bite for Fairfax and perhaps they weren't yet ready for it. James Fairfax was much more cautious than his executives about the proposition. If the PIPs issue had gone ahead, it seems doubtful that the company would have been any bolder. It was still inhibited by the long-standing policy that it would not move on another company without being asked, or at least without being welcome. It was locked into the tactics that had so successfully delivered David Syme. But the big legacy of the PIPs affair was the hardening 'Fairwater' resentment at the JFL management style and aims.

In the eyes of 'Fairwater', Gardiner and Suich, with the backing of James Fairfax, were becoming as wilful and difficult as Henderson and McLachlan had been in the 1960s. Marty Dougherty recalled Warwick saying 'Gardiner is a bigger threat to our family than Henderson was'. Three events to come converted this resentment into a resolve by young Warwick Fairfax that drastic action was needed to bring the company back under control: Rupert Murdoch had launched his second bid for the Herald & Weekly Times (HWT) and defeated Fairfax, which was on the back foot from the start; Sir Warwick Fairfax died; and Fairfax bought HSV7 from Murdoch at what seemed a very high price of $365 million (which included some NSW regional papers) and immediately made a public relations mess of cutting costs and changing programmes to try to improve HSV's image and profits. For the first time, Fairfax's management ignored or underestimated the peculiar sensitivities of the Melbourne market.

In New York in the autumn of 1986 Rupert Murdoch's strategic thoughts returned to the HWT. In Australia, the Federal Treasurer, Paul Keating, had taken charge of the Hawke Government's media policy and was aiming it at breaking up the cross-ownership of newspaper and television stations by one owner in one market. Political leaders from both sides of the Australian Parliament saw

Murdoch when they went to New York. Keating saw him for dinner one night in October 1986 after the Treasurer's regular visit to the International Monetary Fund's annual meeting in Washington. The Murdoch and Packer organisations in Australia were aware of the broad outlines of his proposals. Keating later claimed he had also told Ted Thomas, Fairfax's television boss, and had a favourable reaction. Thomas's recollection was of a brief talk with Keating at an advertising conference to which his reaction, if any, was neutral. In Washington and New York Keating could bring himself up to date on the US cross-media ownership regulations, which were causing problems for Murdoch in Boston, and test his own proposals for Australia on the new US citizen.

The possibility of bans on cross-media ownership by the Hawke Government had been publicly discussed in Australia since mid-October but the policy had not been defined and accepted in the Party and Cabinet rooms. The October dinner in New York was important for sounding out Murdoch's thoughts on the issue. A firmer outline of the proposed policy was put to Murdoch and Packer soon afterwards in Canberra. Max Walsh revealed some of the details in the *Sydney Morning Herald* on 24 October 1988. Walsh wrote:

> Two years ago, early in November, Treasurer Paul Keating met two of Australia's media tycoons, Kerry Packer and Rupert Murdoch, in Canberra. He outlined to the two the Government's proposal to change the then television laws so that licence-holders would not be able to purchase print interests in the same region.
>
> Rupert Murdoch's response was to say that he would beat the gun and bid for the HWT. This was followed by a rather sharp exchange between Mr Keating and Mr Murdoch, which was hosed down by Ken Cowley, Mr Murdoch's top man in Australia, telling his boss to behave.
>
> Mr Keating was not the first politician to give advance information on proposed policy changes to interested parties, but if this information had been used for commercial gain it would have quite devastating political repercussions. As it was, when the Minister for Communications announced the new

policy later in November, Mr Murdoch had an offer on the table
for the HWT within a matter of days.

Significantly absent from that Keating meeting were any
representatives from the other major media groups, Fairfax and
the HWT.

This particular incident is not described in Edna Carew's
biography *Keating*, published last week, but she does relate:
'At a later meeting with Fairfax executives, Mr Keating gloated:
"I've hurt you more than you have hurt me." '

The incident also revealed the fragile relationship between
Keating and Murdoch. They were both people users, acutely aware
of the temporary nature of political alliances. When Keating stayed
at Holmes a Court's country house outside Perth early in 1988,
Murdoch became very cool about him indeed. Murdoch might
have bought the HWT more cheaply than he eventually did if he
could have done so before the media ownership policy was
announced. His reaction at that early November meeting emphasised that the Government had to announce its policy as soon
as possible. Kerry Packer was quietly laughing. He had already
talked with Bond about a Channel 9 television network (Bond
owned 9 in Perth) and who might own it. Would Packer sell to
Bond or Bond to Packer? There was no doubt about the outcome
when Bond's price approached ten figures. Packer knew a lot more
about television than Bond did.

The policy would also force the big Australian media groups
to a fundamental choice: was their future in newspapers or in
television? Fairfax, for example, owned television stations in
Sydney and Brisbane and newspapers in Sydney and Melbourne.
The expansion of its possible television ownership under the
new audience-reach rules, would allow it to buy a station in
Melbourne. But this would jeopardise its ownership of the
*Age*. It could not buy a major newspaper in Brisbane without
jeopardising its ownership of BTQ7. But it could buy either TV
or newspapers in Adelaide or Perth.

Murdoch faced similar but much more serious problems. He
was not in a very strong position in newspapers or television.
His daily newspapers, with the exception of the *Australian* on

Saturday, were struggling. The *Sydney Daily Mirror* was fighting a battle of attrition with Fairfax's *Sun* for a shrinking retail advertising market; the *Daily Telegraph* had lost ground to the *Sydney Morning Herald*; in Brisbane his recently established *Sun* had done Queensland Press a favour by forcing it to enliven its heavyweight *Courier-Mail*; the *News* in Adelaide had always been overshadowed by the *Advertiser*. Only his Sunday papers in Perth and to a lesser extent in Brisbane and his two very successful magazines, *New Idea* and *TV Week*, were leaders in their markets. His Channel 10 TV stations in Sydney and Melbourne were erratic, scoring heavily with specials like the Olympic Games and big movies but spending much of the rest of the time away from the top of the ratings. Apart from a few years in the late 1970s to early 1980s, when television profits were buoyant, there never seemed to be enough revenue to go around three capital city commercial stations.

These factors had made Murdoch take a special interest in the changes taking place at the HWT. John D'Arcy moved down from Brisbane to be managing director in 1985 with a brief to reinvigorate the company. The chairman, Sir Keith Macpherson, was reluctant to release his grip, but eventually he left and John Dahlsen, a director who had been a partner in the company's solicitors, Corr and Corr (later Corr, Whiting, Pavey), moved into the chair. One of D'Arcy's first moves was to get into NSW by buying the provincial newspaper interests of Consolidated Press Holdings Ltd — a mixture of paid and free papers in Orange, the Hunter Valley and the Central Coast centred on Gosford. The price was high at $95 million — $54.9 million in cash and the rest by the issue of 6 195 500 shares. This gave Packer a five per cent stake in the HWT. To Murdoch this seemed like a potential break in the defences the HWT had been building around itself for years.

This view was confirmed when Kerry Packer and John D'Arcy had talks about Packer selling his magazine group into the HWT for a further share swap, which would have given Packer 25 per cent of HWT. This plan broke down when Packer and D'Arcy were both hospitalised for treatment of tumours. The deal perished in the hands of their merchant bankers. Packer immediately sold his HWT shares to Ron Brierley's Industrial Equity Limited (IEL) for $45 million. The HWT also issued more shares: to Associated Newspapers in the UK to take over their long-standing 15 per cent interest in HSV7; to complete the takeover of Gordon and Gotch; for the Leader suburban newspaper group in Melbourne; for a new share issue; and for a share placement to raise more cash. In a year under D'Arcy the HWT had increased the number of shares on issue by a third, about half of which were potentially loose. The policy of strengthening the HWT by performance and growth rather than by the static defence of the old regime, had opened the company up for attack. D'Arcy later said he always knew the fortress would fall but not so soon. That was what some people close to Fairfax thought about a move from young Warwick.

In stockmarket terms, from the end of July 1986, when Packer sold his five per cent to IEL, the HWT was in play, despite the protective web of interlocking shareholdings woven around it. The HWT owned 41 per cent of Queensland Press, which owned 27 per cent of the HWT, which owned 36.7 per cent of Advertiser Newspapers, which owned 11 per cent of the HWT, which owned 59 per cent of Television Broadcasters (ADS7, Adelaide), which owned 11.8 per cent of Advertiser Newspapers. The stockmarket was no longer very impressed with this defence. By the end of September IEL had built up its HWT holding to over 11 per cent. HWT shares had risen from $5.25 at the end of July to over $7 and showed no sign of stopping. Holmes a Court was dealing in the shares, helping to stir up the action. In New York Murdoch could sense that his time was coming. The Government was about to change the ownership rules, the HWT was opening up and the raiders were moving in. If he didn't move soon, time might run out. He had another problem that helped to focus his mind on print as his future in Australia.

In 1986 Murdoch had become a US citizen so that his company could own US television stations. As an American citizen he could not own or control Australian television stations. But he had two: Channels Ten in Sydney and Melbourne. He tried to find a way around this with legal legerdemain and during the HWT campaign even pretended he had nothing decisive to do with News Ltd and the Channels 10 to try and avoid the consequences of his US citizenship.

The HWT takeover documents later filed by News Corporation included the statement:

... (d) Network Ten Holdings Ltd (NTHL) TNCL (The News Corporation Ltd) has less than one per cent of the voting rights in NTHL and accordingly is not deemed to control that company or any of its subsidiaries (which include the licensees of Channel 10 Sydney, ATV10 Melbourne and 4AM Mareeba). Further TNCL asserts that it does not have legal or de facto control of such companies.

The documents pointed out that the Broadcasting Tribunal had sought the Federal Court's legal advice about US citizen Murdoch's ownership arrangements and that important questions of law and fact had still to be decided by the Court and the Tribunal. New directors were appointed to NTHL to comply with the new arrangements. But it was hard for a hands-on operator like Rupert Murdoch to pretend that he was not making all the decisions about these television assets. That and his sudden entrances and exits to and from boardrooms in Melbourne and Brisbane gave the coming struggle for the HWT elements of high and low farce, mainly enjoyed by the Fairfax papers. The jokes did not last long. The Federal Court threw out Murdoch's pretence on 20 January 1987 but he quickly took charge openly of the coming disposal of four television stations, the two Channels 10 he owned, and the two Channels 7 he was about to acquire through the HWT. As a US citizen since 1986 he was not entitled to more than 15 per cent of any of them. But he had the disposition of them. Such was the confusion of television ownership laws.

On 25 November 1986, the Minister for Communications, Michael Duffy, announced the new media ownership rules: no cross-ownership in one market, except for those that already existed, but one television broadcaster could reach 75 per cent of the Australian audience. This was eventually reduced to about 60 per cent in order to secure support of the National Party and ensure the passage of the proposed legislation through the Senate. It still meant one owner could hold four or five television broadcasting licences against the previous two. Although the legislation was months away, the new rules started from 25 November. The previous day Holmes a Court had revealed that he had what he called 'a friendly stake' of 10.33 per cent in Queensland Press.

Two problems confronted Murdoch. At what price should he pitch his HWT bid? It had to be a price the boards of the HWT, Queensland Press and the Advertiser Newspapers could not, in the interests of their shareholders, refuse, but not so high that it became uneconomic for him. And would the Trade Practices Commission throw a block at him as it had in 1979? He had his brokers J. B. Were and Bache, Cortiss, Carr work on the former; his close friend and chairman of News Corporation, Richard Searby, QC, looked after relations and negotiations with the Trade Practices Commission and other government tribunals. Murdoch flew out from Aspen, Colorado, to Melbourne, arriving on the morning of Tuesday, 2 December, to take charge of News Corporation forces in the coming war for control of the HWT group. The board of the HWT was due to meet the next day. One item on the agenda was a proposal from Holmes a Court to merge his and the HWT's West Australian newspaper interests. This may have helped precipitate Murdoch's action. He and Holmes a Court each thought that the other was too close to certain members of the Herald and Weekly Times board.

Over the next two months the action changed the face of media ownership and control in Australia. It also helped convince young Warwick Fairfax that it was time to change the face of the ownership and control of John Fairfax Ltd.

The battles for the HWT were conducted on several fronts: on the stock exchanges, in the courts, before government tribunals, on the front pages and in the boardrooms, in private meetings and over the telephone systems of Australia and North America. On Wednesday morning Murdoch walked into the *Herald* building in Flinders Street, Melbourne, as he had done in 1979, to make his bid of $1.8 billion for the company — $12 a share. The editor-in-chief, Les Carlyon, saw Murdoch walk past his door and immediately rang Max Suich at Fairfax in Sydney. Carlyon, a former editor of the *Age*, had been a Murdoch-watcher from way back. At lunch with Suich a few days previously he had suggested a move by Murdoch was imminent. Suich did not share this view. Carlyon was being wooed by Suich to work for Fairfax and guessed correctly why Murdoch had just walked down the corridor. Murdoch's bid surprised the Fairfax managers, who were well aware that the HWT was in play, but had their eyes on Holmes a Court and Packer as possible bidders. The HWT board late that afternoon said they would recommend acceptance of the bid in the absence of a better offer. Holmes a Court started to feed speculation into the media about his possible intentions and on 8 December had 'preliminary discussions' with the HWT board. Murdoch said he would not increase his offer and on 12 December Brierley sold IEL's 12 per cent stake in the HWT to Murdoch for $12 a share, without an escalation clause giving IEL the right to any increase in the price Murdoch might eventually pay. This caused speculation that a side deal had been done on some other front between the two. Murdoch had his first stake in the HWT. There was some brief skirmishing before the action really started:

*3 December:* Murdoch bids $1.8 billion for the HWT in the morning. The HWT board recommends acceptance of the bid late in the afternoon, subject to not receiving a better offer.

*5 December:* Holmes a Court has 'preliminary talks' with HWT chairman, John Dahlsen, and managing director, John D'Arcy. In succeeding days he keeps the media stoked with speculation about his intentions.

*10 December:* Murdoch says he will not increase his bid above $12 a share.

*12 December:* Ron Brierley sells IEL's 12 per cent stake in HWT to Murdoch for $12 a share ($220.5 million) without an escalation clause to cut him in on a higher bid. Holmes a Court has 15 per cent of Queensland Press.

*19 December:* Holmes a Court tells HWT executives he will decide on making a rival bid the following week.

*23 December:* Holmes a Court outlines to HWT executives a possible bid at $13.30 a share.

*24 December:* Holmes a Court announces a $2 billion bid ($13 a share) through his Bell Group subsidiary, J. N. Taylor Holdings Ltd.

*30 December:* Dahlsen invites Holmes a Court and Murdoch to attend that week's HWT board meeting — Murdoch skiing at Aspen.

*1 January:* Holmes a Court lifts his bid to $2.125 billion ($13.50 a share). He says a bid for Queensland Press is also possible.

*2 January:* HWT board recommends Holmes a Court's new offer, in the absence of a more attractive one. Murdoch suddenly appears at the HWT meeting and says he won't lift his bid above $12.

*4 January:* John Fairfax Ltd bids $910 million for Queensland Press ($20 a share) conditional on Queensland Press selling its HWT shares to Holmes a Court.

*5 January:* Maintaining the alliance, Holmes a Court says he will sell his 15 per cent of Queensland Press to Fairfax.

*9 January:* Murdoch lifts his bid to $15 a share ($2.3 billion) At the same time, through his family company, Cruden Investments, he offers $23 a share for Queensland Press, take or leave the latter by 5 p.m. Queensland Press board leaves it, due largely to opposition by Dahlsen. Stock exchange media index stands at 7100 against 1900 a year previously.

*12 January:* The HWT directors recommend the revised Murdoch bid in the absence of a more attractive offer. News Ltd gets new directors to try and avoid the complications of Murdoch's US citizenship.

*14 January:* Sir Warwick Fairfax dies.

*14 January:* Fairfax lifts its offer for Queensland Press to $24 a share ($1.1 billion), again conditional on Queensland Press accepting Holmes a Court's offer for the HWT.

*15 January:* Holmes a Court and Murdoch do a deal: Holmes a Court sells his 14 per cent of Queensland Press to Murdoch and withdraws his legal actions aimed at confusing Queensland Press. Murdoch sells Holmes a Court West Australian Newspapers Ltd for $200 million and HSV7 Melbourne for $260 million. Murdoch bids $23 for all Queensland Press shares ($1.05 billion).

*19 January:* The Australian dollar falls to 64.2 US cents.

*20 January:* Federal Court throws out US citizen Murdoch's attempt to distance himself from ownership and control of the 10 TV network. Queensland Press accepts Murdoch's $15 a share

for its HWT shares, giving Murdoch 40 per cent of HWT. Fairfax
mounts legal action based on Murdoch's US citizenship.

*20 January:* Bond buys Packer's TV and radio interests for
$1 billion.

*21 January:* Fairfax bids $16 a share ($2.5 billion) for the HWT.

*22 January:* Australian Broadcasting Tribunal (ABT) calls an
inquiry into whether News is controlled by a foreigner.

*27 January:* The HWT board backs Murdoch's bid of $15 a share.

*28 January:* Murdoch starts selling off more HWT assets — ADS7
(Adelaide) to Canberra Channel 7 owner Kerry Stokes. Adelaide
Advertiser delivers its 12 per cent stake in the HWT to Murdoch.

*29 January:* Reserve Bank stiffens its supervision of banks' large
credit exposures for takeovers.

*30 January:* Sir Warwick Fairfax's funeral.

*2 February:* ABT starts its inquiry into Murdoch's bid for HWT.

*3 February:* ABT inquiry adjourned to allow the HWT to consider
selling its own electronic assets instead of Murdoch selling
for them.

*4 February:* Fairfax offers $385 million for HSV7 (Melbourne) and
ADS7 (Adelaide) and four radio stations. The HWT says it will
put them all up for tender.

*5 February:* The HWT board claims 'more than a dozen' bids for
various assets.

*7 February:* Murdoch tells the HWT board that he and Fairfax have
agreed to end the war. Under the truce terms, Murdoch got
the HWT for $2.3 billion; his family company got Queensland
Press for $1.05 billion; Fairfax got HSV7 and a group of regional
NSW newspapers for $365 million. (The regionals actually went
to Fairfax's 45 per cent owned associate, Rural Press, and
Murdoch kept the *Gosford Express* which the HWT had bought
from Packer — thus, with his own *Gosford Star,* gaining complete dominance of the populous NSW central coast market:
advertising rates rose soon afterwards.) Holmes a Court got
WA Newspapers Ltd at a great bargain price; Kerry Stokes got
ADS7 and four radio stations; Westfield and Northern Star
Holdings got two Queensland radio stations and some newspapers. Westfield and Northern Star soon afterwards bought the
10 Network from Murdoch's News Corporation.

The sale of HWT assets which, apart from WA Newspapers, were not substantial or potentially substantial profit earners, reduced the net cost to Murdoch of that company from $2.3 billion to around $1.2 billion. Some of the asset sales were made by agreement with the Trade Practices Commission. But the emergence of Rupert Murdoch with control over newspapers with more than 60 per cent of total Australian-paid circulations was not an issue with the Commission at that time and only with minorities within the two major political parties.

In the middle of the two months action, Sir Warwick Fairfax died on 14 January. His elder son, James, John Fairfax Ltd's chairman, who had first heard of Murdoch's bid for the HWT at Tokyo Airport on his way back to Australia in December, was by then on a cruise ship in Antarctica. Sir Warwick's funeral was delayed until 30 January.

In this summary of the events of those two months Murdoch and Holmes a Court have been identified individually as bidders. Fairfax has been identified as a corporation. This has a purpose. Murdoch and Holmes a Court were their corporations, not only because of their large personal stakes (each had over 40 per cent of his main holding company) but also because they were clearly identified with their enterprises in the public mind, even though neither man's name appeared in the company's title. John Fairfax Ltd on the other hand, was Fairfax, one of the oldest companies in the land, bearing the name of the family that controlled it with nearly 50 per cent of the capital. But the person running the campaign was not a Fairfax. He was Gregory John Gardiner, the group general manager. This difference in the command structure of the three companies engaged in the struggle may not have been decisive in the outcome. Gardiner had the confidence of his board and planned and executed the strategy and tactics with the board's approval. But his campaign was bound to be more cautious and less flexible than those of Murdoch or Holmes a Court. And its objectives were comparatively limited.

Murdoch wanted the lot or what the authorities would allow him to keep. Holmes a Court wanted what he could greenmail out of Murdoch or Fairfax. He particularly wanted WA Newspapers. Fairfax wanted to stop Murdoch. It also wanted Queensland

Newspapers, the Queensland Press subsidiary which published the *Courier-Mail.* Queensland Newspapers had a strong economy based largely on classified advertising as the *Sydney Morning Herald* and the *Age* were. But it was not Fairfax style to make an uninvited or hostile bid for another company. If Murdoch had not bid for the HWT, Fairfax would probably have continued to make clear its policy of friendly intentions towards Queensland Press, hoping that the opportunity would occur for these intentions to be converted into a direct shareholding or some other form of equity arrangement with the big Queensland newspaper group.

Fairfax's friendly intentions were different from those of Holmes a Court. If ever it were forced into making an uninvited bid for Queensland Press it would like a partner, for it would also have to bid for the HWT to secure Queensland Press. That partner, in the absence of anyone else, was Holmes a Court. He and Gardiner had talked in 1985 about how the HWT might be split up if ever they, or one of them, got control of it. One grand strategy would be for David Syme, WA Newspapers and Holmes a Court's *Western Mail,* and Advertiser Newspapers to form a jointly owned Southern Arc. That would leave Queensland Press to John Fairfax Ltd, which would control the eastern seaboard. Such speculations foundered on how the television stations would be divided, particularly who would own HSV7. But they were an accurate enough preview of what was to happen early in 1987 when they were responding to Murdoch's bid.

The three-way takeover struggle for the HWT treated onlookers to a comprehensive display of Murdoch's drive and flexibility. He went in confident that he would acquire the HWT for $12 a share. When he had to raise the price he did. Facing a block at Queensland Press he threw his family company, Cruden Investments, into the fight. He went for Brierley's 11 per cent of the HWT from the start and got it without an escalation clause. Why Brierley, one of the most experienced stockmarket players in the world, would sell without a clause guaranteeing him any higher price Murdoch might pay was one of the mysteries of the campaign. Brierley had been in the box seat. His 11 per cent gave Murdoch the key stake he needed. It meant that Holmes a Court's offer of $13 a share always looked unconvincing, although he was able to lever Murdoch up to $15. Murdoch took Holmes a Court out of the action by selling him WA Newspapers and HSV7 and then gazumped him on HSV7 in favour of Fairfax. He gave away too much to Holmes a Court but achieved his main objectives.

The battle provided an equally fascinating view of the full array of the Great Bamboozler's takeover or greenmail techniques: feint, thrust and withdrawal on the market itself, legal action and the threat of legal action, use of the media to spread speculation and apprehension about his intentions, statements that he might do something soon, theatrical silences, all calculated to create confusion and smokescreens through which opportunities would emerge for the one unconfused player, Robert Holmes a Court. 'Holmes a Court Insists he is Serious' said a headline in the *Australian Financial Review* when he bid for the HWT. That indicated the scepticism about his intentions. Before the bidding started, back on 24 November, when he was asked about his growing stake in Queensland Press, Holmes a Court had suggested that takeovers were no longer his business, pointing out that his group had not completed a takeover for five years. 'If takeovers are our business, then it would seem we have not been conducting our business properly,' he said. His proper business had become squeezing money and sometimes prize assets out of the successful bidder. That was called greenmail since green wasn't as threatening a colour as black. In buying shares in Queensland Press he was going for the key leg of the HWT structure.

Holmes a Court insisted he was serious but serious about what? He had said the 10 per cent stake he had built up in Queensland Press was 'friendly', but friendly to whom? Initially it appeared friendly to Queensland Press, then it was friendly to Fairfax and finally it was friendly to Murdoch. He had added, 'We are always friendly.' Did that mean friendly to everyone all the time? Not many of his targets thought so. He was initially very friendly to Sir Lew Grade at Associated Communications in London. Then he took the company over and got rid of Grade. He had said he regarded BHP as a 'friend' when that company's board was becoming very nervous about his rising shareholding and unstated intentions. 'All my shareholders are friendly and I am friendly to them in return because I work for them all day and they pay my salary. I'm very friendly to BHP on a private basis. Why are they so unfriendly to me in public? I don't want to disturb or disrupt BHP. I'm not doing so. I'm a shareholder and I want to be treated as one.' In fact, he was a very special shareholder in BHP, and in his own company, Bell Group. Six months after the stockmarket crash on 19 October, 1987, he was bailed out of both at prices not immediately offered to other shareholders. Greg Gardiner at Fairfax was very wary about being friendly with Holmes a Court during their 10-day alliance in the struggle for the HWT.

One person with whom Holmes a Court was far from friendly was Rupert Murdoch. Early in December Holmes a Court had tried to contact News Corporation about buying some assets of the HWT (WA Newspapers and HSV7) and the company 'had not bothered to respond'. Murdoch and Holmes a Court had crossed each other previously, first in a takeover battle for Ansett Transport Industries late in 1979. Murdoch thought he had a deal with Holmes a Court to buy Ansett's Channel 10 in Melbourne. He already owned Channel 10 in Sydney and had problems trying to come to a satisfactory networking arrangement with the management of the Melbourne station owned by Ansett. The solution was to buy it — exactly the same solution that led to Fairfax's unhappy purchase of HSV7 early in 1987.

Holmes a Court had made an offer for Ansett that was complex and dragged on. That was one reason why Murdoch made his quick, unsuccessful, bid for the HWT that year. Finally Murdoch took over half of Ansett himself and eventually Thomas Nationwide Transport (TNT) took over the other half. That turned out very well but the difficulty of dealing with Holmes a Court remained with Murdoch. When TNT bought into Ansett, typically, Holmes a Court started to build up a stake in TNT, which Murdoch finally bought at a price above the market to protect TNT. Then Holmes a Court stood Murdoch up over the Ten Network's purchase of television rights to the 1984 Olympic Games. Murdoch led the network of which Holmes a Court's Adelaide and Perth stations were affiliates. Holmes a Court refused to contribute on a network basis. Murdoch was reported to have said, 'I have been hung out to dry.'

None of these encounters, however, compared with what was about to happen at the HWT. Murdoch's takeover bids for the HWT group in 1986–87 made very big profits for Holmes a Court on the shares he held in Queensland Press. In addition Murdoch had agreed to sell him WA Newspapers for $200 million and HSV7 for $260 million, although legally they were not yet Murdoch's to sell. Then Fairfax turned up the heat by taking legal action against Murdoch on the grounds of his US citizenship and offering the HWT, which Murdoch still did not formally control, $385 million for HSV7, shares in ADS7 (Adelaide) and four radio stations. The HWT board felt bound to cover itself by putting these assets up for public tender. Holmes a Court was being gazumped on HSV7. Murdoch had to square him away. Holmes a Court said that could be arranged but that whatever the HWT got above the $260 million he had been going to pay for HSV7 should come off the $200 million he was paying for WA Newspapers. Murdoch (for the HWT) agreed. They then had a mutual interest in maximising the price of HSV7. Holmes a Court put in a tender for whatever Fairfax offered plus $1 million. The tenders were reopened and the bidding became an auction, or a mock auction. Gardiner at Fairfax knew he was being pushed up but, having committed Fairfax to the purchase, finally paid $365 million for HSV7 and the former Packer group of NSW provincial newspapers (but not the *Gosford Express*), which Murdoch thought were relatively worthless anyway and threw them in to build up the price. So the full $105 million difference between the $260 million Holmes a Court was originally going to pay for HSV7, and the $365 million Fairfax eventually paid, came off the price of WA Newspapers which Holmes a Court got for about $100 million. This time Fairfax had been hung out to dry.

Murdoch was battle weary and wanted to get the HWT purchase over and done with. He allowed Holmes a Court to keep, against the strong arguments of News Ltd executives, the 11.6 per cent of Australian Newsprint Mills and 8.3 per cent of Australian Associated Press which went with WA Newspapers. Fifteen months later, Holmes a Court sold them back to Murdoch for a total of

$63.9 million. That brought the cost of WA Newspapers back to $41.1 million. He closed the *Western Mail* with which he had been threatening WA Newspapers' advertising revenues, particularly its classified advertising, but which had been costing him millions of dollars a year in losses, and he sold the WA Newspapers building for $55 million, shifting its operations to the *Western Mail* site where he had installed press capacity capable of producing the daily *West Australian*. Operating staff numbers were substantially reduced with the unions' co-operation and substantial retrenchment payouts. With the profits he made on his HWT and Queensland Press shares, Holmes a Court reckoned that WA Newspapers came to him free plus $165 million cash. It was his sweetest deal.

As he had done with TNT, Holmes a Court then turned his buying attention to Fairfax shares. His increasing presence on the Fairfax share register helped precipitate Warwick Fairfax's bid at the end of August. But, due largely to the 19 October stockmarket crash, he was unable to repeat the greenmail exercise which netted him WA Newspapers earlier in the year.

The war over the HWT ended on 7 February 1987. It left Fairfax with a Melbourne TV station in contravention of the Hawke Government's media ownership policy that took effect from 25 November 1986. The policy was still to be made law but there was no reason to doubt that it would be if the Hawke Government stayed in power, as opinion polls indicated it would. That meant Fairfax could not hold HSV7 and the *Age*. Certainly television ownership laws had been cynically disregarded in stockmarket plays for years. And if Fairfax was cornered in this position it could always sell out of television as Murdoch and Packer had done. There were newcomers around who clearly thought a television network was a licence to print money — a view not shared by those who had owned capital city television stations for years.

The sceptical view about the values placed on television stations in 1987 was supported by figures released in August, 1988 by the Australian Broadcasting Tribunal (ABT). Those figures indicated that the three Sydney commercial television stations had an aggregate after-tax loss of $29 million in 1986–87. The previous year's profit had been $13 million. Gardiner and the television executives at Fairfax had never been able to reconcile the total industry profits revealed by the ABT and those claimed by individual stations. A breakdown of the ABT's total for Sydney stations suggested Fairfax's ATN7 made $3.4 million after tax, Packer-Bond's Channel 9 made $1.4 million after tax, and Murdoch-Northern Star's Channel 10 lost $34 million. But it was Fairfax that was criticised for inefficient management. Although the industry had been very profitable at the beginning of the 1980s it was feeling the pressure of competition from the increasing number of carefully targeted magazines, and radio stations, colour in newspapers and suffering loss of viewers to video cassettes. Big advertisers had more muscle for negotiating advertising rates as mergers and takeovers reduced the ranks of retailing and brand-name industries. Spending and saving patterns had been changed by the tax concessions given to superannuation and home ownership. The new television owners might be able to put the industry back on top of the market as it had been in the early 1980s, but it would not be easy while they serviced the big debts incurred to buy their stations. Packer, Murdoch and eventually Fairfax took the money for their TV stations but they all had an each-way bet on the future by retaining an interest in the companies they sold to.

The HSV7 purchase, coming as it did at the end of the HWT war in which Murdoch and Holmes a Court had got what they wanted, gave Fairfax critics, particularly those at 'Fairwater', extra ammunition. There was more to come in April when HSV7, on instructions from Sydney, made programme changes and attempted staff reductions that caused a major revolt in provincial Melbourne. The strike was given daily treatment by Murdoch's newly acquired Melbourne *Herald* and *Sun*. Fairfax's television boss, Ted Thomas, was overseas at the time and the depth of the Melbourne reaction to these changes was underestimated in Sydney. HSV7 lost audience ratings and finally reinstated the retrenched people. It had been a logical move poorly timed and poorly executed. By April Warwick Geoffrey Oswald Fairfax had virtually committed himself to moving on his family company.

The HWT outcome left Holmes a Court, towards the middle of 1987, at the peak of his fortunes. On paper he was a billionaire.

He had, or appeared to have, one way or another, 30 per cent of BHP. He had substantial holdings in Texaco in the US, in Standard Chartered Bank and Sears Plc in the UK, and in Pioneer Concrete in Australia. He had a large, profitable newspaper dominating the Western Australian market, two television stations, great houses in Perth, Melbourne, London, an island off the Queensland coast, theatres in London, a horse stud and an art collection of great quality. Wherever he went, takeover rumours followed. But the cash flow to support his debts depended on the stockmarket continuing to surge ahead as it had done for most of the past six years. He was holding up an inverted pyramid, balanced on a very small equity base, and adding to the pyramid all the time. He began buying back into Fairfax.

The HWT takeover struggle was remarkable on many counts. It was the biggest ever fought in Australia. It resulted in the biggest newspaper takeover in the world at that time. The four big Australian trading banks were engaged in the action: the Commonwealth Bank backed Murdoch ($1.12 billion); the ANZ backed Holmes a Court ($2 billion); and Westpac and the National Australia Bank backed Fairfax ($1.3 billion each). The banks' arrangement and commitment fees were mouth-watering. The banks were becoming fee-driven. On 29 January, when the war was reaching its climax, the Reserve Bank announced that it had strengthened and expanded its earlier cautionary notice to banks about big exposures that were occurring in their provision of credit lines for takeovers.

The clamour of all these events helped smother a political conflagration, which briefly threatened to engulf the Federal Treasurer, Paul Keating, architect of the new media policy that had helped to start the war. Late on the night of 27 November 1986 Keating admitted to Parliament that he had failed to file his taxation returns for the previous two years. The *Sydney Morning Herald*, the paper at least two Labor leaders loved to hate, flagship of the dreaded Fairfax group, excused Keating on the grounds that Australia could not do without him. The Australian dollar had just fallen to 64 US cents and the international bankers might push it down further if Keating were forced to resign on this issue. Six days later Murdoch bid for the HWT and the issue of Keating's resignation was buried. A key resignation occurred in Perth, however, which had direct significance for young Warwick Fairfax's coming bid. On 16 February it was announced that Willem Bertus Reuter, who had been Holmes a Court's right hand man in the design, financing and execution of his stockmarket plays virtually since he started, had decided it was time to step out of the chairman's shadow. Holmes a Court thought so too. Bert Reuter resigned as general manager of the Bell Group and became a free agent. He was as adept at putting together takeover finance as anybody in Australia. He particularly had the confidence of the ANZ Bank's managing director, Will Bailey.

# Chapter 7

# Bankers Say Yes More Often

In December 1956 the ANZ Bank would not lend John Fairfax Limited £1 million to help finance a rapid burst of expansion in television, magazines and its new Jones Street building. Thirty-one years later it lent Warwick Geoffrey Oswald Fairfax, a 26-year-old tyro with some brief work experience at the Chase Manhattan Bank in New York (enough for him to be described as 'banker' in the annual returns of his family's private companies) but with no experience of publishing or management of any kind, $2 billion to buy his family's company. When problems arose over who had first claims on $340 million the Fairfax company had coming to it (the ANZ Bank's claim was contested by Westpac, the National Australia Bank and some merchant banks), the US-owned Citibank agreed to lend $500 million to pay out the other lenders.

The ANZ's loan to young Warwick Fairfax was the apogee of the spectacular boom in bank debt financing in the 1980s. Debt had never seemed so desirable or available. Instead of being an obligation to be redeemed or repaid at a certain time in the future, it became merely paper to be recycled, with another slice of banks' and advisers' fees to be taken at each recycling. As the quality of debt became debased, more was needed to replace cash for the purchase of assets. If the interest bill became too high it could be replaced by the issue of more debt. Pay In Kind securities (PIKs) became a feature of takeover financing towards the end of the boom. Part of Fairfax's refinancing in 1988–89 involved PIKs. In an era of securitisation, that is, the conversion of large

110

lumps of debt into marketable securities, PIKs were a securitised form of capitalised interest, an anticipation of the non-performing loans that became a feature of bank accounts in the early 1990s.

Deregulation of the banking system increased the competitive pressure on the banks to lend. Freeing up of the foreign exchanges and of the interest rates banks could offer for deposits opened up new sources of funds for the banks to borrow. In the deregulated market credit would always be available at a price. Securitisation took risks off the banks' balance sheets. Fees became big. This was a worldwide phenomenon, but it had particular relevance to Australia. More than 20 new banking licences had been issued, mainly to local subsidiaries of foreign banks, making Australia the most competitive banking market for its size in the world. The new developments in bill finance and easy access to foreign funds enabled the established big four Australian trading banks to avoid the much-resented harness of the Statutory Reserve Deposit system, a hangover from the old tightly controlled and regulated days when the banks had to keep a certain percentage of their deposits with the Reserve Bank at very low interest rates in an attempt to insulate the economy from the sharp fluctuations in the money supply to which Australia, as a big commodities exporter, was particularly prone in an era of fixed exchange rates.

In the 1980s the limits of conventional commercial prudence seemed to be stretched further than they had been in previous booms. Companies without substantial debt were regarded as financial wimps, prime targets for takeover by big borrowers. Conservative managers, who ploughed back most of their profits in order to keep their debt down and their shareholders' equity up, paid their taxes and took a 10- to 20-year view of their responsibilities, became vulnerable. Suddenly the company's share prices would start to rise, a raider would corner 19 per cent of the shares and within two months new owners would have moved in. Sometimes the company's profits and products would be improved; sometimes the new owners would merely eliminate expenses such as research and development outlays and loss-making new products to give the company's results a short-term boost before moving on to the next target; and sometimes the new owners would introduce nothing more than the latest tax avoidance techniques. Sometimes they did none of those things and the company ended up a shambles, or became part of a corporate maze that ended up a shambles.

As usual the market's new fashions were tax driven. The concept that dividend yield was the main determinant of a share's investment attractiveness belonged to an innocent age until it was revived in Australia by tax imputation on dividends after 1987. During the 1950s and 1960s, as markets rose, it dawned on an increasing number of investors that, while they were taxed on their dividends at full rates, capital gains, in Australia at least, were tax free. In North America they were taxed at very concessional rates. Thus it was better to buy shares with a large potential for capital gains, than for dividend yields alone. The shares with the potential were those with high earnings in relation to capital, that is, high earnings per share. If such earnings in relation to the share price were high — that is, the earnings yield was high — or its reciprocal, the price-earnings (p-e) ratio was low, then you were buying the prospect of growth, since those earnings should be the foundation for bigger dividends or assets and shareholders' funds in the future. As the 1980s takeover boom developed, however, these conventional equity investment measurements were overshadowed by EBIT — earnings before interest and tax. That was the takeover indicator. It indicated to the takeover bidder the cash flows available in the company, which could be used to cover the interest on the borrowings needed to take the company over. If EBIT was a bit lean it could be fattened to EBDIT (earnings before depreciation, interest and tax) or OCF (operating cash flow) to give an enhanced version of a company's internally generated cash flows.

The markets became takeover happy. A company's EBIT became vital to stockmarket investors looking for short-term capital gains rather than long-term dividend returns, particularly to the big institutional investors, the superannuation funds and trusts, whose success was being measured in shorter and shorter time frames. They became sprinters rather than the distance runners they had been in the past. Instead of being fairly passive long-term investors, relying mainly on dividend growth for income, they had become active stockmarket players making highly visible capital profits. The big profits came from buying stocks before they came into a takeover play. The takeover aggressors were a new generation of financial adventurers, backed by a new generation of bankers with pressing new sources of funds at their disposal. The best and brightest talents were drawn to the game. The world's top universities and business schools churned out graduates trained in balance sheet analysis, cash flows, takeovers, buyouts, leverage, problem-solving, futures, options, human resource management, arbitrage, negotiation analysis, information technology and the importance of performance, now.

The smartest Australian graduates went to the US business schools to hone their skills and return with a coveted Master of Business Administration (MBA) degree. Most MBA degrees were desirable but none was more desirable than the MBA from the Harvard Business School (HBS). That was the top training ground for the financial boom of the 1980s. US manufacturing industry lost its leadership to Japan, Korea and Taiwan. The talent went instead to where the money was — Wall Street. Of 626 HBS graduates in 1986, the year before young Warwick Fairfax graduated, 3.2 per cent went into computers and 2.9 per cent into automobiles and transport equipment industries. Only 23 per cent went into manufacturing, the rest into services, including 29.4 per cent into investment banking and brokerage, 18 per cent into consulting and 8.1 per cent into real estate. Money was the name of the game. The compulsory course work contained no history studies. The elective courses included a history of industrial and managerial capitalism but not of financial capitalism. Although the school was feeding graduates into the burgeoning financial markets, there was no emphasis on the history of those markets or the culture of individual companies. To most students those studies were irrelevant or of very low priority. The school was there to sharpen money-making skills. History was an indulgence. A cautionary knowledge of previous financial booms and slumps was considered unlikely to impress Wall Street pacesetters like Salomon Brothers, or the junk bond promoters Drexel Burnham Lambert (although Drexel's junk bond pioneer and leader, Michael Milken, had made his and

Drexel's fortunes by studying the history of bonds), or Goldman Sachs, whose Goldman Sachs Trading Corporation had been the most spectacular exploding star of a previous leverage-pyramiding boom in 1929–30.

In the 1980s the market was out of the hands of laymen. The players were the new financial adventurers and their bankers and the fund managers looking for quick profits off their adventures. This was a professionals' boom. The old stockmarket adage 'When the bellhops come in it's time to get out' no longer applied. The bellhops had MBAs and worked for brokers and investment and commercial banks. There was, of course, nothing new in the professionals' boom. Such a boom had happened in the late 1960s when inflation was starting to gather momentum and break up the conservative values of a generation conditioned by the spectre of deflation and the 1930s depression. Money became something to use, not to sit on. The University of Rochester, which had put funds into its fellow Rochester resident, the then little known Xerox company, suddenly became the fifth richest university in the country. The older universities, with their endowments tied up in bonds and steel shares, went looking for other Xeroxes.

(The University of Rochester, through former US Secretary of the Treasury, William E. Simon, later became involved in plans to establish a business school at Sir Warwick Fairfax's country property, 'Harrington Park'. Mary Fairfax had met Simon through his association with Ariadne Holdings, one of the brightest but briefest stars of the 1980s boom [see Chapter 15]).

The performance funds had their first post-war run in the late 1960s. A young funds manager named Gerald Tsai, with a short but impressive performance record, decided to go out on his own and raise $25 million to start his own fund. His underwriters, Bache and Co., raised $274 million the first day the fund opened for subscription and the performance fund boom was underway. So was the cult of the fund management personality and the fund super salesman typified by Bernie Cornfeld, who coined the come-on 'Do you sincerely want to be rich?' to milk people of millions around the world. Their careers were cut short by the 1970 crash when values on the New York stockmarket were halved.

In the late 1960s, as in the 1980s, a good deal of professional investment genius was, as J. K. Galbraith pointed out, no more than a rising market.

President Nixon tried to stop the rot in 1970 by saying that if he had any spare cash he would be buying stock right now. Those who remembered, or who had read their history books, and recalled Herbert Hoover and John D. Rockefeller saying much the same thing in 1929, went for cover. Among the big losers were the hedge funds, which had been theoretically designed to come unscarred through a stockmarket crash. But like all good ideas in the market they had within themselves the makings of their own destruction. When everyone operates on the same signals the exit door quickly becomes jammed. The same thing happened in 1987 when computer-programmed trading was the new sure cushion against a falling market. All it did was magnify the speed and depth of the fall when the break came.

In the 1980s, however, the performance boom went well beyond the stock market into foreign exchange, futures, options, options on futures, debt management and a range of speculative counters undreamed of in the 1960s. Nevertheless, the origins of the 1980s boom went back to the 1960s and 1970s when inflation started to break up the post-war regime of low interest rates, stable exchange rates based on the US dollar, which was in turn fixed to gold at $US35 an ounce, and controlled capital movements.

For 20 years these products of the 1944 Bretton Woods Agreement had served the world well, stimulating economic growth and full employment at reasonably stable prices. Money market traders and speculators starved, but investment in new plant and productive capacity thrived. A series of eruptions turned these flat plains of the 1950s and 1960s into the exhilarating but dangerous peaks and precipices of the 1980s when money markets boomed but physical investment withered. The eruptions began when the authority of the US dollar was undermined by inflationary deficits caused by the costs of the Vietnam War and President Johnson's Great Society programmes being increased without off-setting tax rises. Inflation gathered momentum as governments maintained spending policies aimed at preserving full employment. President Nixon cut the dollar's link with gold, foreign exchange markets opened up and capital started to move freely around the world, at prices set by day-to-day, hour-to-hour, and, as communications improved, minute-to-minute market conditions. The system erupted again when the Third World struck back at the Western world's inflation with big oil price rises during the 1970s, flooding the world banking system with petrodollars. Inflation had broken up the post war order. Keynesian concepts of the need for government intervention to keep employment high fell into disrepute and a world looking for simple solutions to complex problems turned to monetarism. The idea that inflation could be controlled simply by controlling the volume of money appealed on two grounds: it looked easy and it appeared to involve a minimum of government interference. It was and did neither, but it suited and reinforced the swing to conservatism throughout the democratic world.

Money markets thrive on anticipations; the more real or imagined indicators they have to anticipate the livelier they are. For years the London market, and all those based on it, lived from Thursday to Thursday when the bank rate would be announced with due ceremony after the Bank Court's weekly meeting. While monetarism ruled, the markets could live from month to month as they anticipated and reacted to the money supply figures coming from the central banks. Then, as exchange rates were freed and the financial markets became more ingenious at expanding outside the traditional domestic banking system, the money supply figures became less and less relevant. There had always been a problem with the definition of money supply and official targets had rarely been fulfilled. M3, the most commonly accepted version of the money supply, became yet another fallen market idol. Attention switched to foreign exchange rates and concentration on a new regular lunar climax: publication of the monthly balance of trade and balance of payments figures.

This period of great instability in interest and foreign exchange rates fed the futures and options markets as farmers and miners, exporters and importers, and borrowers and lenders unloaded risks on to the money markets and the money dealers unloaded risks on to each other. They had another platform for takeoff. Deregulation and instability coincided with a revolution in communications. Computer screens linking the financial markets of London, New York, Sydney, Tokyo, Hong Kong and Frankfurt made the world one big continuous market operating 24 hours a day. As the number and range of new securities multiplied, the speed with which they were traded accelerated. Both factors added to the apparent liquidity of markets. At any moment billions of dollars and yen and D-marks could be in orbit as risks were unloaded or accepted.

The separation and securitisation of the various risks involved in financial transactions — risks arising from changing interest rates, maturities, exchange rates, saleability — opened up apparently limitless opportunities to lend, borrow, hedge and speculate and gave markets apparently great depth to absorb enormous volumes of selling without major catastrophes. When the axe fell on 19 October 1987, the new financial technology helped precipitate an enormous selling wave. The central banks, however, pushing funds into the system, provided the depth by enabling the markets to experience the biggest vertical fall in history without dragging whole economies down with them. Inflation had helped create these new markets by tearing down the old stable-rate order, but full exploitation of them was restrained by fears of more inflation and the devastation it could cause. It was not until 1983, when the inflation bogey had been squeezed out of the US system by 20 per cent interest rates and falling oil prices, that the world money markets were ready for the biggest financial boom in history.

The US banks, awash with petrodollars in the 1970s, had already thrown history and caution into the shredder by pushing loans at Central and South American countries and Eastern Europe, which led to the Third World debt crisis of the 1980s. In this they were led by Citibank, the former First National City Bank of New York, whose chairman, Walter Wriston, was determined to make it the biggest, most profitable, most complete financial institution in the world. He pushed billions at Latin American countries on the dictum that 'countries do not fail to exist'. That was true, most of the time. But for an unconventional banker, he made the conventional mistake of confusing sovereign countries with businesses. Countries don't go into liquidation and disappear. But how does a bank recover its debt if the country won't pay? The bank can't seize its assets. The US banks ignored history. In February 1988, Anatole Kaletsky reported in the *Financial Times*:

> Nearly every country involved in the debt crisis of the 1980s defaulted on its foreign debts between 1931 and 1933. Practically all the defaulters of the 1930s had previously defaulted in the 1870s. And most of the Latin American countries that were already independent nations in the 1820s defaulted then as well. These defaults were not just transitory or small scale disturbances. They figured just as prominently as the latest debt crisis in the financial news in America and Europe and they caused massive losses for tens of thousands of investors who had put their fortunes in Latin American bonds.

Citibank continued to maintain that Wriston was right, that by recycling the petrodollars into the Third World, particularly into Latin American countries, the banks had been doing the world a favour. Recycling was the operative word. Many of those dollars found their way back into the banks through the accounts of corrupt Third World officials and politicians. But the loans remained as assets of the bank of increasingly doubtful value against which the banks made increasing provisions for possible or probable loss.

There was a trap in making those provisions too. If, as prudence suggested, the banks provided wholly, or substantially, for the loss of those Third World loans, that would only encourage the Third World countries to repudiate their debts. The last and best fall-back for the banks was the assumption that their own Governments would come to their aid, that the stability of the banking system was too important to allow it to collapse under the weight of Third World debts. In making that assumption they would probably be correct. One way or another the taxpayers of North America would end up underwriting the US banks' loans to Eastern European Bloc and Central and South American countries. The only matter to be settled would be the price of the underwriting.

As in the foreign exchange and domestic capital markets, lending to foreign governments this time around was in the hands of the professionals. The US leader was Citibank. In Australia the most exposed bank was the ANZ, largely through its recently acquired UK-based subsidiary, Grindlays. One of the big shareholders in Grindlays had been Citibank.

The big boom starting in 1983 spread through all capital and money markets. The Reserve Bank of Australia noted that Australian banks were growing faster overseas than at home. The ANZ was at the front of that push overseas. It was the only one of the Big Four remaining Australian trading banks with overseas origins. It had been formed in 1959 as a merger between the Union Bank and the Bank of Australasia, both of which were London based, formed during the 1830s sheep and property boom in Australia. The ANZ transferred its domicile from London to Melbourne in 1976 and when the urge to internationalise became overwhelming in the 1980s, took over Grindlays, an old UK bank with operations mainly outside the UK.

The Australian exchange rate was freed on 9 December 1983 and most bank deposit and interest rate restrictions were removed the following year. The Reserve Bank, after fighting a rearguard delaying action against the banks' move into merchant banking, rapidly dismantled controls in the face of this market tide. The banks in turn rapidly established their hegemony over the sophisticated forms of financing, which had been developed outside the banking system during the decades of official regulation. The pressure of competition lifted sharply when new banking licences were issued, most of them to banks with substantial foreign ownership, including Citibank. Competition to lend became intense as world stockmarkets boomed and company raiders flourished, using funds provided or guaranteed by banks to buy what they saw as undervalued or underborrowed companies.

In March 1985, Robert Holmes a Court revealed, in evidence at a US Federal District Court hearing, that two of his bankers, Westpac and Standard Chartered, lent him funds on the security of his BHP shares. They allowed him to draw down 85 per cent to 90 per cent of the value of the scrip he lodged. Holmes a

Court acquired the BHP shares in stockmarket raids that raised the price of BHP shares. He was thus able to use those inflated share values to borrow for more stockmarket raids. The banks fuelled the stockmarket spiral. If physical assets appeared inadequate to support the loans being offered, then new assets could be created. Brand names, which had never appeared with values in balance sheets before, were valued to give greater appearance of weight and security to the assets. With publishers, the brand name equivalent was the newspaper or magazine masthead. In 1984 Rupert Murdoch's News Corporation Ltd put over $500 million into the balance sheet as masthead valuations. Apparently this gave comfort to the company's big lenders. In June 1987 John Fairfax Ltd valued its mastheads and television licences at $997 million. Five years previously they had no value at all in the balance sheet. In 1986 they were valued at $87 million. The 1987 total included $616 million for the mastheads of Sydney and Melbourne metropolitan newspapers. By 31 December 1987 the company's mastheads were valued at $1.3 billion. That was for a balance sheet used in the refinancing of Warwick's debt. They were projected to be worth nearly $2 billion in 1990.

There were reasonable arguments for substantial masthead valuations. The *Age* and the *Sydney Morning Herald* were assets of great value in themselves, of greater value than the buildings and plant through which they were produced. One hundred and fifty years of effort had gone into each of them. They were virtually impregnable in the markets as long as the best and most creative talents continued to be committed to them. But it could not be pretended that brand names and mastheads were the same as real property. The mastheads' value depended on the vigour and inventiveness of editors and publishers and printers and advertising sales persons. If they faltered, so did the masthead's value. In Melbourne the *Argus* had once been stronger than the *Age* but the *Argus* had fallen in 1957. In Sydney the *Sun* had once been much stronger than the younger *Daily Mirror* but the *Sun* folded in 1988. It had not been included in the 1987 Fairfax masthead valuations. In his August 1987 estimate of John Fairfax Ltd's asset values, Tryart financial architect Bert Reuter put Fairfax's interest in a joint *Sun-Mirror* afternoon newspaper at $30 million.

Later it appeared at $50 million. That was on the basis of the highly confidential but ultimately unproductive talks that had taken place between Fairfax and News Corporation on possibly merging the two papers. By the time Warwick made his bid, the joint afternoon newspaper concept was a dead duck. But the Tryart team apparently thought it was still alive.

Prudent lenders would once not have regarded a masthead as security. But prudence was being redefined in the 1980s as pressures increased on managers to perform and expand and lenders to compete. At times it seemed that business and accounting practices were succumbing to a monetary version of Parkinson's Law: asset values expanded to fit the loans available. The redefinition of prudence, the stretching of accounting standards, the new emphasis in the big law firms on aggressive use of the law for their clients, were all products of the takeover-and-debt-driven boom. In 1989 the accounting profession was having some new thoughts about the treatment of masthead and brand-name valuations which, if generally accepted, could cause a major headache for big borrowers like John Fairfax group and News Corporation (see Chapter 15).

The combination of apparently undervalued brand names and mastheads and prospective Earnings Before Interest and Tax (EBIT) made two industries particularly attractive to serious raiders and therefore to those who tried to anticipate them. Those two industries were breweries and media, particularly newsprint media, although the new takeover kings and princes thought television and radio stations were still licences to print money too. In the 1970s Australian breweries and newspaper companies had spent millions upgrading their plants and fighting union resistance to new work practices, mostly out of their own resources. They had low borrowings, were ready to make substantially higher profits from their new plant investments. Their EBITs were about to grow rapidly.

The breweries had another special asset that could be securitised: hundreds of hotels. They had great brand names: Foster's at Carlton and United, Fourex and Tooheys at Castlemaine Tooheys. John Elliott at Elders IXL took the former and Alan Bond at Bond Corporation the latter. They liked what they had done so much that they went overseas looking for more. Bond also liked the media and bought Kerry Packer's television and radio networks for $1 billion. But the richest prizes of all evaded their grasp: the *Age* and the *Sydney Morning Herald* with their hundreds of pages of classified advertising were the big beneficiaries of the newspaper technology revolution. Their cash flows were growing strongly but they were secure from raiders as long as the Fairfax family, with about 50 per cent of the voting shares, stuck together. A minority interest in a cash-rich company was not much good to a raider heavily in debt, as Robert Holmes a Court discovered after 19 October 1987. Some of his minority holdings weren't even cash rich.

The big brewery and television takeovers were financed by banks, partly with funds drawn from abroad. The financing of takeovers, then the refinancing of the takeover debt, became one of the banks' most spectacular activities. Not only were they being driven by competition and the access to new sources of funds tapped through their overseas branches and affiliates. The take-over operators themselves were given more freedom to move by new company and taxation laws.

In 1981 an exception was introduced to the general prohibition against a company helping to finance the purchase of its own shares (Section 129 of the Companies Code). With the informed approval of the members of the company in general meeting and in the absence of objection within 21 days by creditors and other specified parties, funds could be passed from the company to the purchaser of the shares. This cleared the way for a takeover bidder, often with a two-dollar shelf company as the bidding vehicle, to borrow funds to buy a company and then quickly use that company's funds to repay the borrowings. This was not without problems if a substantial creditor objected, as Tryart and the ANZ Bank discovered in the Fairfax takeover. And there was a tax trap in it as Fairfax later discovered. But the Section 129 exception greatly facilitated the provision of bank backing for takeovers, particularly for the new financial adventurers. Then, from 1984–85 onwards, Section 80 of the Income Tax Act was amended to allow the losses of one company in a group to be offset against the profits of another, provided they had common ownership. This meant that the losses of a takeover company caused substantially by the interest on its borrowings could be offset against the profits of the company it had taken over. The way was open for the acquisition of big profitable companies with small borrowings by small companies with big borrowings.

Changes in superannuation taxation rules and practices also helped fuel the stockmarket by making superannuation and its offshoots, approved deposit funds and deferred annuities, the last big tax havens, particularly for high income earners. Billions of dollars flooded into the funds. As with the banks, competition forced the pace and extended the boundaries of conventional prudence. Actuaries competed with each other to measure the performance of funds. The funds competed with each other, on the basis of the performance measurements, to attract new money. The performance periods became shorter, from a year to six months to three months. The fund managers were on a self-propelling spiral. To perform they had to buy shares in special situations, particularly in takeover situations. They became speculators, hoping to get off the spiral before it fell apart, but afraid of getting off too early and becoming known as stodgy performers.

Between January 1983 and the spring of 1987 the Australian all ordinaries share index quadrupled in value, with only a short pause in the middle of each year to catch its breath. The rise accelerated after mid-1986. In New York, London and Tokyo the leading share averages trebled. Bank financed takeovers continued as share prices rose. The Reserve Bank of Australia, pleased with its deregulation initiatives, became increasingly concerned at the large credit exposures of the banks to individual clients. These were often not shown on the bank's balance sheets for they were in the form of guarantees. The Reserve's Supervision Unit, originally set up in August 1984, to handle the entry of new banks, had its work greatly expanded, as the banks and foreign exchange markets were let loose, in supervising the prudence with which the banks were exercising their new freedom.

On 5 January 1986, the Reserve Bank announced that it had asked each bank for a statement of policy in respect of large individual or related exposures and that it be kept informed of all exposures above 10 per cent of the shareholders' funds of the banking group. On 29 January 1987, in the middle of the $2-$3 billion takeover battles for the Herald & Weekly Times (HWT) and Queensland Press being waged between News Corporation, John Fairfax and Robert Holmes a Court's Bell group, the Reserve announced that it had reviewed these arrangements. It had now asked each bank to give it prior notice of the bank's intention to enter into any such large exposure. The bank should be able to show that the proposed exposure would not result in it undertaking an excessive risk. The Reserve carefully pointed out that this was in line with practice in other countries. The banks were clearly pushing at the limits of the Reserve's strictures. In its annual report for the year to 30 June 1987, the Reserve reiterated this message and mentioned specifically that it had reviewed with individual banks their involvements in the provision of large credit lines for the finance of takeovers of companies.

In August, as the Reserve's annual report waited to be tabled in Federal Parliament, and the stockmarket hit new peaks day by day, Bert Reuter was arranging a $1.3 billion loan, quickly raised to $1.7 billion and finally to $2.1 billion, from the ANZ Bank to buy John Fairfax Ltd. He found a willing lender. The Australian stockmarket boom, which had started in 1983, had entered its final spasm. The New York market had already peaked, as had London. Tokyo had also peaked but had one last fling in October. The Australian market, after its mid-year pause, charged on regardless until mid-October. John Fairfax shares were at the front of the charge. As the ANZ prepared to back W. G. O. Fairfax's bid, the market valued the company at around $2 billion. A year previously it had been $560 million and the year before that also $560 million. There was nothing in the recent trading performance to justify the share price rise. Operating profits after tax had been flat for three years. But the market's fever was at its height. The ANZ, which had had the Fairfax bank account for 60 years, lost it in 1983. Gardiner had become increasingly unhappy with the bank's commitment to Fairfax. The overdraft limit had been unchanged for years. The Bank seemed less than enthusiastic about financing the HWT share purchase in December 1979. The company had then gone into the market and found merchant banks eager to support it. Gardiner raised the possibility of splitting the account with the National Bank soon after he took over as group general manager, but Sir Warwick Fairfax, an old and substantial client of the ANZ, was not convinced. In 1983 Gardiner brought more forceful arguments to the board recommending that the account be split between the ANZ and the National (David Syme's bank). Sir Vincent Fairfax, mindful of the family's long-standing personal links with Westpac's predecessor, the Bank of NSW (which handled the Channel 7 television subsidiary's account), suggested that Westpac be considered too. The account was split between the National and Westpac. Gardiner and Cotton took the news to the ANZ.

When Fairfax needed $2 billion to go into the market against Murdoch in his second bid for the HWT in December 1986, the ANZ was again offered part of the action. It was already committed for that amount to the third bidder, Robert Holmes a Court's Bell Group. The prospect of getting back the Fairfax account, and taking the National out of David Syme, was a factor in the ANZ's willing commitment of funds to Tryart in August 1987. But the major factor was the revolution in banking, which in turn had fed and been fed by the debt-and-takeover-driven stockmarket boom.

To the ANZ Bank, funding the Tryart takeover was a straight assets deal: the Bank lent Tryart funds (eventually about $2 billion) for the takeover. Tryart sold off Fairfax assets to repay the Bank, and the Bank got a fat fee, interest and the continuing Fairfax-Syme business. It was probably the Bank's biggest single commitment, ever. The loan application was made by Bert Reuter on 19 August 1987. It took less than nine days for the loan to be processed through the senior management and the Bank board's credit committee, which said a lot about Reuter's ability to prepare a loan application and his standing with the Bank. (The Bank's credit committee consisted of the chairman of the board of directors, Sir William Vines; the managing director, W. J. Bailey; the deputy chairman, M. D. Bridgland, who was also chairman of ICI Australia Ltd; D. C. L. Gibbs of Gibbs Bright, whose family had been on the board of the ANZ and one of its predecessors, the Union Bank, for several generations; C. J. Harper, a professional company director; and R. A. D. Nicholson, deputy managing director and chief operating officer of the Bank.)

Reuter's first approach to the Bank was on the basis that James, John and the rest of the family would stay in — that no funds would be needed to buy them out. The first facility was thus for a total of $1.3 billion (which assumed an upper price limit of eight dollars a share). The Bank notified the National Companies and Securities Commission (NCSC) that these funds were available to Tryart for its bid. Reuter realised, or was alerted to the fact, that the NCSC would only acknowledge that $1.3 billion would cover the cost of the bid if agreements were in place with James, John and other family members that they would not sell their shares. It was impossible to do this as surprise was a key element in Warwick's bid strategy. So Reuter made a second application for $1.7 billion to cover the possibility that the family would accept the bid. At the decisive meeting of the Tryart team in Carnegie Fieldhouse's office on Friday, 28 August, Reuter spent much time walking between the office and the facsimile machine outside waiting for the Bank's facility letter to come through. It did. Warwick launched his bid at $7.50 a share on Monday, 31 August.

All of the Bank's contacts were with Bert Reuter. The key Bank executives did not meet Warwick Fairfax until after the Bank's first commitment was made. The ANZ's general manager of corporate banking, John McConnell, had first met Reuter when he had arranged the finance for Holmes a Court's bid for the HWT in December 1986. But Reuter's contacts with the ANZ's managing director, Will Bailey, went back a long way before that to 1973 when Bailey had been corporate manager in South Australia and Holmes a Court had taken over J. N. Taylor Holdings, a South Australian engineering company.

At a mergers and acquisitions seminar run by Arthur Andersen and Co. in Perth on 25 February 1988, Reuter used the Tryart-Fairfax bid to illustrate his basic formula:

It has been my experience that the best way to approach the Bank is to submit an application that reflects and answers all of the financial data that a bank executive requires to submit to his credit committee or board. This incorporates, of course, many 'what if' situations if the assumptions built into the model are not met. This is vital and demonstrates that all these possible situations have been focused upon by you and you have a solution for each. In other words you are on top of the situation.

Neither the Bank nor Tryart was on top of a number of 'what-if' situations on 28 August 1987. The NCSC had forced them to anticipate one: 'What if the other members of the family decided to accept Tryart's offer? But not another: 'What if the stockmarket came a cropper and reduced the asset values on which the Bank's quick turnaround was based? Or another: 'What if the key Fairfax executives left (the Tryart bid was clearly a vote of no confidence in them and the Fairfax board) and Warwick's new team proved not up to the job? Or another: 'What if other creditors objected to the ANZ Bank getting direct access to Fairfax's cash flows? In August the Bank seemed not particularly concerned with the future management of the company. Later, when the asset sales ran into trouble, and the Bank had to look to a much bigger, longer-term commitment than it thought in August, concern for the company's continuing management became paramount.

Of the four main developments leading up to the takeover of John Fairfax Ltd — the changing balance in the family, growing differences between the 'Fairwater' Fairfaxes and the company's management, the Labor Party's desire to break up certain media ownerships, and the banking revolution in the 1980s — the last was the most important. Without the Bank young Warwick might still have been getting some experience in the marketing department of John Fairfax.

# CHAPTER 8

# SOMETHING'S GOING ON OUT THERE, BUT WHAT?

More than a thousand people, some of them mourners, packed St Andrew's Anglican Cathedral in Sydney for the funeral service of Sir Warwick Fairfax on 30 January 1987. It was a great Sydney occasion. Sir Warwick had died on 14 January, aged 86. His elder son James was then on a cruise ship in Antarctica. His second son Warwick was at Harvard. The two weeks between death and funeral gave Mary Fairfax, the family and the company time to organise an oratorical and ceremonial event to honour a Fairfax who had been close to, but not too directly engaged in, political and cultural events in Australia for the previous 50 years. Present were ex-Prime Ministers, the NSW Premier, Opposition leaders, State Governors, the Chief Justice of the NSW Supreme Court, senior public servants. The Prime Minister, Robert James Lee Hawke, was represented by the Minister for Transport, Peter Morris.

The funeral service reflected his ecumenical, intellectual interest in religion. Prayers were read by his parish priest, Canon Whild, of St Mark's, Darling Point, the occasional address by the Rt Rev. Bruce Wilson, vicar-general of the diocese of Canberra and Goulburn, and the blessing by the Rt Rev. Ewen Cameron, Bishop of North Sydney. The choir led the singing of 'Onward Christian Soldiers' and 'Holy, Holy, Holy, Lord God Almighty'. The operatic soprano Jennifer McGregor, sang Mozart's 'Alleluia, Exultate, Jubilate'. His family read from the Bible, from the book he had been working on for years, *Purpose*, which included a quotation from the Sanskrit, Upanishads: 'Now a person consists of purpose. According to the purpose a person has in this world, so does he become on departing hence. So let him frame himself for purpose.'

The *Sydney Morning Herald*'s senior reporter, Evan Whitton, began his report on the service in the next morning's newspaper with a reflection on things temporal:

In the way of things, Prime Ministers and Premiers necessarily come and go. One such, as Sir Warwick Fairfax's funeral service at St Andrew's cathedral reminded me yesterday, once seized on me at a function to tell me what he was going to do to the Fairfaxes.

The hour was late; the Premier was perhaps overtired. He had been to two functions; his black tie was off, his white shirt undone; his language was lurid as to content and detail.

The task of our trade is to observe phenomena, however bizarre. I offered no rejoinder. After what seemed like a non-stop 10 minutes, the Premier's wife, happening by, said to his minder, 'You'd better get him out of here; he's on about the Fairfaxes again.'

The minder tactfully muttered a word. As the Premier dutifully turned to leave I offered a suggestion that appeared not to have occurred to him: 'Mr Premier, the Fairfaxes have been in this town for 150 years — it seems likely they'll be around for a while yet.'

A year later the Fairfaxes were still around but only one, young Warwick Fairfax, was at the *Sydney Morning Herald*. Because of what Warwick had done, the Fairfax company's financial condition was critical and new advisers had been called in to help solve its problems. The chairman of the advising company, Whitlam Turnbull and Co., was a former Premier of NSW, Neville Wran. He had become a confidant of Mary Fairfax. The public servant who had helped him run NSW, Gerry Gleeson, also became a valued adviser to Mary and to the key family companies, The Rockwood Pastoral Co. Pty Ltd, and Tailer Investments Pty Ltd.

It was a notable funeral. More notable still, in the light of subsequent events, was what did not happen afterwards. A family, with control of one of the great newspaper companies, facing a new generation of ownership of a substantial part of the capital following the death of the patriarch, might have been expected to meet, like a political coalition after an election, to discuss the company's and the family's future, to work out an understanding about how to preserve control, while accommodating each other's ambitions for themselves and their heirs. No such meeting occurred. Perhaps such arrangements had been made before the old man's death. The family came together at the funeral but did not meet as one family after that. The gulf between 'Fairwater' and the rest of the family widened. The terms of Sir Warwick's will were not revealed to the rest of the family. Sir Warwick Fairfax's main interest in John Fairfax Ltd had been held through The Rockwood Pastoral Co. Ltd which owned about 11.3 million shares at his death — 11.3 per cent of the total capital. He also had 34 372 shares in his own name — in effect, his original director's qualification. It had been assumed that the Rockwood shares would go direct to young Warwick. The fact that his mother, Mary Fairfax, had an interest in the Rockwood shares only seeped out as the financing of young Warwick's moves on John Fairfax Ltd became known.

Warwick also had a beneficial interest in the 11 million Kinghaven shares that James Fairfax had committed to him 18 months previously. James still controlled the votes attached to those shares and the income from them. But they would go to Warwick when James died and James could not sell them, or any rights attached to them, without Warwick's consent. Mary Fairfax had 1.1 million shares she had accumulated over the years in her company Acrux Holdings Pty Ltd. She liked to emphasise that she had been a successful businesswoman and was rich in her own right. Her shareholding in the company was based on 180 000 shares she acquired from her husband in the new share issue in 1961, not long after they were married. Warwick Oswald Fairfax's original root stock of over 25 per cent of the new public company in 1957 supplied some thriving cuttings. Young Warwick had a rare and rich inheritance. But for some time, he had been thinking that it was not enough.

Late in December 1986 Warwick and Marty Dougherty had lunch at the 'Pancakes on the Beach' restaurant at Bondi where they reinforced each other's distrust of the Fairfax management. In statements prepared for the court case about Rothwells's $100 million fee (the fee case), their recollections differed about key aspects of their conversation. Warwick recalled that he said to Marty, 'It will be 20 years before I will be in a position to do anything about it' and Marty replied, 'You might have to make a takeover bid for the company'. Warwick said, 'A takeover? That is a bit drastic. And besides, how could it be possible?' Then he recalled Marty saying, 'At some stage during the next three or four years you will probably have to do something like that.' Marty claimed that the conversation was similar to conversations that he had had with Warwick ever since 1984, that it was Warwick who had, over those years, put forward the idea that he would have to move to take over the company, and that that idea was fostered and encouraged by Mary Fairfax. Who thought of and proposed the takeover first? One possibility was not raised in the fee case: that it was inspired by Rupert Murdoch.

As a retained adviser, as well as one of his many ex-editors, Dougherty had kept in touch with Murdoch and kept Murdoch in touch with Fairfax affairs. He and Mary Fairfax had recently dined with Murdoch in New York. Murdoch was well aware of 'Fairwater' dissatisfaction with the Fairfax management. He had a sympathetic ear for Mary's grievances. He had been to dinner at 'Fairwater' when the family's position in the company was discussed. Warwick recalled in the fee case that the main matters discussed on that occasion were Murdoch's and Fairfax's mutual business interests. Murdoch would have liked to own the *Age*, the *Sydney Morning Herald* and the *Australian Financial Review* and was always looking for chinks in the Fairfax armour. He was prepared to make long-term investments in time and attention with the aim of acquiring those products just as he had with other desirable acquisitions around the world. He invited young Warwick to dinner at his home in New York but Warwick declined, feeling that he was not up to Murdoch's league and it was better to stay away. Mary remained Murdoch's potential ally at Fairfax, directly and indirectly through his Ansett Transport Industries partner, Peter Abeles.

Dougherty was visiting the US fairly regularly at this time. He had many interests. As well as his public relations and business consultancy he was working on a development that could be more rewarding than anything he had ever handled. An old friend had come to him with an idea to revolutionise the video cassette hire business. Like many new boom industries this had grown quickly and haphazardly. Video cassettes of movies were made and sold to thousands of small entrepreneurs, who then hired them out for short periods, overnight or for a few days, to people to play on their TV-VCR sets at home. The film cassette maker received one payment for each copy of the film no matter how often the film was played. This posed a problem similar to the one authors and publishers had faced with libraries: they received a royalty only on the sale of their book to the library no matter how many times the book was borrowed or even copied. Dougherty's friend thought he had the answer to this, as far as videos were concerned, with a counting device attached to each tape. Successful application of the new device, Playcount, would probably require an upheaval in the distribution of tapes, but financially it would favour the original makers of popular movie cassettes. Dougherty needed a big partner for development of Playcount and the place to find that partner was in North America. Marty had nerve. He was a gambler and liked high stakes. On a visit to North America in 1986 Marty was giving Murdoch the latest on the growing tension between 'Fairwater' and Jones Street and pondering what young Warwick might do to resolve his problems. Murdoch suggested privatisation. Later, when Warwick made his privatisation bid on 31 August 1987, Murdoch said he wished he'd done that when he was Warwick's age.

After Christmas 1986, Warwick went back to Harvard but continued to talk to Dougherty by telephone and directly when he returned to Sydney for his father's funeral, about what should be done about the company. Apart from the James-John-Gardiner-Suich management, he was concerned about raiders. Although in the market it was assumed that the family had tight control of the company, the family, if it voted as one, controlled only 48.75 per cent of the capital. For all practical purposes this was more than enough for control while the rest of the shares were spread among thousands of smaller shareholders. The retirement funds had over 10 per cent. But the funds' trustees included

Gardiner and other company officers and ex-officers, who were regarded with deep suspicion by 'Fairwater'.

To outside observers, the concern of some members of the family that the total family vote was slightly less than 50 per cent rather than slightly more, reflected their continuing confusion about Fairfax as a public rather than a private company. Their shares represented by far the biggest block of votes in the company. It was unchallengeable. As shareholders they may well have considered that they had a special interest in the company to protect, that they were different from other shareholders. But as directors they were bound to act in the interests of all shareholders. If a high enough takeover bid came along they had, as directors, a duty to recommend its acceptance by shareholders, although they might reject it for their own family holdings. In these circumstances the difference between holding 49 per cent or 51 per cent of the capital was irrelevant. In fact, the directors did have to face this distinction between their private interests and their public duty when young Warwick made his bid. The need to bring the family holdings up to over 50 per cent was of questionable importance, but it seemed important, for cosmetic reasons at least, in the takeover inspired market of the mid-1980s.

In February 1987, as the time came for possible action on all the ideas and speculations, some of which had been floated, some of which were still swimming beneath the surface in Warwick's and Mary's minds, about how young Warwick could take charge of the company now that his father was dead, 'Fairwater' was more active than usual looking for new sources of advice. The ranks of potential merchant banking advisers were limited by Gardiner's widespread use of merchant banks for bill finance. Ever since he had put together the funds to buy 14.9 per cent of the HWT in 1979 he had cultivated these sources of finance outside the trading banks. About 20, apart from the trading banks Westpac and the National Australia Bank, were involved in the company's financing. Socially and professionally he was stitched into the merchant banking network.

'Fairwater' had to be careful not to do anything that might alert him to their aims. Early in February, Mary Fairfax asked her accountant, Peter Done, of Peat Marwick, to suggest advisers who could counsel her and Warwick on strategy. Peter Done suggested Paul Espie or Malcolm Irving. Espie had been chief executive of BA Australia, a subsidiary of the Bank of America, with G. J. Coles and Co. Ltd a substantial minority shareholder. BA Australia had received one of the new banking licences in Australia. It had planned to establish a large retail banking operation. That would require substantial capital investment from both shareholders. But Bank of America, once the world's biggest bank, had run into large financial problems, due largely to undisciplined lending, particularly in real estate. Espie told the two shareholders that without substantial capital investment, their Australian banking plans could not be realised. Bank of America could not afford it. G. J. Coles knew a lot about retailing but little about banking. They scaled down their ambitions and in 1986 Espie left. In February 1987, he was establishing his own low-profile investment company, Pacific Road Pty Ltd. He was one of Gardiner's friends. Malcolm Irving, a former company secretary of Boral Ltd, had worked in merchant banking with Capel Court and Citinational groups before becoming managing director of CIBC Australia, a wholly owned subsidiary of the Canadian Imperial Bank of Commerce, in 1987. CIBC Australia was the company formed out of Martin Corporation, which had employed Laurie Connell in Perth until he went out on his own in 1975.

Marty Dougherty called Espie. Could he meet Mary Fairfax at Carnegie Fieldhouse's office? Espie went. Mary was with Fieldhouse and Dougherty. The talks ranged over a number of Fairfax family concerns: the future of the whole family's share-holdings, in particular those of 'Fairwater'; whether Warwick should join the board; the company's management and its future. Late in the meeting young Warwick came through on the telephone from Boston. Warwick later said in evidence in the fee case that he had had only one conversation, by telephone, with Espie. But Espie saw a lot of Mary Fairfax and Marty Dougherty over the next six weeks. Like other merchant bankers he was sceptical of the need for the family to build up its equity in the company from around 48.6 per cent to over 50 per cent, but thought that if they felt they had to, they should do it without rocking the market. He suggested to Mary that, if Warwick did it, and later a takeover bidder did attack the company, Warwick could gain some kudos for having taken the family over 50 per cent. It could enhance his status in the family. Mary seized on this prospect of glory for her son. But in the next few days Warwick came to his own decision.

On the mid-February weekend, John Brehmer Fairfax was having a rare weekend away from home, fishing along the Upper Queanbeyan River outside Captain's Flat in southern NSW with two friends, a doctor and a stockbroker. John was an outdoor Fairfax. Fly fishing was a treasured pursuit inherited from his father and mother, particularly from his mother who was very good at it. A call from Boston, USA, caught up with him when the fishing party returned in the evening to the small house they were occupying for the weekend. It was Warwick Fairfax with a proposition. He wanted John and his family companies to join him in buying 1.5 million shares in John Fairfax Ltd immediately to lift the family's holding to over 50 per cent of the capital. John spoke guardedly in this phone call, inhibited by the presence of his stockbroker friend who could not be alerted to the enterprise being discussed. But he was initially warm to the idea. It was a chance to cement a relationship with young Warwick. The problem of the minority position of the family, no matter how close to a majority, had occupied his mind for years. His family companies Marinya Pty Ltd and Cambooya Pty Ltd named for the Queensland rural property owned by his grandfather and the nearest town to it on the Darling Downs, had built up their holdings in John Fairfax Ltd by small amounts over the years. They had a lot of shares but not much cash to buy more.

James and his father Sir Warwick had the same problem but they, less frugal than the Marinya Fairfaxes, had been occasional sellers over the years, though in relatively small amounts. A moment of truth had come in 1980. The shock waves from Murdoch's 1979 bid for the HWT and the John Fairfax-Queensland Press defence, were only just passing. What company was now secure from takeover raiders? It had generally been assumed, despite 'Fairwater's' doubts, that the retirement fund trustees would support the company's management or major shareholders in the event of a takeover bid. This failed to acknowledge that the trustees' responsibilities were to the fund members and not to any other interests. That had been emphasised when the trustees of the retirement funds of Waltons Ltd, the Sydney retailers, who were big shareholders in the company, accepted a cash takeover offer from Bond Corporation, rather than join management in a defence of the company. Although the Fairfax funds' trustees had plenty of discretion, in a crunch they could break ranks with the family.

John Fairfax Ltd's acquisition of a 14.9 per cent interest in the HWT at the end of 1979 had meant an end to its special position under the Broadcasting and Television Act. It had lost the grand-father clause that allowed it to have more than two television stations. It had to sell its interests in Canberra (CTC7) and Brisbane (QTQ9). Canberra went to the Perth entrepreneur Kerry Stokes and Brisbane to Amalgamated Wireless (Australasia) Ltd (AWA), a friendly company that had been an original partner with Fairfax in ATN7, Sydney. But the AMP Society had a substantial shareholding in AWA, which meant that it, inadvertently, fell foul of the Act's ownership limits, having more than five per cent of the shares in more than two TV stations. It had to sell down to under five per cent in one of the three companies through which it held its prescribed TV interests.

The AMP had been building up its holding in Fairfax in 1980, but that holding was still the smallest of the prescribed three. So it decided to sell 1.2 million Fairfax shares to satisfy the labyrinthine ownership provisions of the Act. The AMP notified Fairfax management of its intentions. Fairfax retirement funds had already notified the Fairfax board of their wish to buy more shares. So the funds and members of the family were told that the AMP had 1.2 million shares to sell. It would be best all round, certainly best for the market price of Fairfax shares, if such a large parcel were placed privately rather than thrown on to the market. The funds took 400 000. The shares had been selling at around $1.50, one of the great bargains in a subdued market at that time. James Fairfax said that heavy cash commitments would have his hands tied for a year or so. Sir Warwick said he would buy any shares the other family members did not take. Concerned by the Waltons's experience he was against the retirement funds increasing their holdings. In the event, the funds bought 400 000, Sir Warwick 400 000 and the Sir Vincent-John family company Marinya 400 000. That still left the combined family holdings at under 50 per cent but it preserved a balance between Sir Warwick's and Sir Vincent's family holdings.

Young Warwick's plan to increase the family holdings to over 50 per cent in February 1987 thus appealed to John. He returned from his fishing trip to talk it over with his family. They agreed to put $6 million into Warwick's scheme but suggested certain conditions. As usual they were not rich in cash. Neither was Warwick. But he was being debt-educated at Harvard.

Most of the funds would have to be borrowed. The market was very high. Fairfax shares in February 1987 were around $16 and rising. Ever cautious, the Marinya-Cambooya group decided to ask Warwick to consider giving them an option to put the shares back to him at the purchase price if the market went sour and they needed the money — not as a condition of coming in at that stage but as a matter for his consideration. Warwick rejected this out of hand and abruptly ended the discussions. John had felt warmly towards Warwick before this. He felt they could speak the same language about the company and accommodate each other's interests and ambitions in the years ahead until another generation of Fairfaxes took over. John thought they had much more in common than John had with James. But John's and Warwick's expectations of each other in this urgent share purchase proposal showed how little they knew each other. John's growing warmth towards the 'Fairwater' heir went into reverse.

For Warwick, on the other hand, this was the first taste of power, of direct, decisive action on his own account. It confirmed his view that the other Fairfaxes were weak and incapable of decision. James had shown no enthusiasm for Warwick's plan. He took a commonsense view that the family could lift its holding, if necessary, at any time. As Warwick recalled in his fee case statement, he talked about this to Dougherty, who said, 'If that is John's attitude, what is the harm in you doing it on your own? You will get the publicity, you will be seen as doing something in relation to the company and it will make it easier for you when you come back.' Marty recalled Warwick saying in an emotional voice, 'I simply have to do this. I could never forgive myself if I didn't do it.' Warwick also talked to his mother about it. Then he authorised Carnegie Fieldhouse to organise a loan of $35 000 000 from Midland International Australia Ltd to buy 1.5 million Fairfax shares.

When the Sydney stock exchange opened for business at 10 a.m. on Tuesday, 17 February 1987, buyers were offering $18.50 for Fairfax shares, up one dollar from the previous day's final sales. Just before lunch Brent Potts of Potts, West, Trumbell, one of Sydney's smartest brokers, entered the market to record 10 special sales totalling 1.5 million Fairfax shares at $20 a share, then left. Potts had the reputation of being the best off-market broker in the business, of knowing where the key shareholdings were in companies and of being able to assemble parcels of shares at quick notice because of this knowledge. He put together the 1.5 million shares from institutions who understood that they were going to members of the Fairfax family. The identity of the buyer, however, remained a secret until late on 19 February when a letter was delivered to the stock exchange from the solicitor, C. R. Fieldhouse:

I act for Mr Warwick Geoffrey Oswald Fairfax and The Rockwood Pastoral Co. Ltd.

I wish to advise that on 17 February 1987 The Rockwood Pastoral Co., acting on the instructions of one of its directors, Mr Warwick Fairfax, acquired 1 500 000 shares in John Fairfax Ltd at a price of $20 per share for a consideration of $30 million.

This purchase raises the relevant interest of The Rockwood Pastoral Co. Pty Ltd and its associates from 12 543 355 which represents 12.45 per cent of John Fairfax Ltd to 13 953 355, which represents 13.95 per cent of John Fairfax Ltd.

In addition The Rockwood Pastoral Co. may be deemed to be an associate of Serpentine Pty Ltd and its related companies, which holds a relevant interest of 11 331 372 shares, which represents 11.33 per cent in John Fairfax Ltd. Full details according to Companies Form 43 are being prepared and will be filed as soon as possible.

Yours faithfully,
C. R. Fieldhouse.

The letter emphasised that this action was taken on Warwick Fairfax's instructions and not by resolution of the Rockwood board as a whole. Warwick had arrived. Rockwood's board at that time included Mary Fairfax, Max Sandow, former NSW manager of the ANZ Bank (who was also a director of Consolidated Press, a major competitor and rival of John Fairfax Ltd); Sir Rupert Clarke; and J. C. Fletcher, former president of the Rural Bank of NSW, which later became the State Bank. The non-Fairfax directors resigned during the first half of 1988. John Fletcher was replaced as the executive director by Peter Done. The shares the letter had mentioned as held by Serpentine and its related companies were the Kinghaven shares James had settled on Warwick in August 1985.

The Fieldhouse letter resulted in more than a little anguish in the Fairfax company. It was a public document and, as usual, Marty Dougherty handled the distribution to the media of all public statements from the 'Fairwater' Fairfaxes. He released the news that Warwick had been the buyer of the 1.5 million shares to all media organisations, except Fairfax, apparently assuming that Fairfax would know about it. But the Fairfax company did not pick up the news until about 9 p.m. when the chief editorial executive, Max Suich, held a hurried briefing session with Alan Kohler, editor of the *Australian Financial Review*, who told the finance reporting staff of the *Sydney Morning Herald*. They thus just avoided being scooped by every other morning newspaper in Australia on this dramatic event in their own company.

Fairfax shares had been selling at around $13 at the beginning of February. They had risen to $14.70 on 5 February when 531 000 were sold and to $16 on 9 February when Pembroke Securities, a brokerage house controlled by FAI Insurances, sold 1.08 million shares at 50 cents above the market. They continued to rise to $16.45 on Friday, 13 February and $17.50 on Monday, the day before Warwick's purchase was recorded by Brent Potts. They were back to $15.70 by the end of the month. Did Potts pay too much? That depended on his instructions, which remained confidential between him and his client. Was the market aware that something special was on? That seemed likely as the market was alive with buyers at $17.50 on Monday, 16 February. Potts had to talk to a number of people to assemble that parcel. Leaks were inevitable. And the whole market was white hot, setting new peaks during the month. The price paid, however, had its critics among Warwick's later advisers and when the next big brokerage assignment came around, the flotation of David Syme as part of the Tryart takeover in September, it went to another Sydney brokerage star, Rene Rivkin, whose firm, Rivkin James Capel, had links with Wardleys, the merchant bank with strong WA connections. Wardleys and James Capel were both owned by the Hong Kong and Shanghai Bank.

Greg Gardiner was unhappy that the company had not been informed of Warwick's intentions before the 17 February purchase. The company had plenty of market intelligence and could have helped assemble those 1.5 million shares with a minimum of fuss just as it had organised the sale of the AMP Society's 1.2 million shares in 1980. Gardiner felt that, far from stabilising and securing the Fairfax share register, the purchase could encourage takeover speculation by suggesting that the family no longer acted as one, that it could be divided and conquered. Certainly around this time Robert Holmes a Court came back into the market for Fairfax shares, using his well-honed technique of accumulating a parcel then redistributing it into the market through one of his brokers, in this case usually Ord Minnett, placing the shares into the hands of other big players, then rebuilding his own holding, stirring the market, getting action going and being ready to take advantage of whatever eventuated. Holmes a Court thought the Fairfax family edifice might be ready to crack but he did not believe it would crack under a direct frontal assault. His market tactics were aimed at destabilising Fairfax. Warwick's 1.5 million share purchase helped.

But the real message of that purchase was that young Warwick was not coming back to Australia to take his rightful place quietly in the Fairfax company. He was returning as a man of destiny. The signposts were in Fieldhouse's letter to the Sydney stock exchange on 19 February. Close observers of the family believed that the heady experience of that purchase was an important turning point leading to his bid for full control of the company six months later. After years of education, some training in the theory of business, and living in the shadow of his father and mother, he had experienced the exhilaration of the real thing, of resolution and action on his own. Given the necessary resolution, anything seemed possible. Well, resolution and money.

Warwick had borrowed the $35 million to buy the 1.5 million Fairfax shares from the Midland Bank. There was plenty of security for that borrowing in the millions of shares he controlled in The Rockwood Pastoral Co. But the dividend income from those shares would go nowhere near meeting the interest bill. The shares cost $30 million. The $35 million loan allowed for some capitalisation of interest. That debt would either have to be repaid by the sale of other assets or he would have to get direct access to the cash flows of the Fairfax company. The debt was effectively taken over by the ANZ Bank on 20 July 1987. By that time the facility had risen to $37 million.

The prospect of moving on the company was already being envisaged at 'Fairwater'. Within weeks of Sir Warwick's burial it had been decided that young Warwick had to take control of Fairfax. That could only be done with the Rockwood shares as a base. Baring Bros Halkerston were retained to advise 'Fairwater' on how it might be achieved.

In the final months of Warwick's term at Harvard the Fairfax company was confronted once again with the possibility of having to raise new capital. Purchase of HSV7 and the NSW regional newspapers from the HWT had increased its debt by $365 million, most of which ($300 million) was funded by bills drawn on Westpac and the National Australia Bank. James Fairfax, in particular, had supported Gardiner strongly in that purchase. James had been a director and chairman of ATN7 for many years and had seen the frustrations that company had encountered in dealing with HSV7, in trying to put an efficient network arrange-ment together with the Melbourne company when it was owned by the HWT. But the steep increase in debt at high interest rates, without any significant profit contributions from HSV7, would heavily erode Fairfax profits in the next few years. New and complex capital raising proposals, known as the Newco schemes, were again put forward by Dominguez Barry Samuel Montagu, but there seemed no way around the problems of increasing the equity base and ensuring the listing of the new securities on the stock exchanges, while preserving the family's interests without the family making a major contribution. The Newco proposals looked at the possibility of floating off part of David Syme and using it as a separate capital-raising entity. There were proposals for floating the TV network and using that company as a separate fund raiser. That involved another problem: until Australian Broadcasting Tribunal approval was given, Fairfax did not actually own the HSV7 licence, although it had bought the company operating it. But it was allowed to act as if it did own the licence until the Australian Broadcasting Tribunal said otherwise. Bond Corporation had floated Bond Media under similar conditions early in 1987.

Warwick at this stage was being advised on two matters by the merchant bankers Baring Bros Halkerston. After selling out of Martin Corporation to Canadian Imperial Bank of Commerce (CIBC), Barings had teamed up, in what to them was a much more comfortable arrangement, with ex-Potter Partners stockbroker, Keith Halkerston. Murdoch's News Corporation had been one of Halkerston's clients. James Fairfax was told Barings Halkerston would be advising Warwick on the company's capital raising plans. He was not told of their role in advising Warwick and Mary on how to increase their shareholdings and influence in the company. This advice was mainly handled by another Barings director, Mark Burrows. Halkerston and Burrows were well known to Gardiner. He knew Halkerston was advising Warwick on the capital-raising plans but he did not know of the firm's role as advisers to 'Fairwater' on a creeping takeover of John Fairfax Ltd. Nor were Halkerston and Burrows aware that Espie was advising 'Fairwater' on a wide range of matters, including Barings's advice. Espie had never been given a specific brief, nor a retainer. His 'Fairwater' engagement was broken off by mutual consent at the end of March. The capital raising problem was one Gardiner had been wrestling with in one form or another since 1981 but the outlay for HSV7 had made that problem much more acute than it had ever been. Baring Bros Halkerston had their own ideas about using the TV stations for raising funds, which were put directly to James and John Fairfax without Gardiner being present.

Those proposals did not survive. Neither did the Newco plan. Although on Fairfax standards the company was heavily borrowed and could use a new equity capital injection to bring its borrowing ratios down, by the standards of many other companies, including Murdoch's News Corporation, its borrowings were very comfortable. The equity capital-raising problem could again be postponed, particularly as the company might have to sell its television interests.

Warwick had asked Barings in February what he should do next. In a report dated March 1987, Barings outlined the options. Rockwood's interest bill on the Midland's $35 million loan was running at nearly $7 million a year. Current dividend on the 1.5 million shares the loan had bought was $187 500 a year. Rockwood's income had no prospects of meeting its interest bill. It could capitalise the interest for a while, that is, not pay it but add it on to the loan. It could sell the shares at a substantial loss. It was, in Baring's words, logical to move forward. Warwick and Mary could aim at acquiring Fairfax's newspaper assets but they needed to avoid family confrontation. They could look at 'the addition of value to Fairfax by way of improved management strategies'. But if they made a bid for control of John Fairfax Ltd, they might have to offer $20–$25 a share if the family supported the bid, $25–$30 if they did not. (This was before the two-for-one bonus issue announced on 21 May.) A pre-emptive takeover strike was attractive but would cost $1.5 to $2.25 billion at a price range of $20 to $30 a share. The sale of the television assets would reduce this but it would still be very costly. They could have an equity partner, but that would jeopardise the purpose of the bid — to control the family heritage. The fall-back position was to pursue schemes for the rearrangement of the company's assets and gradually build on the Rockwood shareholding.

Marty Dougherty saw Warwick in Boston soon after Warwick received what he regarded as this fairly negative advice from Barings. Warwick recalled Marty suggesting Kevin Parry as the possible partner Barings had recommended Warwick should have. Parry was another Perth adventurer who had built a precarious financial structure on his basic furniture business. His best asset was the Newcastle television company he had bought a couple of years previously. He was also one of the clients Mary Fairfax introduced to Marty. The thought was that Parry might be interested in taking the television stations out of Fairfax. Warwick had lunch with Kevin Parry's son Stephen at the Jockey Club restaurant in New York on 4 April. The Parrys failed to come up with a firm proposition, although Mary Fairfax continued to support Kevin Parry as a potential buyer of Fairfax's television network. Parry's empire fell apart soon afterwards. Marty had another candidate. He had watched the rise of the Perth accountant Laurie Connell, who had become one of the fastest deal-makers in Australia's west.

Connell had started work in the Department of Industrial Development (DID) in Perth, then worked with Poon Brothers, caterers to remote mining camps and drilling rigs. In 1969 he joined Martin Corporation, a young merchant bank then owned by Wells Fargo, United Dominions Trust, Baring Bros, Cater Ryder and the Chartered Bank. With so many owners the reins were fairly loose on this newcomer among the relatively few, fairly staid, merchant banks in Australia at that time. Connell became Martin's money market dealer in Perth. He opened and built up the company's interest in the commercial bill market and became WA manager of Martin Discounts. Connell's energy and drive were outstanding. He was a short, compact, round man and became known as the Little Steamroller, a reference to his physical stature and his capacity to get things done his way, to flatten obstacles that would have stopped people of less drive and confidence. During those years at the DID and Martin Corporation he formed close links with people who later played key roles in the attempted rescues of his company, Rothwells: Brian Yuill, later of Spedley Securities; P. K. Lucas; Tom Hugall; and W. A. Burgess, managing director of Winterbottom Motors and former State manager of IAC (Holdings).

At Martin Corporation he also formed the most important relationship of all — that with Alan Bond. Martin Corporation had started financing deals with Bond Corporation in the early 1970s. Connell and Yuill, with W. A. Burgess of Winterbottom Motors, put together the finance that helped rescue Alan Bond from his pressing financial problems in the late 1970s by enabling him to buy Burmah Oil's Cooper Basin oil and gas shares just before they took off in 1979. The South Australian Government forced Bond to sell more than half those shares to reduce his holding to under 15 per cent, which he did late that year at nearly three times the price he had paid for them. He sold the rest in 1982 for an overall profit of over $150 million on an outlay of $36 million, paid in instalments. That profit enabled him to repay funds he had borrowed to buy Swan Brewery. It put him back on the acquisition trail when his critics, as they had in the past and would in the future, thought he was about to sink under the burden of debt. The Bond-Connell-Yuill business relationship became seamless, with important consequences for the Fairfax takeover in 1987–88, and even more important consequences for the Government of Western Australia.

Marty had never met Connell, but thought he could be a buyer of a small investment-type company in North America. In April he went down from Boston looking forward to meeting Connell at a dinner in New York with venture capitalists and deal makers of mutual interest. Connell was looking at the possible US takeover. He seemed everything Marty had anticipated and more. Marty raised with Connell the possibility of becoming involved in a very big Eastern States takeover. Warwick authorised him to pursue the contact. Back in Australia Marty saw Connell at the Regent Hotel in Sydney and revealed that Fairfax was the company involved in the takeover play. He outlined the major share-holdings: Warwick and his mother had 14 per cent, the rest of the family 36 per cent, the super funds 10 per cent. The public had the rest. Barings had advised against a bid. What did Connell think? According to Marty, Connell said, 'It can be done with a powerful investor and if the family doesn't sell. But the family's interests would be to sell, so big assets sales would be necessary to fund the takeover.' Marty said, 'Warwick is sure the family will stay in. He wants a plan.'

Dougherty and Fieldhouse flew to Perth for further talks with Connell. Barings were still involved in discussions with 'Fairwater' at this stage. In mid-April they had been looking for a possible chief executive to run the company if and when Warwick moved in. Mary Fairfax suggested that they might consider working with the man who said he could do what Warwick wanted, Laurie Connell. But if Halkerston and Connell talked, Gardiner must not know about it. Barings said this was unacceptable to them, as it probably was to Connell. So Barings bowed out. For 'Fairwater' ambitions, Connell alone had the right stuff: boldness, decision, resolve. On 29 April, he engaged Bert Reuter to work on the project.

The next day Dougherty and Fieldhouse met Connell in Perth, where Connell put forward for the first time the idea of a joint venture between himself and Warwick for the takeover. Dougherty met Reuter later that day. The team was coming together. Warwick was still in New York. He had attended the December Fairfax board meeting in Melbourne when the counter-strategy to News Corporation's bid for the HWT had been discussed. He would not be able to accept the board's regular invitations to attend meetings until May. But he was, by the end of April, as his commitment to a takeover bid took shape, already slipping easily into the two roles he would be playing in the coming months. There was the public role as the young Fairfax heir, his academic education completed, about to return from Harvard, already taken into the inner councils of the company and preparing to work in it. And there was the private role, of Fairfax the planner and plotter of a daring takeover bid for the company, engaging the services of a group of can-do merchants to help him in his clandestine task. He played the two roles faultlessly until the end of August, when the private Warwick went public.

The four separate forces that led to the end-of-August takeover bid were coming together. Warwick had dramatically changed the power balance within the family with his February purchase of 1.5 million shares. Relations between 'Fairwater' and the Fairfax management were falling apart, although the latter seemed unaware of it. The Hawke Government's proposed media owner-ship legislation had broken up one old media empire in the HWT and caused the other, John Fairfax Ltd, to make a controversial and potentially destabilising step in buying HSV7. And young Warwick Fairfax had shown that he was deep into the debt culture of the mid-1980s by borrowing $35 million to buy 1.5 million Fairfax shares in February. He was confident with debt, conditioned by his two years at Harvard to think big with it, and by his Fairfax inheritance to take a long view of money. Time was on his side. But as the company's subsequent US financial adviser and Mary Fairfax's friend, Bill Simon, later said, 'Warwick's trouble is that he knows what two dollars is worth but not what $2 billion is worth.'

Back at the Fairfax offices in Jones Street Gardiner had to report to the April board meeting a stalemate on capital raisings. The company had not raised equity capital for 21 years. Now the company's borrowings totalled $450 million at high rates with very adverse effects on profits. It was becoming increasingly apparent that, in the absence of a suitable capital raising, the company would have to sell assets, and TV assets were the logical ones to sell. As Gardiner pointed out to the board, a $450 million debt in a company capitalised on the stockmarket at over $1.5 billion, would not have been a matter of concern to many of the rising companies of that time. But it was to the conservative Fairfax company.

The country newspapers it had agreed to buy from the HWT at the time of the HSV7 purchase had been passed on for purchase by the Fairfax affiliates, Rural Press and Macquarie Publications of Dubbo. But that would probably involve those companies in new capital raisings to which Fairfax would have to contribute. Rural Press had also bought the Central Coast and Hunter Valley newspapers owned by Fairfax itself through Newcastle Newspapers, and the Tamworth *Daily Leader* owned by News Corporation. Although Gardiner and the Fairfax board had been widely criticised about the HSV7 purchase, he and James Fairfax remained firmly convinced of its logic. If the Hawke Government's cross-ownership provisions failed to become law, but the wider television reach provisions did, Fairfax could keep HSV7 and make it more profitable. If the ownership provisions did become law, Fairfax could sell the three Channel 7 stations as a network, a prospect that looked increasingly attractive. Gardiner, like many others who had been in the industry before 1987, did not believe TV profits could justify the prices established by the Bond Corporation purchase from Kerry Packer or the Westfield-Northern Star purchase of the two Channels 10 from Murdoch. It was becoming a good industry to get out of at these prices. Bond was having trouble getting investment commitments to shares in Bond Media, the new company he was floating through brokers A. C. Goode and Co. and Rivkin James Capel, to take over his TV and radio interests. In addition, the new TV station owners might not respect the old agreements between the networks and affiliates that had helped contain the prices of imported films and programmes. Those fears were, in fact, soon realised. If Fairfax had still had only ATN7 and BTQ7 to sell, the potential buyers would be more limited. In fact they could narrow down to one: Robert Holmes a Court. With a three-station network on the East Coast, Gardiner felt the company could look forward to more potential buyers.

Those were useful strategic arguments. But in Melbourne at the end of April as Warwick's takeover team came together, Fairfax was coming under heavy and damaging fire from trade unions, the public and the Victorian State Government over its decision to retrench 78 HSV7 staff. That followed the axing of several less-than-successful Melbourne-based programmes. HSV7's ratings fell. Industrial action by the unions threatened to spread to Fairfax newspapers in Melbourne. Michael Duffy, the Hawke Government's Communications minister who came from Victoria, suggested the Australian Broadcasting Tribunal might have to look at HSV7 staffing in considering Fairfax's application for transfer of the licence. Early in May, HSV7 reinstated all the employees sacked two weeks previously.

The company was being criticised on strategic grounds for paying $320 million for HSV7 and on tactical grounds for the clumsy attempt at cost-saving retrenchments which even its former owners at the HWT acknowledged were necessary for HSV7's profitable survival. The new media legislation passed through the Senate on 3 June, adjusted to ensure the National Party's support by reducing the maximum reach one owner might have from 75 per cent to 60 per cent of the Australian market. Gardiner always believed that the recent media policy would not last, that the huge capitalisations of the new TV networks were unsustainable and that the structure built on the 25 November announcement would collapse. Two and a half years later the last two expectations looked like being realised. But the logic of his reasoning about the industry's future did not mean that the policy would be changed.

The Hawke Government had called a general election for July. If it fell, a new government might introduce ownership legislation, which could make Fairfax's position with HSV7 more comfortable. But Hawke, with the endorsement of the *Sydney Morning Herald* and the *Age*, won with an increased majority in the House of Representatives, though with a decreased percentage of the total vote.

Fairfax was looking for offers for HSV7 alone or for the three stations as a network. At least the shareholders were happy. On 21 May the company announced a two-for-one bonus share issue, capitalising part of its asset revaluation reserves. Many companies were making bonus issues at that time to beat new tax laws, which would make such issues taxable in shareholders' hands after 30 June unless they were made out of share premium reserves. One share selling at $15.40 on 15 June thus became three shares selling at $5.15 on 16 June. Strong buying continued on the stock exchange. By early June, Holmes a Court's companies had built up their holdings to 1.8 per cent of Fairfax and Thomas Nationwide Transport (TNT), run by Sir Peter Abeles, Murdoch's partner in Ansett Transport Industries, had nearly three per cent.

From Jones Street, the TNT presence on the share register (much of it apparently through the company's superannuation fund) looked disturbing. Abeles had had no reason to feel warmly about Fairfax after the *National Times* investigations of his US business. They had upset his good friend, the Labor Prime Minister, R. J. Hawke. Apart from being Murdoch's partner in Ansett, Abeles was a visitor at 'Fairwater' and had employed Marty Dougherty as an adviser, just as 'Fairwater' did. Conspiracy theories flourished at Jones Street and 'Fairwater'. Ever since the takeover battle for the HWT in December and January, the Fairfax management had suspected that the 'Fairwater'-Dougherty-Abeles-Murdoch connection posed a threat to the company's security.

Macquarie Bank had been briefed to look at various alternatives for selling the Fairfax TV interests and became involved in a complex proposal to sell HSV7 to BDC Holdings, a company controlled by Kerry Stokes, into which he had sold his Canberra television station, and forming a joint company to handle the other television interests. Stokes was being advised by the BDC minority shareholder, AFP Investments. The scheme involved a lot of debt, which made Gardiner nervous. He had another possible buyer in mind: Christopher Skase, the ambitious young controller of Universal Telecasters, operator of QTQ9 in Brisbane. Skase and Gardiner had talked business previously. In the second half of 1986 Gardiner had toyed with the idea of buying the 15 per cent of AWA that Skase had built up in preparation for his unsuccessful takeover bid for that company. They were both well out of it. Skase sold elsewhere at a profit and AWA later disclosed substantial losses from foreign exchange operations. Fairfax had sold Skase the Brisbane radio station 4MMM and Gardiner had kept him in mind for possible future deals.

The July Federal election victory for Labor confirmed Fairfax's commitment to sell. Talks continued with Skase's advisers. But it was Skase himself who did the deals. His energy and mobility were important elements of his image as one of the daring young entrepreneurs of the new economy developing around the Pacific Ocean. On 16 July he called Gardiner from the Mount Kenya Club near Nairobi to lift the status of the talks about buying the TV stations. Four days later he called from Hawaii. On Thursday, 23 July he met Gardiner in Sydney and by 2.30 a.m. Friday the deal had been signed. Murdoch's newspaper, the *Australian*, announced the impending sale that morning and nearly got the price right at $800 million. It was a shock to the Macquarie Bank, which had been, until then, negotiating confidently with Kerry Stokes and his advisers. And it was a shock to Mary Fairfax, who rang Gardiner and criticised him for not continuing to talk to Kevin Parry who later claimed he would have paid more than Skase.

Gardiner and the Fairfax board did not take Parry's share swapping plans seriously. He lost his company after the 19 October crash. But Gardiner had been careful to keep Stokes as a reserve if the Skase deal fell through. The Fairfax papers followed on 25 July with most of the details. Fairfax had sold its TV interests to Skase's Universal Telecasters for $750 million — $25 million deposit already paid (of which $21 million went to the Albert family company, which had held six per cent of ATN7 since it was formed), $440 million due by 30 November and $285 million by 31 August 1990. The delayed payments were in effect interest free loans from Fairfax. Discounted at 15 per cent, the deal was worth about $700 million to Fairfax in July 1987 dollars. In addition Fairfax was to invest $100 million in Qintex group shares and convertible notes in November.

Some important elements of the deal were not revealed at the time. Skase had an option to put the television assets back to Fairfax for $285 million before 13 October 1990 (by which time he would have outlayed $444 million) or for $385 million after that but before 13 April 1992 (when Skase would have outlayed $729 million). And the Fairfax papers were entitled to $15 million worth of free advertising on the network over the next three years. Fairfax also agreed to underwrite any losses of HSV7 Melbourne of over $100 000 a week up to 31 January 1988. From 1 February to 31 July 1988, Fairfax and United Telecasters would share any losses equally. Fairfax was also restricted in dealing with its Qintex securities until after 1990. Fairfax could well afford to make these concessions.

At the time the deal was made Fairfax was much stronger financially than the pyramid of companies controlled by Skase. Fairfax reinvestments in Qintex, the put options and the under-written losses were sources of comfort to Skase's bankers at the time. Less than a year later the positions were reversed. Warwick's takeover had loaded Fairfax with an unserviceable debt, and Skase was able to restructure the deal to his own advantage, although he had been four weeks late with his November instalment. But in July 1987, Gardiner was able to point out that, in November, Fairfax would be virtually free of debt and poised for substantial new growth in Australia and overseas. Less than two weeks after the Skase deal was signed, Kerry Stokes also decided TV was a good thing to be out of at those prices. He sold his TV interests to Northern Star Holdings for $225 million.

Warwick Fairfax had joined the company at the end of June. A programme had been prepared for him to meet the editors and managers, to familiarise himself with the people and products behind the company's revenues and profits and assets. He seemed diffident, awkward, even detached, which was not surprising for a 26-year-old tyro mixing with veterans of the Sydney newspaper wars. He had been kept informed of all the Fairfax problems and possible solutions in the previous six months. Gardiner was meticulous about this. The possibility of Warwick joining the board immediately had been raised. Gardiner was keen on it as a demonstration of family solidarity. John B. Fairfax thought it might be difficult for Warwick to be a director and work in the marketing department in a fairly junior capacity at the same time. It was really a matter of timing. John had spent 18 years working in the company as journalist, advertising manager and manager before joining the board and knew the value of that experience. On the other hand it would be logical for 'Fairwater' to want a representative on the board. In the last few months before Sir Warwick died, they had looked for someone to attend board meetings as his alternate director. Sir Rupert Clarke had attended a board luncheon in Melbourne just before the HWT battle. He was a director of Rockwood. His wife and Mary Fairfax were friends. Then after Sir Warwick's death it was thought Carnegie Fieldhouse would attend with a watching brief for the 'Fairwater' interests. But that did not happen and the vacancy remained. Young Warwick was attending meetings by invitation and preferred to let it continue that way. Looking back, there was an ominous logic in that. If he had been a director he would have found it difficult to mount a surprise takeover bid for the company. Attending the board meetings as an invited guest, he got all the information without having to shoulder a director's responsibilities.

For the next three months, from the beginning of June until the end of August, Warwick Fairfax lived the double life. During most working days he went to the Fairfax office and through the familiarisation routines laid on for him by the senior management. He worked in the marketing department under Peter Gaunt. That was the expected, public Fairfax. Outside the office he worked on his role as the unexpected, private Fairfax, planning the company's takeover with his new advisers.

Unaware of the threat from within, the Fairfax board and management were becoming increasingly concerned about possible threats from without. By 24 August Holmes a Court had acquired 3.2 per cent of John Fairfax Ltd's shares, up from 1.8 per cent in June. The share price had risen from $4.50 to over six dollars in three months. On 1 August, Murdoch's *Weekend Australian* had headlined a story forecasting the company's coming fall with relish: 'Sound of a Tumbril in the Fairfax Camp'. The *Australian* kept it up with stories speculating on a move from either Holmes a Court or Sir Peter Abeles's TNT, Murdoch's partner in Ansett. The shares continued rising strongly, topping seven dollars on Wednesday, 26 August. At that price the shares yielded less than one per cent from the prospective dividend and were certainly not being bought for long-term investment. Those prices would only be justified by a takeover bid at more than seven dollars a share. Without knowledge of such a bid, buyers at those prices were facing an awful downside risk. But downside risks were far from the market's mind in August 1987.

On 26 August Gardiner reassured the board that none of the directors was being bugged. This followed a claim by Derryn Hinch, the morning announcer and stirrer on the Fairfax-owned Melbourne radio station 3AW, that a Fairfax director had been bugged. The board had its usual monthly meeting the next day, Thursday, 27 August, a week later than usual. Christopher Skase came to lunch. He and the Fairfaxes were investing in each other. Gardiner and John B. Fairfax and their wives had been on a month-long trip through America and Europe and the meeting had been delayed for their return.

The main item on the agenda was approval of the television sale to Skase's Universal Telecasters. Gardiner and Suich also reported on security problems. Earlier that month, while Gardiner was overseas, his house was reported to have been illegally entered. Nothing had been taken, but there were indications that the telephone system had, at some time, been interfered with, providing possible access for a listening device in the basement. Gardiner and Suich both thought that their houses had been under surveillance earlier in the year when unknown men had inquired about them from neighbours. Derryn Hinch had got a garbled version of the investigations by Fairfax's security staff and the electronics experts they had retained. Something was going on out there, but what? Although the company, relying heavily on family solidarity, was still sceptical about the takeover speculation boiling up in the market, there had been discussions about what action might be taken in the event of a takeover bid, particularly while Gardiner and John B. Fairfax were away during July and August.

Young Warwick had appeared to be settling in to the company. In August his absences from the office appeared to be increasing but who in the marketing department was going to question him about that even if they wanted to? Warwick was living with four friends of similar religious interests in North Sydney. He stayed within his own social circle as, generally, did the other Fairfaxes. In a show of solicitousness for his half-brother's progress, James asked Warwick to lunch at the Bangkok restaurant in East Sydney. They talked about what he was doing, how he was feeling his way into the company. Relations between the two remained cordial but opaque. Warwick was well into his takeover plans but revealing nothing. At the board meeting on 27 August he listened impassively to the reports on security, on the increasing attacks on the company by the State and Federal Governments, and on growing criticism of the company's financial performance, mainly about the HSV7 purchase.

There was also discussion about a merchant banker's report that Robert Holmes a Court had said there were three Australian companies he thought particularly desirable: BHP, Westpac and John Fairfax Ltd. Whether he meant it or not, remarks like that from Holmes a Court stirred possums everywhere. Only when the rapid rise in the company's share price to over seven dollars was mentioned did Warwick show some reaction by partly covering his face. Gardiner was talking to the board at the time. Suich mentioned this gesture to him later, suggesting that something might be going on. But the suspicion was too thin to flourish. In any event it was too late. The next day Tryart received approval from the ANZ Bank for the loan Warwick needed to make his bid for the company.

# CHAPTER 9

# THAT GREAT, FAT CASH COW

Some preliminary work had been done, mostly in Perth, on the proposed takeover of John Fairfax Ltd by the time Warwick's takeover team met in Sydney for the first time in Carnegie Fieldhouse's offices late in May 1987. Dougherty, Reuter and Fieldhouse had met in Perth during the first week in May and then in the third week in Sydney. The planning and talks revolved around the joint venture Connell had suggested. Warwick had no money. That was basic to all the discussions and plans made after his father's death, from the purchase of the 1.5 million shares in February onwards. But a joint venture with Connell? How did Warwick think he could sell that to the rest of the family? Warwick was neither completely naive nor gullible as the family discovered when he made his bid after sitting in on their board meetings, and as Connell discovered when the chips were down. The joint venture could have been step one to eliminate the outside shareholders. Step two would eliminate the family. Step three — well, Connell's usefulness might have a limited life.

The joint venture was to be a 50–50 relationship, with Connell and Warwick each putting up $25 million in equity capital in the bid vehicle that would be formed to buy the public shareholdings and half the superannuation funds' holdings — a total of 42.75 per cent of the capital, or at that time, 42 750 000 shares. This was before Fairfax announced its two-for-one bonus share issue in June. It was based on a range of bid prices from $17.50 to $25 a share and envisaged the subsequent sale of the company's electronic interests for $1000 million ($850 million for the television stations, $200 million for Macquarie Broadcasting). Part of this $1000 million would be used to invest $550 million in convertible preference shares in the bid vehicle. Connell would also put $200 million into these preference shares. The plan depended on the family staying in. Reuter from the outset advised that Warwick should talk to and condition the family to this concept — a course Warwick flatly rejected. Reuter noted in his working papers after meeting Fieldhouse and Dougherty on 5 May:

> It is the belief of Carnie Fieldhouse and Martin Dougherty that the family will not sell their shares under any circumstances. If this is correct then Warwick must be given the ammunition to convince the family to back his management push. Warwick clearly wants to be in control of any bid vehicle.

Reuter was a shrewd and experienced takeover tactician. In a preliminary report to Connell dated 12 May on the proposed media acquisition, code-named with his typical whimsy 'Giornale Dynasty' (Connell was in Italy at the time), he recorded: 'the Heir [Warwick] wanted Connell to join him [the Heir] in acquiring control to make "long overdue management changes".' Reuter noted that Connell planned a major public float to consolidate his interests in one public vehicle. 'It is intended to use this new public vehicle to develop the investment in Dynasty Corporation,' he wrote. A major assumption was that the family would stay in. Reuter was concerned that Connell would be up for $225 million and that this would have to be borrowed. How would Connell avoid a cash drain? He was still looking at a $20 bid. And in notes prepared for a meeting with Warwick three days later on 15 May, Reuter considered that $20 a share was the break-up value of the company. That valued the company fully at $2 billion. The late September bid of $8.50 a share (after the bonus) by Tryart valued the company at over $2.5 million.

In his 15 May notes Reuter wrote: 'A bid for 100 per cent cannot be sustained on borrowings as earnings do not cover the interest shortfall.' He thought some creative accounting could overcome some problems. But on his figurings in May the joint venture looked anything but a bonanza for Connell. Perhaps, with Connell putting his own funds in, the figuring was more conservative than it became in August, when the deal moved on to the $100 million fee basis. Problematical at $20 in May, it became 'do-able' at $8.50 (the equivalent of $25.50 pre-bonus) in September. Reuter said they knew more about the value in the company then.

These were merely financial hypotheses, however. The real issue as far as Warwick was concerned was where control would lie. It was proposed that he should have four directors and Connell three. Connell suggested equal board representation, with Warwick having the casting vote as chairman. At these meetings Reuter suggested that Warwick should start conditioning the rest of the family to his plan. But Warwick was firm: they should spring the bid on James, John, Vincent and Gardiner — paralyse them to stop any counters. The joint venture plan did not get beyond this conceptual stage. It always looked shaky. How could Warwick expect to sell the family on a plan that had them being overshadowed by Connell? But it emphasised that, whatever form the bid finally took, Connell and Warwick Fairfax would have to depend on each other's total commitment to the project and be confident of each other's capacity to see it through.

A few days later, on 8 June, Warwick and Connell met for breakfast to settle their mutual reservations. Connell recalled this as their first meeting. Warwick was about to return to Boston for his graduation ceremonies. Connell wanted to know whether he had the stomach for the battle ahead, which could get very rough indeed. Warwick felt he had to move soon before the existing management ran the company aground or it fell to a takeover predator who would offer enough to seduce one branch of the family into breaking ranks. He appeared not too concerned with the prospect of having to sell off assets to reduce his takeover debt and satisfy greenmailers. His main concern at the end of the day was to own and control the *Sydney Morning Herald*. Connell recalled that Warwick did not want his mother involved although she would be heavily committed through her shares in Rockwood and Acrux. Warwick's commitment satisfied Connell.

And Connell must have satisfied Warwick, whose main source of information about the West Australian had been Connell's new friend and admirer, Marty Dougherty, who joined them in the latter part of the meeting. Warwick was a critic of Fairfax's management. Dougherty was a critic of Fairfax's editorial policies. Some of his clients had been treated critically by Fairfax newspapers. He thought the Fairfax press was anti-business and lacked balance, a view that Warwick must have found congenial since it reinforced his general criticism of how the company was being run. Connell left no doubt about his dislike of, and contempt for, the press of Australia. The Fairfax papers had recently given him a hard time.

In February 1987, as Warwick's takeover ideas were germinating, the editors of the *Sydney Morning Herald* decided it was time to publish a major profile of someone who personified the rising generation of bare-knuckled businessmen from Western Australia. That someone was Lawrence Robert Connell, 40, horseman and deal-maker, who was well on his way to becoming the second richest of Perth's newly rich. The richest was another horseman, Robert Holmes a Court. Connell was challenging his very close friend, Alan Bond, the yachtsman, for second position. Ben Hills was assigned to the Connell story. It was published in the *Good Weekend* weekly magazine inserted in the *Age* in Melbourne on 3 April and in the *Sydney Morning Herald* on 4 April.

Less than three weeks later, Dougherty put the Fairfax proposition to him. Laurie Connell then had at least three good reasons for joining Warwick Fairfax in the project to take over John Fairfax Ltd: the concept was challenging; there would be a lot of money in it; he would get his hands on the company that had just published what he considered the most unfair, biased, scurrilous piece yet written about him. Connell complained bitterly to Marty Dougherty whom he had recently met in New York.

Connell had not always had a good press, even in Western Australia, where the media, not unlike most media around the world, tended to pull their punches on local heroes. Hills laid it all out. Laurie Connell had made a lot of money quickly. Only 12 years previously he had left Martin Corporation, a merchant bank owned partly by Baring Bros but mainly by the Canadian Imperial Bank of Commerce (CIBC), which later bought out Barings and changed Martin Corp.'s name to CIBC Australia. Connell found them a bit stuffy and set up on his own.

Now Connell was succeeding Baring Bros Halkerston as adviser to Warwick Fairfax. He was going to do the deal Baring Bros Halkerston advised against. Later, in the court case about payment of the $100 million fee, the financial projections prepared by Bert Reuter, on which Tryart's bids were based, were criticised by Malcolm Irving and Michael Smith, managing director and investment banking director of CIBC Australia. Connell had left before either of them joined the company. Early in 1987 he was planning to float his interests into a public company in which his shares would be worth over $275 million. He was also planning a $20 million house on the banks of the Swan River. (Both plans evaporated as the market turned against him.) He had between 300 and 400, or maybe it was 200, horses at his stud properties in Western Australia, New Zealand and England.

In 1982 he had taken over a small Brisbane company, Rothwells Ltd, and given it the Connell treatment. Rothwells had been a menswear store, selling socks and suits to a couple of generations of Brisbane's middle classes. It had been taken over by a New Guinea entrepreneur, J. K. Dowling, and some associates. The menswear business was sold off and turned into a fledgling investment company when Connell raided it, beating a small Melbourne company, Qintex, run by a young ex-journalist, Christopher Skase, in a short takeover skirmish. In March 1983 Rothwells claimed it had been granted Queensland's first 'merchant banking licence'. That was a bit of financial licence since there was no such thing as a merchant banking licence. But it was a money market dealer registered under the Financial Corporations Act and the Reserve Bank reluctantly tolerated the use of merchant bank as a descriptive term by such companies. Rothwells thrived in the rising market. In 1987 Connell reported a $16 million profit after tax. Unlike some of the other new entrepreneurs, Rothwells appeared to pay taxes at the full rate. Connell pointed out that a $1000 investment in Rothwells had grown to be worth $16 000 in the five years he had been running the company. That was a month before the crash. After Connell's own interests, the Colonial Mutual Life Office and the AMP Society were among the company's biggest shareholders. The institutions were not so keen on some other Western Australian entrepreneurs.

Rothwells had a vital special attraction for Connell: it was a listed company, which had paid dividends for the last 15 consecutive years and thus ranked as a trustee investment in Western Australia. That enabled Rothwells to accept funds on deposit from investors and institutions, including those of government instrumentalities, which would otherwise have been unavailable to him. Connell was a big punter on the race track and a lavish spender with his winnings.

On the way up there had been a number of incidents that Connell preferred the media to forget. Hills's article recalled them in careful detail. On 3 October 1975, Connell went to the races in Kalgoorlie and heavily backed a horse called His Worship running in the Bernborough Handicap at Melbourne's Sandown racetrack that afternoon. His Worship won. But he had won before some bets were laid. The race broadcast had been held up in Perth and not transmitted to Kalgoorlie until after the race was run. It was not the first time this had happened in Australia. On 2 October the stewards found Connell guilty of 'a dishonourable action' under Australian Rule of Racing No. 175(a) in that he 'bet or caused to be placed bets on His Worship after the race had been run, a fact not known to the bookmakers with whom the bets had been placed'. He was barred from the track for two years. That conviction may have cost him election to the WA Turf Club committee. It was raised against him during his unsuccessful application for Perth's third TV licence. In January 1988, his trainer, George Way, was barred for 20 years for failure to ensure that one of Connell's horses was not doped. No charges were laid against Connell, who maintained ignorance of the whole affair.

Connell liked horses. Their attraction had a new dimension after 1985. In August 1985 the Hawke Government introduced an amendment to the Income Tax Assessment Act allowing generous new annual depreciation write-offs on bloodstock, 50 per cent on stallions, 33 $1/3$ per cent on mares. The new law could have been made for Connell, a horse lover with profits sprouting out of the booming stockmarket, who knew a tax break when he saw one. He was one of the biggest yearling buyers in Australasia. Some reports said he had 210 horses, others that he had 400. Ben Hills reported that controversy had dogged his business dealings too:

> Late in 1985 he made his first reported appearance in the courts [apart, that is, from a charge of refusing a breathalyser test]. The case involved a company called Protective Research Industries, which had the right to a product it boasted would 'make window cleaning a chore of the past'. A hot, new issue, and Connell, the court was told, was the 'puppet-master'. A Perth businessman named Chris Burbury claimed he had been cheated out of a $1.5 million investment in the company, because a post-dated cheque of his was rushed by taxi to the bank before he could arrange funds to cover it.
>
> The case enthralled Perth's business community for days and then abruptly collapsed as Burbury was given his shares, and issued a statement saying he was making no allegation of impropriety against Connell. Then in June last year, Christopher Quinlan, the former general manager of another Connell company, Vital Technology, took action in the Supreme Court in an attempt to check the company's books to see whether 'any director had made improper profits which should have gone to the company'. After a secret hearing which lasted nine days, Quinlan's application was rejected and, once again, Connell was vindicated . . .

Protective Research Industries and Vital Technology were typical of the technology companies that mushroomed around Rothwells and became involved in a web of loan transactions that finally imploded in 1988 when all of them collapsed.

Connell was a hard man to cross. He had organised finance for fellow Perth entrepreneur, Yosse Goldberg, to take over the Fremantle Gas Co. for $24 million. He was said to have charged the gas company a fee of $225 000 for introducing them to Goldberg. Thirteen months later the gas company was sold to the WA Government for $39 million. Connell charged Goldberg's company a fee of $5 million for organising the sale. It also appeared that he split the profit with Goldberg after the finance, provided by the Standard Chartered Bank, had been discharged. At deals and fees, Laurie was the ringmaster.

In the WA Parliament, the Liberal Opposition leader, Bill Hassell, launched a censure motion against the Government over the gas company deal. Connell took the matter up with the parliamentary Liberal Party claiming he was 'mortified at the imputations and innuendos' cast upon him and asked to meet Liberal MPs 'to place them in possession of the proper facts'. Hassell refused to go to Connell's office, lost his authority in the Party and was sacked on a motion moved by a close drinking mate of Connell's. Connell had his eye on media properties. He had unsuccessfully tried to buy the Perth *Daily News*, a poor relation of the rich *West Australian*. He did not like journalists, believing them to be envious of other people's success. Ben Hills later recalled that when he interviewed Connell for his *Good Weekend* article late in February 1987, he had asked the horse-loving dealmaker what he thought about the *Sydney Morning Herald*. Connell said he would 'love to get hold of that great, fat cash cow'. In May he had the chance to do so with or through Warwick Geoffrey Oswald Fairfax. This time the introductory fee was due to Martin Dougherty.

In five or six years Dougherty had built up a special relationship with the 'Fairwater' Fairfaxes. Marty had grown up in Casino in northern NSW where his father and mother had a hotel, the Charcoal Inn. Later they came to Sydney and Marty started work as an articled clerk in a small solicitor's office. After three years he decided the practice of law was not for him and talked his way into a cadetship in journalism at John Fairfax Ltd. He was hired by News Corporation to work on the *Australian* and became production editor when Ken Cowley, future managing director of News Ltd in Australia, was production manager. He went to Melbourne to work on the Melbourne *Herald* as magazine editor, a job that left time to work on Saturdays on the *Sunday Observer*, then owned by the magnetic journalist-economist Maxwell Newton. The *Observer* was edited by John Sorell. Marty, as usual, was very busy on a number of fronts. Newton developed big problems with the Tax Commissioner and went to North America. Sorell became news editor at Channel 9, Melbourne, and Dougherty returned to News Corporation to edit *Truth* in Melbourne before going back to Sydney to edit the *Daily Mirror*.

He had differences with some board members over editorial policy towards the 1980 Moscow Olympic Games, which the Fraser Government, following the US lead, had boycotted. Dougherty quit and became NSW manager for International Public Relations. He left 18 months later without regret on either side and set up his own public relations company, Dougherty Communications. Murdoch remained friendly, and introduced him to Peter Abeles at Thomas Nationwide Transport, who became a client.

That brief period at the Melbourne *Observer* later changed Marty Dougherty's life. Through John Sorell he met Jeanne Pratt, a former journalist. Jeanne Lester had married Richard Pratt, whose family owned Visyboard, one of Australia's biggest packaging groups. Richard, who had been an actor, was managing director of the company. He was very rich and becoming richer. He was eventually to become regarded as a potential buyer of all or part of John Fairfax Ltd. Jeanne Pratt and Marty Dougherty got along well. Like Marty she was busy. (She listed her recreations in Australian *Who's Who* as: reading, writing, theatre, scrabble.) They formed a partnership to produce a poster for the Swedish pop group, Abba, then visiting Australia. Jeanne Pratt later told *Times on Sunday* reporter Geoff Strong:

> Marty said it was a good thing to do, to put out a poster, because he was looking for something to do, he needed some money at the time, so we had it printed. I suppose we broke even; Richard said we didn't, he said he subsidised it. He said I'll never make money because you shouldn't fall in love with your project.

Jeanne Pratt was patron of the Victorian State Opera and the Opera Foundation of Victoria. That developed her friendship with another, even busier opera lover, Mary Fairfax. (She listed her recreations in Australian *Who's Who* as: working, the arts, writing, poetry, sculpture, fashion, entertaining, reading, swimming, talking, travel.) The two women had much in common. They came from middle-European migrant families, had gone to school in Sydney and then to Sydney University. They were interested in the arts, particularly theatre. They were lively, extrovert. They had both married rich men and were able to indulge their interests.

One day in Sydney in the early 1980s Jeanne Pratt was due to meet Mary Fairfax for coffee at the 21 restaurant in Knox Street, Double Bay. The 21 was one of several coffee house-restaurants in that suburb with an Austro-Hungarian atmosphere. It had a special nostalgic appeal for people who had fled Europe just before the Second World War or during the Russian invasion of Hungary in 1956, many of whom, with a good eye for property values, had clustered around Double Bay. As she crossed Knox Street, Jeanne met her old friend Marty Dougherty and asked him to join her and Mary Fairfax at the 21. She told Geoff Strong, 'He is such a jolly fellow and mixes anywhere, a totally charming Irishman. I think she and Marty got on from the beginning.' Marty became a regular visitor at 'Fairwater'. Marty was tall, blue eyed, pink, freshly-laundered. He had a nice easy way with people he wanted to be friendly with, which was most people. Later, after Mary Fairfax turned on him and the takeover started running into trouble, he described her as 'the only former friend I've ever had'.

Sir Warwick Fairfax at this time was over 80, in the last decade of his life. He had few close friends. That did not matter. All his life he had been used to spending long periods alone without being lonely. As a boy he had grown up virtually alone at 'Fairwater', the only child of a mature marriage. In the last years of his life he was finishing his book *Purpose*, spending many weekends at 'Harrington Park', near Narellan, where he kept most of his reference books and could retire to his own private retreat. But in his final months he became virtually confined to his bedroom at 'Fairwater'. Gardiner called on him there to report on latest events at the company, with Mary present. Warwick was still capable of being sharp with her for her vigorous interruptions. But his life was nearly exhausted.

Just before Christmas 1986, Mary held a family dinner party at 'Fairwater'. James sat at the head of the table. Before dinner they all went to pay their respects to Sir Warwick, sitting in a chair beside his bed, frail, but still with them. It was a deeply sentimental occasion, an effort by Mary to enfold them all. But the distances between them remained, in some cases unbridgeable. John B. Fairfax, in an unguarded moment soon after the takeover, told London *Observer* reporter Lindsay Vincent:

I was especially hurt [by Warwick's bid] because I had a good relationship with Warwick and the potential for harmony in our family had never been greater. The only reason we split was because of his mother. She was always hypocritical in her dealings with us, talking about family love and all that bullshit. Ever since she put her beady eyes on Sir Warwick, this is what she wanted.

Marty Dougherty had one special link with the Fairfaxes. His grandfather, William Gibbons, had worked for John Fairfax & Sons as a reader for 35 years. Gibbons, in the manner of the best readers who performed a vital function in the newspaper production process before being eliminated by the technology revolution in the 1980s, was a guardian of the *Sydney Morning Herald*'s accuracy and English usage. The Fairfaxes liked that sort of family connection.

Marty Dougherty often breakfasted with Sir Warwick at 'Fairwater' and walked with him along Seven Shillings beach in front of the house. He became a business adviser, involved in plans to subdivide a tract of 'Harrington Park'. The funds released from this were to have helped young Warwick Fairfax build up his equity in John Fairfax Ltd. On 16 August 1986 the *Sydney Morning Herald* reported that the Department of Environment and Planning had approved an executive housing development on the 800 hectare property. The first stage included plans for 2800 home sites on about 320 hectares. This would develop into a $500 million mini-city of 5300 home sites. Sir Warwick said that his family company, which owned the estate, did not intend to develop the property — it would be sold to a development group 'in the near future'. Marty Dougherty handled the press release. Four years later no progress had been made. The up-front costs of the development — the provision of water, sewerage and other services — would be enormous.

Young Warwick Fairfax was overseas as Marty Dougherty became close to the 'Fairwater' family. He spent the three years to 1981 at Oxford University, worked at the Boston investment bank, Gordon H Begg and Co. and then at the Chase Manhattan Bank in New York. They were lonely years for a reserved young man of limited interests. At Oxford he was attracted to a group of young Christians, went to a retreat with them and became converted to a Christian fellowship, deeply committed to group discussions, support and prayer. In America he became a member of the very well-endowed fundamentalist Christian fellowship movement in which Republican Senator Mark Hatfield and the former Democratic Senator Harold Hughes were prominent. So was Arthur Burns, chairman of the Federal Reserve Board.

The fellowship was cellular, meeting often as breakfast prayer groups, sometimes for retreats, crossing denominational and political boundaries but satisfying an apparently deep need for spiritual comfort and support in post-Vietnam and post-Watergate America. It emphasised personal guidance, which suited the self-centred political mood of the time. One of its prominent converts was Charles Colson, one of President Nixon's chief lieutenants, whom Eric Sevareid of Columbia Broadcasting Service (CBS) had called 'the toughest of the White House tough guys'. Colson was largely influenced in his conversion by Tom Phillips, president of Raytheon, and by the supportive figure of Doug Coe, who was sustained by financial sources in the movement so that he could carry on the fellowship's work fulltime. Phillips had been converted by Billy Graham but the fellowship worked much more discreetly than Graham. It worked from small groups rather than through great revivalist meetings.

Back in Australia Warwick maintained the fellowship connection. While the takeover was being planned and executed he lived with some fellow members in Neutral Bay, rather than with his mother at 'Fairwater'. His fellow members included Ross Cameron, son of an outspoken Right Wing politician, Jim Cameron, who established a prayer group in the NSW Parliament with the help of his close friend, Neil Pickard, a member of the State Legislative Assembly. The prayer group, also known as the Kingfisher Group, included the Transport Minister, Bruce Baird, the president of the Legislative Assembly, Johnno Johnson, and, later, the Health Minister, Peter Collins. Ross Cameron's brother, John, was married to Bev King, daughter of Peter King, an executive director of the Van Leer packaging group. It was this connection that led Warwick to offer King the chief executive's job at the Warwick-owned John Fairfax Ltd. Ross Cameron was offered a job on the staff of Mark Hatfield in America. His father Jim was a trenchant critic of the media. 'The media worships Neophilia, it always goes for what is new and novel, and away from what is enduring and permanent. It is overwhelmingly cynical, and always sees things from a diseased, malaised viewpoint,' he told the *Times on Sunday*. He thought the 'media barons', particularly at Fairfax, had lost control to the employees.

Cameron's criticisms were thus added to those of Packer and Murdoch, Hawke and Keating, and Marty Dougherty, Laurie Connell and Mary Fairfax that the company was out of control. Cameron believed that the world needed saving from humanism, from the idea that humankind could save itself. He wanted a return to 'spirit-based values' and saw some hope in the dismissal of the Unsworth Labor Government in NSW. In an interview with the *Times on Sunday*, he emphasised that the established prayer groups were connected with the highest centres of power. He said groups existed in about 50 of the world's parliaments, and that Doug Coe was 'dealing constantly with Prime Ministers and Cabinet Ministers'.

This emphasis on the fellowship's connections with, and appeal to, those in positions of power, sat oddly with the Christian emphasis on humility and compassion. Charles Colson, in his book *Born Again*, had emphasised the importance of C. S. Lewis's book *Mere Christianity*, in his own conversion. He quoted C. S. Lewis: 'Pride is a spiritual cancer; it eats up the very possibility of love, or contentment, or even common sense.' C. S. Lewis's words seemed to Colson to sum up what had happened to all those at Nixon's White House. Humility was not a virtue commonly associated with politicians or with newspaper publishers. Jim Cameron believed that political parties tended to be populated by 'plasticine people, who are all things to all people — capitalists to capitalists, socialists to socialists ... unknown, incontroversial people, with no armour-piercing potential'. Cameron used armour-piercing words, but had a humour and charm that could be more effectively disarming.

In those critical three months of June, July and August 1987, the counsel and advice young Warwick Fairfax was seeking and getting outside the Fairfax office appeared much more positive than what he was getting inside the office. At Jones Street he was being passed around to polite but busy and, after their first meeting, not particularly interested managers and editors who were not engaged by his manner. The senior executives mapped out a familiarisation programme for him and broadly left him to it apart from the occasional inquiry about how he was going — a look-after-the-new-boy-for-me attitude, which Warwick may have found patronising. Working in the marketing department, under the control of Peter Gaunt, he was exposed to some management meetings that did not impress him. He came closer to confiding his concerns to Gaunt than to anybody else in the company. Laurie Connell, Bert Reuter and Marty Dougherty were a different matter altogether. They all had a big vested interest in Warwick and the takeover project. If Warwick had doubts or fears about the wisdom of what he was embarking on, they were not likely to be reinforced by these advisers. Connell might strongly question Warwick's commitment but that only strengthened it.

At the Fairfax offices in Jones Street Warwick was a very privileged object of some curiosity, but no immediate consequence. At the takeover planning sessions at C. R. Fieldhouse's offices in the city, he was leading a crusade, and his advisers were unlikely to knock it. By August the takeover project had a momentum of its own. Warwick Fairfax would have found it hard to turn back. He was not alone. By the end of August the ANZ Bank had become part of the project's momentum. The Bank also found it hard to turn back. They were in the grip of Newton's first law of motion. Even an external force as big as the coming stockmarket crash could not stop them.

Fieldhouse's offices became planning headquarters for the takeover. Carnegie Richmond Hallett Fieldhouse had the most richly furnished and endowed offices in Sydney, discreetly located on two floors of Hope House, Macquarie Street, Sydney headquarters of one of Fieldhouse's clients, Lang Hancock, the West Australian iron ore magnate. Hancock then owned the building. It was named for his first wife. He had a penthouse on the top floor. Fieldhouse occupied the second and ninth floors. In his mid-fifties, Fieldhouse was the oldest of the takeover group. When the action started he remained behind as adviser on the home front, while the active front line role was taken over by Aleco Vrisakis, of Blake Dawson Waldron, one of the most effective of the new generation of lawyers attuned to the debt-and-tax-driven takeover boom. Vrisakis left the Blake Dawson Waldron partnership on 31 December 1987. Carnegie Fieldhouse had focused on taxation early in his career and had come some distance since writing *Cut Your Income Tax: A Practical Guide to Bigger Taxation Savings for Wage Earners, Shop-keepers and Small Traders*, published by Angus and Robertson in 1964. In 1987 Fieldhouse had a small, rich practice, probably the most exclusive in Australia. His name, unlike Vrisakis's, rarely appeared in the press.

A rare profile in the *Law Society Journal* in 1983 described the office and the practice:

> ...what strikes the visitor most of all about this office is not the view from it — other lawyers have splendid views too — but the furniture and the books. The furniture ... is from nine-teenth and eighteenth centuries, finely worked German examples and English crafted oak, solid, distinctive, but not overdone.
>
> The most striking of these pieces is an early walnut con-ference table capable of seating 16, with the somewhat rare characteristic of being an extension table, even though it is circular.
>
> Nobody knows how many legal books there are on the ninth and second floor offices of C. R. Fieldhouse, solicitors, but they run into thousands. It is a major legal library, and certainly one of the very best anywhere in the country...
>
> Among the rare sets: the complete *Laws of Hong Kong* in 22 volumes and kept up to date weekly, a complete set of *Powell on US Real Property* in 13 volumes; *US Current Legal Forms* in 14 volumes; the *Revised Reports of England dating from 1785* in 152 volumes, as well as the *English Authorised Reports* and *Halsbury's Statutes of England*; the *American Law of Mining* in five volumes; the *Taxation of European Countries* in 10 volumes; *Canadian Tax and Canadian Sales Tax Law*; *American Corporation Law*; complete *American Federal Income Tax Law*; *American Federal Excise Tax*; *US Federal*

*Estate and Gift Tax*; *German Tax*; all *American Tax Treaties*; *African and South American Tax*; *European Tax Planning*; *Taxation in Middle Eastern Countries*; all *United States Tax Cases*, right up to date [there are believed to be only a few sets in Australia]. In fact, almost every worthwhile international tax text and report known to practitioners.

Often he uses his library when he is preparing material to be sent overseas for an opinion. 'It's very much an international tax library, set up for the type of family clients that I have.'

C. R. Fieldhouse had only about 20 clients, all on retainer, all families, the article stated. It concluded:

When Carnegie Fieldhouse reaches the lift that takes him down to the Rolls Royce that takes him home to 'Killara' [which is furnished in the same style as his office suite], the last thing he sees is a framed, illustrated message of sorts that must bring a smile to the faces of his clients: 'Riches are always restless, it is only with poverty the gods are content.'

Fieldhouse's library emphasised a major preoccupation of his clients: tax. The Australian film industry's generous tax concessions for investors beckoned Fieldhouse's clients in the 1980s. Lang Hancock became the major investor in *Mad Max*. Fieldhouse himself became executive producer of *Now and Forever*, a film that fell well short of the critical and box office acclaim of a motion picture of the same name made in Hollywood 50 years previously. In 1987 he was playing a behind-the-scenes role in an unfolding drama of high and low finance, family ambitions and intrigue, a drama with a character and story line to match any of the motion pictures he had helped to produce and finance.

(In 1989 after the Colonial Mutual Life bought the Hope building for a major redevelopment project, Fieldhouse moved, with Hancock, to equally stylish offices at Double Bay.)

Bert Reuter went to North America for holidays with his American wife Andrea in May. In June he moved to the Regent Hotel in Sydney, which became a joint planning headquarters with C. R. Fieldhouse's offices for the takeover bid. The problems involved in ownership and control of the joint venture plan appeared insoluble. The two potential partners had different aims. Warwick Fairfax wanted to secure control of the newspapers. Laurie Connell wanted to maximise his profits, but also to own and influence influential newspapers. His half of John Fairfax Ltd could be included in the new company he planned to float, giving a huge stockmarket value, and a big lift in status, to his diverse private interests.

In July the joint venture plan was abandoned and the $100 million fee arrangement took its place. The several versions of how this happened are outlined in Chapter 16. Although there were claims that the $100 million fee was cheap compared with what Connell was going to get out of the joint venture, there was little evidence that Connell was unhappy with the fee arrangement. His plans to float his private interests, including his proposed equity in Fairfax, and pyramid his personal fortune to $300 million had fallen through. Eastern Australian markets were sceptical of his operations and Ben Hills's *Good Weekend* article published early in April had not helped. The National Companies and Securities Commission (NCSC) had started to look at some of his companies' dealings. In March 1987 the NCSC had been tipped off about possible share manipulation between Rothwells, an associate, Vital Technology, and various Connell companies. This had broadened into a substantial investigation, which was eventually called off in a deal with Aleco Vrisakis acting for Rothwells, and perhaps Connell, late in October. Without a strong underwriting and continued support in the Eastern markets a flotation of the size Connell contemplated early in 1987 could fall very flat and become an embarrassment. The fee arrangement would allow Warwick to have sole control and Connell to do what he did best — make deals. Rothwells's own position was precarious. The NCSC later claimed the company's balance sheet at 30 June 1987, had been rigged to the extent of $323 million.

The rising price of Fairfax shares was becoming an even more urgent concern to them than it was to the Fairfax managers at Jones Street. A successful bid by Warwick, alone or perhaps with other family members, would depend on getting total ownership of Fairfax in order to control the cash flows to service the very big debt required to finance the takeover. It had become increasingly evident that such a requirement left great scope for greenmailers to move in, threaten the bid by buying up, say, 10 per cent of the shares, and thus becoming able to demand very special concessions before they would sell their shares and allow the bid to achieve its objectives. Holmes a Court was assuming an ominous position on the Fairfax share register and Kerry Packer was waiting in the wings. Murdoch had not yet appeared but at some stage he might have to be appeased. The market and his advisers were pushing Warwick into action, into the fee-based deal with Connell. There was another danger. Security had been tight, but as the final plans took shape and all the financial and legal commitments were being made, the possibility of leaks increased.

Bert Reuter made the formal application to the ANZ Bank for funds to finance the bid on Wednesday 19 August. About then the Fairfax board papers for the meeting to be held later that month went out to directors and, as a matter of courtesy, to Warwick. They contained final profit estimates for the 1986–87 year and estimated results for July against the 1987–88 budget, which had been prepared for the June board meeting. Fairfax's information systems were first class. The August board report figures immediately became available for the takeover financial planning. They also contained detailed breakdowns of all subsidiary trading results, details of the sale agreement with United Telecasters and cash forecasts. This would be vital information for Connell and Reuter in planning the asset sales which would be needed to repay substantial amounts of the ANZ's loan.

Few takeover bidders could have been so well informed about the company they were about to bid for. Without actual experience of the Fairfax operations, they still made errors of interpretation of the figures they had before them, but the overall picture was there in substantial detail. The August report's profit estimates for July also showed the adverse effect a new, free real estate weekly was having on the results of the *Canberra Times*. Kerry Packer later complained bitterly that he had been misled by the *Canberra Times*'s buoyant profit results and forecasts shown to him when he bought the paper in September. Reuter and Connell said they were not shown the August board papers.

In mid-August Marty Dougherty went to New York for negotiations with the American Broadcasting Corporation (ABC) about taking a position in Playcount. ABC was attracted, but not yet hooked, when Warwick Fairfax rang Dougherty suggesting that he return to Sydney immediately to prepare for the takeover action. Marty had a tricky choice to make: he could stay in New York and try to clinch the ABC deal, which could mean a lot of money to him if Playcount developed as he hoped it would, or he could return to the more certain monetary and personal rewards of the Fairfax takeover. He had substantial fees coming or in prospect from Warwick Fairfax, from Connell, from the sale of Dougherty Communications and from a contract as future managing director (editorial) of John Fairfax Ltd. It was no choice. With luck he might have all this and the ABC too. During his years in business Marty had often said he would like to go back to journalism but couldn't afford it. Now he couldn't afford not to. He caught a plane to Sydney and ran into heavy delays on the US West Coast and Honolulu. He landed in Sydney in the morning of Friday 28 August, and immediately rang New York to find out how the ABC negotiations were going. 'The fat lady has sung' he was told — the ABC was coming to the party. He went straight in to C. R. Fieldhouse's offices where the final structure of the takeover was coming together.

On 28 August the ANZ committed itself to provide certain loan facilities for the takeover; Warwick Fairfax acquired two shares in the takeover vehicle Tryart Pty Ltd; and the agreement between Warwick Fairfax and Rothwells Ltd was signed. It was a busy day. In all the discussions, planning and negotiations that had taken place about the takeover in the preceding four months, the deals had involved Laurie Connell personally, acting for himself or his personal company, L. R. Connell and Associates. Bert Reuter had been recruited by Laurie Connell and his fee was agreed with Connell personally, not with Rothwells. Similarly, Marty Dougherty's side of the deal was coming from Connell. Marty was also getting fees from Warwick Fairfax, who later said he was surprised that Marty was also being paid by Connell for the Tryart deal.

On 18 August, as the final shape of the bid was being decided, and Connell's role had been that of an adviser only commanding a block-busting fee of $100 million, he decided to switch his fee to Rothwells. This would enable Rothwells to make an enormous step forward as a merchant bank. No other merchant bank in Australia, perhaps no other merchant or investment bank in the world, had ever charged a fee of this size for a deal like this. The takeover involved the blue-blooded Sydney company John Fairfax Ltd and its equally blue-blooded Melbourne subsidiary David Syme Ltd. The financial facility would be the biggest the ANZ Bank had made; the ongoing deals would make the East Coast merchant banks puce with envy — the flotation of David Syme, the sale of other subsidiaries and properties to reduce the ANZ debt, the total management of the takeover, and of any subsequent issue of shares that Rothwells might consider necessary to deal with the takeover debt. Not only that. If ever a company needed an injection it was Rothwells, as events and investigations subsequently showed. Connell assigned his share of the Fairfax fee to Rothwells soon after the NCSC became interested in the company. The fee was stunning. To justify it, the performance would have to be equally stunning.

Surprise and the appearance of confidence were the key elements of the Tryart campaign. Marty Dougherty claimed later that Warwick Fairfax, when making the bid, owned and controlled only about seven per cent of John Fairfax Ltd capital. But his direct ownership may have covered only the 1.5 per cent of the capital he bought in Rockwood's name in February 1987. The rest of the shares held in Rockwood's name — about 11 per cent of the capital — were held for Tailer Investments on behalf of the two trusts, the Oriolo and Jones trusts, whose beneficiaries were Warwick and his mother. That was how Marty credited Warwick with the 5.5 per cent that took his total holding to seven per cent. But the precise nature of those trusts was not known. Whether his direct interest was 1.5 per cent or seven per cent, its relative slenderness emphasised the need for support from his mother who controlled the other half of the Rockwood shares and her own 1.1 per cent held by her company Acrux Holdings. Warwick held his mother's power of attorney while she was overseas during August and September. His mother's support was vital. With it, on 30 August, he could speak, temporarily, for about

15 per cent of Fairfax's capital. Mary Fairfax's support for her son's takeover venture became particularly critical later in 1987 when the takeover appeared to be a *fait accompli*, and again nearly a year later in 1988 when its refinancing was in the balance.

On 30 August Warwick had no positive power over James's Kinghaven shares. He had a veto right only. He could veto a sale by James but could not force one. Otherwise James still controlled Kinghaven's 11.3 per cent of the capital. James had another 5.5 per cent on his own account. With the support of his mother and his sister Caroline, the James Fairfax group was assumed to control about 19 per cent. The Sir Vincent-John B. Fairfax group controlled about 15 per cent. The Fairfax superannuation funds had about 11 per cent, leaving the public with slightly less than 40 per cent. The AMP Society, with whom the company had had close relations for many years, was the biggest public shareholder with 6.2 per cent of the capital. Warwick said, or Marty Dougherty said on his behalf, that he hoped the family would stay with him in John Fairfax Ltd or perhaps join him in Tryart in some way or other. Connell and Vrisakis were sceptical. The family, or at least the two key members, James and John, had not been sounded out before the bid was made. This seemed a basic weakness in the bid at the outset. If Warwick wanted the family to stay in, why had he so carefully hidden his intentions? As he later made clear in the legal fight about payment of the $100 million fee, Warwick believed that James and John were not too sharp and the less notice they had the less chance Gardiner would have of organising a counter for them. The ANZ Bank had made its initial facility available on the assumption that the family would stay in.

The initial concept had another hairy assumption — that the superannuation fund trustees could be convinced that they should sell only half their shares, thus further reducing the cash outlay required to gain control. The basic objectives of the bid as it was envisaged at the end of August remained that Warwick should gain control without running into a large, long-term debt; that the family should remain in but with a substantial cash return to them (which had been the objective of the plan Sir Warwick had put to the board 10 years previously); and that the company should keep its newspapers. These objectives were not so far away from those Baring Bros Halkerston had been working on in the early part of 1987 without finding an acceptable solution.

Tryart's bid was a high risk operation, which was all the more reason why it should not appear so. A major concern of Warwick's advisers was that the appearance of confidence should bluff out Holmes a Court or Packer or any other potential bidder from making a counter bid. The bluff was hardly necessary. Even though he might directly own only 1.5 per cent, Warwick controlled, had an interest in, or a veto over the sale of, over 30 per cent of the company's capital. Any outside bidder, to have a chance of gaining over 50 per cent of the capital, would have to dislodge one of the other substantial family shareholdings. And even a holding of over 50 per cent could be of doubtful value to a counter-bidder since, without 100 per cent or a complex deal with Warwick, he would not be able to get his hands on the company's cash flows to service his takeover debt. The price Warwick was about to offer was high at $7.50 a share. Any outside counter bidder would not only have to offer more for each share, but offer it for more shares since Warwick did not, initially at least, have to buy the shares he already controlled or influenced.

Nevertheless, the less time the bid took, the less time there was for greenmailers to move in, or for the unexpected to happen, for things to go wrong. The takeover battle for the Herald & Weekly Times, nine months previously, had been a classic precedent. Murdoch had faced a situation with some similarities to that now facing Warwick Fairfax. He had to price his bid high enough to win the support of a family of companies (as Warwick eventually had to do to win the support of a family of individuals); he had to plan to meet as many foreseeable contingencies as possible; he had to make the bid as surprising and execute it as quickly as possible to keep the greenmailers out; and, when the action started, he had to be ready to change his plans to meet rapidly changing circumstances. In military terms, he had to recognise that few plans survived the first contact with the enemy.

The Tryart bid would be particularly susceptible to green-mailers since Tryart needed complete control of Fairfax to get its hands on the cash flow to service the debt. The first move from the Tryart camp was to take place early on the night of Sunday 30 August, when Warwick would call on James and John Fairfax and Greg Gardiner to announce his intentions. That, in itself, took some planning since Warwick's capacity to handle such confrontations was unknown. There was a rising sense of urgency, with the adrenalin surging, as the Tryart plans were discussed at the meeting Marty Dougherty joined early on Friday 28 August, at Fieldhouse's office. Apart from the strong rise in the market price of Fairfax shares in the previous two weeks, particularly in the previous week, which might have suggested a leak from somewhere in the Tryart camp, the security of Warwick's planning, after five months, had been remarkable. Takeover speculation about Fairfax was still focused on outsiders. But the rising market was increasing the pressure on Warwick to make the final decision to move that weekend. Warwick claimed Connell, Dougherty and Reuter all emphasised Holmes a Court's presence in the market, predicting a move from the West Australian raider early the next week, pushing Warwick to make the final commitment. That meant signing the Tryart agreement with Rothwells to act as adviser for a $100 million fee. Reuter and Connell wanted the fee to be paid when the offer became unconditional. But Warwick would still have no money by that time. Tryart would not have access to Fairfax's funds until the takeover was complete, the new board had moved in and the necessary notices and shareholder meetings had taken place. In effect, John Fairfax Ltd would have to pay the fee.

In private conversations with Warwick and Marty Dougherty, Fieldhouse said the fee was too high and might be negotiated down. Warwick later claimed, in the fee court case, that Marty had urged him to sign, that Marty had warned him that Connell would walk away unless that $100 million fee was formally agreed, that it was cheap compared with what Connell would have got out of the joint venture. Marty denied all of this and claimed Warwick had drawn the joint venture comparison. There was also the problem of the fee due to the ANZ Bank if they went ahead, as the Bank's commitment and line fees for the takeover finance. Connell said he or Rothwells would lend Warwick $10 million to pay the Bank's fees.

Fieldhouse tried to play for time. He had, as usual, sent the agreement document to Phillip Street for opinions, in this case to David Bennett QC and David Bloom QC. Fieldhouse said they had not had enough time to consider the agreement in all its ramifications. Warwick finally signed for Tryart and Rockwood and Connell for Rothwells. The agreement was not ratified by formal resolution by Tryart directors until November. And then the minute recording the resolution could not be found. With the Tryart agreement signed, the team got on with more strategy talks and planning for Warwick's visits to his family and to Gardiner on Sunday night. Vrisakis suggested Warwick should make a point of asking James and John directly whether they would accept the offer. This would help establish their status as Warwick's associates or not, under the Takeover Code.

Warwick had worn his diffident, compliant, family member mask in public for five months, and it was decided he should continue to do so right up to the last moment. He had been invited to the twenty-first birthday party of Kerry and Rosalind Packer's daughter, Gretel, to be held on the night of Saturday 29 August. That was 24 hours before he would be calling on his half-brother to tell him he planned to take control of the company. Should he go to the party at the Packers' mansion at Bellevue Hill or should he stay with the Tryart team for the final countdown before Sunday night's surprise calls? It was decided he should go. Those who met him at the party found him even more reserved and detached than usual.

On Saturday morning Warwick rang Gardiner to ask where he would be on Sunday night, should he, Warwick, want to contact or call on him. Warwick also wanted to contact James and John. James Fairfax was weekending at his country house 'Retford Park', near Bowral, and John was having his first weekend away from Sydney since the weekend in February when Warwick had asked him to share the buying of those 1.5 million shares. James would be back at his Darling Point, Sydney, house at 5.30 p.m. on Sunday, and John back at his Centennial Park house at 9.30 p.m. The call to Gardiner rang bells immediately. He called Rodney Halstead of Mallesons Stephen Jaques to tell him that the event they had thought might happen one day could be imminent. He called James at Bowral who had just cradled the telephone after talking to Warwick about the Sunday night appointment. Then he went off to lunch at the Suntory, an elegant Japanese restaurant in Kent Street, to talk about plans for a Fairfax international publications division.

As the Tryart team continued their planning sessions in the early afternoon of Saturday, 29 August, the three Fairfax executives Warwick planned to get rid of met to talk about their plans for expansion in North America and the UK.

The company had just announced its intention to launch *Sassy*, a new magazine aimed at the teenage market in America. *Sassy* was modelled on *Dolly*, a very successful magazine developed for the Australian market by Fairfax's magazine offshoot. The company's New York manager, Anne Summers, was also talking with the owners of the feminist magazine *Ms* about a possible takeover. Kerry Packer had talked about buying *Ms* a year or so previously, but his US magazine advisers had swung him against it and he had bought his way out of the deal at the last minute. *Ms* was a high profile property but was not profitable. *Sassy* was a risky venture, which could cost several millions to establish, but the possible rewards were large.

Fairfax's consumer magazines, run by the subsidiary, Fairfax Magazines (formerly Magazine Promotions, formerly Sungravure) were profitable at last, after a long, very chequered and usually unprofitable history. The parent company, John Fairfax Ltd, was prepared to back their expansion overseas. But the most dynamic magazine growth in the group had come from the business division centred on *Business Review Weekly* (BRW). This was run separately from the consumer magazines. The BRW group, domiciled in Melbourne and half-owned by David Syme Ltd was run by a former *Australian Financial Review* journalist, Robert Gottliebsen, with a board of directors that included Max Suich, Fred Brenchley, and Greg Taylor of David Syme as chairman. The BRW group seemed to magnify much of what was considered right and wrong about Fairfax. It had had some brilliant successes in the market place, particularly with BRW and *Personal Investment*, but was inclined to excesses of enthusiasm driven by Gottliebsen's restless energy, backed by a confident board. It was bigger on creative energy than on control.

In 1985 Fairfax had bought a 50 per cent interest in a small but very profitable New Zealand company, Fourth Estate Holdings Ltd, publisher of a business weekly, *National Business Review* (*NBR*), of *New Zealand's Business Who's Who* and a legislation newsletter. This was a beachhead in the New Zealand market from which a daily business newspaper matching the *Australian Financial Review* could be developed, plus New Zealand versions of *BRW* and *Personal Investment*, giving Fairfax dominance of newspaper and magazine coverage of the developing trans-Tasman economic union. Gottliebsen and Brenchley were eager to develop *NBR*. It was quickly converted from weekly, to bi-weekly and then on 15 June 1987 it was launched as a national business daily. This was a long-term investment and required careful management, but it had helped whet their appetites for more. Gottliebsen returned from meetings in New Zealand concerned mainly with *BRW*, late on Friday 28 August. He was also concerned about hearing that day that Consolidated Press was changing *Australian Business* from fortnightly to weekly publication on 1 October. This would bring it head on with *BRW*. He stayed overnight in Sydney for meetings on Saturday morning at Jones Street with Fred Brenchley and David Love, Fairfax's partner in a highly regarded economic analysis unit, Syntec. There were strains in the partnership and Fairfax was offering to buy Love out. Gottliebsen and Brenchley then went on to lunch with Max Suich and Greg Gardiner at the Suntory. They talked about plans for major international expansion in business publishing.

Preliminary merger-takeover talks had already been held with a Kansas-based company, American Business Journals (ABJ), and links had been discussed with EMAP, a profitable business publishing group in the UK.

ABJ had started a successful weekly business newspaper in Kansas City and developed more in a number of cities in America. Then it had bought another publishing group to give it reach over 38 cities. It had run into problems with this expansion and was operating at a loss though forecasting profits. Fairfax planned a survey of how ABJ publications were performing in each of those cities. If they liked what they saw, they would make an offer for ABJ. In the UK they wanted to develop a Money Show (a

money-based trade fair, which had been very successful as a joint
venture in Australia and New Zealand) and a *Personal Investment*
magazine. EMAP was regarded as a possible partner for the UK
Money Show.

When Fairfax first looked at ABJ the shares were cheap. But
news of talks between the two companies had been leaked into
the markets and ABJ shares had started to rise strongly. This was
just before the peak of the 1987 stockmarket boom and the share
price rise was starting to undermine the deal's prospects before
Tryart's takeover bid obliterated it altogether. The deal was dead
before the 19 October stockmarket crash. So was the prospect
of buying into EMAP in the UK. But on the afternoon of Saturday,
29 August, the ABJ deal was still well up on the Fairfax agenda
and the talks at the Suntory restaurant went on until about 4 p.m.,
while at the Regent, Tryart's team planned the next night's moves.

On Sunday James Fairfax left 'Retford Park' at around noon to
join a small luncheon party at the Mittagong country house of
his fellow Fairfax director, Sir David Griffin. He excused himself
from the lunch relatively early, explaining that he had to be back
at his Darling Point home in Sydney by around 5 p.m. Warwick
called on James at 5.30 p.m. James Fairfax's house stands on the
northern point of Darling Point, the harbour at the bottom of
the garden. Warwick came by himself. The limousine that brought
him waited, took him back to campaign headquarters at the
Regent, then took him and Bert Reuter to Gardiner's home
and waited. Warwick was then dropped off at John Fairfax's
house. The car took Reuter back to the Regent and returned to
pick up Warwick.

Warwick told James that he intended announcing, the next
morning, a bid for the shares in John Fairfax Ltd and hoped for
James's support. Few details of the financing or the mechanisms
for the bid were discussed. James took it calmly. Of all the
Fairfaxes, he felt by far the biggest obligation towards his young
half-brother and his immediate reactions were not totally
antagonistic. But James would not commit himself to support
the proposal. He thought Warwick should wait for at least
another 24 hours before making the public announcement. But
that was not part of the Tryart plan, which was to keep the time

between the courtesy calls on the Fairfax directors and the public announcement to a minimum. Although for most of the following month Marty Dougherty for Tryart continued to maintain that they were confident that the family would support Warwick's bid, the impact of nearly everything they did was to ensure the family's alienation.

In his calls on James and John that night Warwick went in alone. When he called on Gardiner, Reuter went with him. They sat in an attractive, informal living room overlooking a front terrace, Reuter in the chair his former boss Robert Holmes a Court had occupied one night months previously, when he had called on Gardiner to talk about possible mutual television interests. Holmes a Court's proposition was as coolly received as the one Warwick Fairfax and Bert Reuter were about to put. Warwick made a few introductory remarks, then said he would let Bert explain what they were proposing. Reuter said the market was alive with takeover rumours and that they expected a takeover bid for the company any day, perhaps early in the week that had just begun. Warwick was making his bid before that could happen, that is, announcing it the following morning as soon as the market opened. He said they had received bank approval for the bid's financing late the previous week. Warwick was making his bid in the interests of the family, to keep the predators out. Warwick Fairfax took up the conversation. He said he would like the existing management to stay, particularly Gardiner, to whom he suggested a new employment contract with higher salary and other inducements. Gardiner said he thought it was inappropriate to talk about Tryart's takeover intentions and offer him bigger inducements at the same time. It seemed obvious to Gardiner that, if Warwick took over, there would be no room for Gardiner to act as an effective chief executive any more. He was right. Fairfax and Reuter gave few details about the mechanics of the bid and the structure of John Fairfax Ltd afterwards, but Reuter emphasised that they had the funds and they had to move now. Gardiner was proving as hard-shelled as they had expected.

Warwick's appointment with John B. Fairfax had been arranged for 9.30 p.m. but it was 10 p.m. by the time he knocked on the door of the house in Lang Road, Centennial Park. He was greeted by John's wife Libby who, with a polite sense of family obligations, as they waited for John, spoke about an invitation for Warwick to dine with them at home in the near future. In months past, when relations between Warwick and John had been warm and promising, Warwick had talked with John and Libby about how they saw the company's future and their children's role in it. This was a matter dear to them, as John had a lifetime commitment to the company and hoped that commitment would be carried on by his children. Whether Warwick knew it or not, his takeover plan threatened John much more than it threatened James or Greg Gardiner. This was the most sensitive of his visits that Sunday night. John was prepared for the unexpected. Warwick said he had devised a way of privatising John Fairfax Ltd, which would secure its future by eliminating the ever-present possibility of it being raided. As he outlined his plan John Fairfax realised he was talking about a takeover raid that would leave John and his family in a very subservient position. Instead of looking forward to a future in which he could succeed James as chairman and see his own children enter the company before probably handing over to Warwick, John now faced an immediate future with Warwick as dominant shareholder and boss. His options were clear: he could go along with Warwick's plan, organise a counter bid, or sell out. As the days went by the last became by far the most attractive option. His immediate reaction on Sunday night was to say he totally opposed Warwick's proposal.

Warwick went back to the Regent to assess the night's work and plan the next day's moves. The late night session at the Regent considered delaying the bid for a day and dismissed it. Despite James's coolness and John's outright hostility to the bid, Warwick was convinced the family would come around and support him. That left the offer price to be decided. The market had outstripped a $7.25 bid. It was decided to go for $7.50.

Connell came late to the meeting, after the $7.50 price had been decided. He agreed with the price. He then made two telephone calls. The first was to the Prime Minister, R. J. Hawke, to tell him about the bid announcement planned for the next day. Connell had entertained Hawke on his boat in Perth. He was strongly connected with the Labor Party in Western Australia.

He was an earthy, can-do operator, who made the business of making lots of money look easy, attributes that appealed to some Labor politicians. He was also a big racehorse owner and punter, activities Hawke liked, and had become a substantial art collector. Hawke had recently had him appointed to the Australian National Gallery Council, an appointment he had to resign later in the year when Rothwells claimed all his attention. Connell knew Hawke had no sympathy for the existing regime at Fairfax. Then he rang Sir Peter Abeles to try and line up TNT's shareholding and was told Holmes a Court was calling on Abeles the next morning. That built up the apprehension about an imminent bid by Holmes a Court and the need for urgent action by Warwick to forestall him. Connell asked Abeles not to talk to Holmes a Court before Connell talked to Abeles. Holmes a Court called on Abeles the next morning. It was a sociable meeting between two men of affairs. Abeles had already committed his shares, or was about to commit them, to Kerry Packer.

Throughout August Bert Reuter had worked on new proposals for Warwick to make his own bid for the company, still code-named Dynasty. The basic objectives were for the Heir (Warwick) to have effective control of Dynasty without retaining 'long-term exposure to high level debt'; for the family and superannuation funds to stay in but for the bid to be structured and financed for a possible family sell-out; and for Dynasty to retain its print media assets. The plan envisaged a large cash return to the family to ensure their support and a public share flotation of David Syme Holdings which would include the *Australian Financial Review*, all of *BRW* magazines and Fairfax Magazines. Syme, under Reuter's direction, would become the vehicle for growth. By this time Fairfax had sold off its television interests to Skase's Universal Telecasters. Reuter still assumed that Macquarie Broadcasting could be sold for $200 million.

Like most of the other capital reconstruction plans for John Fairfax Ltd that had been put forward over the past 20 years, a cash return to the family was central. 'It is our understanding that the family has been assets rich and cash poor for years and would be attracted by substantial cash returns,' Reuter wrote. The assumption was that the cash payment would be a tranquilliser:

it would keep James and John and his family quiet as continuing shareholders while Warwick assumed control of the company. Reuter's workings at this stage were based on a bid price range of $7–$8. The market price in mid-August was just under $6. He looked to substantial savings in operating costs when Tryart took over. 'The general overhead structure in badly managed companies is very indulgent,' he wrote. Reuter had been through many takeover exercises with Robert Holmes a Court but had been particularly conditioned by his experience with Associated Communications Corporation (ACC) in London. ACC's chairman, Sir Lew Grade, in his book *Still Dancing*, complained that the Holmes a Court team even sacked Katie, the tea lady. Soon afterwards they eased Grade out too.

Reuter had originally asked the ANZ Bank for a facility of $1.31 billion, to cover an offer of $7.50 a share, based on the assumption that the family would stay in. The ANZ had agreed to this by letter on 28 August and notified the NCSC that this financing was in place to support Tryart's coming bid for John Fairfax Ltd. Whether the NCSC pointed it out or it suddenly occurred to Reuter independently, late in that final week before the bid, the $1.31 billion was inadequate. Tryart's bid would, under the Companies Acquisitions Code, have to cover all the shares in which Warwick did not have an interest. The NCSC would require evidence that finance was available to cover the family receiving and accepting the same offer as the other shareholders. Reuter rang the Bank in Melbourne and lifted his requirement to $1.76 billion. The Bank executives agreed but it had to go through a credit committee meeting at 9.30 a.m. on Friday.

As the meeting in Fieldhouse's office proceeded on 28 August, transferring Tryart to Warwick, finalising the Tryart Agreement with Rothwells, Reuter was keeping an eye on the facsimile machine outside for the ANZ letter offering the $1.76 billion facility. Eventually it arrived. The ANZ had written two letters to Tryart dated 28 August, one offering $1.31 billion and one offering $1.76 billion.

Bert Reuter continued to adjust his takeover financing figures right up to Sunday, 30 August. The final bid analysis in his own handwriting dated 30 August summarised the proposed offer: $7.50 cash, or $4.50 cash plus three Syme shares for every Fairfax share, or 15 Syme shares for two Fairfax shares. The financial analysis relied heavily on the proposed Syme flotation to reduce the cash cost of the bid, which had to cover 224 million Fairfax shares, that is, all but Warwick's own interests. At $7.50 a share that would cost $1.625 billion. Costs associated with the bid were estimated at $136 million — a total require- ment of $1.76 billion. Reuter thought that the Syme share alternatives would be widely accepted, including a big reinvestment in Syme shares by the Fairfax superannuation funds, reducing the cash outlay to $1.143 billion. That assumed the Syme shares could be sold at $1.20. The TV sale to Skase and the proposed sale of Macquarie Broadcasting would reduce this to $231 million. The company already owed $450 million to its bankers. The takeover would thus increase the overall Fairfax debt to $681 million. More asset sales would be needed. He roughed out the possibilities: *Canberra Times*, $100 million; *Rural Press*, $50 million; property lease back, $100 million; *Newcastle Herald*, *Illawarra Mercury* and Community Newspapers, $75 million; Australian Newsprint Mills shares, $200 million; Total $525 million.

The expectation that Syme shares could be floated at $1.20 was optimistic. That valued the reconstituted Syme holding company at nearly $1 billion. But when Rene Rivkin, as broker for the Syme issue, canvassed the AMP Society to test their reaction to this proposal, the AMP's investment managers said they would look for Syme to sell at 15 times 1988–89 earnings before they would be interested. That would reduce the current valuation of the company from $988 million to $810 million. Reuter reduced the valuation on Syme shares from $1.20 to one dollar on the proposed issued capital of 824 million shares. That was the sum that resulted in the two alternative Syme share exchange offers Tryart made on 31 August. More asset sales would be needed to reduce the group debt after the takeover. Bert Reuter had small, neat, round, upright handwriting, which ran in immaculate horizontal lines across the paper. Occasionally, as he sum- marised his workings over that 29–30 August weekend, it became a hurried scrawl.

At around 11 p.m. as the Sunday night meetings wound up, Warwick rang Sir Eric Neal, one of the non-family directors to tell him of the next morning's announcement. He asked Neal to tell the other outside director, Sir David Griffin. He left it to John to tell the oldest, longest-serving member of the board, John's father, Sir Vincent Fairfax.

# CHAPTER 10

# LAURIE CONNELL'S GREAT JUGGLING ACT

At 8.45 a.m. on Monday, 31 August 1987, the Sydney stock exchange received a letter from Warwick Fairfax outlining Tryart's takeover bid:

The Manager — Companies
Australian Stock Exchange (Sydney) Ltd
Exchange Centre
20 Bond Street
SYDNEY NSW 2000

Dear Sir

Tryart Pty Ltd ('Tryart') proposes to make offers to acquire all of the shares in John Fairfax Ltd ('Fairfax') to which it is not entitled.

Tryart is a company owned by Warwick Fairfax, the son of the former chairman, the late Sir Warwick Fairfax. The directors of the company are Warwick Fairfax, Bert Reuter and Martin Dougherty.

The offers will be part of a restructuring of the Fairfax Group. This will involve the transfer to the present wholly-owned subsidiary, David Syme and Co. Ltd ('David Syme') of three highly profitable assets from the Fairfax group. They are the group's magazine division, the *Australian Financial Review* and the 50 per cent interest in the *Business Review Weekly* (BRW) division not presently owned by Syme. David Syme presently owns the *Age* and other newspaper interests.

David Syme will be owned 45 per cent by Fairfax and the balance will be offered to existing Fairfax shareholders through the offer. Application will be made to the Australian Stock Exchange Ltd to list the shares in David Syme.

The Tryart offer to Fairfax shareholders is $7.50 a share; OR three shares in David Syme plus $4.50 in cash for each Fairfax share; OR 15 shares in David Syme for every two Fairfax shares.

The cash component of the offer price is being funded by the ANZ Banking Group Ltd.

It is proposed now to register a Part A Statement and to despatch the offers as soon as possible.

Yours faithfully,
W. G. O. Fairfax, Chairman.

The news would have been distributed immediately to brokers' offices over voice-line and through the Jecnet and Reuters Economic Services systems to stock exchanges and subscribers throughout Australia. The letter came from Rothwells's office in the AMP Building at 50 Bridge Street, but carried the address of Tryart's registered office — 19 Hamilton Street. Warwick was, in a sense, already in residence at John Fairfax Ltd. Nineteen Hamilton Street was the official address of John Fairfax Ltd's downtown city offices in Hunter Street. The building, known as Hardie Chambers, had been built in the 1880s and had stood next to the Warwick Buildings in Hamilton Street built by Sir James Reading Fairfax and owned by John Fairfax and Sons until they were sold to the AMP Society in the 1940s. The Warwick buildings were demolished and Hamilton Street truncated when Australia Square was built by Lend Lease Corporation in the 1960s.

Hardie Chambers survived, as did its Hunter Street neighbour, Hunter House. In 1955 they became part of one of the remarkable property deals R. A. G. Henderson did for Fairfax with the AMP Society. The two properties, Hardie Chambers and Hunter House, were bought for about £100 000, first in the name of Henderson and then transferred to the AMP Society. They were then leased to Fairfax for 25 years on a fixed rental with options to purchase at the end of that time at a depreciated value, or to renew the rental for another 20 years. A similar deal was done for the company's big Jones Street building developed in the late 1950s.

The deals reflected the mid-1950s assumption that long-term bond rates would go no higher than the then current four per cent, inflation was out of the question and basic land values would not increase. The windfall profits for Fairfax in the 1980s were enormous. In Hunter Street, Falkingham bought the next building but one to Hunter House in the 1970s and then Gardiner filled the gap by buying the building next to Hunter House soon after he became chief executive in 1980. Falkingham had actually concluded a verbal arrangement with the AMP Society to buy Hunter House and Hardie Chambers for less than the option price on the grounds that a renewal of the lease would be even more costly to the AMP. But Gardiner did not press that point. First, and overwhelmingly, Henderson, then Falkingham, then Gardiner, had put together some of Sydney's best real estate for a song. Historically this was the city's Fairfax precinct. The old *Herald* building, completed in 1929 on a site the firm had occupied since 1856, was just across Pitt Street, a flat-iron shaped building with its nose in Hunter Street, now owned and occupied by Westpac Banking Corporation. Sir Warwick Fairfax had his city office at 19 Hamilton Street after he retired as chairman of the company in 1976. The Rockwood Pastoral Co.'s registered office was there at various times. Sir Warwick and Lady Fairfax had bought the Grand Hotel on the opposite side of Hamilton Street in 1986. The Warwick tearooms had once occupied the 19 Hamilton Street basement. Fairfax had looked at a joint development of the Hunter Street properties with Lend Lease Corporation. But there were problems with National Trust classifications of the buildings and it had been decided that this was a job for a professional developer alone. It was decided to sell the properties. Gardiner wanted to use the funds to buy another, more suitable building, for Fairfax's inner city headquarters, perhaps even the old *Herald* building itself. That led to problems after the Tryart takeover since Mary Fairfax thought the Grand Hotel should be included in any sale for redevelopment. Her terms were not agreeable to Fairfax. By that time the company needed the money from the sale of those buildings to help fund Tryart's debt. They were sold in 1988 to

Leda Holdings for $37 million. Most of them had been bought for under $1 million in 1981 because of arrangements made 25 years previously by the reviled Henderson.

News of the takeover was broken publicly by the top rating radio talker John Laws on the Fairfax-owned Sydney radio station 2GB. Laws told his listeners soon after starting his programme at 9 a.m. to expect a bid from Warwick Fairfax for the family company. John Laws was one of Marty Dougherty's clients. Marty had advised him on his contract with 2GB, which included a clause to the effect that, if 2GB's ownership changed, the contract could be broken. When Tryart took over Fairfax, Laws used that clause to leave 2GB for rival station 2UE, owned by Bond Media. That was the beginning of the end of the Macquarie Broadcasting Network. The Laws broadcast was a small public relations masterpiece. This is what Marty's client Laws said about Marty's clients Warwick Fairfax and Laurie Connell and their companies:

> Big business news of the morning is that a firm called Tryart will make a bid for the Fairfax organisation. It will make a bid of $7.50 per share for the Fairfax organisation, which would value the company at about $2¼ billion. Tryart, for your edification, is a company that is owned solely by Warwick Fairfax, 26 years of age. Today he will make a bid to buy the farm back — in other words, buy the family company at the age of 26, supported by Rothwells, the Western Australian merchant bank headed up by Laurie Connell, one of the world's most astute bankers, who sees a great deal of potential in this young man.
>
> Quite an extraordinary achievement if he pulls it off and today is the day that we will find out if 26-year-old Warwick Fairfax, the son of the late Sir Warwick Fairfax, ex-chairman of the Fairfax board, is able to buy it back.
>
> Today is the day he tries: $7.50 a share, putting a value of $2¼ billion on the Fairfax organisation and supported in total by Laurie Connell, the financial adviser on the bid and supporting him totally with the bank being Rothwells, the Western Australian merchant bank.
>
> So there is a collection of people and if a fellow like Laurie Connell and the Rothwells Bank from Western Australia support

a 26-year-old, so there is plenty of life in the young; 26 years of age, today making a bid for the company, $7.50 a share.

We will watch that one with interest.

Many Fairfax executives learned of the proposed takeover from Laws's news report that morning, including the chief editorial executive, Max Suich, and Macquarie's managing director, Bob Johnson. The news did not make the first editions of the two Sydney afternoon papers, the *Sun* and the *Daily Mirror*, but was all over the front page of the *Mirror*'s second, on the streets soon after midday. In the *Mirror*'s later editions it was upstaged by a story about the law's growing leniency towards child criminals. In Melbourne the *Herald* carried a long, very well-informed piece by Terry McCrann anticipating an imminent bid, with most of the bid's details. It was written before the bid was announced, but the formal announcement had been made at the Melbourne stock exchange by the time the *Herald* was on sale. McCrann anticipated a counter-bid from Robert Holmes a Court. His story was used by the *Daily Mirror* in Sydney.

A press statement from Bert Reuter at Rothwells and Marty Dougherty at Dougherty Communications had Warwick Fairfax saying:

Privatisation will provide stability for the Fairfax group. It will give shareholders the opportunity to continue to participate in present significant and profitable assets of the group and to benefit from future media expansion through a new listed company. It will also end the takeover speculation that has dominated discussions of the Fairfax group in recent years.

The press statement also revealed that 'advisers on the offer are the merchant banking group Rothwells Ltd'.

John Fairfax Ltd's response to Warwick's takeover letter was swift and cool, delivered to the Sydney stock exchange at 11.25 a.m.:

The Manager — Companies
Australian Stock Exchange (Sydney) Ltd
Exchange Centre
20 Bond Street
SYDNEY 2000

Dear Sir

The Board of John Fairfax Ltd has a copy of a letter dated 31 August provided by Tryart Pty Ltd to the Manager — Companies, Australian Stock Exchange (Sydney) Ltd.

The Board has no additional information available other than that contained in the letter and the subject has not been discussed at any stage by the Board. The Board awaits any other information which might be forthcoming including formal details contained in the Part A Statement.

Until the Board has this detailed information, and has had the opportunity to evaluate it, it strongly advises that shareholders should not sell or otherwise dispose of their shares.

Yours faithfully,
I. S. Cumming (Group Company Secretary)

That remained the company's position for nearly two months. The Part A Statement, which Warwick Fairfax 'proposed now to register' on 31 August, was not registered until 9 October and then had to be adjusted for the 19–20 October stockmarket crash.

Neither the company, nor the Fairfax family directors, made any attempt to deny publicly the claims that the family were supporting Warwick in his bid, which Marty Dougherty very successfully peddled to the media, including the Fairfax newspapers, for the next three weeks. That campaign was important for Tryart to appear to be starting from a strong shareholding base in John Fairfax Ltd. The company and the family made only a feeble attempt to counter that campaign, apparently assuming that if they did, and successfully isolated Warwick, he might sell out, possibly to Holmes a Court or some other raider. In fact, James and John B. Fairfax might have killed this bid at the outset by publicly stating that they would not accept it for their own shareholdings. But that would be flouting their obligation to all the other shareholders. Such considerations did not bother some company directors in the 1980s. But Warwick's bid posed a moral dilemma for James, John and Vincent Fairfax: how could they say no in their own family interest when that might stop a once-in-a-lifetime offer for all the other shareholders? The dilemma was resolved by saying yes. Warwick made that easy by paying far too much for the shares.

Warwick confirmed the correctness of the fear that he might sell out during the fee case. Under cross-examination on 24 October 1988 he said he had been prepared to sell out if the family opposed his bid and would not deny that he had told Bert Reuter that he would sell 'even to Holmes a Court'. A memorandum from Max Suich to the editors on 2 September 1987, suggested that, when the newspapers carried a report of Warwick's advisers claiming that the family was behind him, it should be pointed out that neither J. O. nor J. B. Fairfax confirmed any such claim. But then, neither did they deny it. The qualifier was soon forgotten in the newspaper reports. By not denying Marty's claims from the start, they played into his hands. The Fairfax newspapers were misled by both sides, by commission from one, by omission from the other.

If Warwick did decide to sell, the family would not be big borrowers to relieve him of his shares at prices then ruling. But how many shares did Warwick have to sell? It was apparently assumed that he controlled the Acrux and Rockwood shares — about 14 per cent of Fairfax's capital. In fact he controlled neither holding when the chips were down. His mother controlled Acrux and at least half of Rockwood. In a story rich with ironies the greatest irony of all would have been for Mary Fairfax to sell her shares to Robert Holmes a Court from whom she had claimed for years that she was concerned to protect the company. But anything was possible and the company remained silent while Marty went to work. Warwick was a master of disguise. For months he disguised his intentions from the board and the family, then for another three weeks he disguised the weakness of his bid's base. He was successful in both deceptions partly because the family and the company's controllers believed what they wanted to believe.

Apart from the formal Fairfax letter to the Australian Stock Exchange and the mixture of disbelief, shock and excitement that Warwick's bid caused at Fairfax and all other media companies, there were three notable responses to the takeover news on 31 August. Rupert Murdoch said: 'I wish I'd had the guts to do it when I was 26'. When Murdoch was 26 he was planning his first takeover bid — one of his few unsuccessful bids — for Advertiser Newspapers Ltd in Adelaide (partly by offering shares with limited voting rights so voting control would not be watered down), a company he finally snared in 1987. 'I congratulate James Fairfax, I mean Warwick Fairfax,' Murdoch said. He predicted that the bid would succeed but not at $7.50 a share. The stockmarket thought so too. Fairfax shares were traded from $8.00 to $9.00 during the day. Bert Reuter said he expected other players to take part in the game, but that their intention would be to 'muddy the waters' rather than propose a serious alternative. Reuter knew Holmes a Court better than most newspaper reporters and columnists did.

The Great Bamboozler started stirring and muddying the waters the next day. He was 'not disinterested in Fairfax', Holmes a Court told reporters. He was concerned at 'certain aspects legally' of the bid and the reflotation of David Syme Ltd. 'An unconditional bid has been announced but it does not appear capable of being carried through,' he said. These were familiar opening gambits from him: a hint at a possible counter bid and a nod in the direction of possible legal action. One of his companies, J. N. Taylor Holdings (which Bert Reuter had run until February 1987) reported that it had sold 2.9 million News Corporation shares for $55.4 million. This added fuel to speculation that he could be getting ready for a Fairfax bid. Within 24 hours of the bid's announcement, one of Tryart's three alternative offers fell through. Canvassing of Fairfax institutional shareholders had indicated an overwhelming support for the third alternative: 15 shares in David Syme for two Fairfax shares. If all the outside shareholders accepted this, Syme would have a capital of $2 billion. That was nearly 50 times Syme's reconstructed profits after tax as optimistically projected by Tryart. Reuter suggested the Syme shares should be rationed, pro-rata. Vrisakis said the NCSC would not wear that. The 15-share exchange alternative was dropped. That cooled the market a bit on Tuesday, bringing the shares back from $9.20 during the day to $8.40 at the close of trading. Enthusiasm for the Syme share exchange however suggested that any Syme share issue involved in the bid did not need to be underwritten. Rivkin James Capel were appointed brokers to the Syme issue involved in the second alternative.

Rivkin James Capel had been the obvious first choice by Rothwells to handle the Syme float, just as it had been the obvious choice to handle the Bond Media float earlier in the year. Wardleys Australia, the local merchant banking offshoot of the Hong Kong and Shanghai Banking Corporation, had bought 15 per cent of Rivkin's firm when he and Brent Potts and other partners split in 1984. When the bank took over London brokers James Capel in 1986, the stake in Rivkin was lifted to 50 per cent and the firm was renamed Rivkin James Capel. Wardleys had advised and backed Alan Bond in his rise as a global takeover operator. Bond and Connell were inseparable. So when Connell wanted a big thinker to handle the Syme float, it went to the Wardleys associate, Rivkin James Capel. The Bond Media shares had not been easy to place and those who took them were showing big losses. The shares, floated at $1.55 earlier in the year, were selling at around $1.08 early in September in what was still a bull market. Those who bought them at this price later showed even bigger losses. Rivkin James Capel suffered a heavy blow in mid-September when Rene Rivkin entered hospital to have a benign brain tumour removed. That meant a loss in momentum to the marketing of the Syme shares when it was most needed. Rivkin returned to the market on 21 October. The partnership with James Capel was dissolved in December.

On Tuesday, 1 September, Marty Dougherty started the campaign of disinformation about the family's intentions (that is, James's and John's family intentions), which continued for the next three weeks. Warwick, Marty said, 'knew that nobody in the Fairfax family would break ranks' and that all were solidly behind the bid. That was a bit rich. One of the reasons for making this bid Warwick gave when he made the rounds on the previous Sunday night was fear that one of the predators then roaming the market could split the family. The family said nothing. In fact, from early in the first week in September, it was obvious to Tryart that the family was not solidly behind Warwick's bid. But the propaganda was maintained while Tryart built up its position, particularly while it took out the two threatening minority shareholders, Kerry Packer and Robert Holmes a Court. Laurie Connell claimed that the Fairfax family was supporting Warwick in a 'very tangible way'. Connell told an ABC reporter: 'He has been meeting with them and talking with them and working with them to achieve the result of stabilising the Fairfax controlling interest in Fairfax'.

Packer had been critical of the Fairfax management and board of directors for some years. His criticisms had been inflamed by the Goanna affair. He and his advisers thought Fairfax was very indulgently run, that costs, like journalists, were out of control, and that the company's operations could benefit greatly from the tighter controls and efficient management exercised at Consolidated Press. Rupert Murdoch shared those views, substituting News Corporation for Consolidated Press. At Consolidated Press the death of Sir Warwick Fairfax was seen as the loss of a key bonding element in the company. The purchase of HSV7, the subsequent industrial strife in Melbourne and the sale of the Seven Network to Christopher Skase, all appeared to confirm Consolidated Press's view that cracks were opening up in the company's formerly solid facade. Fairfax shares were rising strongly in the market to prices which could not be justified by profits. Packer decided he should be ready for any play in Fairfax assets.

In the early months of 1987 Fairfax management had watched a sizeable holding of shares being accumulated largely in the name of Beaglemoat Nominees Pty Ltd. They had served notice on Beaglemoat requiring the beneficial ownership of those shares and had been told the shares were being held for TNT superannuation funds. They kept a close eye on this as TNT's managing director, Peter Abeles, was regarded as a possible adversary, or a friend of possible adversaries. The Fairfax management was deeply suspicious of the Abeles-Murdoch, Abeles-'Fairwater' connections. The Beaglemoat purchases were very well timed. By mid-August Beaglemoat and associated holdings totalled between three and four per cent of Fairfax's capital. Packer and Abeles had mutual business interests. They had both used the services of Marty Dougherty. Packer rang Abeles and it was agreed that, if and when TNT wanted to sell, Packer should have first right to buy.

This development leaked into the market late on Wednesday 2 September. For the next three weeks the market was treated to a contrast in tactics between Packer and Holmes a Court. Packer then spoke for about four per cent of Fairfax. In the first week of the bid Holmes a Court had about four per cent. Either could move to 10 per cent and be in a position to stymie the bid. Tryart could not compulsorily acquire minor holdings, until it had over 90 per cent. Packer chose to stay at four per cent and make it clear that he could and would move to 10 per cent if necessary. Holmes a Court continued to buy strongly in the market right up to when he got all that he could out of Tryart, paying up to nine dollars a share and lifting his holding to around nine per cent to keep the pressure on the Tryart team. They were both very threatening presences in the market. But Packer's threat was implicit. Holmes a Court paid heavily to make his explicit. In the end he made a profit of about $30 million out of his Fairfax shares but could not consummate his agreement to buy Fairfax assets.

Perhaps, also, Holmes a Court's information about Fairfax and Tryart was not as good as Packer's. The Beaglemoat shares, possibly to avoid double tax and stamp duty, had not been transferred to Packer by the time Fairfax's share register was ruled off for Tryart's finally successful offer in November. So the takeover money went to Beaglemoat Nominees and then presumably to the TNT superannuation funds. But five days after the Abeles-Packer share deal was leaked to the market on 2 September, when the sale was confirmed by Sir Peter Abeles, he spoke as though the shares were held by TNT itself. He said TNT had bought the shares as an investment, not with the intention of becoming a media player. 'We had surplus cash and we judged it as a good investment,' he said. 'Our business is not in the media, we are a transport company and we just thought, let's take our profit and go.' TNT, or the superannuation funds, got the profit and Packer had the use of the shares as a lever to get strategic assets out of Fairfax.

While this was going on Aleco Vrisakis had moved quickly to quash doubts about the legality of Tryart's commitment to offer David Syme shares before it had control of John Fairfax Ltd.

Holmes a Court had criticised this aspect of the bid. On Wednesday, Tryart announced that the NCSC had cleared the bid of any breaches of company law. Tryart was out canvassing the institutions for their reactions. They generally anticipated an increase in the bid.

At Jones Street, Gardiner and James Fairfax decided to ask the Tryart team to come in and explain how the bid was supposed to work. Sunday's calls by Warwick and Monday's public announcements had been short on detail. Warwick Fairfax, Connell, Reuter, Dougherty and Vrisakis went to the Jones Street offices on Thursday morning to make their presentations. They met first in James Fairfax's office on the north-east corner of the 14th floor, with James, John Fairfax, Greg Gardiner and Rodney Halstead from Mallesons. Bert Reuter had a well-developed sense of humour and soap opera melodrama. His takeover planning had been code-named Dynasty with John Fairfax Ltd known as Dynasty Corporation and Warwick Fairfax as the Heir. In the early planning, when Connell had been in Italy, he had called it Giornale Dynasty. For this 3 September presentation he had constructed a chart, headed 'Fairfax Galaxy', to show the company's proposed structure after the purchase by Tryart, assuming James and John remained as shareholders.

The scheme was designed (as Sir Warwick's mid-1970s scheme had been and Gardiner's participating preference issue scheme of 1985 had been) to put a solid cash windfall into all the Fairfax family shareholders' pockets immediately, thus satisfying what was generally assumed to be their most urgent need and thus, presumably, going a long way towards winning their support. That misjudged James and John, particularly John, who had a strongly dynastic attitude to the company. Certainly they were interested in cash. But the Galaxy plan also clearly delivered control of John Fairfax Ltd to Warwick Fairfax. The Heir was a very dominant sun in this galaxy.

The outline of the plan was fairly complex, and Gardiner suggested that they move into the conference room on the southern side of the 14th floor where Connell and Reuter could use a wall-board for explanatory diagrams. The Galaxy plan was to take place in five steps: Tryart to borrow $1.2 billion from the ANZ Bank;

David Syme's share capital to be written up from $12 million to $874 million; Tryart to lend Syme $450 million to buy certain assets from Fairfax on condition that the loan be converted into preference capital; Tryart to pay $750 million cash to accepting Fairfax shareholders and distribute $450 million of Syme ordinary shares to those Fairfax shareholders who wanted them or to the underwriters/brokers. Fairfax would then subscribe for $1.2 billion in Tryart preference shares (including conversion of the $450 million loan). The $1.2 billion, to repay the bank, would come from the $450 million from Syme, $712 million from the discounted value of the television sale to Skase, and $150 million from the sale of half Macquarie Broadcasting and the 15 per cent investment in Chris Skase's Universal Telecasters Ltd.

There would be enough cash for a special $200 million dividend to the family shareholders remaining in the company. Warwick would end up with nearly 64 per cent of Fairfax's capital, James with 18 per cent, John with 16 per cent and the rest with 2.1 per cent. It was a snap. No it wasn't. John and his advisers thought that being left in a minority position in a private company controlled by an unknown Warwick Fairfax, who probably stood eventually to control James Fairfax's 18 per cent too, was not an acceptable long-term proposition. There was no future for John or his family in the Galaxy plan. They would be very small, lonely planets attached to and dependent on, a very big sun.

The plan seemed so clearly unacceptable that some wondered why it had ever been presented. It certainly helped raise family resentment against Warwick's bid and was the first major step towards Warwick having to buy out James and John. That may have been seen by members of the Tryart team as the most desirable outcome from the start. It would certainly solve a potential conflict of interests for James, John and Vincent. As directors, if they went along with Warwick's bid, they had a duty to get as much out of him as possible for the shareholders. But if they were going to continue as directors and shareholders, they had an interest in keeping the cost of the bid as low as possible to limit the company's future debt. Once they decided to sell, the conflict disappeared and, supported by group general manager,

Greg Gardiner, they could apply themselves to getting as high a price as possible for all shareholders.

That altered the whole economics of the Tryart bid. Marty Dougherty continued to maintain, speaking on Warwick's behalf, that the rest of the family were right behind Warwick. By the end of the first week, K. M. G. Hungerford was advising James, Lloyds was advising John and Macquarie Bank was advising John Fairfax Ltd. Tryart's Part A takeover statement was to be two weeks later than expected. Institutions were being briefed on the flotation of David Syme Ltd with a capital of around $850 million — more than the whole of John Fairfax Ltd had been capitalised at in the market a year previously. Fairfax shares were selling well above Warwick's offer price at $8.80. Pressure was mounting for a lift in the $7.50 bid price but Connell said no, that was not on. Connell speculated that Packer might be after a stake in Syme as part of a deal to buy him out of his small but threatening stake in Fairfax. Dougherty said that Packer 'had not indicated he was hostile and in terms of families they are on very friendly terms'. Packer said nothing; nor did the Fairfax family. But as the time came to buy Packer and Holmes a Court out, Connell was rapidly confirmed as the dominant force in the Tryart team.

They were making and remaking tactics and strategy on the run. Apart from the flotation of David Syme, the only asset sale envisaged when the bid was made was that of half of Macquarie Broadcasting. Very early in the game, when it was thought the family might stay in, they considered leaving Holmes a Court with the prospect of being an impotent minority shareholder and squeezing him to sell his Fairfax shares without having to offer to sell him assets. Holmes a Court saw that and returned the squeeze by buying more Fairfax shares and building up his own propaganda offensive. Once it became obvious that family members were sellers and would have to be bought out, then the sale of assets to Holmes a Court and Packer became imperative because Tryart needed the money to help fund the bigger takeover debt. The combination of having to buy out the family and a one dollar rise in the takeover price per share, added $650 million to the takeover debt. Assuming that the cash to come from Skase and the Syme flotation was safe, Connell had to raise $800 million from asset sales instead of only $150 million from the sale of half Macquarie Broadcasting and the equity in Universal Telecasters. Of Connell's two aims — to secure the Holmes a Court and Packer holdings and to raise funds by selling them assets the second became as important as the first as the cost of the takeover mounted.

This was to be a classic greenmailing encounter. Tryart needed full control of John Fairfax Ltd to get access to its cash flows to service the takeover debt. That made it particularly susceptible to greenmail as Packer and Holmes a Court quickly realised. Under the takeover code they could not be paid more for their Fairfax shares than other Fairfax shareholders. They had to be satisfied with assets, sold to them at a price they found acceptable, but which could not be seen as a preferred price, and which Tryart needed to be as big as possible to help liquidate the soaring ANZ debt. Connell had to get $800 million out of these asset sales. In addition, Packer and Holmes a Court might both want the same assets. This was a bargaining point for Connell, who, in effect, had to woo and screw these two hard-heads at the same time.

John B. Fairfax and his advisers were also thinking that, since it appeared that he would be leaving the company, he should make a bid for some of the assets that could form the nucleus of a future publishing enterprise for him and his family. John B. Fairfax was at the head of the queue. The more bidders there were, the better it was for Laurie Connell's great September juggling act as he kept all the Fairfax negotiable assets in the air until he could place them in satisfied hands at the right price. It was a pretty good act, particularly as, although he knew the titles of the assets he was juggling, he didn't really know what was inside them. At a generous merchant banking fee of one per cent of the $800 million of assets involved it would have been worth $8 million — if all the deals had been consummated. It was a pretty good act, but it could not survive the stock-market crash on 19–20 October. Neither could Connell's other big act, Rothwells.

The second week opened with some predictable horseplay between Holmes a Court and Connell. From London Holmes a Court said he was still buying Fairfax shares at above $7.50 and considering legal action. He said he planned to build a substantial shareholding in Fairfax. But decisions about further purchases would be made on a day-to-day basis. He was sceptical about the David Syme share issue. He warned, 'The duty directors bear is that, if they are selling [assets], to accept the highest price … If assets are going to be disposed of, it is known that there is a Melbourne Cup field after them.' Connell thought Holmes a Court's comments were 'humorous' and said the bid would go ahead at $7.50. There were problems, however. If Tryart was to give an accurate picture in its Part A Takeover Statement of what assets were to go into David Syme and how it would be capitalised, it would need sensitive information from John Fairfax Ltd about the individual sales, earnings and assets of the *Australian Financial Review, BRW* group and other assets, including David Syme itself. Fairfax was seeking legal advice about whether it should provide this.

On Tuesday Warwick came to see James about the takeover bid and the future. It was a friendly enough session, but James pointed out that the absence of any discussion with him or any other director or family member before the night of Sunday 30 August, meant that Warwick's bid had to be regarded as hostile. The half-brothers spoke by telephone a couple of times after that during September, but by the end of the month all communications had been broken off by Warwick. James rang and wrote inviting him to lunch, but Warwick was never available and then there was no response at all. They did not meet again until the company was handed over on 7 December.

Holmes a Court was buying shares at nine dollars and his holding was now close to five per cent. Rivkin James Capel, as brokers to the proposed Syme share issue, continued canvassing institutions for support. The phoney lull was broken when, on Thursday, 10 September the *Australian Financial Review* published details of the brokers' draft document projecting David Syme's earnings, which Rivkin was using as part of the hard sell to the investment markets. The document forecast profit increases of 18 per cent for 1987–88 and 39 per cent for 1988–89, based on increased revenue and cost savings of $17 million annually. Syme would have a capital of 824 million one dollar shares and assets of $1.1 billion. The *Age* was valued at $500 million, the *Australian Financial Review* at $300 million, BRW group at $150 million, other Fairfax magazines at $100 million, the other Melbourne and suburban newspapers at $70 million and the regional papers at $30 million.

The draft revealed that Reuter was to head up David Syme. It was later claimed that this was window dressing to help impress the investors as Reuter had established his credentials as a cost-cutter when Holmes a Court had taken control of Lew Grade's Associated Communications group in London. The new owner's rationalisation programme would involve the closure or sale of loss-making operations and stringent cost reassessment throughout the company. Reuter had previously, in pre-31 August exercises, which were the clear forerunners of this draft, expressed his opinion that the company was poorly controlled. The document did not specify closures but noted losses by the Melbourne throwaway *Winner's Weekly*, BRW group magazines' *Triple A* and *Money*, and consumer glossies *Harpers Bazaar*, *Good Housekeeping* and *Portfolio*. 'Most of them could be either curtailed or sold reasonably quickly and it is estimated that this could add about $9 million pre-tax to group profit,' Rivkin James Capel said.

This was dynamite. The document emphasised the extent of the information the Tryart team had about Fairfax operations, presumably from the board reports Warwick had received as an invited guest at board meetings and during the couple of months he was doing the rounds at Fairfax. It also emphasised the Tryart team's low opinion of Fairfax's management and control and the implicit threat to jobs throughout the company contained in the easy assumption of closures and cost-savings.

At Gardiner's suggestion, Warwick rang senior executives, including Suich, Brenchley and Anderson in Sydney, Gottliebsen and Taylor in Melbourne and John Hemming at Fairfax Magazines, to try and hose down any fires the *Australian Financial Review* report might have caused. He denied the statements and implications of the Rivkin James Capel document, told the executives they were all important to the company's future and possibly talked too much to be convincing. The executives were not impressed. Suich put to him that some closures, rationalisations and asset sales must be on the agenda. Warwick denied that.

Warwick was maintaining the family unity line. Suich, as chief editorial executive, suggested that Warwick talk to the editors, particularly to Alan Kohler at the *Australian Financial Review* and John Alexander and Chris Anderson at the *Sydney Morning Herald,* to establish some understanding with them. Warwick said he would do that. But he did not. He agreed to meet Suich and Brenchley at 4 p.m. after the board meeting on 17 September to discuss the nature of the new company and sound out their ideas about the company's future. The appointment was cancelled. Further notes and calls from Suich and Brenchley were ignored. There was no contact for six weeks. They assumed they were being frozen out.

In Melbourne, however, Greg Taylor was offered a service contract. He was the only one of the very top echelon of executives to stay with the company. Gottliebsen also stayed. He told Warwick he thought he, Warwick, would have trouble with his advisers, largely on the basis of what Gottliebsen saw as basic weaknesses in the Rivkin James Capel document. Deeper within the employee ranks, however, particularly among the journalists, the Rivkin James Capel document lit a fuse of apprehension which exploded three months later, after the new management moved in, bringing the company to a major crisis.

By the end of the week, leading institutions were becoming wary of the high capitalisation and earnings projections for the proposed David Syme company. As with Bond Media, they thought it might be better to wait and buy the shares after they were issued and listed and selling at a discount below their one dollar issue price. Fairfax shares closed the week at nine dollars with Holmes a Court still buying, emphasising to Tryart that he would want prize assets out of the Fairfax group before he would sell.

Marty Dougherty was very busy during the weekend of 12–13 September holding the official Tryart line of family unity. The *Times on Sunday* reported that Warwick had offered members of the Fairfax family shares in Tryart as one of several options for their involvement in the bid. If all the family came in that would give Tryart 50.01 per cent of Fairfax before launching its bid for the public shareholdings. Marty Dougherty, for Tryart, said only that Warwick remained 'extremely confident' of the bid succeeding, the family being united in its approach. This was followed on Monday with a report in the *Sydney Morning Herald* that Warwick Fairfax expected to reach formal agreement with other members of the family 'today or tomorrow' to unify them behind his bid. Dougherty said, 'We are absolutely certain that the family will continue its 150-year-old tradition of unity in the publishing business. Warwick Fairfax has been extremely confident all along that the family will not be disunited.' The family and the company said nothing.

Holmes a Court, back from London at his country property near Perth, said that a share deal between Tryart and the family 'would be very dicey stuff. It could involve differential offers to the family and the public which could offend the Takeovers Code'. The *Sydney Morning Herald* reported:

Sources close to Mr Fairfax have said that his bid was never intended to extend to other members of the family, but that condition was not stated in the original announcement of the offer made two weeks ago.

Full details of Tryart's offer were expected at the end of the week. The propaganda war was being fought by Dougherty for Tryart and Holmes a Court for his Bell group, but by nobody for the rest of the Fairfax family. Holmes a Court told the *Sydney Morning Herald* again that he would lift his holding to over 10 per cent unless he was offered the chance to buy some Fairfax assets. He would not allow his stake to be bought by Warwick Fairfax unless his stipulation on assets was met.

On Tuesday 15 September, Holmes a Court turned up the heat a few more degrees by buying 3–4 million shares at nine dollars. Most of them came from institutions, including the AMP Society, which unloaded 1.4 million of its total holding of around 20 million shares. The AMP was clearly testing the market and nine dollars appeared to be the ceiling. At the same time it was revealed that Holmes a Court, through his Bell group, had written to Fairfax asking for financial information, which might assist him if Bell decided to make a counter bid. But the Fairfax board had not yet decided whether and when the company's auditors, Touche Ross and Co., should give Tryart the information it wanted. The board was due to meet on Thursday. Holmes a Court bought a further 400 000 shares on Wednesday at nine dollars, lifting his holding to over seven per cent, including an option over a parcel of one per cent. His increasing equity was seen as not only a threat to Tryart's future access to Fairfax's cash flow, but also to the plans for selling assets into David Syme and then refloating the company. While Holmes a Court was increasing his pressure through the market, Lloyds had targeted which assets could be bought for John B. Fairfax and his family, and their price. The case for an increase in Tryart's offer price, as the family determined that their only course was to sell and make sure that all share-holders got as much as possible, had also become irresistible and virtually acknowledged by Tryart. Once that was established, all the assets of Fairfax, apart from the *Age* and the *Sydney Morning Herald*, were up for sale to the minority shareholders. The cost of the takeover rose by $650 million and the amount to be recouped from the asset sales to $800 million. That virtually ensured that the *Australian Financial Review* would have to go in order to make up the $800 million. But that in turn would reduce the size of the David Syme flotation since the *Financial Review* would no longer be available to Syme.

The ANZ Bank was facing a commitment surging towards $2 billion instead of $1.3 billion. The Fairfax board met on Thursday, 17 September, and later released a preliminary statement of 1986–87 profits. Although television had had a very difficult year and radio profits were down, the metropolitan newspapers had been very profitable and group profits before tax had risen by nine per cent to over $80 million. A big rise in the provision for income tax — common that year as companies absorbed the cost of employees' fringe benefits, which had previously been tax deductible — had trimmed the net result by six per cent to $42.2 million. There was a further $91 million capital dividend from Australian Associated Press, paid out of profits from the sale of Reuters shares. The board raised the dividend for shareholders, said the new year had started very strongly for the main news-papers and repeated their advice not to accept Tryart's $7.50 a share offer until Tryart's Part A Statement explained its proposals in more detail. Only 20 000 shares were traded on the exchanges, mainly at nine dollars. The next day, Friday, Tryart and John's and James's financial advisers agreed that the takeover price would rise from $7.50 to $8.50 and that John and James would sell at this price.

Connell was in Sydney talking asset sales, meeting Packer at Packer's office in the Consolidated Press building in Park Street and the Lloyds advisers to John B. Fairfax, Peter Mason and Brian Wilson, at Rothwells's offices in the AMP Building, 50 Bridge Street. Although, in targeting desirable Fairfax assets to buy, John was attracted to the *Australian Financial Review* for which he had once sold advertising space, and to the *Canberra Times*, of which he had been general manager for some years, there were problems with both. They were probably outside his price range, especially the *Financial Review*. The *Canberra Times* faced pressure on its profits from a free real estate paper and the *Financial Review*'s precise results were hard to extract from the overall Jones Street operations. What John needed were well-managed, stand-alone assets. Lloyds targeted those: the substantial minority or 50 per cent interests in Rural Press; Macquarie Publications (run and substantially owned by John Armati at Dubbo); Eastern Suburbs Newspapers in Sydney (half-owned and run by the Hannan family); Stereo FM Brisbane Ltd, a cash box since the sale of its radio station; and the *Queanbeyan Age*. These were assets in which Greg Gardiner had spent much time building Fairfax's equity over the previous seven years. Total price was $78 million. John B. Fairfax and his advisers had picked relatively small but sweet plums from the Fairfax tree. The *Australian Financial Review* was not only at the top of John B. Fairfax's list but at the top of Holmes a Court's and Packer's as well.

Packer did not know Connell before these meetings. Although they had a mutual interest in horses, they liked different kinds of horses. Connell owned racehorses, hundreds of them. Packer liked betting on race horses but was not a heavily committed owner of them. He owned polo ponies and since he had fallen in love with them, he seemed to have lost most of his enthusiasm for betting on race horses. If the two men found a rapport, it was not based on four-legged animals but an admiration for the way they each did business. When Connell looked for rescuers for Rothwells at the end of October, the first person he rang was Kerry Packer. Although there had been speculation in the press, inspired by Connell's remarks, that Packer could be interested in backing his magazines into a reconstituted David Syme, there was little substance in this. Packer was not interested in taking a subordinate position in the company, below a Tryart-owned John Fairfax Ltd. When he had talked with John D'Arcy about backing his magazines into the Herald & Weekly Times (HWT) a year previously, he had been looking at becoming the biggest independent shareholder in that company, subordinate to nobody. Now, with Fairfax assets in play, he had his eye on the *Australian Financial Review*, *BRW* business magazine group, the Fairfax consumer magazines and *Australian Property News*, a strategic publication in the burgeoning national property advertising market in which Fairfax, through the *Australian Financial Review* and Murdoch through the *Australian*, had already developed substantial and growing stakes, but in which Consolidated Press had none. Negotiations between all parties were entering their final week, the offer price had been settled between Connell and James's and John's advisers and Macquarie Bank for the Fairfax board at $8.50, and Lloyds had fixed the assets they were buying for John, but the newspapers continued to be mesmerised by Marty Dougherty's family-unity campaign. Speculation continued that the family would be brought in to Tryart. In the Melbourne *Herald* Terry McCrann called it 'a truly brilliant exercise in disinformation by Warwick's bunch of musketeers'. At least the market had the message: on Monday 21 September, the shares dropped to $8.30.

Direct, face to face, talks with the Lloyds advisers or with Kerry Packer were no problem for Connell. They were a short walk or a short car ride away in Sydney. But he had to catch Holmes a Court when and where he could. Holmes a Court would be in Melbourne on Monday and Tuesday for board meetings and the annual general meeting of BHP in which he had a 30 per cent shareholding. Connell and Vrisakis flew to Melbourne on Monday to start realistic talks with him at his Melbourne office.

Such talks with Holmes a Court were never easy. His first claims were for the *Age* and the *Sydney Morning Herald*. He was less serious about the latter than the former. Packer had made a similar ambit claim. Connell dismissed them both. Eventually the negotiable assets were on the table — virtually everything but the *Age* and the *Sydney Morning Herald* — with price tags attached.

At the *BRW* group Gottliebsen was becoming increasingly concerned about the fate of the magazines in his charge, particularly concerned that they might fall into the hands of Kerry Packer, whose *Australian Business* magazine had just changed from fortnightly to weekly publication to compete head on with *BRW*. The business magazine market was highly competitive, *BRW* had the upper hand, Packer's *Bulletin* magazine had been hurt by the new business publications, and Gottliebsen was convinced that if Packer got his hands on *BRW* it would be shredded. While Connell was talking to Holmes a Court in Spring Street, Gottliebsen saw Dougherty at Connell's penthouse suite at the Melbourne Regent hotel. Dougherty assured Gottliebsen that *BRW* was not for sale separately.

Of all the journalists who had followed, and been followed by, Holmes a Court in his remarkable career, Gottliebsen was probably the closest. At dinner on Tuesday night after the BHP meeting, Holmes a Court gave Gottliebsen Connell's Fairfax For Sale list, which included the *BRW* group at $100 million and the *Australian Financial Review* at $300 million. Holmes a Court said he had been told he could have either but not both. Packer was seen as a rival bidder for both. In fact, Packer thought the *Australian Financial Review* a very desirable property — but $300 million? That was a bit high for a newspaper that would have to be printed and published by Fairfax under contract for some years before it could be separated out from the Jones Street factory. That could be very messy. In any event, Connell was virtually forced to earmark the *Australian Financial Review* for Holmes a Court.

Packer had unique claims to the Fairfax consumer magazines. Holmes a Court did not want them. If Packer also took the *Financial Review*, only small pickings, apart from the *BRW* group, would be left for Holmes a Court who wanted the *Financial Review* and would pay for it. Holmes a Court could then be topped up with some other publications and Macquarie Broadcasting as his contribution to the $800 million Connell wanted out of this sale. That would leave the *BRW* group to go into the David Syme float, which was now without the *Australian Financial Review.*

There were problems with the sale of the *Australian Financial Review* as Packer had anticipated and Fairfax and Holmes a Court later discovered, although none would have stopped a determined buyer. The problems of separating the *Financial Review* from Fairfax were always assumed to be more formidable than they actually were.

Gottliebsen was still obsessed about *BRW* falling into Packer's hands. He flew to Sydney on Wednesday to see James Fairfax, Greg Gardiner and Max Suich and urged them to do what they could to keep *BRW* out of the enemy's hands. Tryart's takeover bid had, however, immobilised them. He then saw John B. Fairfax, thinking he might be interested in buying the business magazine group. But *BRW* was already off the Packer agenda.

While Gottliebsen was lobbying Fairfax executives, Tryart was coming to an agreement with Kerry Packer at Consolidated Press. Packer would take Fairfax consumer magazines and the *Canberra Times* and its free offshoot, *Canberra Chronicle*, to top his contribution to Connell's $800 million up to $250 million. John B. Fairfax's contribution had already been settled at $78 million. That left $470-$480 million to come from Holmes a Court. The *Canberra Times* sat oddly with Packer's other assets. Consolidated Press had sold nearly all its newspaper interests in the previous few years. It was assumed in the trade that, when the time was ripe and the furore about all the recent takeovers in the industry had fallen away, Murdoch would emerge as the owner of the *Canberra Times*. After the HWT takeover early in 1987 he was going quietly for a while. He did not want to provoke unduly the extreme Left Wing of the Australian Labor Party who, if Murdoch bought any more newspapers immediately, would be calling for a Royal Commission into the ownership, control and other arrangements of the Australian Press.

Tryart's deal with Packer was fixed in a hurry as Connell and Vrisakis had to get to Sydney Airport. Holmes a Court had offered to send his Boeing 727 to Sydney to pick them up. Dougherty stayed to conclude and sign the deal with Packer. This 23 September agreement was done on the run and read like it. They did not bother about a deposit or a payments schedule. The agreement was vague about the precise assets being bought and sold and reflected sizeable gaps in what both parties knew about Fairfax's operations — about the current profitability of the *Canberra Times*, about whether the *Good Weekend* magazine supplement carried in the *Sydney Morning Herald* and the *Age* each week was part of the newspaper or the magazine division, about the status of *Australian Property News*, or what rights the Hearst Corporation of the USA had over the magazines being published under licence: *Cosmopolitan*, *Good Housekeeping* and *Harper's Bazaar.* But Packer was covered on two vital points: if he wanted to close any of the magazines, Fairfax had to pay any damages or other costs to any franchisor for such magazines; and he was covered against the unknowns of the Hearst agreement and the *Good Weekend.*

Packer would have been better off with the *BRW* group than with the *Canberra Times.* He was not a long-term holder of the Canberra paper. With *BRW* he could have rationalised the business magazines, stopped *Australian Business*'s losses and looked after the *Bulletin.* But *BRW* would not have made up the numbers for Connell. Packer in any event would probably have had problems with the Trade Practices Commission (TPC) if he had bought *BRW.* He continued to probe Fairfax for ways of rationalising the business magazine market after the TPC had told Consolidated Press in November 1987, that acquisition of *BRW* would probably be unacceptable.

For Connell, however, for all the gaps in the Packer agreement, it was a big breakthrough. With Packer now satisfied, he could close with Holmes a Court, formally sign up James and John B. Fairfax, and perhaps get that Part A Takeover Statement registered at last. The Takeover Code allowed two months from the public announcement of a proposed takeover offer for the formal offer, complying with all the Code's requirements, to be made to shareholders. The Part A Statement, outlining the details of the offer, its purposes and its financing, had to be registered with the Corporate Affairs Commisssion 14 days before that. Tryart had until 16 October to lodge that Part A Statement if it was to avoid asking for a deferment.

Connell and Vrisakis flew with Holmes a Court from Canberra to Perth that night. The Great Bamboozler called up his well-developed tactics of exhaustion, tactics that had helped get the better of Murdoch in the past. During the five-hour flight to Perth he talked of matters of mutual interest — art, horses — but not much about the purchase of Fairfax assets. The broad outlines had been agreed in Melbourne, but Holmes a Court was a lawyer. Packer was prepared to have his deal summarised on two sheets of paper, leaving the holes to be filled in later. Holmes a Court wanted a detailed contract.

After the 727 landed in Perth they sat in the aircraft talking over the finer points of the deal. Connell might have been exasperated but he did not exhaust easily. Holmes a Court's lawyer, Martin Bennett of the Perth firm, Keall, Brinsden, was working overtime. Holmes a Court's own time was running out, but he was not one to appear in a hurry. He was due to leave on Thursday night for London for Standard Chartered Bank meetings, then to go on to Washington, wearing his Standard Chartered tie, for the International Monetary Fund (IMF) annual meeting. The IMF had turned this into an annual get-together for world bankers, fiscal politicians and civil servants.

On Thursday 24 September, he turned up the pressure a few more notches by going back into the market, buying 4.6 million more Fairfax shares at nine dollars, lifting his holding to over nine per cent of the company's capital. He was on the brink of being able to block the whole strategy of the bid. Negotiations continued between Connell and Vrisakis for Tryart, and Holmes a Court and Bell executives for the Bell group. Connell threatened to leave as the Bell people seemed to become bogged down in minutiae. Holmes a Court was fresh. At around 11 p.m. he, his wife Janet and Connell and Vrisakis had dinner and talked about the prospects of anything but the Tryart-Bell deal. Martin Bennett returned with another draft contract after dinner. The deal was finalised at 3 a.m., Friday 25 September. Holmes a Court had postponed his departure for London until Friday night.

Under the 25 September agreement, Tryart and W. G. O. Fairfax agreed to sell Bell Group or WA Newspapers, subject to Tryart taking effective control of Fairfax:

- *Australian Financial Review* and associated assets;
- *National Business Review* and associated assets;
- *Times on Sunday* and associated assets;
- non-exclusive rights to certain news services;
- shares in the issued capital of Australian Associated Press Pty Ltd (6.34%) and AAP Information Services Pty Ltd (5.78%);
- shares in the issued capital of Australian Newsprint Mills Holdings Ltd and Australian Newsprint Mills Investments Pty Ltd (7.10%);
- Infoline and Moneywatch businesses and associated assets;
- Macquarie Radio Network and associated assets.

It had been a big, exhausting, satisfying week. But as the direct talks with Holmes a Court opened, an event occurred that was to undermine it all. The stockmarket on Monday hit and fell back from its five-year peak.

Connell had got the right mix of assets to build up Holmes a Court's purchase price to $475 million and the total for the Fairfax assets to just over his target of $800 million. But he had done it with a secret twist to the Holmes a Court deal. It was not disclosed at the time, nor in the formal takeover documents that followed in October, that Holmes a Court had an option to put Macquarie Broadcasting back to Fairfax/Tryart in six months for $158 million — $33 million more than he paid for it. If he put it back he would have what he really wanted for $319 million. Macquarie Broadcasting was included to make up the numbers, to complete the sums on which the ANZ Bank's financing was to be based. Connell had pushed Holmes a Court to buy it. He was selling it for $125 million. He told Holmes a Court it was worth $150 million. Holmes a Court said, all right, if it is worth that, give me an option to sell it back to you if I decide I don't want it.

There was another reason for the option. Packer had failed to get the *Australian Financial Review* but had agreed to co-operate with Connell on a plan to extract at least $350 million for the *Financial Review* out of Holmes a Court. He wrote Connell a letter offering $350 million on the understanding that he would get half of whatever Holmes a Court paid over $320 million. Connell showed Holmes a Court the letter, which was a two-edged sword. If he sold the *Financial Review* to Holmes a Court for less than $350 million, Packer might challenge the sale since he had signed a letter offering $350 million. The Macquarie put option helped build the total deal to an apparent $475 million which could include $350 million for the *Financial Review*.

Macquarie did not fit in with Holmes a Court's grand plans. In an interview from Washington on the following Monday, when the deals were announced, he told Steve Burrell of the *Financial Review*, 'Radio I don't really know much about. I have very clear plans in mind in relation to print, but radio is a bit foreign to me.' All the other purchases had a place in the third of the asset groupings Holmes a Court was then establishing: steel and resources (BHP, Texaco, Bell and Pioneer Concrete); banking (Standard Chartered); and media, especially print media (WA Newspapers) and particularly business print media (the *Australian Financial Review* and *National Business Review* in New Zealand). Merchant bankers and others, trying to rationalise Holmes a Court's share purchases (possibly with a view to what they could sell him in the future) may have been reading too much into them to invoke a grand strategy. But there was no doubt that he was particularly drawn to print and television. And this was the strategy the Fairfax board had heard of at their August meeting, when Holmes a Court's remarks about BHP, Westpac and Fairfax being the most desirable companies in Australia had been reported to them. His special interest in newspapers was reflected in his careful extraction of Australian Associated Press (AAP) and Australian Newsprint Mills (ANM) shares from Connell. Fairfax was well aware of his focus on the business press. He had for months been trying to get access to the Dow Jones services in Australia controlled by the *Financial Review*.

Holmes a Court's purchase price of $475 million was to be payable $50 000 on execution of the agreement, $124 950 000 on settlement and the balance six months later, interest free.

Settlement was to take place 90 days after Tryart got effective control of Fairfax and after Tryart had given seven days notice. For all the detailed haggling that had gone into this agreement, it was potentially windier than the Packer agreement. The *Australian Financial Review* was not a direct subscriber to AAP news services. For years it had not been allowed by Fairfax management to use AAP services, being a Johnny-come-lately to the Australian newspaper world dominated by Fairfax and the HWT, and, as a national newspaper, presenting problems to the balance of power between the two. Finally, it was allowed to use AAP business news in the early 1970s, when Murdoch briefly wooed the *Financial Times* services away from the *Australian Financial Review*. The *Financial Review* continued to use AAP services after the *Financial Times* returned, but it was not a direct subscriber.

Tryart had no obligation to sell AAP and ANM shares with the *Financial Review*. But Holmes a Court wanted to build up the small holdings in those companies which he had got out of Murdoch with WA Newspapers seven months earlier. And Tryart wanted to build up his purchase to $475 million. The articles of the AAP and ANM companies provided that, if any shareholder wanted to sell, the shares had to be offered to the other shareholders first. Holmes a Court was well aware of this as he was already a shareholder in those companies through WA Newspapers. But the biggest shareholder in the AAP and ANM companies, apart from Fairfax, was Rupert Murdoch's News Corporation, again through the HWT takeover. If Fairfax was selling, News Corporation was entitled to first bite of most of them. This was not acknowledged in the Tryart-Holmes a Court agreement. The AAP and ANM shares were to be sold to Holmes a Court. This was news to the AAP and ANM boards which, in effect, controlled all share transfers. Acquisition of those shares would be a remarkable achievement for Holmes a Court. Only a year previously he had been knocking on AAP's door, wanting a share of AAP for his fledgling newspaper, the *Western Mail*, and being knocked back. Now the Tryart deal would give him ownership of over 14 per cent of AAP, controlling the balance of power between the two major shareholders, Fairfax and News

Corporation, in the vital Reuter-linked news service. He would also have a similar stake in ANM.

The purchase of *National Business Review* (NBR) in New Zealand owed something to Holmes a Court's close association with Bob Gottliebsen of Fairfax's *BRW* magazine group. Gottliebsen had been associated with NBR, as a director of its holding company, Fourth Estate Holdings Ltd, ever since Fairfax had bought 50 per cent of Fourth Estate two years previously. Fourth Estate held much more than NBR, including *New Zealand Business Who's Who*, a legislative newsletter, the building which housed the operations in Wellington, and the newly launched *New Zealand Personal Investment* magazine. But NBR was the main product and Gottliebsen, when telling Holmes a Court of what a good investment Fairfax had made in Fourth Estate, habitually referred to it as NBR. Holmes a Court's own interest in New Zealand, and his long-distance thinking about media interests, were reflected in the 10 per cent stake he had built up in Wilson and Horton, Auckland-based publishers of the New Zealand *Herald*. Remembering Gottliebsen's enthusiastic but shorthand description of the Fairfax investment in New Zealand, he bought NBR in the Connell sale, instead of Fourth Estate Holdings, which would have given him all the assets.

On Friday Connell and Vrisakis returned to Sydney. Holmes a Court went off to London. At the peak of his career as a stockmarket operator, wherever Holmes a Court went, takeover rumours and speculation followed. In London it was suggested that he was about to buy the *Times* from Rupert Murdoch, who had just bought 14 per cent of the Pearson group, publishers of the *Financial Times*.

In Sydney over the weekend James and John Fairfax spoke by telephone about the events of the previous four weeks. They were committing themselves to breaking with the enterprise their great great grandfather had started 146 years previously. All of their advisers strongly recommended acceptance of Warwick's revised bid. It could not be matched. At $8.50, on most generous criteria, the shares were fully if not over-valued. That was the problem of Warwick, his mother and the ANZ Bank. James and John and his family were going to be very cash rich. But the fact was they were presiding over a substantial dismantling of the Fairfax publishing group, although the cornerstones, the *Age* and the *Sydney Morning Herald*, remained. The sale of the *Australian Financial Review* was a particularly heavy blow. But the logic appeared inexorable. When Warwick made his bid they had three options; they could counter-bid; they could go with him as shareholders in Tryart; or they could sell out. Warwick's bid was too high to over-bid with any financial prudence; they were unwilling to put themselves in his hands as minority shareholders in his private company; they would have to sell. Once that was determined they had to get the best price for all shareholders. Unfortunately this meant the *Financial Review* had to go. Eventually it meant a lot of other key assets had to go too. But as directors their duty was to shareholders, not to Warwick's private company.

James Fairfax would have liked more time to be absolutely sure the alternatives had been exhausted, just as he had wanted more time between that visit on Sunday night and Warwick's announcement of the bid. But Warwick had gone away. By accident or design that branch of the family tended to be away at decisive moments in the company's history. That was a small problem for Tryart's advisers too. An announcement about the revised takeover offer and the asset sales had been scheduled for Sunday night, 27 September. Marty Dougherty had rung journalists early on Sunday afternoon to warn them an announcement was coming. It had to be postponed for 24 hours. But that hardly mattered. Marty's warning call had alerted the journalists, who rounded up their contacts. Monday morning's newspapers had the bones of the story. They all forecast a higher bid, sale of the *Financial Review* and other assets to Holmes a Court, and the consumer magazines to Packer. They were unaware of the deal with John B. Fairfax. Lloyds involvement in the Tryart negotiations remained one of the best-kept secrets of that month's hectic dealing.

Tryart announced details of the revised offer and the proposed asset sales later in the day. The staging of Holmes a Court's $475 million payment was not revealed. Nor were his put option on Macquarie Broadcasting and his purchase of shares in AAP and ANM. Nor was the fee of $100 million payable to Rothwells for handling these and other matters. In addition to the offer of $8.50 cash a share, there was an alternative of $40 cash plus 11 Syme shares for every six Fairfax shares. Warwick's advisers were keen to have a listed company for future market plays. Fairfax would sell Syme its 50 per cent of the *BRW* magazine group and some other business publications for $20 million, leaving the restructured Syme much smaller than was originally intended.

Details of the new Syme capitalisation and flotation were given later in the week. Tryart made reassuring statements about continuity of employment and superannuation benefits for the staff being transferred with the assets being sold. This was to become a major concern for the staff, many of whom thought they were being sold like cattle. A big danger was that they would not be. As Tryart's formal offer later disclosed, the 23 September agreement with Packer did not mention staff. The 25 September agreement with Holmes a Court's Bell Group mentioned only that Bell would be entitled to offer employment to Fairfax's staff working on the assets Bell was buying.

James and John Fairfax, in prepared statements, referred to their problems with Warwick's bid. James said:

> In negotiations over the past four weeks a solution that would have kept the group together has been sought. However, once the Tryart bid put the company on the market, it became inevitable that significant assets would have to be sold. It is important that the *Sydney Morning Herald*, the *Age* and the *BRW* group of magazines will remain under Fairfax control. The Tryart bid was launched with no prior warning to the board and despite repeated requests that it be delayed to see if a better course of action might be found.

John B. Fairfax said:

> We have considered carefully all the options available to us and we have decided that, in the absence of any higher offer being forthcoming we will accept the revised and increased offer by Tryart Pty Ltd to purchase all our shares for $8.50 a share. All shareholders in John Fairfax Ltd will benefit from the increase of one dollar a share, which we have negotiated

with the offeror. We have advised the board of John Fairfax Ltd of our decision today.

James and John also revealed that they, and Sir Vincent Fairfax, would continue as directors of John Fairfax Ltd with James as chairman. This seemed an untenable position, the result of a decision based on sentiment, concern for the staff and the newspapers, and a desire to salvage some face from what, to the public, could appear a too-eager sell-out, leading to the dismemberment of a fine company. As directors they would be assuming onerous responsibilities for the guidance of a company they had just sold out of because they did not want to be subordinate to the new major shareholder. Their commitments to continuing as directors fell apart over the next two months. James Fairfax also revealed that, apart from accepting Tryart's offer, in the absence of any higher offer for the 5.53 per cent of the capital he controlled, he had terminated his interest in the Kinghaven shares, representing 11.3 per cent of the capital, which were being held in the Guilford Bell trust he had set up in 1985 for Warwick. James had sold to Tryart his claims to future income on those shares for $22.7 million. They would now be completely controlled by Warwick.

At Jones Street, about 300 Fairfax journalists met and unanimously expressed deep concern at the sell-off of Fairfax assets and renewed a call by the Australian Journalists' Association for a Royal Commission into the media. Earlier in the day Max Suich had addressed *Australian Financial Review* journalists. He had spoken to Holmes a Court early that morning in Washington. He said Holmes a Court had assured him that staff would continue in their jobs and that superannuation would be protected. This was much more than was promised in the Tryart agreement. Suich said:

I do not believe he will give up on the *Times on Sunday*. I genuinely believe the acquisition will keep that newspaper alive. He has a fund of ideas as to where it might go and what it might do. He will be a tough employer and a good one, I expect. It is an opportunity to set up a separate, independent and distinctly different publishing operation in this country.

There were other concerns. Kenneth Davidson, the *Age*'s liberal economist wrote:

> The implied conflict of interest between Murdoch's media and aviation interests pale into insignificance by comparison with the potential conflict between Holmes a Court's interests as Australia's biggest share trader and proprietor of Australia's only financial daily.

That was a problem John B. Fairfax addressed in more detail in a speech in November, which finally cut any links he might have had with a Warwick-owned John Fairfax Ltd. Suich was supporting and comforting the journalists. But the sale of the *Financial Review* and the *Times on Sunday* had virtually confirmed in his own mind that there was no place for him on the new, reduced, Warwick-owned John Fairfax Ltd.

Market analysts and commentators spent the rest of the week trying to work out what this new takeover format meant for Tryart/Fairfax's ultimate debt burden. Most guessed the debt would end up at around $500–$600 million. Tryart's advisers would not, or could not, specify what the final figure would be. Bert Reuter told Martin Peers of the *Financial Review*, 'Obviously there is going to be some debt left in Fairfax but at a very manageable level.' He did not specify the level. Reuter denied any need to close the *Sun*, or any need for further asset sales, saying everything that was to be sold had been announced. The David Syme structure was being recalculated to include BRW magazines only, instead of the originally proposed inclusion of BRW, the *Australian Financial Review* and Fairfax consumer magazines. Rivkin James Capel was now looking at Syme shareholders' funds of $495 million, Fairfax owning 45 per cent, and after-tax profits rising from $19.8 million in 1986–87 to $33.5 million in 1988–89. Ace cost-cutter Bert Reuter was still to fill the top position in the company.

The Federal Treasurer, Paul Keating, made his first public comment on the Fairfax break-up, declaring that all the changes in media ownership in the past nine months 'were a very good thing for Australia'. He said the media shakeout started by the Hawke Government's new media policy announcement on

25 November 1986, was at the end of the road. 'There's nothing left to shake out,' he said. Four months later he was being asked by the UK publisher Robert Maxwell if there would be any official objections to Maxwell buying the *Age*, which might have to be sold to help relieve Fairfax of its debt. If policy was consistent, Keating and the Foreign Investment Review Board might have had some problems in refusing Maxwell permission to take over the *Age* after allowing US citizen Murdoch's News Corporation to take over the HWT a year earlier. But this was a matter of politics, not logic. Maxwell got the cold shoulder.

Tryart finally registered its Part A Statement with the Corporate Affairs Commission in Canberra on 9 October. The Statement revealed details of the 23 September agreement with Packer and the 25 September agreement with Holmes a Court for the first time, but still did not reveal Holmes a Court's put option on Macquarie Broadcasting. It also revealed details of Syme's restructuring. Fairfax would transfer all the capital of David Syme & Co. Ltd to David Syme Holdings Ltd, which would issue 499 999 999 one dollar shares to Fairfax as consideration. Fairfax would then transfer at least 275 000 000 Syme Holdings shares (55 per cent of the total) to those nominated by Tryart for one dollar a share, paid by Tryart. Those shares, more if necessary, would be used to satisfy Fairfax shareholders opting for the takeover alternative of Syme shares and cash. If all the public Fairfax shareholders opted for this alternative, Syme Holdings would have to issue them over 300 million shares and Fairfax's equity in Syme would fall below 40 per cent. But this was highly improbable. It was much more likely that the cash/share acceptances would involve less than 275 million shares, so the acquisition of these shares had been underwritten to assure Fairfax of a $275 million return (less fees) from the Syme float. It was assumed the underwriter would be Rivkin James Capel, which was to be broker to the originally-planned Syme flotation.

As days passed, institutional Fairfax shareholders continued to have reservations about accepting the cash/Syme shares alternative offer. Bond Media shares, which were floated at $1.55 in February, were selling at $1.05. Some big investors took the view that it was better to take $8.50 cash now and possibly buy

Syme shares at under one dollar later, when the underwriters were unloading. In the third week in October, a week after the Part A Statement had been filed, it was revealed that the Syme issue would be jointly underwritten by Rivkin James Capel and Rothwells, Laurie Connell's merchant bank. Under the 28 August agreement between Tryart, its associates and Rothwells, Rothwells had agreed 'to engage a suitable underwriter to underwrite any issue of shares which is advised by Rothwells in the future as a means whereby in whole or in part the Offeror may deal with its indebtedness in respect of the takeover offer'. Now Rothwells said one suitable underwriter was Rothwells. In fact, Rothwells was on the verge of needing a massive underwriting itself. Alan Deans, the *Sydney Morning Herald*'s investment editor, reported that nearly 20 institutional sub-underwriters had been arranged, about half said to be based in Melbourne, but Rivkin James Capel had declined to identify the composition of the panel. There was some speculation that Holmes a Court's Bell Group was among them. Holmes a Court still desired the *Age* and a piece of the $275 million share underwriting could be the way in. Connell himself was apparently to assume half of Rothwells's share of the underwriting.

# CHAPTER 11

# NO ONE ELSE COULD HAVE DONE IT

By the third week in October the long-term debt prospect for Tryart-Fairfax still did not look comfortable. Full cash acceptance by Fairfax shareholders of Tryart's offer would cost nearly $2 billion to be financed by the ANZ Bank. The proposed Syme flotation and the asset sales to John B. Fairfax, Kerry Packer and Robert Holmes a Court would bring in nearly $1.1 billion. That would leave the takeover debt at around $800 million. There was also the undisclosed Rothwells takeover fee of $100 million. And if Holmes a Court decided he did not want Macquarie Broadcasting and put it back to Fairfax, the proceeds of the sale to him would be down $158 million. Those two items would rebuild the takeover debt back to over $1.1 billion. There were the Skase payments to come to Fairfax from Skase's Universal Telecasters: $470 million on 30 November and $285 million in August 1990. But $100 million would be going back to Qintex Australia or Universal Telecasters to buy shares and notes in that group. Discounting the 1990 payment, the Skase debt might be worth around $700 million. Some leakages in that contract were not discovered until November. The Tryart advisers still anticipated getting $200 million back out of the superannuation funds. That still left a gap of around $200 million between the takeover debt and its repayment. And it ignored the claims of the National Australia Bank and Westpac, which were owed $150 million each for the financing of Fairfax's purchase of HSV7 earlier in the year and the claims of the group of merchant banks, which were owed $150 million on the same account and for working capital.

Further substantial asset sales, as well as heavy reliance on reinvestment by the superannuation funds, seemed inevitable if the residual debt was to be manageable. The Fairfax board had not yet met to consider the takeover offer. James and John Fairfax had spoken for their own and John had spoken for his family's shareholdings. But there were also two outside directors, Sir David Griffin and Sir Eric Neal. Griffin was a lawyer and Neal a former managing director of Boral Ltd, a company that had grown substantially by takeovers. They were well aware of the care they had to exercise in acting in the interests of all shareholders, particularly the public shareholders who held nearly 50 per cent of the Fairfax company's capital. It had been suggested that both, or one of them, might act as a conciliator between Warwick, James and John to try and bring them together and avoid the partitions now facing the family and the company. But if an independent director did that, he could jeopardise the very handsome offer Tryart was making to all shareholders.

The company's own legal adviser was also advising James and John. Fairfax had its own financial adviser, Macquarie Hill Samuel. Neal suggested that the two outside directors should have their own independent advice in this situation to ensure that they fulfilled their legal obligations. The other Fairfax board members readily agreed. Neal nominated Gerald Wells of Murphy and Moloney, one of the city's leading commercial solicitors, who had handled Boral's work for many years and was deputy chairman of that company. Boral had been probably the most successful takeover operator in Australia, first as a defender against Caltex in the 1950s, then as a predator in the 1960s of undervalued companies such as Mt Lyell Mining and Railway and Huddart Parker, the coastal shipping firm, and continuing, with funds generated by those raids, as a buyer of building materials companies until it had built up one of the biggest, most coherent and successful industrial groups in the country. Boral's and Gerald Wells's takeover experience were unmatched.

The Fairfax board was due to meet on 26 October to consider the Part B Statement it had to make to shareholders in response to Tryart's Part A. In the third week of October, however, as the underwriters to the Syme flotation were revealed as Rivkin

James Capel and Rothwells, ominous tremors started to appear in the five-year stockmarket boom. On Monday 12 October, the Australian all ordinaries share index lost 35 points following a big sell-off in Wall Street, which had given the New York market its worst week of the year. On Tuesday the market was down again following bad days in New York and London. A rally on Wednesday again took an overnight lead from overseas but on Thursday the slide accelerated. The Australian market lost $4 billion in value following a record one-day loss on Wall Street. That left the Australian all ordinaries index seven per cent below its 21 September peak. On Friday New York slumped again, closing down 9.5 per cent for the week and 17.5 per cent below its late August peak. Most ominously, 340 million shares were traded on Friday. This was no technical adjustment as the analysts like to call occasional, but nerve-testing retreats in a long-term rising market. This was a rush for the parachutes.

The Australian market is on its own on Monday mornings. Only the New Zealand market opens before it. The big overseas markets, from which it usually takes a lead, especially since foreign exchanges were freed up in the earlier 1980s, are still closed for the weekend. On Monday 19 October, the Australian market was in a state of extreme nervous apprehension about what the New York and London markets would do that night. Selling pressure knocked $9 billion off the market's total value during the day. The *Australian Financial Review* page one headline on Tuesday morning told what had happened overnight: 'World Markets Collapse'. Few buyers were prepared to face the avalanche on Tuesday: $55 billion was wiped off stockmarket values as the index fell by over 500 points. By the end of the week it was under 1300, about half its September peak.

For Tryart, Aleco Vrisakis maintained a bold front. 'These market aberrations do not affect the basis on which the bid was put together,' Vrisakis said. Nor would the market's fall affect the Syme flotation, he said. That was fully underwritten by Rothwells and Rivkin James Capel. The *Financial Review* reported that sub-underwriters were examining their agreements to see if they could be cancelled. Fairfax shares fell to $7.50 as Tryart directors re-affirmed that the bid would not be cancelled. According to

Warwick Fairfax's evidence in the subsequent fee case, Connell said that, although the underwriting agreements were firm, they should not be tested. It was not the sort of thing one did, he said. In fact there were no written underwriting agreements. Tryart's Part A takeover statement had said that the Syme share sale 'will be underwritten'. No underwriter was named and no underwriting agreement was mentioned. Court action would be inevitable if Tryart tried to enforce whatever agreements existed. Connell was chairman and managing director of Rothwells and knew its desperate financial state after 20 October, possibly before that. Rothwells couldn't underwrite anything.

Connell personally was apparently to share Rothwells's underwriting commitment either as joint underwriter or as sub-underwriter. After 20 October Wardleys were involved in all legs of the underwriting arrangements. Their involvement with Rothwells and Connell was mentioned briefly by Neil McPhee, QC, in his opening address for Tryart in the fee case (see Chapter 16). And they had a close ownership connection with James Capel. When the Syme flotation had to be cancelled, as Bert Reuter later recalled, he decided to put the onus on Rivkin James Capel. Rene Rivkin was still out of action.

Reuter rang Rivkin's partner, Stephen Anstice, and asked were they ready to proceed with the underwriting. Anstice had to ask Wardleys in Perth for instructions. Back they came: the underwriting was off. Anstice's memory differed; he thought the underwriting was called off by mutual agreement. There was nothing else to do. The crucial question was whether the whole Tryart takeover venture should be cancelled. The National Companies and Securities Commission (NCSC) may or may not have agreed to cancellation or postponement or to revision of Tryart's $8.50 offer. The matter was raised by Warwick's advisers but not developed. Cancellation or postponement of the offer would mean unwinding the big asset sales to John B. Fairfax, Kerry Packer and Robert Holmes a Court. It would also mean breaking the contracts to buy James's and John's shares at $8.50. None of those problems seemed insurmountable. Nor was there anything new in breaking an underwriting agreement because of a falling market.

One of the proposed Syme share issue underwriters had, three months previously, withdrawn a bid because of a falling market. Rene Rivkin was the driving force behind Oilmet Investments Ltd, which, in July 1987, had cancelled its bids for two Sydney-Japan investment trusts, citing a fall of over seven per cent in the Tokyo share market's Nikkei index as its escape clause. After the 19–20 October crash Oilmet withdrew, with the NCSC's approval, a five-month-old takeover bid for QBE Insurance group. The bid was to be financed by a $400 million facility from NZI Securities, secured against QBE shares. But the fall in the price of those shares had eroded the security. Oilmet could not make up the difference so NZI withdrew the facility and the NCSC agreed to Oilmet withdrawing its bid.

In the fee case, Malcolm Irving and Michael Smith of Canadian Imperial Bank of Commerce (CIBC) Australia, giving evidence as competent merchant bankers, said they would have advised Warwick to take whatever action he could to cancel the bid, including an approach to the ANZ Bank about the $100 million fee, thus giving the bank a reason for cancelling its $2 billion takeover facility. If the ANZ had then told the NCSC that the takeover funds were no longer available, the case for NCSC approving withdrawal of the bid would be overwhelming. Rothwells did not press an application to the NCSC. Warwick himself believed that the market crash should work in his favour. It would scare off any potential counter bidders and ensure the bid's success; $8.50 had looked attractive before the crash. Now it was irresistible.

This confidence was not shared by his mother, the joint and so far silent Tryart backer, Mary Fairfax. On the afternoon of 20 October, after two days in which the Australian stockmarkets had been nearly halved in value, Warwick, Bert Reuter and Marty Dougherty had been discussing the latest market developments in Reuter's rooms at the Regent Hotel. A hotel manager knocked on the door. Lady Fairfax was in the foyer wanting to see her son. 'Don't send her up,' Warwick said. His mother then wrote a note from the Regent's foyer arguing strongly that the offer be withdrawn and sent it to Reuter's apartment. Warwick read the letter, crumpled it up and threw it in the wastepaper basket from which Reuter later recovered it. Having backed the bid, Mary

Fairfax became increasingly apprehensive and agitated about her financial prospects after 19–20 October.

Warwick was charging on. The crash had ensured his bid of success. He would be 27 years old on 2 December and hoped to be in control of John Fairfax Ltd by then. On 20 October, however, it was apparent that the bid would have to be restructured for the third time. The original full Syme share exchange alternative had not lasted 24 hours. Then the price had to be raised to $8.50, knowing that the family was selling out. Now the partial share exchange alternative would have to be dropped because of the market's crash. Apart from Connell's concern that the underwriting agreement should not be tested, the fact was the underwriting was no longer feasible. Sub-underwriters had seen or experienced what had happened with Rivkin James Capel's previous big media underwriting, Bond Media, whose shares were now selling at less than half their issue price. Connell did not want to press the underwriting issue. Rothwells could not afford it. The whole market could not afford it. The Syme issue was scrapped. Tryart would have to find $275 million from the sale of other Fairfax assets to replace the $275 million from the Syme flotation.

Waiting in the wings, as ever, was Rupert Murdoch. Fairfax had two important strategic assets of value to any Australian newspaper publisher: 50 per cent of Australian Newsprint Mills (ANM) and 43 per cent of the two Australian Associated Press (AAP) companies. Reuter rang Maisey at the ANZ Bank: the Syme issue was being canned, but the sale of Fairfax's shares in ANM and AAP would raise $275 million to take its place. That was OK with the banker. Marty Dougherty was deputed to handle this sale with his old friend Ken Cowley of News Corporation. The sale of these strategic Fairfax assets to News Corporation was arranged over the weekend of 24–25 October and the agreement signed early the following week. Then the Trade Practices Commission stepped in (see Chapter 13).

News Corporation ended up with little of those two sales, but Murdoch kept coming. The obvious financial problems at Fairfax and Holmes a Court's Bell Group resulting from the 19–20 October crash suggested some key assets were still in play. In

November Cowley approached the Trade Practices Commission (TPC) with a feeler: how would they feel about News Corporation buying the *Australian Financial Review* and the *Canberra Times?* The TPC was still under the control of Robert McComas, the chairman who had sanctioned the purchase of the Herald & Weekly Times and subsequent adjustments to the ownership of some of its assets which had been criticised by Murdoch's opponents as being merely cosmetic. This time he told Cowley it was not on. But Murdoch was indefatigable. Few doubted that he would be back sometime, somehow.

By 24 October Warwick's bid was being threatened by two other events: depositors had started taking funds out of Connell's merchant bank Rothwells at an increasing rate; and in London and New York, Merrill Lynch withdrew a $1.1 billion bond issue for Bell Resources because of volatility and adverse changes in the market. Merrill Lynch were not as sensitive as Laurie Connell claimed to be about the sanctity of underwriting agreements. Merrill Lynch had left Holmes a Court short. If world markets had held up for another week he might have been able to hold his Bell companies together. Now the collapse in values of his big investments in BHP, Standard Chartered Bank, Sears, Pioneer Concrete, and Texaco had him hobbled. The legs were falling off — had fallen off — two of the big September asset sales Connell had put together: Syme could not be floated for $275 million and Holmes a Court, still maintaining a confident face in public, faced a liquidity crisis that would end up costing him control of the Bell companies he had built and the assets he had in play to create his resources, banking and media empires.

Seven weeks after the bid was announced on 31 August, Tryart was looking at the third major restructuring of the bid's finances. Laurie Connell would have to come on with a new juggling act. But his talents and energies, and those of his legal adviser, Aleco Vrisakis, were required elsewhere. The 20 October crash had caused a rush on non-bank institutions by people suddenly more concerned with security than with yield. They wanted their money in the safest place — under the bed or in a bank, a real bank. There were heavy withdrawals from many fringe financiers. Rothwells's trustee status, which had enhanced its attraction for funds, made it specially vulnerable to a rush for withdrawals. Solicitors, company directors, stockbrokers and others who had placed funds in their care or trust, or who had recommended clients to place funds, with Rothwells at relatively high interest rates owed a duty of care to those clients and rushed to get those funds out of a company whose assets were shrinking rapidly after Monday 19 October.

The run on Rothwells's funds gathered momentum during the week. By Thursday the company had run over its credit limit with its bankers, the National Australia Bank. The word quickly spread through Perth's financial district. On Friday afternoon, Tim Treadgold, finance editor on the *West Australian* newspaper, had a telephone call from someone in Rothwells offices at 77 St George's Terrace, telling him there was a queue of people in the foyer waiting for their money. Treadgold, a photographer, and another reporter quickly covered the 400 metres from the *West Australian* to Rothwells. They found about 30 very tense people in the lobby, none willing to talk. This was every man for himself. Nobody there was interested in spreading the news about Rothwells problems until after they had their money. They had their own places in the queue to protect. Eventually someone passed Treadgold a note: 'We're here to get our money out'. Some threatened the reporter with violence. The newspapermen were asked to leave by Rothwells's staff. Treadgold refused and asked for Connell. Told he would be forcibly evicted, he rang the *West Australian*'s police roundsman and another photographer who could report and photograph his eviction for the next morning's newspaper. Beyond the lobby, in Rothwells's offices, desperate attempts were being made to find funds to meet the depositors' demands. Westpac finally gave some temporary accommodation. The depositors were called from the lobby to the inner offices and paid with cheques on Westpac.

Treadgold returned to the *West Australian* to write his story. He rang Alan Deans at the *Sydney Morning Herald* to alert him to expect the story as part of the news exchange system between the two papers. The *West Australian*'s lawyers advised against publication on the grounds that the story was damaging to Rothwells. The editor took that advice. But Treadgold had given the details to Alan Deans who summarised them in three potentially explosive paragraphs in the *Sydney Morning Herald*'s page one lead story that Saturday. The story pulled together the latest stockmarket developments in Australia and overseas five days after the crash. It reported the cancellations of Robert Holmes a Court's $1 billion European fund raising for Bell Resources, a $277 million share issue by Boral and a $116 million raising by an oil hopeful, Petroz NL. Then:

> In Perth angry clients gathered in the foyer of Rothwells merchant bank and demanded to see its chairman, Mr Laurie Connell, or other executives.
>
> The clients were believed to be seeking funds owed by the merchant bank. It is believed that Rothwells's troubles stem from a clearing bank it dealt with which was taking a conservative stance in the wake of the stockmarket crash. Many clients are known to have been paid yesterday.

The *Times on Sunday* picked up the Treadgold story on Saturday and began developing it for the next day's issue. The three paragraphs also rang alarm bells for Fairfax chief editorial executive, Max Suich, and his successor-elect, Marty Dougherty, but for exactly opposite reasons. Suich saw it as an important news story, which had to be handled very carefully to avoid any accusation that the Fairfax papers engineered a run on Rothwells. Dougherty, who had been on a $10 000 a month retainer from Rothwells to look after its image in the Eastern States, saw it as an irresponsible story that should be held out of the papers. To journalists this crystallised the threat they saw from the Tryart takeover, which would result in Dougherty becoming the editorial boss of John Fairfax Ltd.

Dougherty rang Suich and argued that the story was being vastly over-played; there were runs on many institutions; it was unfair to single out Rothwells. The Dougherty-Suich telephone exchanges were not cordial. Suich would not accept Dougherty's line but was concerned that the *Times on Sunday*'s treatment should be well balanced and not be seen as scare-mongering or as relishing the chance to stick the boot into a company that was playing a big part in an unpopular takeover. He faced a perennial newspaper dilemma: if a company holding millions of dollars on deposit from the public was known to be in difficulty, should the paper report it and risk aggravating the problem (and probably attracting a damages suit) by causing a run on the company by depositors wanting their money? Or should the paper play safe, and not report the company's problem, thus allowing those in the know to withdraw their funds while new deposits continued to be accepted and the majority remained ignorant of their increasing risks? The problem recurred with every boom — and bust — business cycle. Few complained about stories which boosted highly speculative money-raising companies, which mushroomed during a boom and ultimately resulted in heavy losses to the public when the inevitable crash came. But stories warning of a company's hazardous financial conditions were extremely hazardous for the publisher, as the *West Australian*'s lawyers had recognised in advising the editors not to publish the Rothwells story.

Suich went into the Fairfax offices on Saturday morning to discuss the story's treatment with the *Times on Sunday*'s acting editor, David Jenkins. He emphasised the need for caution and balance. Jenkins saw it as the biggest story of the weekend and proposed leading page one with it. Suich came in again in the afternoon to argue against this. He proposed changes to the story. They had an alternative lead story about President Reagan blaming Congress for the market crash. As the 4 p.m. first edition deadline approach Suich went against using the Rothwells story as the lead. It was given single column treatment on page one without a photograph of the depositors gathered at Rothwells offices late on Friday waiting for their money. Jenkins continued to argue by telephone with Suich at home, urging that Rothwells replace Reagan for the second edition. By this time, the editor-in-chief of the *Sydney Morning Herald*, Chris Anderson, who was also responsible for the *Times on Sunday*, had entered the argument on Jenkins's side. Suich came around to their point of view, though he remained against publishing the photograph. Jenkins misunderstood this and ran the story and the photograph as the lead for the second edition. The story remained very cautious.

Unknown to the *Times on Sunday* a desperate rescue operation for the company was already under way. But the *Times on Sunday* story ensured that the rescue had to be in place by Sunday night, in time for a big play in Monday morning's newspapers before Rothwells opened for business. Connell had sent an SOS to Bond Corporation the previous Thursday, talked to Bond's managing director, Peter Beckwith, who had put him in touch with James Yonge, managing director of Wardley Australia, a merchant banking arm of the Hong Kong and Shanghai Bank. Beckwith also called Alan Bond in Rome, who returned to Australia immediately. The rescue package was put together by Yonge, Bond and the Western Australian Government, relying heavily on the networks each had established to enlist contributors to the rescue. The Government provided a guarantee for $150 million, which secured accommodation from the National Australia Bank to meet further cash withdrawals. A group of Australian businessmen put up, through their companies, over $100 million in preference shares. Rothwells itself made an ordinary share issue for $55 million, and arranged to sell assets for $30 million.

Laurie Connell claimed on Sunday night that Rothwells was one of the most conservatively geared institutions in the country, that it was in excellent shape, that profits were up 50 per cent on the previous year and that depositors could continue to invest 'with confidence'. Connell claimed to have put in $70 million of his own money. Heavy withdrawals continued the following week. One year and one week later, after the Western Australian Government and its instrumentalities had continued to pour money into the company, Rothwells went into provisional liquidation. Laurie Connell had left the board. The provisional liquidator, Ian Ferrier, pointed out that the 1987 rescue had concentrated on Rothwells's liabilities instead of its assets. Much of its funds had been invested in its satellites, which were as fragile as eggshells when the crunch came. The company and its attempted rescue became a focal point for the incestuous, and, for the Western Australian taxpayers, costly relationship between the Western Australian Labor Government and various business and financial institutions in that State.

Rothwells's 20–27 October crisis had important consequences for the Tryart-Fairfax takeover. It removed Rothwells as an underwriter of the proposed Syme float. Rothwells had to be rescued with cash injections totalling around $300 million to pay its depositors. It could not afford to meet any underwriting liability, particularly the liability likely to arise in a stricken stockmarket. Connell returned to Perth and became preoccupied with his own and Rothwells affairs. After that whirlwind September and October he played little part in coping with Tryart's increasing problems until his resignation in March. Rothwells surrendered its securities dealer's licence on 22 November in circumstances only later revealed by the NCSC in court actions involving Connell and Rothwells. Tryart's fee was sold to Bond Media and, when Tryart refused to pay the $100 million in June 1988, it became the subject of an epic Supreme Court case in Sydney before Justice Giles (see Chapter 16). The intervention of Bond Media made a settlement before the case began virtually impossible. Bond Media sued for payment of the $100 million. Tryart cross-claimed against Bond Media and Rothwells for $160 million damages, plus $68 million from Bert Reuter and Martin Dougherty for breach of duty as advisers to and directors of Tryart. Dougherty's interventions on behalf of Rothwells on 24 October and afterwards soured his relationships with Fairfax journalists before he took over as managing director, editorial, on 7 December. That in turn led to a major crisis, which resulted in Dougherty's forced resignation in February 1988.

When the Fairfax board met at last on 26 October to consider its response to the Tryart bid, Rothwells's future looked so uncertain that the Fairfax board was told it was understood that Wardleys would move into the advisory position if Rothwells fell out. That could further have complicated the status of the $100 million fee. Rothwells stayed in. Nobody was told when it lost its securities dealer's licence on 22 November. Tryart's bid at 26 October consisted of two alternatives: $8.50 cash for each Fairfax share or $40 cash and 11 Syme shares for six Fairfax shares. The proposed capitalisation of David Syme had been recast and reduced again to eliminate the *Australian Financial Review* and Fairfax Magazines. These had been in the original proposed Syme holding company but had been sold to Holmes a Court and Packer. Syme would now buy only the 50 per cent of the BRW group it did not own and Rydges Publications from John Fairfax.

The October crash was about to eliminate this revised version too. Tryart had approached the NCSC for permission to drop the Syme share exchange option altogether because of the crash. Vrisakis was in Melbourne putting this to the Commission. In Sydney, Mark Johnson of Fairfax's advisers, Macquarie Hill Samuel, was telling the Fairfax board that, in a break-up of the company after 19 October, the assets would probably realise less than $8.50 a share; that if the $8.50 offer was not there the shares would probably be worth $4.30-$5 in the market; and that there was a strong case for recommending that shareholders accept the bid. He left the boardroom to take a call from Melbourne. The NCSC wanted to know if Fairfax would agree to a bid of $8.50 cash only, that the cash plus Syme shares alternative be dropped. That was no problem. Macquarie Hill Samuel's advice was easy, simple and unqualified: the Fairfax board should recommend the offer of $8.50 cash.

As the Fairfax board decided to recommend the bid in its cash only form, the shares fell to $6.80. The buyer at that price faced a quick capital profit of $1.60 a share. At Rothwells a stitch and paste-up job was done on the Tryart offer document. A white paper patch carrying the brief message: 'please note: Syme share offer deleted' was pasted over the Syme share alternative on the cover and a letter dated 27 October, signed by W. G. O. Fairfax, stapled over the first page, covering his previous letter, dated 24 October, which had included the alternative offer.

Fairfax directors' recommendation, that shareholders sell to Tryart, was dated 28 October, the day of John Fairfax Ltd's last annual general meeting of shareholders as a public company. At the meeting, the chairman, James Fairfax, regretted the break-up of the Fairfax group to help pay for Tryart's takeover, stressed the need for an independent press and defended the purchase of HSV7 and subsequent sale of the Seven Network. The move out of television, he said, was designed to eliminate the group's debts, and leave a substantial group cash surplus to help fund substantial growth in newspapers and magazines. He did not need to point out that, in helping to precipitate his half-brother Warwick's takeover bid, the television deals had achieved the exact opposite. Instead of being debt free, the company would be assuming a debt of over $2 billion. The meeting lasted 30 minutes. It was sparsely attended. There were no questions. No Tryart representatives were there.

With the Fairfax board's recommendations behind it and the market price emphasising its attractions, Warwick's offer was rushed. In a week his holding in the company had risen to 84 per cent and the bid was declared unconditional. Among the acceptors were the Fairfax superannuation, long-service and other funds established for employees' benefit, which held over 35 million Fairfax shares. At $8.50 a share the funds faced a sudden cash injection of nearly $300 million. It was this, or a large part of it, that Tryart's financial advisers had hoped to recycle by investing the funds back into Fairfax or into Tryart itself, thus filling a big gap in the refinancing programme. By mid-November, as they discovered more about the funds, they had been forced to re-examine their expectations though they still hoped to get about $76 million out of the long-service fund and they thought there was a way of getting $200 million out of the retirement fund by investing the money with an institution that would then lend it to Fairfax.

Despite the uncertainty about these funds as a source of cash for the company, and the stringency facing Holmes a Court's companies, the ANZ Bank still looked at the takeover facility as being largely self-financing through the quick asset sales arranged in September and October, when the ANM and AAP sales to Murdoch had replaced the Syme flotation as the source of $275 million. Even after the 20 October market crash it was still believed that funds from most of the asset sales would come through by 31 December. The ANZ had wanted to see the asset sales agreements before agreeing to finance the $8.50 bid at the end of September. They were considered watertight. The Bank was not shown the Holmes a Court put option on Macquarie Broadcasting. It was apparently confident that Holmes a Court would fulfil his contract despite the 20 October market crash. The Bank was happy with the ANM and AAP sales to Murdoch even though they faced possible problems with the Trade Practices Commission.

Documentation for the ANZ Bank's $2.1 billion facility came through on 10 November. On that day a prospective programme for the handover of the company, including reconstitution of the Fairfax board with Tryart-nominated directors was agreed between the two companies. In addition, Fairfax agreed that Tryart could be represented at any board meetings before the company was handed over and that Tryart could have full access to Fairfax employees and business information. Marty Dougherty and Aleco Vrisakis, as Tryart's representatives, attended the last Fairfax monthly board meeting on 19 November 1987. Warwick had last attended a board meeting — as a guest — on 24 August. He had not been asked after the takeover bid was announced but now that he was in control with over 90 per cent of the shares, the old board and management were concerned to hand over the company in good order and condition. They had hoped that Warwick himself would turn up on 19 November and that reconstitution of the board, when the company was handed over, could have been settled then. It was still assumed that James and John would continue as directors though this looked increasingly doubtful.

On 7 November John Fairfax had addressed the Regional Dailies of Australia Association in Sydney. He warned of the dangers to journalistic integrity posed by the media carve-ups of the past year. He pointed to the close relationships with the Commonwealth Government of the new media owners and the potential conflicts of interest facing a stockmarket player like Robert Holmes a Court as owner of the *Australian Financial Review*. And he said a potential problem for Warwick Fairfax was the involvement in Tryart of Martin Dougherty, whom he described as 'a former newspaper man but more recently a public relations man'. The prospect of James and John sitting on the John Fairfax Ltd board with Warwick and his advisers seemed increasingly remote. All the other directors had signed their resignation letters. Gardiner, Suich and Brenchley had all resigned independently and for their own reasons. Gardiner had realised from the outset that there was no place for him in a Warwick-controlled company. He had one year to go of a four-year contract and before agreeing to pay him out the Fairfax board checked with Tryart. There was no objection. Suich had determined to go when the *Financial Review* and *Times on Sunday* were sold to Holmes a Court. Brenchley had a big personal commitment to the Jones Street plant and its products and was the last to resign. They were all paid out early in November after the offer became unconditional but stayed at work for the transition period until the company was formally handed over on 7 December.

Gardiner used the 19 November board meeting as an occasion to emphasise the glowing health of the company that was about to change hands. A month after the 20 October crash, Fairfax, he said, was trading at record levels. The *Sydney Morning Herald* was particularly strong. It and the *Age* were still increasing their shares of the classified advertising markets in Sydney and Melbourne. Only the *Canberra Times* was suffering — from the drain on its advertising revenues caused by a competitive, free real estate paper. The *Illawarra Mercury, Newcastle Herald,* the Community Newspapers, Macquarie Broadcasting, Fairfax Magazines, and the BRW group were thriving. Non-television profits were up 25 per cent. As part of the TV network's sale to Skase's companies, Fairfax products would be entitled to $15 million worth of free advertising on ATN7, HSV7, and BTQ7 over the next three years. 'The board and senior management hand over to Warwick Fairfax and his team a very vibrant operating group,' he said. Seven years previously (when Gardiner took over) the company had been capitalised in the market at $74 million, which did not rank it among the top 100 company capitalisations in Australia. The previous year's profits had been $9 million after tax. The 1986–87 profit had been $45 million after tax and Tryart's bid capitalised the company at $2.55 billion, twelfth largest of the companies listed on the Australian Stock Exchange. Even at half Tryart's bid price, at $1.275 billion, it would be 30th largest.

Then he confirmed the existence of a few time bombs the Tryart guests should have been aware of, even if they hadn't been fully appreciated. Merchant bankers, Gardiner said, had been calling about their facilities. In addition to the $300 million Fairfax had borrowed from Westpac and the National Australia Bank to help buy HSV7, it had about $200 million in unsecured debt to about 20 merchant banks, including those that had advanced funds specifically for the HSV7 purchase. The company they had lent to was about to be transferred to a new owner $2 billion in debt. The banks were naturally becoming very concerned about their access to Fairfax's future cash flows, including the funds to come from Skase and from other assets sales. The merchant banks' inquiries were an early warning signal of big problems to come in January and February.

Gardiner also reported to the board, and its guests, the completion of arrangements the board had approved to preserve the tremendous cash windfall the retirement and long-service funds had received from the takeover for the exclusive benefit of fund members. This was another rare aspect of the Fairfax takeover: the immediate cash benefits were shared substantially by the employees through the retirement and long service funds. John Fairfax and Sons Pty Ltd had started one of Australia's first retirement funds early in the Second World War.

The deed, dated 30 June 1941, commemorated the 100th anniversary of Fairfax ownership and conversion of the original *Sydney Herald*'s title to the *Sydney Morning Herald*. The fund was not named in the deed but was initially known as the John Fairfax and Sons Staff Pension Fund. It later became the John Fairfax Retirement Fund. It was managed by the AMP Society but a general fund within the Retirement Fund was invested exclusively in John Fairfax shares. The fund was built on joint contributions by staff members and the company but for many years members who left before retiring age (65 for men, 60 for women) took with them only their own contributions plus interest. The company's contribution stayed with the fund. Normal staff turnover and growth during the 1960s and 1970s meant that the general fund built up rapidly when the company's shares were cheap. On top of that, Fairfax expanded its capital ten-fold between 1972 and 1987 by bonus share issues. For those who, like the Retirement General Fund, bought Fairfax shares during the 1970s at $1.50–$2, the bonus issues had cut the cost of the shares to 30 cents or less by the time Warwick made his $8.50 takeover bid in 1987. There were no complaints from shareholders outside 'Fairwater' about the company's financial management.

By the time Warwick made his bid, the various funds held nearly 12 per cent of the company's capital. The Retirement General Fund held 14.67 million shares, the Long Service Fund (for employees with over 15 years service) held 10.91 million, and the Staff Provident Fund (for employees with over 10 years service) 3.71 million. The remaining shares were held by two smaller staff welfare funds. With non-Fairfax investments added in, the funds were worth nearly $400 million at the end of September 1987. Tryart had from the outset sought to use a substantial part of these funds to help finance the takeover, in effect by recycling takeover funds back as loans to Tryart/Fairfax.

Initially, Reuter had planned to convince the trustees to accept Tryart's offer for only half the funds' shares, thus saving about $123 million at the lower bid price range of seven dollars and $141 million at the then projected higher range of eight dollars. Then it was proposed to talk the funds' trustees into reinvesting their cash into Tryart redeemable preference shares. Other ways were envisaged of recycling part of the funds' $300 million cash windfall back into the company. All were shaky. In March 1985 the Commonwealth tax legislation applying to superannuation funds had been amended to limit to 10 per cent the proportion of a tax-qualifying fund that could be invested in the employing company's own securities. Fairfax funds were exempted from this under a grandfather clause which gave them 10 years to adjust while they continued to hold their original shares. But if and when those shares were sold the 10 per cent rule applied. The most Tryart could have recycled was 10 per cent of the General Fund — say, $30 million — and perhaps the Long Service Fund's $75 million, if the trustees could be persuaded to do so.

In November 1987, the trustees of the funds made changes that ensured that even those prospective amounts would shrink rapidly as fund members left. Provisions of the Retirement Fund had been liberalised over the years: retirement age for women had been lifted to 65 with men and women having the option to retire at 60. And after five years' service members had become entitled to take part of the company's contribution with them if they left, depending on their length of service. When the trustees of the funds met on 4 November to accept Tryart's offer they liberalised conditions much further. Optional early retirement was reduced to 55; members leaving after one year would be entitled to their own contribution plus interest, plus 10 per cent of the balance of their benefit, increasing by 10 per cent a year until, after 10 years' service, the member's full benefit would be paid on leaving. In addition, the Fairfax shares held by the funds had been revalued at $8.50 and the surplus distributed to members as at 1 June 1987. And an excess benefits fund had been established to preserve taxation advantages for those employees now entitled to a retirement payment of more than the last annual salary multiple allowed by the Taxation Commissioner. The changes ensured that the fund members got the full benefit of the takeover. They also made early retirement an attractive proposition for hundreds of employees, many of whom left in the next few months. The funds contracted sharply. Many of those employees had substantial accrued leave, which the company had to pay. The only offsetting benefit for Tryart was that the wealth of the funds and the early retirements would reduce the company's contribution costs in the immediate future.

The retirement fund developments came on top of another, already known to Dougherty and Vrisakis, which would be costly to Tryart. During the previous month the company had signed service contracts, authorised by the board at previous meetings, with 30 editors and managers, entitling them to separation payments of twice final salary plus other benefits if they were dismissed or left the company under certain conditions. In the editors' contracts and at least one advertising manager's contract, these conditions included fundamental disagreement over policy. Individual contracts had been very rare at Fairfax. Tryart, particularly Marty Dougherty, had many changes in mind. That was one reason for taking over the company. Getting rid of editors and managers was going to be very costly. In addition, Fairfax had to bear the increased cost of paying out those people whom Packer and Holmes a Court did not want.

Marty was angry about these contracts, though the one he was then considering for his own employment at John Fairfax Ltd was more generous. When the time had come to talk job specification and remuneration with Marty in October, Warwick had offered him the position of managing director (editorial) at $225 000 a year, plus an unsecured interest-free housing loan worth $25 000 a year, $15 000 a year entertainment allowance, a car of his choice, his home telephone expenses, a travel allowance to take him and his wife overseas once a year, five weeks' annual leave plus 2.5 years' salary and entitlements when he left. Marty had initially rejected these terms. Warwick had also offered him $2 million as a lump sum to compensate him for the work he had done for Warwick and 'Fairwater' over the years and for the loss of the consulting business Marty had to sell to join Fairfax. Warwick had to keep Marty's salary and allowances in line with Cotton's and King's. Finally, towards the end of November he offered to lift the lump sum to $3 million if Marty would accept the original salary package. Marty accepted. He left Fairfax three months later with $3.6 million. But his own salary negotiations did not help him to swallow easily Gardiner's report on 19 November. Tryart had been done. The Fairfax directors, as usual, went down one floor to the directors' dining room for lunch. Dougherty and Vrisakis did not join them.

After two and a half months, which were even more hazardous and trying than Connell and Reuter had warned, Tryart was on the verge of taking control of John Fairfax Ltd. They would not quite make it for Warwick's birthday on 2 December but they would be there a few days after that. There were still plenty of problems in finding funds to fill up the gaps still left after the asset sales to refinance the ANZ's $2.1 billion loan, particularly since the potential contributions from the retirement funds looked uncertain. Nobody had spoken to Westpac or the National Australia Bank or the merchant banks about the $300 million plus owed them for the HSV7 takeover. It was still assumed that the bulk of proceeds from asset sales and Skase's second payment for the TV network would be in by Christmas. The full consequences of the 19–20 October crash had not sunk in or had not been admitted so that the serious financial problems left in the takeover were still regarded as manageable. Serious divisions were also starting to appear at Tryart itself. Connell wanted Rothwells's $100 million fee urgently to help stave off that company's continuing liquidity crisis. The fee was due to be paid in April 1988 but he wanted to discount it to get some of it now. That caused a major split between Connell and Reuter (see Chapter 16). Relations had been cool between them since September. Reuter felt he had been steadily cut out of inner councils since the Rivkin document being used to sell the Syme float to institutions had been leaked to the *Financial Review*. That document had been based on Reuter's projections of savings that could be made in Syme's operations and the leak had been very embarrassing to Tryart. By November, Reuter had become isolated though he was still vital to the ANZ's financing arrangements. As Reuter's counsel said in the fee court case, he was feeling 'somewhat unloved and estranged from Connell' from early November.

The pressure was also telling at 'Fairwater'. As acceptances poured in at the end of October and Tryart's takeover success seemed assured, Mary Fairfax became very concerned about her financial future. The high cost of the takeover could inhibit significant dividend payments on her John Fairfax Ltd shares for years. Under the old ownership, Mary's interests held through Acrux and Rockwood, would, as a result of the company's development under those dreaded managers over the years, have given her a dividend income of over $2 million a year, tax free. This was disappearing. What would she live on? How would she maintain 'Fairwater' and 'Harrington Park'? She rang Dougherty and poured out her fears. She had a strong hand. Her own shares and Rockwood's had to be mortgaged to the ANZ Bank as part of the takeover financing. Acrux and Rockwood had not accepted Tryart's bid, nor was it intended that they should — which was a potential disaster for the group's subsequent tax arrangements. If Mary had accepted the offer for her Acrux shares and her interest in Rockwood, it would have cost Tryart another $180 million.

Vrisakis was deputed to fix this. Out of the crisis came an agreement between Warwick and his mother and the takeover and family companies: Tryart, Acrux, Rockwood, Tailer Investments, One Hundred and Thirty Seven Pty Ltd, and John Fairfax Ltd. Warwick agreed to pay his mother, through Tailer Investments and the Jones trust, $2.9 million a year for life, tax-free and adjusted for upward movements in the consumer price index. They agreed that Warwick could buy or Mary could sell to him her Acrux shares at $8.50, adjusted for any movements in the consumer price index, by or at November 1988. Apart from these amounts, Warwick agreed to give his mother $3.91 million immediately. Her company, One Hundred and Thirty Seven Pty Ltd, would pay $2.3 million for Tailer Investments' interest in the Grand Hotel, Hunter Street, making Mary sole owner of that property. If One Hundred and Thirty Seven wanted to sell the hotel, John Fairfax Ltd had the option to buy it back at One Hundred and Thirty Seven's purchase price.

In return for these arrangements, Mary agreed that Acrux and Rockwood would support Tryart by not accepting Tryart's offer. The agreement was dated 27 October 1987, the day the final amended offer of $8.50 cash only was made for John Fairfax shares, 18 days after the Part A Takeover Statement lodged with the Corporate Affairs Commission in Canberra on 9 October, had said that Rockwood 'is controlled by Warwick G. O. Fairfax' and that Warwick 'beneficially owned' the shares held by Acrux Holdings, three days after the formal document was dated to send to shareholders. It was apparently assumed that when the deals were signed with James and John on 9 October for the acquisition of their shares, Warwick owned or controlled all the family shares. But he had to guarantee his mother $2.9 million tax free for life to gain her support for the disposition of the Rockwood shares, and for an option over her Acrux shares. The arrangement had to be adjusted again in October 1988, when Tryart/Fairfax was being restructured to accommodate the $1.6 billion refinancing of the takeover. Warwick then had to deal with his mother himself. Acrux was finally paid $8.50 a share for its 3 333 333 shares in John Fairfax Ltd. Mary Fairfax ended up with non-voting B shares in John Fairfax Group Ltd in exchange for her Jones Trust shares. The company took over Warwick's commitment to pay Mary $2.9 million tax free for life. In the event of a liquidation, the B shares were entitled to the first $150 million after creditors had been paid (see Chapter 14).

The 27 October 1987 settlement with Mary Fairfax shored up the ANZ Bank's Privatisation Support Facility for $2.115 billion. The first signs of serious problems with other banks emerged late in November when Ron Cotton joined Tryart and started talking with his old associates at Fairfax about the loans from Westpac and the National Australia Bank of $150 million each. Cotton had resigned from the NML Royal Bank on 10 November, when he heard that the ANZ facility was in place. He rejoined Fairfax on 23 November. The National Australia Bank and Westpac were not going to roll over easily. That promised big trouble if the proceeds of the asset sales arranged in September and October did not come through on time.

Those concerns, however, did not overshadow the general satisfaction at having achieved control of the company at last. The old management — Gardiner, Suich and Brenchley — left on Friday 4 December. The old board of directors left on Monday 7 December, and the new board and management moved in. It was celebration time. Warwick invited the takeover team to dinner at 'Fairwater' on Tuesday night: Cotton, Reuter, Connell, Vrisakis, Dougherty, David Frecker and David Selig of Blake Dawson Waldron, who handled most of the legal work, and Sean Gillespie of Rothwells.

Cotton picked up Reuter at the Regent Hotel and drove him out to 'Fairwater'. They discussed the position paper Reuter had written the previous day emphasising the need to monitor closely those asset payments, the Skase contracts and the superannuation funds, which were still substantially beyond their reach. Reuter said he had undertaken to the ANZ to remain on the project until June 1988. He emphasised the need to get Peter King on board as soon as possible. He remained nervous about Connell's presence on the board and the impact this could have on the company's credit and about Marty Dougherty's lack of corporate experience.

During drinks before dinner Mary's two youngest children, Charles and Anna, who had been adopted in the UK during the 1960s, appeared briefly. The compliments were effusive. Laurie Connell recalled Mary Fairfax saying to a group including Reuter, Dougherty, Vrisakis and Cotton, 'No one else could have done the great job that Laurie and his team have done in the takeover.' Mary was the chatelaine, at dinner the only woman at the table. Warwick rose and thanked them all for their work on the takeover. 'Laurie has achieved what others regarded as impossible,' he said.

In evidence given in the fee case it was alleged that Warwick particularly thanked Bert Reuter for 'being able to con the Bank into providing the money to make all this possible'. Warwick denied saying this; it was not the sort of expression he used, he said. Nevertheless, the Bank had provided the funds to make it all possible. And the Bank had been conned. There were no bankers at the dinner.

# CHAPTER 12

# THE JOURNALISTS VERSUS
# MARTY DOUGHERTY

The journalists at Fairfax were apprehensive about the consequences of Tryart's takeover from the time it was announced on 31 August 1987. Fairfax had always been a journalists' company. The managing director had to be a journalist. Other senior executive positions were filled by journalists. The latitude the journalists enjoyed and their pre-eminence in the company, which riled the company's critics, could be limited and undermined by a change of ownership. Their fears became concentrated on two prospects: the arrival of Marty Dougherty, the public relations man, as editorial boss of the company; and the loss of jobs from the closure of loss-making products like the *Sun* and the *Times on Sunday* and other economy measures foreshadowed in the Rivkin James Capel selling document reported in the *Australian Financial Review* on 10 September. The longer the takeover took, the more the apprehensions grew, particularly when problems developed in the deals with Packer and Holmes a Court.

Many of the journalists had reported, and been stimulated by, the takeover stories that had dominated the business pages and sometimes the front pages in recent years. Those stories had concentrated on, and tended to glamorise, the big takeover operators who emerged in the 1980s to change the ownership and structure of many Australian companies. Not much attention was paid to what the takeovers meant to the people who worked for the companies taken over. Now the journalists were those people and it was not pleasant. This particularly applied to those working for the *Australian Financial Review* and the *Times on Sunday*. When, at the end of

September, they discovered they were, in effect, being sold to Robert Holmes a Court, they were stunned. As rumours started to spread during the last week in September that Holmes a Court might be getting the *Australian Financial Review*, Fairfax's chief editorial executive, Max Suich, tried to hose down the journalists' fears. On the night of Sunday 27 September, when *Financial Review* reporters were sure they had the outline of the deal with Holmes a Court, the acting editor, Glenda Korporaal, still sceptical that such a thing could happen, checked again with Suich. She intended running the story on page three of the next morning's paper. Suich said he would ring her back. He came through just on the *Financial Review*'s deadline and said, 'Put it on page one.' Korporaal sent the message, placing the story on page one, on to the sub-editors' VDT screens.

The journalists acted as though they had been mugged. They were about to be sold to a man about whom they had probably written and published more than any other person in the previous six years, someone whose fortunes depended upon taking big positions in individual stocks in a rising market. However highly they regarded him as a newsmaker, they were very wary about him as a prospective owner. The potential for conflicts of interest was awesome. Glenda Korporaal came into the office at 7.30 the next morning to try and see Warwick and talk him out of the sale. At 8 a.m. she went to Rothwells's offices at 50 Bridge Street in the city. He was not yet there. She returned to the foyer of the building to wait and ambush him as he came in, to tell him as strongly as she could that the *Financial Review* staff wanted to stay with John Fairfax Ltd. Warwick came in at 8.20 a.m. with others. Korporaal culled him out and gave him the message. Warwick listened, reserved and unmoved. 'I understand what you are saying,' he said, 'but sometimes these things have to be done.' His mild manner could be deceptive as Dougherty and Connell later discovered. He turned politely and caught the lift to the 12th floor.

The editor of the *Financial Review*, Alan Kohler, was holidaying in Italy with his family, at a farmhouse in Tuscany without a telephone. He called from a public telephone on Monday to make a routine check on what was happening in Sydney and was told he had been sold to Holmes a Court. He checked into a hotel in Florence, spent some hours on the telephone and flew to London on Wednesday hoping to meet Holmes a Court there later in the week. Holmes a Court flew in from America on Friday, a week after he had signed the agreement with Tryart in Perth. He invited Kohler and his wife to the *Phantom of the Opera*, then playing at Her Majesty's Theatre. Kohler pointed out that he had tried to get tickets to that show but it was booked out for many weeks ahead. Holmes a Court said not to worry, he owned Her Majesty's. It came with his takeover of Sir Lew Grade's companies four years previously. They went on Saturday night. Holmes a Court would not be drawn into talking about the *Financial Review*'s future. Kohler accepted his offer of a lift back to Australia in the Bell Group's 727, leaving London next day.

Kohler thought Holmes a Court could not get away from talking about his Tryart purchase on that flight. Holmes a Court had only recently bought the plane from an oil sheikh. The signs were still written in Arabic. The layout included a large ante-room for seated passengers and a bedroom where Holmes a Court slept and thought for most of the next 20 hours. Bell executives were fellow passengers. But the man Kohler wanted to talk to was asleep aft. In Perth Kohler said he would not leave the plane until Holmes a Court talked to him. They had 15 minutes of generalities — editorial freedom, continued commitment to existing high standards … He left Perth for Sydney no better informed about his paper's future than when he left London.

The *Times on Sunday*, losing $5 or $6 million a year, was in a much more hazardous position than the *Financial Review* which was making profits of more than twice that. The *Times on Sunday* editor Valerie Lawson was on maternity leave with a two-week-old baby. She was due to return to work in January but became deeply concerned about how to hold the paper together until it could be transferred to the Bell Group. A couple of days after the announcement of the paper's sale she got through to Holmes a Court at the Jefferson Hotel in Washington, seeking firm commitments from him about the future for the paper and the staff. Had he asked for the *Times on Sunday* in the negotiations with Tryart? Yes, said Holmes a Court, he thought it had a good, long-term future. He said the positions of the staff were guaranteed. All would be offered transfers to whichever company in the Bell Group would be the new owner. How many on the staff, he asked? Forty-five journalists. He thought that was a bit thin. He said they could stand losses for a very long time if he thought they were building something worthwhile. He was interested in the *Observer* in London and would be in the *Times* or the *Financial Times* if they were for sale. 'Bell Group is in a growth phase and will provide a better safety net than Fairfax,' he said. It was 30 September, less than three weeks before the stockmarket crash.

Lawson spoke to him again in Perth, a week later. Tryart's Part A Takeover Statement was still not filed. The problems of unhooking the *Financial Review* and the *Times on Sunday* from Fairfax and hooking them on to Bell Group looked forbidding. Holmes a Court admitted the complexities of the deal. 'This is a cowboy transaction,' he said. He sent a couple of boundary riders to Sydney to keep an eye on his prospective properties and to start planning their transfer. They set up camp initially at the Intercontinental Hotel, interviewing editors, advertising managers and others. On 20 October, the day the stockmarket crashed in Australia, Suich wrote to the editors and managers warning that no confidential information should be given to Bell Group representatives. They should be treated as any other shareholders of the company. After 20 October the Fairfax people found it increasingly difficult to focus the Bell executives' attention on the problems of the coming transfer of the two newspapers. They had been looking at a new building in the city as possible office space for Holmes a Court's new media interests. That became too expensive. Bell's director of personnel, John Reynolds, was cautiously reassuring. 'Things are going ahead, a bit more slowly. We are moving into recessional times, but it's cautious business as usual,' he said. Kohler was not so sure. The executives were no longer staying at the Intercontinental but at the Cosmopolitan Motor Inn at Double Bay.

Holmes a Court had become increasingly hard to contact. Publicly he was maintaining a brave, confident front, but the market crash had cut hundreds of millions of dollars off the values of his investments in BHP, Texaco, Standard Chartered Bank, Sears

Holdings and Pioneer Concrete. He talked by telephone late one night to Kohler and admitted that he would not be able to afford the *Times on Sunday.* Kohler kept that to himself. He had recently attended a lunch Suich gave in the Fairfax directors' dining room for Joe Rogaly of the *Financial Times.* Rogaly was preparing for a major *Financial Times* survey on Australia. The *Australian Financial Review* had held the rights to use *Financial Times* material in Australia for many years, with two short breaks, once in the early 1960s when Frank Packer's Consolidated Press had outbid Fairfax for the rights in order to produce a short-lived *Australian Financial Times*, then in the early 1980s when Rupert Murdoch won the *Financial Times* away from Fairfax to help him produce another short-lived publication, *Finance Week.* The *Financial Times* returned to Fairfax and they had seemed comfortable with each other ever since.

After lunch Kohler and Rogaly went with Suich to his office and they talked about the *Australian Financial Review*'s ownership problems. The conversation stayed with Kohler. When Holmes a Court told Kohler of his problem with the *Times on Sunday,* Kohler realised the West Australian could need a partner. He rang Frank Barlow, executive director of Pearson Group plc, owners of the *Financial Times*, in London. He asked Barlow if Pearson group would be interested in taking part of the equity in the *Australian Financial Review* with Holmes a Court. Barlow was interested. Kohler then rang Holmes a Court and asked if he would be interested in a partner. Holmes a Court said he would if the partner added value to the property. 'What about the *Financial Times?*' asked Kohler. That started weeks of negotiations between Pearson group, Bell and Fairfax, which finally came to nothing when the Holmes a Court contract was cancelled and Fairfax decided to keep the *Australian Financial Review.* But in November–December 1987, Kohler was concerned that, if the paper was to be sold, it go into secure, strong hands. Holmes a Court's no longer looked strong enough. Kohler had asked Fairfax's New York manager, Philip McCarthy, to sound out the Dow Jones Co., owners of the *Wall Street Journal,* about taking an interest in the *Australian Financial Review.* But Dow Jones was preoccupied with its own internal cost and other problems.

McCarthy also talked to Knight-Ridder Newspapers, which owned the *US Journal of Commerce*, as well as major newspapers in Miami, Philadelphia and Detroit. They were not familiar with Australia and assumed it was like Canada with restrictions on foreign ownership. McCarthy pointed out that US citizen Murdoch owned 60 per cent of the Australian press. Knight-Ridder said they would be interested if the *Sydney Morning Herald* or the *Age* became available. The *Financial Times* group was the *Australian Financial Review*'s white hope.

Although Kohler had kept Holmes a Court's news of the *Times on Sunday*'s fate to himself, it was quite evident that the paper's position was becoming increasingly precarious. At the annual general meeting of Bell Group shareholders in Perth on Wednesday 9 December, as the Tryart team was moving in at Fairfax, Holmes a Court had talked about problems with the contract to buy Macquarie Broadcasting and a possible partnership in owning the *Australian Financial Review*. The *Times on Sunday* had not been mentioned. Valerie Lawson spoke to him by telephone on 11 December. Holmes a Court's telephone conversations were notorious for his long, silent pauses, which often seemed to take more time than the exchange of words. Now the pauses seemed longer and his speech seemed to have lost some of its usual studied modulation. He said the *Times on Sunday* was not involved in the partnership talks. He regretted that he had mentioned the *Australian Financial Review* and Macquarie at the Bell meeting on Wednesday. He had not intended to do so. And he revealed the pressure he was under as the Bell Group's growth phase contracted into a state of siege. 'BHP is running a campaign against us. Nobody would say anything if we were talking about trucks and buses,' he said. BHP had been pressured by Holmes a Court during the stockmarket boom. Now the positions were reversed. BHP was negotiating to have Bell removed from its share register.

The next day Holmes a Court rang Kohler and said he was offering a half interest in the *Times on Sunday* with half of the *Australian Financial Review* to the Pearson group. This was confirmed by John Reynolds of Bell to Valerie Lawson. She then rang Barlow in London who said yes, Bell was apparently offering a partnership in the *Times on Sunday* as well as the *Australian Financial Review* and *National Business Review* in New Zealand.

Among the journalists and others at Fairfax there was an increasing conviction that it was now every man for himself. The *Australian Financial Review* was in limbo, the *Times on Sunday* in what seemed like a big black hole. The Tryart-Bell agreement was unclear about how the transfer of staff would be effected. Would they have to resign from Fairfax before joining Bell? If so, what guarantees did they have that Bell would offer them the same jobs they had left? Would they take their accumulated leave and other entitlements with them? Or would they be paid out by Fairfax? Could they be paid without terminating their employment? That river they had to cross looked wider and deeper each day. Journalists on the other Sydney newspapers, the *Sydney Morning Herald*, the *Sun* and the *Sun-Herald*, showed some reservations about taking up the cause for their *Australian Financial Review* and *Times on Sunday* colleagues. They had their own concerns. For the *Australian Financial Review* and *Times on Sunday* people the whole messy business did not inspire confidence in the commitment and managerial competence of their prospective owners who were, in any case, becoming less and less visible. For the journalists on the other, bigger, newspapers, it did not inspire confidence in their new owners. Holmes a Court's 'cowboy' tag seemed increasingly apposite to both sides. Chris Anderson, editor in chief of the *Times on Sunday* as well as the *Sydney Morning Herald*, also spoke to Holmes a Court to try and define his plans, without success. Holmes a Court complained, as he had to Suich and others, about the Fairfax papers nicknaming him Hacca, a familiarity he found offensive.

Marty Dougherty was convinced that the Fairfax newspapers were out of control, irresponsible and that the business pages, particularly of the *Sydney Morning Herald*, were anti-business. Bringing them into line would involve getting rid of the people who ran them, particularly Suich, the chief editorial executive, Chris Anderson, editor-in-chief of the *Sydney Morning Herald* and the *Times on Sunday*, and John Alexander, editor of the *Sydney Morning Herald*. Suich was going, anyway. The *Australian Financial Review* and *Times on Sunday* would become Holmes a Court's worry. In Melbourne the *Age*, too, needed shaking up. Reuter and Dougherty both believed it was absurd that David Syme and Co. Ltd was allowed to run as virtually an independent company.

It was not unusual for a new boss to want to move his own people into key positions under him. Marty had run a very successful disinformation campaign through September, maintaining the public myth that the Fairfax family were friendly to Warwick's takeover and that Warwick was in a strong, commanding position of control over substantial shareholdings in the company. He and Suich had crossed swords over the reports on the run at Rothwells in the week after the 20 October crash. Rothwells had had a good press after its rescue on the weekend of 25–26 October. Soon afterwards Anderson sent two journalists to Perth to report on how Rothwells was standing up after the rescue. The assignment was completely justified by subsequent events. It was also calculatingly provocative to Marty Dougherty, who was shortly to move in as Anderson's boss. It emphasised Dougherty's fundamental problem: he could not protect Rothwells and Connell and maintain high standards of objective journalism at Fairfax at the same time.

Anderson had recognised this when the takeover was announced. After it seemed to be coming together at the end of September, Anderson had seen Warwick with Marty at Rothwells offices at 50 Bridge Street. Warwick had previously asked Anderson to stay on as editor-in-chief of the *Sydney Morning Herald*. At the meeting at Rothwells, Anderson told Warwick and Dougherty that he had strong reservations about Dougherty taking the top editorial post in the company and left no doubt that he, Chris Anderson, would find it difficult to work at Fairfax if this happened. Anderson, a small, compact man, had a mind with a very sharp, hard leading edge. He spoke as directly as he thought when the occasion demanded it. At 41 he was well on top of one of the biggest editorial jobs in Australia and ambitious for new challenges. He had seen the *Sydney Morning Herald* out of the 1982–83 recession and into a position of great prosperity and editorial strength. His ability was recognised at News Corporation as well as at Fairfax, at least at pre-takeover Fairfax. He had been approached to work for News Corporation previously but had refused all offers.

Perhaps prompted by the growing turmoil at Fairfax, News Ltd's managing director in Australia, Ken Cowley, approached Anderson again in October. Would he be interested in moving over as editor-in-chief at News Ltd with a specific brief to develop the *Australian*? Anderson said he would think about it. He told Warwick and Dougherty about the offer. They both said they were keen for Anderson to stay. But he could not see how he could continue to be a strong, effective editor with Marty Dougherty on top of him.

Dougherty had been making his own plans. In New York in July he had met Andrew Clark, who was then working for Murdoch at the *New York Post*. Clark had worked for Fairfax at the *National Times* as political correspondent in Canberra during that paper's palmiest days in the 1970s. Then he had worked for Packer's new business magazine, *Australian Business*, becoming editor for four strenuous years. His relations with the staff were sometimes tense. He was prickly, impatient, obsessive about his journalism. To some journalists these were assets, to others liabilities. They could be very trying. Towards the end of his editorship of *Australian Business* some key journalists left to join the *Sydney Morning Herald*. *Sydney Morning Herald* editor-in-chief, Chris Anderson, lured John Alexander away to become the paper's finance editor. Alexander was followed by Deborah Light, Alan Deans, Mark Westfield, Catherine Armitage, all top reporters. Together they made a team that became important in the struggles to come at Fairfax.

In September 1987, Alexander became editor of the *Sydney Morning Herald* and Deborah Light the finance editor. The paper's business pages had been greatly expanded under Alexander. They were regarded as an important factor in the paper's strong rise in circulation and advertising revenues in the previous four or five years. Dougherty was not an admirer of these pages. They included columns that were sometimes irreverent and disrespectful, and worse still, critical of some of his clients. In October he rang Andrew Clark in New York and asked him if he would be interested in coming back to Australia to a big editorial job. Clark was at a loose end. He had left the *New York Post* to work on a pilot business television programme for

Murdoch but prospects for that did not look bright. Marty called again in November. The job he had in mind was assistant editor of the *Sydney Morning Herald*, possibly becoming editor of the *Sydney Morning Herald* or the *Age*. Clark was hooked. He regarded editorship of the *Sydney Morning Herald* as one of the most desirable jobs in the world.

These developments were unknown to Fairfax journalists who, by early November, were becoming increasingly concerned now that Warwick's final takeover offer was being rushed and the changeover in ownership and control appeared imminent. On 9 November, the Fairfax house committee of the Australian Journalists Association (AJA) resolved that, if Marty Dougherty took over as chief editorial executive while he still had an active interest in a public relations company, a stop work meeting would be called to consider striking until he left Fairfax or left the public relations company; and that a committee be set up to receive complaints from members about the use of editorial influence by the new owners. They were waffly, ineffectual resolutions. Dougherty had virtually committed himself to joining the company subject to negotiations with Warwick about compensation for giving up his business, which he was also in the process of selling. But the meeting reflected the mounting concern of the journalists. Later that month Marty settled for Warwick's offer of $3 million for past work and the loss of his public relations business and officially started at Fairfax as managing director (editorial) at $250 000 a year plus extras.

Early in November Anderson had decided not to accept Cowley's offer of a top editorial job at News Ltd. Cowley asked if he would be interested in a non-editorial management job. Anderson was interested in testing his abilities outside journalism. He let Cowley's inquiry hang in mid-air and told Warwick Fairfax he would continue with Fairfax for six months, emphasising his reservations about working with Dougherty. Relations between Anderson and Dougherty reached a critical point in mid-November when Dougherty questioned the assignment of the two reporters to look again at Rothwells in Perth. Dougherty still had no position in Fairfax. He was particularly steamed up about who the reporters were: Colleen Ryan, a very hard-nosed business reporter who had crossed some of the characters involved in the Rothwells rescue on previous occasions, and Andrew Keenan, the *Sydney Morning Herald*'s crime specialist. Marty said he had had a complaint from 'the West' and asked whether Anderson thought the assignment was wise. Anderson pointed to the editorial justification for the project in terms Marty could hardly argue with. The Rothwells rescue was a big Australian story, involving some of the country's leading businessmen, the National Australia Bank and the Western Australian Government. A year later it nearly brought down the Government. Marty could only say he relied on Anderson's judgement.

But Anderson regarded the incident as another omen of what he could expect when the Tryart team moved in early in December. He thought again of Cowley's question about his interests in general management and spoke to John Alexander about the way things were shaping at Fairfax. Both felt that the time to jump was rapidly approaching. Anderson had recently signed a contract with John Fairfax Ltd in which differences about editorial policy could trigger his departure with maximum entitlements. Marty Dougherty would not mind squeezing the two men out, but if he enabled them to build a case based on interference with editorial policy, the company would be squeezed for a substantial sum in the process. In addition to Andrew Clark, Dougherty had other people lined up for top editorial jobs in the company. Ita Buttrose had been retained by Fairfax under contract, with a year to run, working on *Woman's Day* and the *Sun* when the takeover was announced. When it succeeded she went to see Dougherty. *Woman's Day* was going to Packer. The *Sun*'s days seemed numbered. Was there a job for her? Buttrose had held senior editorial positions with Packer and Murdoch before working for Fairfax. She was probably the best known journalist in Australia. Some, including Anderson, thought she was a better promoter and publicist than she was a newspaper editor. But she was widely liked. Dougherty said she could be editor-in-chief of the *Sun-Herald*. Buttrose met the other key members of the Tryart team at Rothwells and accepted the job.

On 10 December in Melbourne Marty asked Pat Boyce if he would like to be editor of the *Age*. Boyce jumped at it. He had worked at the *Age* in fairly senior editorial positions before parting with the paper when he was denied the second most important position of news editor by the editor, Creighton Burns. Marty had known Boyce since they were at school together in northern NSW. He put Boyce on $5000 a month retainer. The *Age*'s editor, Creighton Burns, was not consulted. Only Ita's appointment had been announced.

Marty had mentioned the possibility of bringing in Andrew Clark to Chris Anderson, but Anderson thought Clark would be going to the *BRW* business magazine group. The Tryart team moved in on 7 December. That night, as the editorial and production floors of the Fairfax building in Jones Street became increasingly active with preparations for the next day's issues of the *Sydney Morning Herald* and the *Australian Financial Review*, Chris Anderson took Warwick Fairfax and Marty Dougherty on a tour of the editorial departments. They paused at the *Sydney Morning Herald*'s business reporters' section to look at a wall covered with cartoons, clippings from newspapers, pictures — items that had excited special comment or gossip. Two stood out boldly: a picture of Laurie Connell with a caption 'Connell for Chairman' and a sheet headed 'The Dougherty Hit List' with a list of Dougherty's known public relations clients. The heading was a half-serious joke, a reminder to watch for barrows being pushed.

The tension increased that night. Marty's brother Paul Dougherty, who had been installed as Marty's editorial assistant, showed the editorial manager, John Richardson, a draft of a statement to be made by Warwick ushering in the new era of ownership, direction and management. It had been passed to Richardson for distribution to all the Fairfax newspapers for publication the next morning. The statement included some clear disparagements and criticisms, not only of past management, but of the past performance of printers and journalists. Richardson called Anderson and said, 'If we print this there will be a strike tomorrow.' Anderson refused to publish. Creighton Burns, editor of the *Age*, objected to the statement and indicated he would not necessarily publish any statement. Richardson suggested a number of changes to eliminate the potentially offensive parts.

Those changes were made. Anderson suggested more in talks with Marty Dougherty and Warwick Fairfax. He had his first taste of Warwick's stubbornness. The final version had most of the stingers removed. The *Sydney Morning Herald* ran it this way on page seven the next morning:

Mr Warwick Fairfax, the new proprietor of John Fairfax Ltd, issued this statement yesterday.

There has been some speculation these past months about my editorial and management philosophy, and that of the incoming management team. Some may have wondered how the company and the newspapers it publishes will be affected.

What we are trying to do is nothing new. Rather we seek to maintain the company and its newspapers firmly within the tradition started by John Fairfax and continued for much of the past 150 years.

Editorially, we seek to report the facts. Nothing more, nothing less. We should strive to keep opinions out of the news reports in our papers and we must not allow the news to be slanted in any way.

When one set of views on an issue is reported, we will continue to ensure fair representation is given to opposing viewpoints. In the same way, we will continue to ensure that our published commentaries cover a variety of opinions.

Our editorials will continue to strive to be balanced and thoughtful. We do not seek to favour any political party or viewpoint.

We do not see it as our role to change Australian society. That would be gross arrogance. It is our more modest goal to equip people with the information they need to make their own judgements.

Within this charter, we will also try our best to be bright, readable and — where possible, and appropriate — entertaining.

Our management philosophy is simple. We seek to create a caring and supportive company, where excellence at all levels is encouraged. It is a rather old cliche, but the success of the company depends on its people. We will not perform well as an organisation unless that supportive environment exists. If we expect loyalty from our people we must show loyalty to them. Every person in this company matters, from the cadet journalist and apprentice printer to the chief executive. We will encourage people to show initiative.

We will treat all people with honesty, openness and respect. These are the goals for which we will strive. They provide a benchmark for what we are trying to do.

In some areas much change is needed, in others very little. Those changes that are required will not happen overnight, they will take a while.

However, our course is set.

In conclusion, and to place these remarks in their historical context, I would like to quote from the first editorial in the first the *Sydney Morning Herald* on 18 April 1831:

'Our editorial management shall be conducted upon principles of candour, honesty and honour ... freedom of thinking and speaking shall be conceded and demanded. We have no wish to mislead, no interests to gratify by unsparing abuse, and reason with a desire, not to gain a point, but to establish a principle. By these sentiments we shall be guided and, whether friends or foes, by these we shall judge others. We have a right, therefore, to expect that by these we shall be judged.'

The authors had either forgotten, not read or hoped their readers had not read, Gavin Souter's *Company of Heralds*. The paper started as the *Sydney Herald* in 1831. It became the *Sydney Morning Herald* in 1842, two years after John Fairfax bought a half share in it. As Souter pointed out, it was not unusual for newspapers aiming for mass circulation to proclaim commitment to principles of neutrality and fairness. In the *Herald's* case it was not long before the paper was letting its prejudices hang out about convicts, emancipists, Catholics, Governor Bourke, Aborigines and one of its competitors, J. D. Lang's *Colonist*.

Anderson sat in his office that night reading the stories about that day's events at Fairfax written for the next day's paper, with Warwick Fairfax and Marty Dougherty looking over his shoulder at the words coming up on the screen of his video display terminal. A long piece by senior reporter Malcolm Brown, describing the who, when, why and how of the change in ownership and control, said Connell's appointment to the board was a surprise. Dougherty wanted that taken out. He also objected to Alan Deans, the investment editor, suggesting that the Macquarie Radio Network probably would not be sold to Holmes a Court due to his option to put the network back to Fairfax. (Holmes a Court confirmed this at the Bell group annual general meeting in Perth two days later, on 9 December.) Anderson knocked back Dougherty's objections. The events of that night convinced Anderson that he should go. He rang Cowley at News Ltd and said he was interested in that management job if it was still going. Cowley was delighted. They talked about Anderson going to News Ltd as chief of the company's Sydney newspapers, still with special responsibility for lifting the *Australian*, and possible deputy to Cowley. Anderson would have to prove himself there against some vigorous competition for executive preferment at News Ltd.

At Fairfax, relations between the editors and journalists on the fifth floor and their new masters on the 14th floor continued to deteriorate. Two days after the new executives moved in Marty Dougherty decided that he and his brother Paul should have VDTs installed in their offices. They could, with access to all the key commands and codes, pick up any story written for any of the newspapers on their office screens before publication or before they were sub-edited. There was nothing unusual about senior editorial managers reading journalists' stories before they were printed in the newspaper. It was common practice before the electronic revolution for the top editorial executive to read reports and leading articles in the form of galley proofs taken from the metal type as it stood in long trays waiting to be assembled into a page form. It was not unusual for Marty Dougherty's predecessors to walk into the reporters' and sub-editors' rooms and, after a word with the news editor, leaf through the galley proofs held on long metal spikes, looking for a story in which they might be particularly interested. This had not worried the journalists. But that was before electronic screens replaced hot metal type. Perhaps there was something sinister and threatening in the idea of someone in a remote office being able to monitor

anything being written by any journalist in the building, particularly if it was someone the journalists did not trust. Big Brother
seemed to be looming over their shoulders. Access to editorial
material held or being put into the system was governed by
priorities. Ordinary reporters had Priority One giving them access
to their own copy and some wire services. Priority Six, the top
priority, gave access to everything. Very few people had that level
but it was understood that there were about to be two more,
the Dougherty brothers.

The technology instructors, who taught new journalists how
to use the system, scoffed at the mounting apprehension on the
editorial floor. It would take a week's solid instruction and practice
to start to feel confident about using the system and more practice
after that to use it efficiently. Marty and Paul Dougherty had had
one lesson. Those who knew them were sceptical that they would
stay in their offices until midnight to check on what was going
into the next day's papers. It was easier and more open to follow
the usual practice and ask the editors. Marty Dougherty was able
to do neither. He did not have an easy working relationship with
the editors. The VDT installed in his office was never used. He
rapidly became preoccupied with the mounting crisis over the
company's finances and sales contracts. But the VDT screens on
the 14th floor became symbols causing fear and loathing to
flourish on the fifth floor. Dougherty's relations with Anderson
and Alexander were cool to frigid.

The day after the news of the installation of the VDTs in the
Doughertys' offices spread through the building, Marty Dougherty
told Anderson about his proposed appointment of Andrew Clark
as associate editor (finance) of the *Sydney Morning Herald*. Bert
Reuter's fears about Marty's lack of experience in running large
organisations were rapidly being justified. Any self-respecting
editor appointed his own staff, including his deputy and
associates. He would probably talk to his chief executive about
senior appointments and the chief executive might suggest
appointments to him, but the decision would be the editor's and
he would wear responsibility for it. Anderson told Dougherty that
if Clark joined the *Sydney Morning Herald* as a business writer
or columnist he would have to report to the business editor and

the editor. Nobody was likely to want that. The business editor, Deborah Light, and the editor, John Alexander, had left the magazine *Australian Business* when Clark was editor. Now he would be reporting to them. Marty Dougherty had other ideas. He thought Clark could take charge of the *Sydney Morning Herald*'s business section, pull it into line, and combine its activities more closely with those of the *Age* in Melbourne. That made the big assumption that the *Age* was malleable. But with Anderson opposed, this idea had to be abandoned. Dougherty still wanted Clark in a senior position on the *Sydney Morning Herald*. They looked for a compromise. Anderson suggested that Clark could be appointed the *Sydney Morning Herald*'s New York correspondent, enabling him to work his way into the paper. But the damage had been done at Jones Street. Word had quickly spread that Dougherty had offered Clark an editor's job on the *Sydney Morning Herald* without Anderson's or Alexander's knowledge. Indignation inflamed the fear and loathing.

At Jones Street the mounting concern about the real or imagined intentions of Marty Dougherty and the new owner led to a stop work meeting on 18 December. The concerns had been expressed that day in a letter from the AJA house committee to Dougherty. He had not replied.

Anderson was now busy on two fronts. His talks with Cowley about moving over to News Ltd, probably as manager of Sydney newspapers, had developed into an audacious plan, which could demoralise Fairfax and strengthen News. Anderson would bring with him Alexander, the *Sydney Morning Herald* editor, and half a dozen key editors and other journalists from the business reporting staff including Deborah Light and the top reporters. The exodus was expected to spread to the general news room. As many as 40 journalists in all could make the jump. Fairfax's marketing manager, Peter Gaunt, was also expected to go with Anderson and other business and circulation people. Whether News Ltd could have coped with such a transfusion or not, it was very doubtful that the donor, Fairfax, could. Unknown to the company's new owner and controllers, this loomed as big a threat to the company's future as the financial crisis developing over the asset sales and the banks. The most important assets finally backing the takeover loan were the company's newspapers. A mass exodus of people who wrote and sold them could undermine their values, certainly undermine the market's perception of their values.

As he became enthusiastic about what might be achieved at News Ltd's *Australian, Daily Telegraph* and *Sunday Telegraph* with an infusion of talent from Fairfax, Anderson had to maintain his equilibrium on the home front. He asked the journalists' house committee if he could address the 18 December stop work meeting and proceeded to try and take some of the heat out of the explosive atmosphere on the editorial floor. He said he had been assured that Andrew Clark would answer to the editor of the *Sydney Morning Herald*, Alexander, and to him, Anderson, and that they would decide what Clark's duties would be. He appealed to the journalists to go back to work and give the new management time to settle in before rushing to judgement on them.

The journalists' representatives saw Marty Dougherty later that day to discuss the issues, mainly the right of the editor-in-chief or editor to hire and fire. Marty agreed that 'as long as the editors enjoy the confidence of the company, the final decision on the employment of staff will rest with them'. He reminded the journalists that he had been a journalist for 20 years, editor of two newspapers, and had never fired anyone. 'The only reason why I am here is that I am a new chap in this organisation and you are wondering what this Dougherty fellow is up to. It is very early days for people to get excited about where I am leading because leading I am. There won't be any doubts in your minds that I will have an influence in the organisation and my dearest hope is that it will be positive and welcome in the interests of quality journalism and of maintaining the traditions of newspapers of record.' He concluded, 'I understand the difference between church and state and I would suggest that in your interests there has never been someone who better understands the difference between the business and editorial side of it. I am committed to Warwick's statement of 7 December.'

A sort of truce ensued. Anderson told Dougherty that he would be standing down as editor-in-chief. Dougherty said all his entitlements would be met and that he, Dougherty, would talk to Warwick and Peter King about a possible departure date. Both men were going overseas for Christmas, Dougherty to Hawaii for a couple of weeks and Anderson with his family to Ireland, England and the Middle East. Anderson planned to be back at the end of January and to leave Fairfax shortly afterwards. He rang Andrew Clark in New York. It was agreed that Clark would not start at Fairfax until Anderson returned. Clark had been shaken by the row his proposed appointment had caused at Fairfax but he was very determined and the journalists' reaction had only strengthened his resolve to return. He thought Anderson was going to a managerial position at Fairfax's former television station, ATN7, an idea as astray as Anderson's original assumption that Clark would be returning to work at the *BRW* magazine group.

Anderson's talks with Cowley had progressed so well that Cowley suggested Anderson organise his holiday itinerary to include a few days at Aspen, Colorado. Murdoch would be staying at his house there. They could talk about plans for the future. Anderson welcomed the chance to spend a few days with Murdoch, whose appetite for involvement in every part of his expanding empire seemed insatiable. At Sydney Airport, as he waited with his family to board the plane for Los Angeles, Anderson unexpectedly met Warwick and Mary Fairfax. Mary was also going overseas. She caught up with Anderson again in London.

At Aspen, in mid-winter, the Andersons fell under the full, persuasive power of the Murdoch spell, which culminated in an irresistible gesture. When the time came to leave for Boston and the flight to London, internal flight schedules were being upset by heavy snow falls. Murdoch had his private jet flown out from New York to take the Andersons to Boston. Those few days at Aspen helped soothe the small, nagging doubts Anderson had begun to feel about how far his authority to make changes would go at News Ltd. It was much more tightly controlled from the top than John Fairfax Ltd. But he was reassured by Murdoch. The companies had radically different cultures, which other top journalists had failed to bridge.

Marty Dougherty and Bert Reuter had left Sydney for their over-seas holidays on 21 December. That left Ron Cotton alone at the helm at Jones Street. Relations between Cotton and Dougherty had become increasingly tense. Dougherty was the stronger personality and was increasingly critical of Cotton's apparent reluctance to act on the company's pressing business and financial problems. There was no chief executive to resolve this. Marty took his complaints to Warwick who kept his distance, saying he was not going to make their decisions for them. Alan Kohler at the *Australian Financial Review* was spending most of his time trying to get Pearsons involved in Holmes a Court's purchase of the paper. This could be the basis of another substantial newspaper publishing group in Australia, a very desirable alternative to Murdoch and what remained of the Fairfax groups.

The *Times on Sunday* was living from week to week with a shrinking staff of journalists. Talks with Bell executives about how the two newspapers would be transferred from Fairfax to Bell had virtually ceased. There was no forward planning. Journalists' time became increasingly occupied with fruitless speculation about the future. The internal communications system spread rumours like a virus: who was leaving, who was being sacked, who was being asked to stay. Very personal messages being sent through the VDT system were sent to the wrong people. Sometimes they flashed up on the screens of people who were being written about rather than their intended destinations.

The problems of the journalists and advertising salesmen who found themselves in this no man's land somewhere between Fairfax and Bell were not high priority with the senior executives in either company. Fairfax was rudderless. The banks were becoming concerned for their competitive claims on the company's prospective cash flows from the asset sales that had not eventuated (see Chapter 14). Reuter was in Seattle and apparently uncontactable. Connell was in Perth with all his fingers in the dyke at Rothwells. Warwick Fairfax was invisible. In Mary Fairfax's eyes there was one person clearly to blame for this deterioration in the company's affairs: her former close friend and confidant, Marty Dougherty. She felt this was confirmed when she heard that Chris Anderson was leaving the company.

Mary Fairfax was in London in mid-January, less than happy about the flat she was using. She rang Fairfax London manager,

Alan Dobbyn, and asked if the company's flat in Fetter Lane, off Fleet Street, was available. Dobbyn said no, it was occupied by Chris Anderson and his family. Mary said she would like to see the flat anyhow. She had never done so. Now that the company was privatised she might have easier access to it. At 9 a.m. on 18 January Dobbyn met her at Fetter Lane. Anderson was out jogging along the Embankment. His wife showed Mary over the flat. Anderson returned and Mary poured out her concerns to him. She urged him to go back to Sydney and help get rid of Dougherty. Anderson was unaware of the pressures on the company over the bank debts and postponed asset sales, which had increased alarmingly in the last three weeks. Mary said she had put up a great deal of equity for the takeover and had been denied a board seat. She feared Dougherty had too much influence on her son Warwick, that the way the company was being run differed from the wishes of her late husband. She wanted Anderson to use his influence to protect the Fairfax newspapers and her son's position. She let her concerns become known to an ever-increasing circle of her friends and acquaintances in Sydney and they inevitably reached Dougherty himself.

That was but one of Marty's problems. He had rung Cotton from Hawaii on Christmas Eve and received an earful of them. He had also had another run-in with *Herald* editorial executives. When Westpac took legal action late in December to ensure the repayment of its $150 million loan to Fairfax, the *Sydney Morning Herald* was bound to report it. Dougherty rang the acting editor, Max Prisk, from Hawaii. He wanted to know why Prisk thought this was worth running in the *Herald*. He questioned its news value and said it was not in the company's best interests to run it. He was on shaky ground. The story was run on 31 December. The next day Marty rang Prisk and apologised for coming on so strongly at him on the previous day but saying he still believed he was right.

Soon afterwards the *Herald*'s investment editor Alan Deans was told by a stockbroker that some of his clients were still waiting for the cheques from Tryart for their Fairfax shares. A reporter, Ian Verrender, discovered three large shareholders who had not been paid. In a takeover of this size, in a market that had been hyperactive until just before the share register was ruled off to decide who should be entitled to the offer, some delays were probably to be expected. But when Verrender tried to contact Dougherty and other executives for an explanation during the day, none was available and his calls were not returned. The executives were fighting other battles. Verrender wrote his story and Prisk, as a matter of caution, sent a copy to Dougherty at around 9 p.m. Dougherty hit the roof and said it was 'a load of rubbish'. Prisk decided to hold the story for 24 hours while it was double checked. It was found to be correct. But that day the company couriered the cheques to the unpaid shareholders. The next day the *Herald* carried a report reassuring the investment community that the final cheques had been paid. Anderson heard the story in London soon after he had seen Mary Fairfax. The incident was confused and probably could have been avoided but it stoked the fires on the editorial floor. Dougherty might have handled it differently under less pressure. To help solve his problem with Cotton, immediately he returned from holidays on 4 January, he had encouraged the appointment of the new merchant banking firm, Whitlam Turnbull, as financial advisers to the company. He was dealing with Kerry Packer and his managing director, Trevor Kennedy, over the assets sale to Consolidated Press and trying to deal with Holmes a Court and his executives over the assets sale to Bell Group.

One morning late in January, Valerie Lawson of the *Times on Sunday* cornered Dougherty in the Jones Street car park and spoke to him for the first time. What was happening about the sale of the *Australian Financial Review* and *Times on Sunday* to Bell? 'Don't worry, you will all be going there in about 10 days,' said Marty. Lawson rang John Reynolds at Bell to check this. Reynolds said there were six major problems with the Bell-Tryart-Fairfax contract, including problems with the sale of the Australian Associated Press and Australian Newsprint Mills shares. It was all totally unsatisfactory, totally one-sided, he said. The deadline was 3 February. On that day the journalists met to protest about the lack of information and direction about the Bell deal. Later that day both companies announced that the deal was off (see Chapter 13). The *Times on Sunday* had a month to live. The

*Australian Financial Review*'s future ownership remained uncertain for some weeks until the Fairfax board committed itself to retaining the paper.

The company badly needed a leader. Peter King had finally committed himself to the job but was not due to start until the beginning of March. Chris Anderson had returned from overseas on 1 February, two weeks after Alexander had returned from Sri Lanka. They were both shaken by the loss of morale among the staff while they had been away, particularly following the conflicts with Dougherty about the banking and share payments stories. There was also a major dispute between the journalists and the newspaper companies about termination payments for employees being retrenched. Final negotiations about the sale of Fairfax Magazines and the *Canberra Times* to Kerry Packer's Consolidated Press had taken place in the offices of Allen, Allen and Hemsley, Packer's lawyers, in a long session on 8 January. Consolidated Press bought most of the magazine titles, but Fairfax kept the physical assets, including the buildings, and responsibility for retrenching or employing the staff Consolidated Press did not want. In Brisbane at the same time Queensland Press had decided to close its losing afternoon newspaper, the *Telegraph*, and terminate the services of staff no longer required.

It was obvious that the futures of the *Times on Sunday* and the *Sun* in Sydney were in doubt. The AJA was determined to extract from the companies a formula for termination payments, which would become a standard for any further jobs lost through newspaper closures or mergers. At the end of the first week in February no agreement on this formula had been reached and the dispute threatened to develop into a strike. The Fairfax company had faced up to some long and bitter strikes in the past but it could not afford to now. With a $2.6 billion debt around its neck, the loss of revenue from a strike was the last thing needed by the company and its bankers. The journalists, too, were nervous about the company's financial future and were perhaps more reluctant to go to the barriers than they had been in the past. But they initially had been told no jobs would be lost and, since few seemed safe any more, were determined to gain a deal that would soften the blow for those who would be retrenched in the future, an attitude no different from that of executives who welcomed, and in some cases sanctioned, the payment of big golden handshakes since precedents were created for when their turn came.

Dougherty had been in and out of these negotiations but, in the second week of February, it seemed that the dispute could erupt into a large scale confrontation at any time. It was over-shadowed by more dramatic events. On Tuesday 9 February, Anderson went to Dougherty's office on the 14th floor and resigned. The news spread quickly through the building. On Wednesday, at 11 a.m., John Alexander was called to Dougherty's office, told of Anderson's departure, and that Andrew Clark had been appointed editor-in-chief of the *Sydney Morning Herald*. Alexander returned to his morning news conference and delivered the news: he, too, had resigned. Eight more resignations quickly followed, including those of the news editor, chief-of-staff, finance editor, investment editor and other senior journalists. More were expected. A mass meeting of Fairfax journalists that afternoon 'expressed its profound lack of confidence in the senior management of John Fairfax and Sons, specifically in Martin Dougherty, and its concern about the continuing erosion of editorial independence of its papers'. The meeting also affirmed that the positions of editor-in-chief and editor 'should be filled only by candidates who have the confidence of the journalistic staff'. Andrew Clark made a placatory speech to the meeting. He was convinced he could handle this situation given a bit of time. The journalists went out on strike until Saturday. Anderson, Alexander and others who had resigned and were not members of the AJA, stayed to bring out the strike-bound editions with Andrew Clark.

Anderson was due to leave the company on Saturday 12 February, when the journalists were due to return to work. Prospects for a smooth resumption of work were not good. The industrial troubles were being fully reported in the *Sydney Morning Herald* and were getting large plays in the Murdoch papers. Events were sapping morale and could soon affect the confidence of readers and advertisers. The bankers were shaken. They would be heavily committed to Fairfax much longer than they thought in 1987. They needed the reassurance of sound, continuous management. It seemed their best hope was Peter King, the chief executive who had yet to take his post at Jones Street.

King had taken his time about finally committing himself to Fairfax. He had committed himself to Australia some years previously by taking Australian citizenship. King was born in South Africa and grew up in Rhodesia. He joined the Anglo-American Corporation there as a management trainee and worked at mine sites and then at head office in Johannesburg for about 14 years, mainly in the purchasing and personnel departments. Then he joined the Van Leer packaging group in South Africa. Royal Packaging Industries Van Leer BV, the Dutch holding company for the worldwide packaging group, was owned by the Van Leer Group Foundation. The Foundation used its funds to support the Bernard Van Leer Foundation which, as the Van Leer 1987 annual report said, carried out 'projects for the benefit of socially and culturally disadvantaged children, primarily those living in the countries where a Van Leer company is established'. King became managing director of Van Leer in Australia from 1982 to 1985. He took Australian citizenship and his daughters stayed in Australia when he went to Holland as one of the four executive directors of Van Leer Packaging Worldwide.

Like many European companies Van Leer had two tiers of directors — a Supervisory Board looking after the interests of the shareholders (in this case shareholder) and an Executive Board which ran the company. King had special responsibility for personnel, strategic planning and quality and geographical responsibility for operations in Asia, Australasia and the European food packaging division. He had met John B. Fairfax at a Harvard Advanced Management course at Mt Pelerin, Vevey, Switzerland in 1979 and they saw each other socially a few times in 1982–85. His job at Van Leer in Holland had him always on the move around the world and, at 52, he had decided that, if and when the opportunity came, he would settle for good in Australia. One daughter had already married there.

King was in Australia on Van Leer business in August 1987. He had never met Warwick Fairfax but they had a connection through the Christian Fellowship network. King had the calmness and confidence of a man of deep though unobtrusive faith. Warwick heard through the network that he could be available for the job Warwick wanted to fill — someone to run John Fairfax Ltd for him, Christian and untainted by Australian ways.

Warwick's executive choices were hardly orthodox: he had made Connell deputy chairman despite warnings that Rothwells would be a millstone around his neck and could threaten Fairfax's all-important standing with the banks; he had made Dougherty managing director, editorial, although Dougherty had limited executive experience in large organisations and was mainly interested in doing deals rather than in the long, hard slog of administrative control; Ron Cotton's appointment as managing director, administration, had something to do with the Christian connection and discounted the fact that the company had let Cotton go in the past; now, without knowing King, he was about to offer him the top job. King had no experience of financial management, which would be Fairfax's top priority in the coming years. He knew nothing about newspaper publishing. But he had other important qualities: he had worked his way up in a big organisation to one of the top jobs; he was very good at handling people, which he regarded as one of the main functions of a manager; and he gave the impression of steadfastness. Wherever these qualities ranked with Warwick when he decided King was the man in August 1987, they had become absolutely vital to the survival of the company six months later.

According to Warwick, he first met King in Sydney on 7 August 1987 and asked him if he would be chief executive officer of John Fairfax Ltd if Warwick made a bid. Warwick said he did not think the existing executives would stay. Six days later King met Dougherty and Cotton briefly in Carnegie Fieldhouse's office before returning to Holland. In the third week in October, when it appeared that the takeover would go ahead and succeed before the stockmarket crash, Warwick flew to Holland and spent some days with King talking about their possible roles in the company's future. King was hooked but not yet landed. He had to go to Asia on Van Leer business and Warwick suggested that they meet Marty Dougherty in Singapore. They would be the three most important people in Fairfax's immediate future. King and Dougherty could get a measure of each other there. Warwick went briefly to London and picked up King at Amsterdam for the flight to Singapore. Marty Dougherty flew in from Sydney.

From the outset Marty made it clear that, as editorial director of Fairfax, he would be responsible to the proprietor, Warwick Fairfax, and nobody else. He said he had no intention of answering to a former packaging executive with no experience of newspapers. They looked at compromises, at them being joint managing directors or King being chief executive officer and Dougherty group managing director responsible for newspaper operations and profits as well as editorial performance. That ignored the titular claims of a status-conscious Ron Cotton but it was more or less the understanding Dougherty had when he flew back to Sydney the next day.

Warwick faced the fundamental problem that dogged the company after Angus McLachlan's retirement in 1969: how to have a clean, direct, management structure leading to one chief executive when the chief executive was not a journalist and could not command the editors. The Fairfax board had tried with Sir Warwick Fairfax as chairman and executive committee of one. Sir Warwick was a journalist but not a manager. Falkingham was a manager but not a journalist. After 1980 they had, substantially at Falkingham's suggestion, settled on the Gardiner-Suich formula with Gardiner the chief executive but Suich answering to the board on editorial matters. It worked because they accommodated and supported each other. If the King-Dougherty arrangement was to work, Warwick would have to be a strong last-man-down and King and Dougherty would have to respect each other's territories. They were looking at a jerry-built version of the 1980 solution, the James Fairfax-Gardiner-Suich arrangement, which had so disturbed Warwick and his mother that they had overthrown it at a cost of $2 billion.

The top management structure was not fixed until King came to Australia on the weekend of 5–6 December. Tryart moved in on Monday, 7 December. King, Dougherty, Cotton and Warwick Fairfax met during the weekend to talk about the future direction of the company. It was on this weekend that King decided to join the company. Warwick would be chairman, King chief executive officer, Dougherty managing director, editorial, and Cotton managing director, operations. This suited Marty who did not look forward to carrying the responsibility for profits. He remained nominally independent of King on editorial matters. And the arrangement satisfied Cotton's territorial ambitions. He would get Gardiner's old office and Gardiner's status in the company.

King left Sydney on 6 December and returned briefly in the second week in January. He went in to the Jones Street building for the first time. It was obvious to him that changes would have to be made. The company was already adrift and the seas were rising. He was due to start at the beginning of March and early in February went to South Africa for a much-postponed visit to his mother. Soon after he arrived in the middle of the second week in February he rang Dougherty in Sydney to check on what was happening at Fairfax. He was in touch fairly constantly by telephone with Cotton and Dougherty. Marty said things were fine, some of the natives were a bit restless about changes being made but that was to be expected and they would get over it. On the fifth floor the journalists had just passed a vote of no-confidence in Marty; they had resolved to go on strike for three days, and key editorial executives were resigning. Peter Gaunt, publisher and marketing director of the Sydney newspapers, had also told Cotton that the Dougherty brothers' management style was making his position untenable, that he had another job offer and was thinking of leaving.

Cotton rang Warwick in Washington and King in South Africa and told them things were becoming increasingly desperate in Sydney. Warwick talked to King. They agreed that they should get back to Sydney as quickly as possible and that King should move in as chief executive immediately. They both arrived in Sydney on the morning of Sunday, 14 February, and spent the afternoon being briefed by Cotton, who then left them to make their decisions. King and Warwick Fairfax saw Marty Dougherty in the new chief executive's big room at the corner of the 14th floor of the Jones Street building early in the afternoon of the following day, Monday 15 February.

In the fee court case later in the year, Marty's counsel George Palmer, QC, described the meeting:

Mr Fairfax, without prior introduction or preamble in this regard, said that he had some criticisms of Mr Dougherty in his performance as group managing director, editorial, of the paper. He listed some of them. Mr Dougherty, as one can imagine, was completely stunned by this unexpected discussion. The most significant of the criticisms which he can recollect directed at him by Mr Fairfax were these: Mr Fairfax objected to Mr Dougherty having appointed Ita Buttrose as editor-in-chief of the *Sun-Herald*; Mr Fairfax objected to Mr Dougherty having appointed Andrew Clark as editor-in-chief of the *Sydney Morning Herald*; Mr Fairfax objected to Mr Dougherty having appointed his brother in an executive role in the group. There may have been others but they certainly were not significant criticisms. Certainly none so significant that Mr Dougherty can remember what they may have been, but of course none of these objections to the appointments had previously been made by Mr Fairfax to Mr Dougherty at the time that they were proposed. He then said to Mr Dougherty that from then on he would have to report to Peter King in relation to editorial appointments.

That cut across the line of reporting directly to Warwick, which Marty had been so blunt about establishing at the outset in Singapore. Nothing, to Marty's mind, could be more calculated to precipitate his resignation. He said, 'You know I won't do that, so you expect me to resign.' Warwick Fairfax said, 'Yes.' As Palmer, QC, described it, Ron Cotton 'was not present when the death blow was struck but he was deputed by Mr Fairfax and by Mr King to wipe the blood off the floor'. Cotton was called in, told by King that Marty would be leaving that day, and asked to draw a cheque for his severance pay. Marty asked if he could stay until Friday, and retired to his office. Cotton came to see him shortly afterwards to tell him permission had been refused; he should leave that day. The severance payment was agreed: $3 million for the services he had given Warwick Fairfax in connection with the takeover over the past year (Marty wanted $5 million but could get no advance on $3 million); and two and a half years' salary and other entitlements that had also been agreed in Marty's conditions of employment. Marty had been due to take delivery of a new company Mercedes Benz that day. He would have to pay for that.

Marty received two letters from Warwick that day — one with Tryart letterhead recording the $3 million payment, the other with Fairfax letterhead recording the salary termination payment. The $3 million was paid to Marty's private company, Tabulum Holdings Pty Ltd, the salary to Marty himself. Marty had grown up near Tabulam, a small country town in northern NSW. He had formed his company when he was living in Melbourne, and named it for Tabulam but mis-spelled it Tabulum. He had formed Dougherty Communications Pty Ltd, when he set up his public relations business in the early 1980s, sold it to Ogilvy and Mather, the US advertising company early in 1984, then bought it back early in 1987. He sold the business again in 1987 before he joined John Fairfax Ltd. Marty and his brother Paul left late that afternoon on 15 February.

King asked the editors to meet him in the 14th floor conference room at 5 p.m. Some asked whether this was just a social occasion, thinking they would skip it, if it was. King's secretary said, 'I think you'd better come.' Buttrose (*Sun-Herald*), Kohler (*Financial Review*), Lawson (*Times on Sunday*), Andrew Clark (*Sydney Morning Herald*), John Richardson (editorial manager), Ron Cotton and Peter King sat at the round conference table. John Benaud, editor of the *Sun*, had left after the last edition and was unavailable. King told them cheerfully that Marty Dougherty had decided to leave the company — immediately. It was the first time they had met King. He radiated stability, confidence and good cheer. The meeting lasted half an hour as King consulted the editors about how this should be announced and let them know he would be accessible to them all. Afterwards, those who did not have a paper to produce, went down to Richardson's office for a couple of stiff drinks. Kohler went back to the *Financial Review*, and Clark, half punch drunk from the events of the past few days, back to the *Sydney Morning Herald* to oversee a story that made him the editor-in-chief with the shortest tenure in history. King had said at the meeting that discussions were to be opened with Chris Anderson and John Alexander for their return. Valerie Lawson went to break the news to Deborah Light, finance editor of the *Sydney Morning Herald*. Light turned to her reporters, 'Boys,' she said, 'Go and get the beer.'

It was King's first day in the office. He called Chris Anderson at home and asked him to come in and see him and Warwick Fairfax the next morning. He asked Anderson to come back as editorial chief of Fairfax with a place on the board. For Anderson this meant breaking his agreement with Cowley at News Ltd. The Fairfax job was risky considering the company's financial condition. At Fairfax he would be on top, at News he could still get lost in the ruck of executives competing for Cowley's job. He told King he could not return and accept Dougherty's appointments. He could not become a director of the company while Laurie Connell was on the board. And he was worried about the company's debt. The first was no problem. He could decide which, if any, of Marty's appointments would continue and he would appoint all future editors. On the second, King said not to worry, Connell would be going, though that would take a little time. On the third, well, he could make his own mind up about the risks involved in the debt. They were going to rethink their strategy about what debt to carry and what assets to keep and Anderson as a director would play a major part in that.

Anderson rejoined as group editorial director (when Cotton left nine months later he also became managing director) on the board of John Fairfax Ltd and immediately pushed King to close the *Sun* and the *Times on Sunday*. He announced the closure of both papers to angry meetings of journalists on the morning of Monday 14 March. The *Times on Sunday* had published its last issue the previous day. The *Sun*'s issue for Monday was abandoned. The *Daily Mirror*'s circulation jumped by over 100 000. John Fairfax Ltd, under Warwick Fairfax, was proving as pragmatic as Murdoch and Cowley at News Ltd had anticipated (see Chapter 13). All the other resignations were withdrawn with some relief as not all of those who were going were comfortable with the idea of putting a new career on the line at News Ltd. John Alexander was made editor-in-chief of the *Sydney Morning*

*Herald* and Andrew Clark withdrew to consider his position. He became London manager of John Fairfax Ltd. Pat Boyce, Marty's editor-elect of the *Age*, was told his retainer was finished. Ita Buttrose, editor-in-chief of the *Sun-Herald*, was dismissed by Anderson a few weeks later.

On 16 February the journalists accepted a revised company offer on retrenchment payments, including an *ex gratia* payment of $4000 to each employee, plus other entitlements. That night Marty Dougherty issued a statement on his resignation after three months with the company:

> Regarding my resignation as group managing director, editorial, of John Fairfax Ltd, I believed it was time for me to go back to a business environment outside newspapers.
>
> I did something historical in helping Warwick Fairfax and Laurie Connell plan and execute the takeover of John Fairfax Ltd. It was the biggest takeover in Australia's history.
>
> Many experts, including some in the media, said we could not do it. But we did it, as a team. It was enormously exciting and the most personally rewarding event in my business life.
>
> Warwick and I remain close. I believe in him and his vision and his management team. I expect to help him as an adviser in many ways — including takeovers — over the next decade.
>
> He will be a great publisher of newspapers and a great proprietor. He has my absolute support — and I believe I have his. He will solve the current difficulties and any others that crop up.

Marty became less cordial after Warwick and Peter King decided not to pay the $100 million fee to Rothwells, and Marty and Warwick ended up on opposite sides in court.

The journalists welcomed another piece of news that week. When Anderson's appointment to the board was announced, Ron Cotton told them that Fairfax would not be selling any assets to the British media baron Robert Maxwell, who had made a $1 billion bid for the *Age* and other assets. That third week in February 1988, was a major turning point for the company. Not only was the crisis with the journalists over, a new approach to the refinancing of the takeover debt, which had grown out of the ANZ Bank's original commitment of $1.3 billion, had begun. The company would keep what it regarded as its core assets, including the *Age*, the *Australian Financial Review* and the BRW business magazine group, and live with a much bigger debt. It was risky, but if it worked Fairfax would continue as a substantial national publishing company. The alternative could mean financial anorexia, starving the company of assets to reduce debt, in an exercise unrelated to the company's long-term well-being.

# CHAPTER 13

# THE DEALS, KEATING AND FAIRFAX

Federal Treasurer Paul Keating was never far from all the dramatic events that changed the face of media ownership in Australia from 1986 onwards. He orchestrated the new media policy, which precipitated the subsequent takeovers and deregulated the foreign exchanges and the banking system that financed them. Soon afterwards he had to face the paradox of the political economy of the free markets that were advocated so strongly by the economic dries in the 1980s: free markets soon create situations that demand political intervention to limit the damage. Keating, Hawke and their Government's agencies soon found themselves intervening in the consequences of the takeovers they had helped to create. In 1988 Keating had to move quickly to limit the inadvertent damage he could have caused the company with the tax amendments foreshadowed in his 25 May Economic Statement that year. And, in the 1990s, the success or failure of his economic policies could make or break the financial strategy to which the company was committed.

When it was assumed that the David Syme share issue, which was to have raised $275 million to help repay the ANZ Bank, would be cancelled, on 21 October 1987, Marty Dougherty was despatched to replace the funds with the sale of Fairfax's 44.5 per cent interest in Australian Newsprint Mills (ANM), 38.3 per cent of Australian Associated Press (AAP) and 37.6 per cent interest in AAP Information Service (AAPIS). AAP's only, but very significant asset, was its 7.7 per cent interest in Reuters. Dougherty went straight to his friend Ken Cowley, managing director of News Ltd.

Murdoch and Cowley wanted to see Warwick Fairfax succeed in his takeover. They thought that a Warwick-owned Fairfax company would be more pragmatic than the one James Fairfax and Greg Gardiner had run; that is, it would be a company driven by reasonable business interests, a competitor, but a reasonable competitor, instead of the rogue publisher Fairfax had appeared during the last 10 years.

So when Dougherty contacted Cowley he had an immediately sympathetic reception. Cowley agreed to take assets from Fairfax to make up the $275 million. The ANM and AAP shares were the obvious assets but they would not do much for News Corporation's cash flows. In New York, Murdoch was prepared to help Warwick but was not too impressed with the idea of spending $275 million for assets paying meagre dividends in which he already had significant strategic stakes. Dougherty agreed to include the *St George Leader* in the $275 million to sweeten the deal. News Ltd was to pay $120 million for the AAP and AAPIS shares, $150 million for the ANM shares and $5 million for the *Leader*, which could be very profitable, contribute a useful cash flow and fill a strategic gap in Murdoch's suburban newspaper perimeter around the city of Sydney. Even so, the cost of holding those big additional equities in ANM and AAP suggested that Murdoch had in mind selling them on again if and when he found the right buyers. In the meantime he would be paying $275 million to Fairfax, or Tryart, on the proposed settlement date around 21 December, thus helping it to meet its cash forecasts.

The Trade Practices Commission (TPC) upset the timing of that arrangement on 18 December when it requested News to suspend its ANM and AAP purchases, a request supported by an injunction granted by the Federal Court three days later. The TPC had been alerted to the proposed sale when it was reported in the *Sydney Morning Herald* on 23 November. The $275 million Tryart had first expected from the Syme float and then from News Corporation, was disappearing again. The TPC, and later, the Foreign Investment Review Board (FIRB), did Tryart a favour. It eventually received about $290 million for the ANM and AAP assets, and kept AAPIS and the *St George Leader*.

That was after the new merchant bank, Whitlam Turnbull and Co. Ltd, got into the act. The bank had been formed the previous year to combine the talents and connections of Malcolm Turnbull, the aggressive young lawyer who had recently beaten the UK Government in the Spycatcher case; Nick Whitlam, an aggressive young banker who had worked at Morgan Stanley before becoming chief executive of the State Bank of NSW; and Neville Wran, lawyer and former Premier of NSW; with the money of Kerry Packer and Larry Adler (who had made his FAI insurance group one of the most successful stockmarket operators of the decade). Packer and Adler put up $25 million each. Wran was to be chairman. But Adler had other ideas. He was actively involved in all his interests and thought he or Packer should be chairman. Packer was more relaxed. Turnbull had worked for him as journalist and counsel, he knew Wran very well, and it was not his style to insist on status or position in all the companies in which he invested. There was another problem. The two big shareholders were active in the stockmarket, particularly Adler, who took speculative positions in many companies. Whitlam Turnbull would be seen as their associates and tend to be excluded as advisers to companies sceptical of the imaginary walls within merchant banks that were said to avoid conflicts of interest. This was a potential problem when Whitlam Turnbull went to Fairfax. How could a Packer-owned company be seen to be advising Fairfax on financing and asset disposals in which Packer was, or could be, financially or strategically interested? Packer had bought Adler out of Whitlam Turnbull for $25 million in October 1987, three months after the company started. Packer then had $50 million invested in Whitlam Turnbull but most of it was apparently lent back to Consolidated Press at no interest. The market was made aware that Packer would be reducing his investment when a more suitable shareholder could be found, as one was by April 1988. Packer withdrew from the company in June. But when Turnbull first made contact with the Fairfax company early in January, Packer dominated Whitlam Turnbull's ownership.

The merchant bank's offices were in the Consolidated Press building. Turnbull, acting for Packer, had, with Aleco Vrisakis, drafted the Tryart-Packer asset sale agreement at the end of September. Nevertheless, as Whitlam and Turnbull became involved with Fairfax, they were able to reassure the Fairfax executives that the company was distancing itself from Packer and would soon break with him altogether.

By the time Turnbull arrived at Fairfax on 6 January the Packer sale agreement was in the final stages of renegotiation. Whitlam Turnbull took no part in that settlement but were heavily involved in most of the other asset sale negotiations and renegotiations. They had been looking for a way into the Fairfax action ever since Warwick and his team moved in on 7 December. Wran had suggested to Dougherty in mid-December that Fairfax might be able to use the bank's services in its post-takeover financing. Turnbull had left a similar thought with Dougherty just before Marty went to Hawaii. Turnbull was holidaying at Palm Beach when Dougherty phoned to suggest he come into the Fairfax offices on 6 January.

When Turnbull arrived the Fairfax executives were recovering from their first full confrontation with the ANZ Bank over the perilous state of their finances. Turnbull waited in the reception area. Warwick Fairfax walked by. They knew each other and went to talk in Warwick's office. Turnbull quickly realised his company's great opportunity to become involved in one of the biggest corporate restructurings in Australia's history. Dougherty introduced him to Cotton who told him the First National merchant bank had to be paid $13 million by 11 a.m. the next day. Fairfax did not have the money. Its lines with its merchant banks had been frozen. Turnbull turned up the next morning with a cheque for $13 million. Whitlam Turnbull then organised the $500 million from Citibank to repay Westpac, the National Australia Bank and the threatening merchant banks (see Chapter 14). On 1 February they were mandated to go into all the takeover's problem areas: the retirement funds, asset sales, the Skase, Holmes a Court and News Ltd contracts and valuation of the company's mastheads.

There was a delicate game of dominoes to be played in the Holmes a Court and News Ltd deals, involving ANM, AAP and AAPIS shares. The TPC had frozen the sale of those shares to News Ltd but later lifted its freeze on AAP and AAPIS. The FIRB, however (under Paul Keating), which was involved because Murdoch was a foreign citizen, would not allow the AAPIS sale to go through, since a foreigner would have virtually total control of Australia's internal news service. The AAP sale was allowed since the assets involved were shares in Reuters, a foreign company.

The ANM shares were a different matter. Fairfax had 50 per cent. If they were to be sold to someone other than Murdoch it would help if Holmes a Court's ANM shares went to Murdoch to build his holding up to 50 per cent too. That had to take place in two steps. Holmes a Court was a shareholder in the ANM, AAP and AAPIS companies through his purchase of WA Newspapers from Murdoch a year previously. He had talked Connell into selling him some more out of the Fairfax holding in September 1987 to go with the other assets he was buying. But he had not squared that purchase away with Murdoch who, as the other shareholder in the three companies, had pre-emptive rights over any shares for sale.

Whitlam Turnbull was concerned that Holmes a Court might want to go to litigation about that, string out the talks that had been going on about the implementation of his contract to buy the *Financial Review* and other assets and, knowing Fairfax's urgent need for funds, finally offer to settle on a much reduced price. This was an accurate reading of Holmes a Court's past form but may have over-estimated his financial capacity in January 1988 when he was liquidating the main assets of his public companies to reduce their debt and keep them and his vast private fortune afloat.

On 19 January three Fairfax executives and a Blake Dawson lawyer went to Perth to negotiate the operating agreements under which Fairfax would print the *Financial Review* and *Times on Sunday* for Holmes a Court's Bell Group. Late on 20 January the talks broke down on the issue of what equipment Fairfax was actually selling to Bell under the 29 September agreement. Holmes a Court still clung to a plan to sell half the *Financial Review* to the Pearson group for around $130 million. Bell took action in the Western Australian Supreme Court on 21 January, seeking to clarify the Fairfax agreement.

The Fairfax people were about to leave Perth when they had a call from Connell's secretary suggesting that they meet the Bell executive John Reynolds, without lawyers, to put together a timetable for settlement. The Fairfax team returned to Perth on 27 January for more talks with Bell. The two sides seemed to be coming together on most points when, after noon on 29 January, the Dawson Waldron lawyer with the Fairfax team had a call from David Frecker of Dawson Waldron in Sydney telling them to break off the talks. At Fairfax headquarters in Jones Street, Sydney, it had been decided to stop the filibuster and call Holmes a Court's bluff. On 26 January Tryart gave Bell group notice to complete the contract to buy the Fairfax assets in seven days.

There were different versions of how this came about. Ron Cotton, in his evidence statement, said that on about 27 January he accepted Blake Dawson Waldron's recommendation that a notice to complete should be served on Bell. In his view the Bell matter had to be brought to a head so they would know whether to start looking for alternate buyers for the assets involved. The next day Turnbull, Dougherty and Cotton discussed the matter. Cotton later reported that Dougherty had said Connell had suggested a course of action to settle the matter with Holmes a Court and that Turnbull had said the Connell approach was worth trying.

In the next day or so Frecker told Cotton that T. E. F. Hughes, QC, had advised that Tryart-Fairfax should appear to be ready to settle with Holmes a Court on the due date, 3 February, thus forcing the choice of whether to proceed or abandon the deal. On 1 February Holmes a Court disputed Tryart's 26 January notice to settle. The next day, 2 February, the deal was called off by mutual consent to a rescission *ab initio* of the agreement made on 29 September.

On one version these initiatives came from Connell. Vrisakis, then in New Zealand, had spoken with Holmes a Court about the legal rescission. In Whitlam Turnbull's progress report to Ron Cotton on 15 February, however, Connell and Vrisakis were not mentioned. They did say advice had been sought from T. E. F. Hughes, QC, and 'your solicitors' (Blake Dawson) and that 'the termination of the contract constitutes a major success in our efforts on your behalf'. Warwick Fairfax announced the retention of the *Financial Review* on 3 February. So did Whitlam Turnbull.

Pearson group continued to look at the possibility of taking an equity in the *Financial Review*, but the price was high and Fairfax was no longer willing to sell.

Having retained the shares it was to have sold to Bell, Fairfax then had 50 per cent of ANM and 44.6 per cent of AAP. Cancellation of the Bell agreement enabled Whitlam Turnbull to go ahead with the domino game. An alternate buyer for Fairfax's ANM shares was found, with News Ltd's agreement, in Fletcher Challenge, the big New Zealand based newsprint producer, at a price substantially higher than that News Ltd was to have paid. Turnbull also organised a 10-year newsprint supply contract based on the New York posted price, which looked good for Fairfax so long as the Australian dollar was worth around 74 US cents or more and the US newsprint prices remained stable or fell.

Those factors worked for Fairfax in 1988–89, but not as well as they would have if the contract had been based on the New York discount price, the spot market price that fell rapidly as capacity exceeded demand in America. But they were an additional risk for Fairfax. Since he had given up, temporarily at least, ideas of a publishing empire, Holmes a Court was prepared to sell his ANM and AAP shares too. So Fletcher Challenge bought the Fairfax shares in ANM and Murdoch bought the Fairfax and Bell shares in AAP and the Bell shares in ANM. The TPC and the FIRB approved both deals, but Keating and the FIRB would not approve the sale of AAPIS to Murdoch. This gave Fairfax $290 million ($222.5 million for the ANM shares, $67.5 million for the AAP) plus retention of the AAPIS shares and the *St George Leader*, instead of the $275 million Murdoch was to have paid for the lot. And Holmes a Court received $63.9 million for assets valued at $6.4 million when he had bought them from Murdoch a year previously.

Murdoch's AAP purchase ran him foul of Reuters' Articles of Association since he was not allowed to own more than 20 per cent of the voting shares in that company. Reuters itself eventually bought the AAP shares from him in May, an outcome he may have had in mind in the first place. The renegotiation of the News Ltd contracts, however, meant that, instead of receiving $275 million from News at the end of December, Fairfax received

$222.5 million from Fletcher Challenge early in April and $67.5 million plus $1.3 million interest from Reuters for the AAP shares in May.

There were domino elements in the asset sales to John B. Fairfax and Kerry Packer too, since the assets of one involved printing arrangements with the other. Packer had let Connell know early in December that he was not happy with what he was paying for the *Canberra Times*, that the figures he had been given, on which he based the purchase price, did not represent the trading position of that newspaper in September 1987. The *Canberra Times*'s profits in 1987–88 were, in fact, running well below the previous year's profits due to competition for property advertisements from a new, free newspaper run by the real estate agents. Connell thought the Packer contract was watertight.

In what was to become a Greek chorus for the renegotiation of the asset sales early in 1988, Dougherty told Ron Cotton, 'Leave it to Laurie, Laurie will sort it out.' Cotton took a team from Fairfax to meet Consolidated Press executives on 15 December to discuss the contract. At the end of two hours of what seemed reasonable discussion, Don Bourke, finance director of Consolidated Press, dropped a hand grenade on Cotton. He (Cotton) realised, Bourke said, that the $250 million Consolidated Press had agreed to pay for the Fairfax assets would be reduced by $15 million because of the agreement. Agreement? What agreement? Cotton knew nothing of Packer's letter of September offering to pay Connell $350 million for the *Australian Financial Review* for Connell to use in negotiations with Holmes a Court.

Bourke and Trevor Kennedy, managing director of Consolidated Press, took Cotton outside to enlighten him. Then they went to see Kerry Packer. Cotton said he would have to refer to Connell about the said $15 million. Packer said, 'Yes, do that, by all means. And whilst you are at it, tell him that I am not paying the price for the *Canberra Times* for the profit figures I was given do not stand up and I am just not going to pay that. Ron, if you're interested in a proposition to resolve the position then give me the *BRW* group and we will call it square.'

Gottliebsen's fears about Packer's designs on *BRW* were fully justified. Cotton said the *BRW* group was not for sale, although

Whitlam Turnbull later included it in one of the alternate combinations being offered to Murdoch early in February. Murdoch agreed to buy *BRW*, but none of the other business magazines, and the Syme half of the *Sunday Press*, the small Melbourne Sunday paper in which he owned the other half through the Herald & Weekly Times (HWT). But *BRW* was not for sale and that proposal fell through.

Just before his 15 December visit to Consolidated Press, Cotton had a call from Peter Chegwyn, finance director of News Ltd, asking for the latest accounts of Federal Capital Press, holding company for the *Canberra Times*, 'because Packer and Murdoch have been holding discussions about Packer on-selling it to Murdoch and the only question at present is one of price'. Cotton checked with Don Bourke who confirmed Packer's interest in selling. Cotton sent the accounts to Chegwyn.

On 12 November, Ken Cowley, managing director of News Ltd, had sounded out the TPC on a couple of propositions. What would the TPC's reactions be if News Ltd proposed to buy (1) the *Australian Financial Review*, (2) the *Canberra Times?* Cowley's approach was a political exploration. Certainly the *Canberra Times* sat oddly with Packer's other publishing interests and might be bought if the price was right, and Holmes a Court's finances suggested he would not go through with the *Financial Review* purchase, which could put it back on to the market. But neither possibility would be worth pursuing if the TPC said no.

The TPC had allowed News Ltd's takeover of the HWT to go through with comparatively little interference after receiving certain undertakings from News Ltd. But there had been widespread criticism of its decision. Leaders of the Labor and Liberal Parties had supported the decision, but the rank and file, particularly of the Labor Party, had been highly critical of a decision that put about 60 per cent of Australia's newspaper circulations into Murdoch's hands. There was pressure for a public inquiry into the ownership of Australian media. Murdoch was highly sensitive about these matters.

If News Ltd wanted to buy more newspapers in Australia to fill the gaps in its extensive portfolio, it had to clear two hurdles: the TPC and public and political opinion. The TPC was first. Cowley was turned back on both propositions. The TPC said that purchase of the *Australian Financial Review* was not on. Nor was purchase of the *Canberra Times* but the TPC could be prepared to listen to further argument about the *Canberra Times.* In a letter to Cowley on 19 November the TPC chairman W. R. McComas, said any newspaper acquisition by News Ltd would now be looked at very carefully before the Commission could be satisfied that it should not intervene. News Ltd had also asked about acquiring the *West Australian.*

But those strictures would not stop Packer and Murdoch exploring the possibility of a future deal on the *Canberra Times* and exchanging information on it. Packer would also be interested in the price Murdoch would put on it. He could be a seller at any time if the price and any other conditions were right, as he was in June 1989 when he sold the paper to Kerry Stokes of Perth. But in December 1987 he was very angry about the *Canberra Times*'s profits being well below those on which his purchase had been based and intended to use this to lever the purchase price down. Cotton said Connell's advice was: 'We will let Packer sit for a week or so and sweat'. Packer relaxed at his Palm Beach house. He was due to go overseas on 11 January.

At the end of the first week in January all the sweating was being done by Fairfax and ANZ Bank executives about when the money from the asset sales would start to arrive. On 7 January, in a conference telephone call between Dougherty and Cotton in Sydney and Peter King in Holland, Dougherty was authorised to deal with Packer before he went overseas. Connell ('Leave Kerry and Robert to me') could not be in Sydney before 11 January. He said he had a meeting scheduled for that day with Robert Holmes a Court in Perth to talk about Fairfax buying the Australian Newsprint Mills (ANM) shares Holmes a Court had acquired from Murdoch a year previously. Marty Dougherty wasted no time. On 8 January he reported that the contract with Packer had, with a few adjustments, been settled for about $215 million instead of $250 million. Fairfax would keep the Fairfax Magazines Pty Ltd property at Joynton Avenue, Sydney, and three small consumer magazines Packer did not want: *Smash Hits, Countdown* and *Portfolio.* Fairfax would also keep *Australian Property News,* which had never been part of the consumer magazine group. 'Kerry also wanted the *Spectator,* but he is not getting it,' Dougherty said.

The details were settled at a long meeting the following weekend in the offices of Allen, Allen and Hemsley, Packer's lawyers. In effect, Packer bought Federal Capital Press Pty Ltd (the *Canberra Times*) and Fairfax Magazines Pty Ltd. But he acquired only the titles and the staff he wanted with Fairfax Magazines and left the assets and staff he didn't want with Fairfax. Packer had knocked about $30 million net off the original purchase price and left Fairfax with the cost of retrenching or redeploying the unwanted staff.

At Consolidated Press headquarters in Park Street, Fairfax Magazines became very profitable. Consolidated Press's cheque for $211.6 million came through the day after the agreement was reached. By the end of that week ending 16 January the two main elements of the assets sold to John B. Fairfax were settled and paid for: $20 million for Fairfax's 48.15 per cent interest in *Rural Press* and $28.5 million for the 49.76 per cent interest in Stereo FM Brisbane Ltd.

A couple of weeks later the sale of Fairfax's one-third interest in the Queanbeyan *Age* was settled for $1.5 million and on 19 February final settlements of the assets sale to John B. Fairfax was made with the payment of $17 million for Fairfax's 50 per cent interest in Eastern Suburbs Newspapers Pty Ltd. The $11 million sale of the 49 per cent interest in Macquarie Publications had broken down. During Greg Gardiner's time as chief executive, Fairfax had encouraged and helped finance the expansion of the Macquarie Publications printing plant at Dubbo. The company was run and substantially owned by John Armati, who had developed it into a very successful printer of metropolitan magazines as well as publisher of the Dubbo newspaper and other publications serving central and western NSW. Expansion had involved substantial borrowing, which Fairfax had been comfortable with but which might sit less easily with the much smaller enterprises John B. Fairfax was putting together. The deal was called off. Fairfax retained the 49 per cent of Macquarie Publications, which, like Eastern Suburbs newspapers, continued to print magazines sold to Consolidated Press.

While Whitlam Turnbull was working on the Holmes a Court, News and Skase contracts, Wardleys had been mandated to look for new buyers for the Macquarie Broadcasting Network. Bob Johnson, managing director of Macquarie Broadcasting, had told Cotton late in December that his contact at the Bell group had told him that all talks about the transfer of Macquarie were off. Wardleys was one of the most entrepreneurial of the Australian merchant banks, reflecting in part the rather swashbuckling style of its parent company, the Hong Kong and Shanghai Bank.

The Bank provided the funds and Wardleys the advice for some of Alan Bond's big takeovers. At an 8.30 a.m. meeting with Cotton, Kerry Roxburgh of Wardleys had said that he was aware that a group named Sonance, headed by Sir Frank Moore, a well-known Queensland businessman, and including the Hong Kong-Sydney publisher, Sally Aw, was interested in the Macquarie Network. There were two other interested groups, neither of which made an offer that seemed capable of completion. In February, after the Bell agreement had been cancelled, Sonance offered $98 million for Macquarie — less than half the value Reuter had placed on the network six months previously. The purchase was completed early in April.

Sonance then set about selling most of Macquarie's radio stations and other assets. Mary Fairfax bought the substantial 2GB building for $15 million.

Paul Keating was in Europe at the end of January-early February 1988, attending the big annual get-together of businessmen and financiers at Davos, Switzerland, when Robert Maxwell, the UK publisher, asked to see him urgently in London. Maxwell's *Daily Mirror* was a major competitor with Murdoch's *Sun* in the UK mass market. He wanted to know what Keating's reaction would be to a Maxwell bid for the *Age* or other parts of the Fairfax group. Maxwell knew that any bid he made would be a highly political exercise. While he and his executives were talking to Keating, he had a couple of his newspaper photographers come in and take pictures of this meeting with the Australian Treasurer. Keating was not impressed. He said a bid by Maxwell, like any other, would be considered on its merits when it was made.

Maxwell was encouraged. He had sent a team to Australia to look at Fairfax's assets and acquisition possibilities after the Holmes a Court agreement was cancelled on 2 February. On 8 February Maxwell Communications put a 'basic outline of an offer to acquire certain assets' in a letter to the directors of John Fairfax Ltd, c/- Whitlam Turnbull, 60 Park Street. This was an ambit offer of $1.2 billion for nearly everything except the *Sydney Morning Herald* and the *Sun-Herald*, signed by the two leaders of the team in Australia, Richard Baker, the deputy managing director of Maxwell Communications, and Kevin Maxwell, a director and son of Robert. It was followed four days later by a new offer, addressed to Malcolm Turnbull and signed by the chairman himself 'Bob'. This was $1.1 billion for all of David Syme plus half the *Australian Financial Review* and half the investments in ANM and the AAP companies. It valued Syme at $700–$800 million.

Whitlam Turnbull, on Fairfax's instructions, countered on 3 March by offering Maxwell all of Syme, except its shares in AAP and its joint venture interests in BRW and Electronic Publishing. Maxwell replied on 8 March with an offer of $1 billion for all of Syme plus half of Fairfax's interests in ANM, AAP, and AAPIS, or $650 million for the package Fairfax offered on 3 March or $350 million for half of David Syme. They were playing gin rummy with Fairfax's assets.

Fairfax was sending out a number of signals at this time. In a statement published in the *Sydney Morning Herald* on 17 February, Ron Cotton said that John Fairfax Ltd aimed to maintain a strong NSW media base after it completed its asset sale programme. He said part of David Syme might be floated off or sold but certainly not to Robert Maxwell. Cotton said that John Fairfax and Maxwell 'did not have the same views in relation to price and approach to business'. This was a soundly based policy statement, at least a month ahead of its time. Cotton persisted in his view that no deal would or should be done with Maxwell.

Whitlam Turnbull and Peter King flew to Paris for meetings with Maxwell executives and their advisers from Bankers Trust on 21 March. The following day Robert Maxwell himself arrived with his chief editorial director, a former *Daily Mirror* editor, Mike Molloy. Games followed. It was agreed that everyone was talking about the sale and purchase of David Syme. Maxwell suggested that he write his highest price on a piece of paper and place it in an envelope and the Fairfax representatives write their lowest price on a piece of paper and place it in an envelope. If the Fairfax price was lower than the Maxwell price, then the middle price between the two would be the contract price and the deal would be done. If Fairfax was higher than Maxwell there would be no deal and everyone could go home. This sudden death solution did not appeal to Turnbull who talked prices privately with Maxwell. Maxwell's top price was $805 million, Fairfax's lowest $950 million. Fairfax might have to push more assets into Syme to get Maxwell up. Turnbull persuaded Maxwell to leave his $805 million offer on the table until 13 April. The next day in London, however, in talks that included Warwick Fairfax, Maxwell said he had other opportunities in Europe and thought three weeks was too long. The offer deadline was later shortened to 2 April. This was all becoming fairly irrelevant except that Fairfax was establishing a benchmark price that could be used with other potential buyers.

Maxwell and Fairfax, or Whitlam Turnbull on behalf of Fairfax, had been sparring with each other for nearly two months without getting close to a decision. Whitlam Turnbull had argued in February that the sale of David Syme for $800 million-plus was the most 'bankable' financial strategy for Fairfax. It would reduce the takeover debt to manageable proportions. They worked hard to get the deal done. But the hardening opinion at Fairfax, especially from Anderson, was that the company should keep its remaining newspaper assets, that the *Age*, the *Sydney Morning Herald*, the provincial newspapers and the *BRW* magazine group, made a group of quality products rare in world publishing. It should be held together and a long-term financial strategy developed based on that premise. King, the former packaging executive, was also becoming increasingly impressed by the assets now in his charge. The Fourth Estate factor was at work.

After the Paris meeting with Maxwell, King met Warwick Fairfax in London. Anderson telephoned them from Sydney. Financial logic, as well as sentiment and intuition, was swinging him around to keeping the *Age*. Any buyer of that newspaper, even Maxwell, would have to rely on its future cash flows to finance the purchase. Whether Fairfax stayed as it was or shrank further, it would still need four or five years before it could get its earnings up to service its residual debt. It would probably have a better chance of doing this with the *Age* than without it. King and Warwick Fairfax were coming to the same view.

Terry McCrann had written a seminal article in the Melbourne *Herald* on 24 March headed 'Warwick, Go or Stay, but Just Decide'. He argued that there was a yawning gap between what Fairfax had to get to justify selling and what a buyer could sensibly pay. If Warwick Fairfax sold the *Age* at a sensible price to the buyer he would be throwing away one of his two key properties without any net financial gain to Fairfax. McCrann argued that Fairfax and the ANZ Bank were in this together, and that Fairfax should remind the Bank of this. Politicians had buried the Maxwell option. McCrann described the 'almost pathetic and largely pointless activity dragging on with the *Age* ... [as a] ... very public exercise in corporate self-laceration'.

The Saturday before McCrann's article appeared Nick Greiner had led the Liberal Party back to power in NSW in a swing that had a national message for the Labor Party ominously like the national message Neville Wran's victory for Labor 12 years earlier had had for the Liberal Party. For Hawke and Keating it was not a time to make unnecessary unpopular decisions. The door, which had never opened very far, closed on Maxwell. Wran's victory in 1976 had eventually led to the destabilisation and partial dismemberment of John Fairfax Ltd. Greiner's victory helped make sure that what remained was kept intact.

Prospects of a deal with Maxwell were always clouded by politics. Keating's opinion at the outset in February had been that Maxwell's main value would be in setting a price an acceptable Australian buyer would have to think about matching. He had told Anderson that, if Fairfax was going to sell the *Age* to Maxwell, it should be done quickly to have half a chance of beating the political outcry that would follow. He asked to be kept informed.

On 18 March Anderson wrote a memorandum to King outlining his view of the politics of the Fairfax/Maxwell situation. He speculated on Keating's relations with Murdoch, on Keating's desire for a powerful media counterweight to Murdoch (Keating had been concerned about the outcome of the HWT takeover ever since it happened) and on Keating's relations with the *Sydney Morning Herald*. If the memorandum meant that Anderson was canvassing Keating's support for a Maxwell takeover of the *Age* the logic of it did not last long. Cotton had already stated Fairfax's basic policy of maintaining a strong presence in NSW. McCrann's article on 24 March helped swing Anderson to the view that the *Age* should be retained before he rang King in London. But the 18 March memo contained two boomerangs. In it Anderson suggested that, if the Maxwell offer was to be entertained 'I'd like to see another foreign player in the market to muddy the waters, like Canadian Conrad Black of the UK *Telegraph* group'. Whitlam, Turnbull, King and Warwick Fairfax met the UK *Telegraph*'s chairman, Sir Frank Rogers and senior executives in London. The *Telegraph* took three copies of Whitlam Turnbull's information memorandum on David Syme. Other London publishers — United Newspapers, Lonrho, Associated Newspapers — were also interested in the information memorandum but the *Telegraph* seemed the most interested by far. King and Fairfax flew on to North America to see Conrad Black, the main shareholder. In London the *Telegraph* set about arranging lines of finance and preparing an offer. But Fairfax had gone cold on selling the *Age*. The *Telegraph* did, however, buy the *Spectator* for $4.5 million. This was later reduced as the *Telegraph* clawed back about $500 000 for debts not revealed in the *Spectator*'s accounts warranted by Fairfax at the time of the purchase. The second boomerang was the memo itself. On the flight to Paris King gave it to Turnbull. A copy of it turned up in the documents subpoenaed from Whitlam Turnbull in the fee court case.

The Labor Party's rank and file had become restive enough over Murdoch's purchase of the HWT. The prospect of more foreign ownership of Australian newspapers could cause an outright rebellion, a Royal Commission of inquiry into media ownership and a return to the Labor Party-media trench warfare, which first Wran and then Hawke and Keating had tried to limit and then eliminate. The fact that Maxwell was a Labour Party supporter in Britain was by no means a plus for Labor in Australia. In its prime, in the 1940s and 1950s, the London *Daily Mirror* had been politically influential, partly through the strength of its journalism, partly because it reflected the spirit of the times. In the 1980s the *Daily Mirror* had been backing a loser in the British Labour Party. Murdoch's *Sun* was winning the circulation war and backing Margaret Thatcher. The Fairfax-owned *Age* had given the Australian Labor Party some carefully measured, but never ideological, support. A Maxwell-owned *Age* could cost Labor votes for letting him in. Maxwell's entry would not be popular with the Liberal Party either. Murdoch's takeover of the HWT had divided both parties. Maxwell's entry would deepen the division. Nationally, Maxwell would have few friends if he did make a bid for the *Age*. In Melbourne he would have none. Local reaction to the Maxwell prospect had been very hostile. Friends of the *Age* had tried to save the paper from the Fairfaxes in the early 1980s but they had settled down and learned to live with the very low-profile owners in Sydney. The flamboyant Maxwell was a different matter.

David Syme, like the parent John Fairfax Ltd in Sydney, was a journalists' company. On 12 February and 11 March Syme employees met and resolved that the *Age* 'must not become an organ to peddle the views of a person, a political party or an interest group'. They were backed by 'A Message from a Few of our Readers' run as an advertisement in the *Age* on 28 March. The readers included the chairman of BHP, the president and secretary of the Australian Council of Trade Unions, a former Police Commissioner, the Anglican Archbishop of Melbourne. The journalists and important readers formed a vocal interest group with grass roots support no government could ignore.

If Keating thought, like Macbeth, that if the deed was to be done it should be done quickly, the time for action came and went one day early in February. By early April Prime Minister, R. J. L. Hawke and Treasurer Keating were publicly stating reservations about foreigners buying any more major Australian newspapers, especially Maxwell buying the *Age*. Hawke virtually vetoed such an event on 8 April.

The supercharged political reaction in Melbourne not only confirmed the change in Fairfax's basic strategy to one of keeping rather than selling the *Age*, it must have helped to condition the ANZ Bank to accommodate that change in strategy. As a Melbourne-based bank, the ANZ had enough problems on the public relations front at that time, partly arising from its $2 billion loan to Warwick Fairfax, without being seen as the bank which, as a result of that loan, forced the sale of the *Age* to Robert Maxwell.

A few local groups had expressed an interest in buying all or part of David Syme, but not at prices anywhere near the $800 million Maxwell had talked about. The groups included one headed by John Dahlsen, former chairman of the HWT, and a director of the ANZ Bank. This group included, among others, Robert Holmes a Court. Murdoch thought they had been too close during the HWT takeover action. Hudson Conway Ltd, a Melbourne property company, was the most visible and audible of these interested parties. Hudson Conway had been visible and audible during the previous stirrings about the *Age*'s ownership in the early 1980s. When Whitlam Turnbull had been looking at the possibility of factoring the Skase debt in February, Hudson Conway's chairman, Sir Roderick Carnegie, had expressed an interest in his company acquiring the debt and the notes Fairfax was taking up in Skase's company. Nothing came of it.

In March, Hudson Conway directors, including Conway, Lloyd Williams and the stockbroker John McIntosh, had arranged to call on Syme's managing director Greg Taylor to talk about the *Age*. Taylor was surprised to find television cameras outside the building to record their arrival for that night's television news. They seemed to be eager to be seen as potential buyers. But nothing came of that, either. Lloyd Williams later described Whitlam Turnbull's figure of $800 million for David Syme as 'outrageous'. He wondered when the Fairfax group was 'going to get to grips with what the market value is'. He had ideas about restructuring the Fairfax debt. Some thought that a key player had been missing when the TV cameras had been running outside the David Syme building, that when Hudson Conway showed an interest in the *Age*, Lloyd Williams's good friend Kerry Packer could not be far behind.

Whitlam Turnbull's other big job for Fairfax was renegotiation of the Skase contract. Under the original heads of agreement

Skase had made in July 1987 to buy the Fairfax television assets, he had agreed to pay $25 million on signing, $470 million on 30 November 1987 and $285 million three years after signing, a total of $780 million. Of the $25 million on signing, $21 million was earmarked for the Albert family company, which had been a shareholder in ATN7 since it was formed. Of the $470 million due on 30 November, $100 million was earmarked for Fairfax's investment in Qintex group securities, and $12.5 million represented the present value of advertising Fairfax was to get on the Seven Television Network in future years. And of the $285 million due in 1990, $55 million was earmarked for investment in more Qintex group securities.

The deal would put Fairfax in a strong financial position. Skase was stretched and Fairfax was prepared to support his purchase with reasonable financial terms. After Warwick's takeover the positions were reversed in favour of Skase. But at July 1987 the deal appeared to leave a net $604 million cash for Fairfax, of which $230 million was due in 1990, plus its investment in Qintex plus its television time to come. By the time the agreement was legally documented four months later the payout on signing was reduced to a net $4 million and the 30 November payment was reduced to a net $382.5 million, after Fairfax had made its $100 million investment in Qintex on that date. Fairfax would also underwrite the losses on the Melbourne station to the tune of around $30 million. The total consideration in the legal contract remained unaltered at $785 million but Skase's immediate cash outlays had been trimmed back. They were trimmed back a good deal further when he failed to meet the 30 November deadline for the $382.5 million. He finally paid $282.2 million on 21 December and a further $60 million on 31 March.

Whitlam Turnbull then turned to the problem of liquidating the $285 million due from Skase in 1990, the $55 million Fairfax was due to invest in more Qintex securities by then, and the $100 million it had already invested in the Qintex group. Skase was in no hurry. Any settlement would cost him money. If anybody knew, or should have known the relative positions of the two companies it was the ANZ Bank. Skase and Fairfax settled in the middle of 1988 in a complex arrangement, the reporting of which was confused by Skase's need to be seen to have been greatly fortified by the settlement. The media was still portraying Skase as the great deal maker.

In essence Fairfax sold its $100 million of Qintex Australia convertible securities to the AMP Society for $55 million. Fairfax had had an agreement with Skase that it would not sell those shares for three years without Skase's consent. The AMP Society was a more than welcome replacement for Fairfax on the Qintex ownership register. But the price of Qintex Australia shares had been nearly halved since 30 November when Fairfax put in its $100 million and the AMP discounted its purchase price for that fall. Instead of paying $285 million in October 1990, Qintex paid $129.8 million to Fairfax in July 1988 and $70 million in December 1988. The securities Qintex was to have issued to Fairfax for $55 million by 1990 were placed elsewhere, the proceeds helping to pay Fairfax that $70 million. Fairfax also paid Qintex $28 million in quarterly instalments to satisfy the underwriting of HSV7's losses plus $4 million for other settlement adjustments.

It was complex and the net outcome was more than $200 million less than the $785 million nominated as the purchase price of the Fairfax television network a year earlier. But Fairfax needed the money and Qintex had a debt off its books and the AMP Society as potentially its second biggest shareholder. The AMP ended up with egg on its face and the Chase-AMP Bank with a substantial bad debt provision when the Qintex group went into receivership a year later. Fairfax had been forced to do itself a favour by discounting itself out of Qintex in mid-1988.

The sellers of all three television networks in 1987 had helped finance the highly inflated prices the buyers paid. Of the $1050 million Bond paid for Packer's Nine Network and other radio and television interests, Packer provided $200 million by taking up convertible redeemable preference shares in Bond Media, the company into which Bond transferred all his broadcasting assets, and a further $50 million in options to buy more Bond Media shares. Packer also sub-underwrote part of Bond Media's ordinary share placement. The National Australia Bank provided $800 million bridging finance for the Bond purchase and also a joint underwriter for the Bond Media share placement in the Bank's stockbroking subsidiary, A. C. Goode and Co. The underwriters were left with 27 per cent of the Bond Media float — 71 million shares at $1.55 each, of which Packer took 8.6 million as sub-underwriter. He sold them at a loss soon afterwards.

Bond Media's own cash outlay for the Packer TV purchase was $5 million. It was a classic Bond play in pushing up asset prices with other people's money. The National Australia Bank was a willing participant. Packer's 50 million options were to take up 50 million shares in Bond Media at $1.55 at various times up to 1991. Bond Media shares never looked like reaching $1.55. And Packer had the right to put those options back to Bond Corporation at one dollar each early in 1989, which he did. After some arm twisting he received the money in two payments of $25 million each. His preference shares ($200 million) were redeemable on 3 March 1990 or convertible to ordinary shares at $4.65 a share by 31 March 1990. The redemption date passed without Packer getting his $200 million. Eventually, he had to convert his preference shares into ordinary shares in Bond Media in a complex deal to buy control of the company since he could not get his $200 million in cash.

Murdoch also saw the original values of his Ten Network sale eroded by the stock market crash. Murdoch made a clean cash haul on the sale of HSV7 to Fairfax for $320 million plus $45 million for country newspaper interests in NSW. But the earlier sale of his two Channel 10 stations to Westfield Corporation for about $800 million was more complex. Westfield put the two stations into Northern Star Holdings and at the end of the asset-share exchanges Murdoch's News Corporation had 36 million shares in Northern Star (14.9 per cent of the capital) at an average price of about three dollars a share. That holding had to be reduced to five per cent to comply with the Federal Government's ownership rules. In May 1989 News Corporation sold 22.75 million shares to the Daily Mail and General Trust, owners of Associated Newspapers in London, at $1.51 a share. That was about 50 cents a share over the market price of Northern Star shares at the time, suggesting that the price was the result of previous agreements between Murdoch and Northern Star's owners, Westfield. There seemed no reason why the Daily Mail and General Trust should have paid more than the market price to lift its holding to its limit of 20 per cent.

News Ltd appeared to lose about $20 million on the sale and still had about 11 million Northern Star shares on its books. By September 1989 the shares were down to around 50 cents when Westfield quit its big investment in the television company at a loss of about $500 million.

Only Fairfax was forced, by Warwick's takeover, to sell out and take its losses on the chin as Westfield Corporation did a year later. In the event, that turned out to be a lucky escape. A year later its Qintex securities would have been worthless and it would have been in the long queue of Qintex's creditors.

In the 7 December 1987 memo Bert Reuter circulated as the Tryart team moved into Fairfax, he emphasised the importance of having all the asset sale contracts made in the second half of 1987 by the old and new Fairfax managements settled on their nominated dates. This included discounting the Skase and Bell contracts and reinvestments by the superannuation funds. On Reuter's schedule they should have brought in $1970 million by 31 January 1988. Six months later, when all the anticipated transactions had been renegotiated, replaced or cancelled they had yielded a total of $1310 million — $566 million from Skase, $744 million from the rest. The company retained the *Australian Financial Review* and some other assets. But it was nowhere near repaying the ANZ Privatisation Facility and it still owed nearly $500 million to Citibank. By the end of the year it had about $1.5 billion to refinance (see Chapter 14). The asset transactions had rearranged and streamlined the engine room. But the company also had major problems with its superstructure. Tryart had borrowed about $2 billion for the takeover, which had to be repaid or refinanced. As the funds came in from the asset sales they were parked in a special account with the ANZ, and later transferred as interest-free loans up to Tryart and then to the bank to repay the takeover debt. By late May 1988 about $1 billion had been transferred in this way. There appeared to be no tax problems in this. Under Section 108 of the Income Tax Assessment Act an advance to or loan by a private company to a shareholder is treated as a dividend to the extent that the

Commissioner reckons it is made out of a distribution of profits. Any payment so reckoned is regarded as a dividend paid at the end of the financial year in which the payment is made.

The asset sales had made substantial capital profits for John Fairfax Ltd. But the assets had mostly been held for a long time and the profits attracted little tax for the operating company. As it passed the sales proceeds up to Tryart as loans, those loans could be regarded as dividends but that would be all right since the dividend was being paid to a company within the same group and it too would not be taxed. Paul Keating could have wrecked this. On 25 May the Federal Treasurer, in a major economic statement, introduced a new round of tax reforms. For unfranked dividends paid after 25 May the intercorporate concession would be denied to the private company receiving the dividend unless it and the company paying the dividend had been members of the same group of companies for the whole year of income. (Unfranked dividends were dividends paid from untaxed profits.) The object of the change was to stop private companies deferring the payment of tax. But it trapped Tryart, which had only become a member of the same group as John Fairfax Ltd in November 1987 — five months into the year of income — and still did not wholly own that company. About $1 billion had already been transferred to Tryart. On a possible reading of Section 108 the company could be up for nearly $500 million in tax.

Tryart was not trying to defer the payment of tax. It was trying to pay down a debt with which it was barely able to stay afloat. Another $500 million for the Tax Commissioner would sink the company. It had just started complex negotiations for restructuring the $1.5 billion outstanding with the ANZ and Citibank. The possible tax liability threatened these negotiations. Chris Anderson pointed out these potential traps for Fairfax in long discussions with Keating. Anderson knew his way around in Canberra as he did around Macquarie Street, Sydney.

When the Minister for Transport, Peter Morris, introduced the amending legislation to the House of Representatives on 31 August (Keating was away), it contained a couple of transitional clauses, one of which allowed through dividends deemed by Section 108 to be paid after 25 May but declared before that date — that is, the $1 billion that had been passed by John Fairfax Ltd to Tryart. The amending legislation was passed through the House on 19 October, through the Senate on 8 November and given the Governor-General's assent on 21 November.

Fairfax had escaped that accidental tax hazard but many problems remained. The companies had to be restructured to cope with the refinancing then being planned and to avoid future tax traps. Tryart's name was changed to John Fairfax Group Pty Ltd (JFG) on 22 July. JFG then, as a matter of urgency since funds were no longer being passed up from John Fairfax Ltd and the other subsidiaries while they were only partly-owned, proceeded to buy out the minority interests in John Fairfax Ltd still owned by Acrux (Mary Fairfax), Rockwood (Mary and Warwick Fairfax) and Kinghaven (Warwick Fairfax). The restructuring was vital if the company was to survive the high risk financing course to which it was now committed.

Mary Fairfax rebelled as she had in November 1987. She was committed to sell her Acrux shares under the November 1987 agreement but not for her Rockwood interests held through the Jones trust. Her agreement to the sale of the Rockwood shares to JFG was essential and needed urgently. King and Anderson said the position was intolerable. They told Warwick to issue the ultimatum: either his mother agreed and signed or he would put the company into liquidation. If Warwick did not deal with his mother, King and Anderson would quit. Mary signed on 1 October. The balance sheet engineering is explained in the End Notes to this chapter.

JFG's second major structural problem also stemmed from its debt. Although, after 1990, the problem of whether intercompany loans were really taxable dividends would be resolved, and losses within the group could be offset against profits of other companies within the group, JFG, the holding company, would be a big accumulating loss maker, which would soon make its balance sheet look very odd indeed. The company needed substantial profit earning assets of its own to correct this. The solution was to transfer to JFG the Sydney-based income earning assets previously held by JFL — that is, the *Sydney Morning Herald*, the *Sun-Herald*, the *Australian Financial Review*, the business magazines and the *Good Weekend* magazine. That was done in January 1989. But it involved another major tax problem. Those assets were valued at $1 billion. JFG paid its subsidiaries that amount for the assets with money borrowed from JFG Finance. The subsidiaries then lent the money back to JFG at no interest, enabling JFG (nee Tryart) to repay the remaining takeover debt to the ANZ Bank. That $1 billion sale could incur State Transfer Stamp Duty of around $50 million. Fairfax's legal advisers, Freehills, approached the NSW Government for a waiver of the duty. The assets transfer was an internal matter. The Fairfax takeover had already been a financial bonanza for the NSW Treasury from Stamp Duty on the share transactions and subsequent registered mortgages and charges.

The State Government granted the waiver. When this was later revealed in *Australian Business* magazine it caused a brief political flurry. The State Labor Opposition tried to be indignant about this special treatment of its old enemy Fairfax. But there were adequate precedents for the waiver. Labor's main criticism was about the size of the waiver. It was big because it flowed from the biggest takeover in Australia's history. Labor's indignation faded. Perhaps it was overcome by the irony of the situation. Freehills had been legal advisers to the NSW Labor governments. Nick Greiner had terminated that relationship when the Liberals came to power, and spread the Government's patronage among other leading law firms. He was doing Freehills no favours.

At a chance meeting in Tokyo late in August 1988, Paul Keating told Max Suich, the former Fairfax chief editorial executive, 'I've just saved Fairfax $500 million.' That could have been true. But he first could have cost them $500 million. It was a continuation of the ambivalent relationship Keating had with the Fairfax organisation over the last decade. One Fairfax newspaper had attacked him. Others had supported him. He had aimed to unsettle the Fairfax company with the new media legislation he had championed in 1986. But he had become concerned at the outcome of the HWT takeover battle which, early in 1987, turned Murdoch from a relatively weak newspaper owner in Australia into the strongest with 60 per cent of the market. Keating knew that outcome bought no long-term commitments from Murdoch, who ran luke warm and cold on Keating. Murdoch backed winners. He was the ultimate pragmatist. News Corporation's debts and high gearing ensured that. Fairfax's debt would make it more pragmatic too.

The high-priced takeovers of 1987 would leave all the Australian media companies extremely nervous about running against popular opinion and risking adverse reactions from readers, viewers, listeners and advertisers. Debt could tame the Fairfax newspapers, but they were still likely to differ widely from Murdoch's group and take a more rigorous line on a big range of issues and Keating would have preferred a more even market balance between the two than that which emerged from the events of 1987. It was not in his, or the Labor Party's interests, to see Fairfax weakened further by accidental tax imposts. But his concerns would buy him no special favours from Fairfax either. Editorially, most of the company's newspapers had supported him and his policies as Treasurer, and backed the Labor Party in Federal elections while he and Hawke had publicly abused them. Soon after Keating ensured that his new tax laws would not accidentally trap Fairfax, the *Sydney Morning Herald* started to turn against his policies. Its editorials and columnists became increasingly critical of his handling of the economy. Keating, his Treasury advisers and the advisers to the Governor of the Reserve Bank had all underestimated the strength of private investment in 1988–89. Everything had come good at once and his critics at Fairfax wrote of the need for greater restraint, urging Keating to abandon the tax cuts he had promised as part of a new wage accord with the trade unions.

The *Australian Financial Review* was inclined to see things more Keating's way. The *Sydney Morning Herald* became supportive again when the Federal Budget was presented in August 1989. Australia and the John Fairfax Group were walking the same tight rope. The expanding economy in 1988–89 had produced record profits before interest and tax for Fairfax, profits well ahead of those forecast when the refinancing was being arranged in April–May 1988. The banks were happy. But the expansion in the economy had also greatly increased the overseas trade deficit. Keating was relying on high interest rates to slow the economy down but they were doing nothing to correct the balance of payments deficit, and the Australian dollar remained high on the foreign exchanges. Fairfax's future was riding on the outcome.

# CHAPTER 14

# JUST RIDE
# THE BANKS OUT

In financing the Fairfax takeover the ANZ Bank was dogged by
Murphy's law from the start. If anything could go wrong, it did.
When Bert Reuter took the deal to his friend, the bank's managing
director, Will Bailey, and the Bank's general manager of corporate
banking, John McConnell, in the second last week of August 1987,
it looked like a big but fairly straightforward financing operation,
rich in its fallout in fees, interest and the acquisition of the Fairfax
and Syme accounts from Westpac and the National Australia Bank.
The ANZ would lend Warwick Fairfax or his takeover vehicle, the
money to buy the John Fairfax Ltd shares, there would be a rapid
selldown of highly marketable assets to repay the loan and the
ANZ would resume the client banking relationship with Fairfax
that it had lost to Westpac and the National Australia Bank in
1983. It would also pick up David Syme from the National Australia
Bank. It looked like a bigger, richer, version of the type of takeover
financing the banks had enjoyed and developed in the mid-1980s.
The assets involved were first class. The stockmarket was charging
ahead. The Reserve Bank was concerned about the banks'
exposure to individual corporate plays but there should be no
problems in syndicating the ANZ's loan for the Fairfax takeover,
thus keeping the ANZ's own exposure within the Reserve's
guidelines. A big, quick assets play followed by a long-term
banking relationship with two blue chip clients. Bert Reuter was
delivering a rare banking treat.

Six months later the Bank had a serious public image problem.
The Fairfax takeover was a mess, the stockmarket crash in October

had revealed the perilous condition of some, though not yet all, of the big, bewildering corporate groups ANZ and other bank loans had helped to build, such as Ariadne Australia, the ANZ's Third World loans received regular attention in the media and the development of the Reserve Bank's new prudential guidelines focused attention on the quality of all bank assets. With good dividend yields carrying substantial tax advantages after the introduction of tax imputation, bank shares, as a group, had recovered strongly after the crash. But ANZ shares, due to market concern about its lending policies, lagged behind those of the National Australia Bank and Westpac.

The ANZ's initial offer of $1.31 billion as the support facility for Warwick's proposed privatisation of John Fairfax Ltd had to be amended immediately. The amount did not cover, as the Companies Takeover Code required, the possibility that the other members of the family would accept the offer. When Reuter suddenly realised, or was alerted to, the error, he called the Bank, asked for the facility to be lifted to $1.75 billion and waited in Carnegie Fieldhouse's offices for the higher facility to be approved by the Bank's credit committee and the new facility letter to come through on the fax machine.

The first letter had mentioned a maximum price of eight dollars a share and that the funds were 'only sufficient to acquire those shares not already owned by the immediate Fairfax family [as discussed]'. The second letter mentioned a maximum price of $7.50, which could be increased with the Bank's written consent, but that the funds were 'only sufficient to acquire those shares not already owned by Tryart and its associates'. Tryart's associates at that stage were The Rockwood Pastoral Co. (owned by Warwick and his mother), Acrux Holdings (owned by his mother) and Kinghaven (owned by James Fairfax but with Warwick having a veto over the disposal of Kinghaven's shares). These shareholdings totalled 25.28 per cent of John Fairfax Ltd's capital.

Although it seemed to be assumed, when the bid was made on 31 August, that Warwick controlled and would not have to buy these shares, he ended up paying for control of all of them. Neither the Bank, nor Warwick's advisers, nor the National Companies and Securities Commission (NCSC), nor the board of John

Fairfax Ltd, appeared to question, with any great diligence, the nature of Warwick's claims over, or interests in, the shares held by Rockwood and Acrux. It was only at the last minute, on 27 October 1987, that Vrisakis secured Warwick's claims to those shares, or perhaps more accurately, his mother's support for the takeover financing.

The Bank's facility included a condition that, before Tryart could draw on the funds provided, the Bank required a charge over the shares held by Rockwood and Acrux and unlimited guarantees from the two companies. When that happened in October 1987, Mary Fairfax, who owned Acrux and had a substantial say in Rockwood, objected and had to be paid for her support. The Bank's August letter offering the takeover finance acknowledged the Reserve Bank's increasing concern at large exposures by providing that, if official policy towards commitments such as the ANZ was making to Tryart changed, the facility could be renegotiated or cancelled. The offer also provided that, if John Fairfax Ltd became an associate of Tryart, the latter would use its best endeavours to ensure that the 'proceeds from John Fairfax Ltd's recently announced major [that is, television-broadcasting] asset disposals will be ... applied expeditiously towards repayment of the facility'. This led to the confrontation with Westpac and the National Australia Bank at the end of December over who was to get the first major payment from Christopher Skase's group for the television assets he bought in July.

Another provision was that, if it was proposed to float any of Fairfax's subsidiaries or divisions, then an underwriting agreement would have to be arranged 'to the satisfaction of ANZ, in a form and with a party(ies) that is acceptable to ANZ'. The flotation of David Syme in one form or another was always part of the Tryart plan until just after the 19–20 October stockmarket crash. It was certainly part of the plan when Tryart's Part A Takeover Statement was registered with the ACT Corporate Affairs Commission on 9 October. The Part A Statement could not be altered without the ANZ's consent. The Statement said only that the proposed Syme share issue would be underwritten. No underwriter was named and no underwriting agreement mentioned. Rivkin James Capel, and later Rothwells, had been mentioned as underwriters during the course of the takeover. There appeared to be no written agreement and the status of whatever understandings existed was never tested. Rothwells was publicly named as an underwriter, presumably with the ANZ's approval, only a few weeks before having to be rescued from a liquidity crisis on 24–25 October. It had been leaking badly for some time. The ANZ had been one of Rothwells's bankers. The bank should have known Rothwells's condition.

The offer also provided that 'If, in the opinion of either Tryart or ANZ a significant change should occur in the relevant financial markets and that such change materially affects the facility, then the parties will enter into discussions with a view to arriving at a mutually acceptable solution'. The stockmarket crash of 19–20 October put that to the test. Neither party invoked this clause. Warwick Fairfax decided to go ahead and the Bank stood behind him, in contrast to Merrill Lynch's withdrawal from the $1 billion it was raising for Robert Holmes a Court's Bell Group at that time. By that time, as the takeover price rose to $8.50 and the family decided to sell out, the takeover facility had risen from $1.75 billion towards the $2.114 billion finally offered on 10 November. (The acquisition actually cost $1 948 708 000 including stamp duties, fees and interest up to 7 December 1987). Then the Bank's problems really began. Reuter's proposals and projections supporting his applications to the Bank had never included the $100 million fee payable to Rothwells, since Warwick did not want that revealed and Reuter and Connell agreed that the Bank did not need to know about it. If anybody at the Bank asked what Rothwells was getting, the reply was not recorded. Presumably it was assumed that Rothwells's fee was included in Reuter's workings with 'Other fees and costs ... $21.9 million'. Before the bid was made Warwick had also insisted that nobody should talk to Westpac or the National Australia Bank about their $150 million loans to Fairfax for fear they would tell Fairfax's chief general manager, Greg Gardiner, and thus alert him to the coming takeover bid, spoiling Warwick's dawn-raid strategy. After the bid was announced on 31 August this constraint no longer applied. But it was not until Ron Cotton joined Tryart late in November and learned from a former colleague at Fairfax that Westpac and

National Australia Bank expected early repayment that the prospect of a clash between the banks was faced. By agreement with Fairfax, Tryart had had access to all Fairfax information from 10 November.

Reuter was in contact with the ANZ constantly throughout the takeover during September and October, advising the Bank about the changing terms of the offer and the asset sales to John B. Fairfax, Kerry Packer, Rupert Murdoch and Robert Holmes a Court. The Bank was not told of the agreement with Holmes a Court giving him the option to put the Macquarie Network back to Fairfax for $152.8 million within six months. The Bank saw copies of the sale agreements before lifting its facility to cover the final $8.50 offer price, but the option agreement with Holmes a Court was not disclosed.

Reuter was not involved in any of the asset sales but was the link man with the Bank. In his workings for the revised bid, which emerged at the end of September when the price of $8.50 had been agreed with James and John Fairfax and the three big sales agreements had been made, he showed a total cash outlay for the takeover of $2044.6 million (assuming all outside shareholders accepted the bid) offset by $1829 million from asset sales, leaving a continuing deficit of $215.6 million. This he proposed to cover with an issue of preference shares or convertible notes to 'say company funds', that is, the retirement and long-service funds. That was a big 'say' but seemed to be accepted by the Bank.

The omitted Rothwells's fee of $100 million was not large beside the projected outlay of over $2 billion but it was large beside the projected deficit of $215.6 million. Its omission was rationalised on the grounds that it would not be payable until the following April and then would be paid by Fairfax and thus did not come into the current Tryart financial exercise.

A 'Strictly Confidential' cash projection, dated 29 September, included Rothwells's fee and showed a deficit of $317.7 million reduced by $111.7 million from the long service and retirement funds ($76.7 million from the former and only $35 million from the latter, acknowledging that only 10 per cent of the latter would be available under the existing tax regime), leaving $206 million to be refinanced. A cash flow projection Reuter sent to Bruce

Maisey of the ANZ on 28 October, the day after Tryart's takeover offer finally went out to Fairfax shareholders, showed a deficit of $219 million to be met by the proposed share or note issue to the funds, although Reuter's 'Strictly Confidential' estimates a month earlier had limited the funds' contribution to $111.7 million. The Bank did not appear to question the capacity of the funds to reinvest in Fairfax.

None of this was publicly known at the time. As far as the market was concerned the ANZ was financing the biggest takeover Australia had known and there was no real need to question it until the market crashed on 19–20 October and then Rothwells had to be rescued five days later. In the shaky days that followed, when Mary Fairfax tried to get Warwick to call the whole thing off and the David Syme flotation was replaced by the sales of Australian Newsprint Mills (ANM) and Australian Associated Press (AAP) shares to News Ltd, the shares of John Fairfax Ltd fell to $6.80, despite Warwick's determination to go ahead with the bid at $8.50. That valued the 258 million shares Warwick was acquiring at $1.75 billion against the ANZ's facility of around $2 billion. Counting in the 42 million Rockwood and Acrux shares, Warwick said he controlled or beneficially owned — a very debatable claim since he later had to pay his mother for her share of them — the company was being capitalised at just over $2 billion.

This market behaviour was an aberration, as Vrisakis claimed, but it indicated what Fairfax shares would have been worth if the bid was not made. They would have been worth a lot less than $6.80. Tryart's Part A Statement had said that 'repayment of amounts drawn down under the [ANZ] facility will be secured by charges over the John Fairfax Ltd shares owned by Tryart and its associates and by other security'. As far as the shares were concerned the ANZ was creating its own security. The value of the shares was being propped up by Warwick's offer, which was being financed wholly by the Bank. If it did not lend the $2 billion, the shares would not be worth $2 billion or anywhere near it.

When Warwick determined to go ahead with the bid at $8.50 and the option of an approach to the NCSC for permission to postpone or alter the bid had been allowed to evaporate into thin air, the Bank went with him all the way. On 25 October the

Bank said it had no plans to pull out of the facility arrangement, although John McConnell said that 'we could probably pull out if we wanted to'.

It was a bold decision, in marked contrast to Merrill Lynch's withdrawal from the Bell Group capital raising. But instead of accolades, the Bank's reputation for prudence and judgement took a bath. It had seen the asset sale agreements and approved the substitution of the ANM and AAP share sales for the David Syme flotation. As far as Bert Reuter was concerned these were water-tight contracts, as good as money in the bank, and the ANZ seemed to agree with him. They all fell apart. Instead of having $1.4 billion in the bank from the asset sales by 31 December, plus $220 million from the retirement and long-service funds, the company had only $280 million from the pre-takeover television sale to Skase, and that was a month late and was being claimed by Westpac, the National Australia Bank and a number of merchant banks. Financially the ANM and AAP share sales looked better for the ANZ's purposes than the Syme issue. But like all the other asset sales, the Murdoch agreements ran into trouble too.

Whether the ANZ acknowledged it at the time or not, the 19–20 October market crash killed the simple, seductive grand strategy of backing Warwick's bid — that is, a big loan followed by a quick assets sell-off, then a continuing client banking relationship with an easily accommodated working capital facility. The quick assets sell-off was off. Worse still, Westpac and the National Australia Bank were not inclined to help the ANZ out of its difficulty by agreeing to roll over the $150 million advances made to Fairfax earlier in the year.

On 27 November, four days after he joined Tryart as prospective managing director, operations, of the Fairfax group, Ron Cotton spoke to Barry Moore, group chief accountant of Fairfax, about the company's finances. It was Tryart's first inquiry about the $500 million Fairfax owed its pre-takeover bankers and other lenders. Moore told Cotton that he would not be rolling over the Westpac and the National Australia Bank bill facilities of $150 million each because the banks would be paid out of the $340 million they were then expecting from Skase. Moore had drafted a letter to the two banks telling them to expect to be repaid at the end of the month. Cotton spoke urgently to Reuter who said that, although nobody had spoken to the two banks, they were expected to continue those facilities as the company's bankers. Moore was asked to contact the two banks and ask if they would extend their facilities. He told Cotton he was also being asked by the merchant banks about the company's future banking relationships.

The National Australia Bank was first to confront the Tryart team. On 1 December Geoff Armbruster and David Maybury of the National Australia Bank saw Reuter, Cotton and Moore and told them that the Bank expected to be paid out of the Skase monies, that its $150 million had been provided to help buy television assets in the first place, that it had been concerned for the company's security after the big asset sales, and that it should not be taken for granted. That was six days before Tryart moved into Fairfax. Cotton asked for 30 days grace to which the National Australia Bank agreed. They saw Bob Stutchbury, senior manager of corporate banking at Westpac two days later. Reuter argued that the Westpac and National Australia Bank facilities were for working capital, unrelated to the takeover finance, and that they should be rolled over.

On 3 December Westpac offered to extend its facility from 30 November to 29 January. The question of who might be the company's future bankers was left up in the air. But Westpac and the National Australia Bank seemed to be in no doubt that they would be out and the ANZ would be in, and therefore the ANZ should take over responsibility for the working capital. That, however, could have added up to $500 million to the funds the ANZ was already committing to Fairfax for the takeover and could cause problems with the Reserve Bank's prudential guidelines, even though the ANZ had syndicated part of the $2.1 billion facility. The syndication's extent and terms were never revealed.

The failure of the asset sales to produce funds on time had the ANZ over two barrels. Westpac and the National Australia Bank had their fingers on the triggers and were not unwilling to pull them. The ANZ had a $158 million shock from another quarter on 9 December when, at the Bell annual general meeting in Perth, Robert Holmes a Court announced that the group would probably be exercising the put option on Macquarie Network. That would mean $158 million off the $475 million (discounted to $457 million) they expected to get out of Holmes a Court. It was the first the Bank, or Cotton or Reuter, had heard of the put option. It fell on the Bank's executives like the news about Rothwells's $100 million fee had fallen a month previously. In the meantime, Skase was late with his first substantial payment of $340 million and it was sinking in to the Tryart financial architects that there were very big problems in recycling the Fairfax retirement fund's money. That would yield about $200 million less than they had anticipated. Reuter thought there might be some way for the funds to lend the money to an institution like the AMP Society or the National Mutual and for the institution to lend it on to Fairfax. But that looked dicey. The view from the ANZ's head office at Collins Place was becoming daily more overcast.

On 10 December Cotton and Reuter met McConnell and other bank officers in Melbourne. McConnell was very tough about the secret put option. The Bank executives were coming under pressure from their board of directors who in turn were starting to feel the flak from outside as the foundations of the Bank's commitment to Fairfax started to wobble. The National Australia Bank was pressing its concerns about being disadvantaged by the proceeds of asset sales being used to repay the ANZ and on 15 December the ANZ wrote to Fairfax reminding the company urgently that its facility required the debt to be discharged in full from the proceeds of asset sales within six months. The prospect of this happening was disappearing rapidly. Bert Reuter went on holidays to Seattle for six weeks. He did not reappear in Sydney until late in January. Two days later on 17 December the ANZ wrote to the National Australia Bank promising a resolution of their dispute. Time was running out for a negotiated settlement to this conflict between the three banks. On 11 December, after Mary Fairfax had been squared away, for the time being, John Fairfax Ltd shareholders (that is, Warwick and his mother) had passed a resolution under Section 129 of the Companies Act enabling the company to provide financial assistance to Tryart in the funding of the takeover, that is, enabling Fairfax to pass the proceeds of the asset sales to Tryart and then to the

ANZ Bank. The resolution was advertised as required by law. The advertisements appeared in the *Sydney Morning Herald* and the *Canberra Times* on 12 December and the *Age* on 15 December. It gave creditors, debenture holders or shareholders 21 days to apply to the Supreme Court to oppose the resolution. That caused a tense round of negotiations between the banks and with Fairfax. Following their 17 December letter, the ANZ met the National Australia Bank. The latter countered with a letter on 22 December stating that the ANZ's proposals were unacceptable and if the National Australia Bank's counter-proposals were not accepted by 23 December then action would be taken to protect its position.

While this was going on Skase was late with his $340 million payment, thus putting Tryart/Fairfax in default with the ANZ's $2.1 billion facility. When Skase's payment was negotiated down from $340 million to $280 million, payable on 21 December instead of 30 November, the ANZ waived the default and approved the rearranged Skase payments schedule. Six months previously Fairfax had been generous to Skase, selling him the TV stations on terms that were seized upon by Fairfax's critics, including Warwick Fairfax, as signs of incompetence. James Fairfax and Greg Gardiner had regarded the terms as reasonable and helpful to a vigorous young entrepreneur whose finances were stretched but who they thought was worth backing for long-term investment and a continuing investment in the TV industry, which they thought would one day be shaken up again, and which they might re-enter on favourable terms.

Warwick's takeover had reversed the situation. Skase now had the bargaining position and Fairfax had to give him even better terms, with the ANZ Bank supporting both. Cotton said that, throughout the negotiations with Skase, he was comforted by the ANZ's assurances that Skase would pay. Nevertheless on 22 December, when Skase's company made its first payment of $280 million instead of the $340 million outlined in the schedule of anticipated asset sales when the ANZ's $2.1 billion facility had been negotiated, the ANZ wrote to Cotton wanting to know why. Fairfax explained by letter the next day.

On 21 December the Federal Court granted the Trade Practices Commission (TPC) an injunction restraining News Ltd from completing the ANM and AAP share sale agreements. Marty Dougherty, who had made the agreements, went to Hawaii on holidays. Ron Cotton had asked Barry Moore to seek legal advice from David Frecker of Blake Dawson Waldron about the status of the Westpac, National Australia Bank and merchant bank loans to Fairfax as against the ANZ loan to Tryart. Generally, his advice was comforting to Fairfax and Tryart, though Westpac was probably in a stronger position than the National Australia Bank since its $150 million facility had been specifically made for the HSV7 purchase and was subject to tougher default conditions than the National Australia Bank's. Of the 18 other banks, Bank of America and the Mitsubishi Bank were probably in a position to force repayment of their loans. Frecker advised that Fairfax should respond selectively but quickly to requests for information. On Christmas Eve there were further discussions between the banks and Fairfax.

The banks had been unable to agree among themselves about how their claims on Fairfax's funds should be met. McConnell at the ANZ had found his counterparts at Westpac and the National Australia Bank intractable. He rang Cotton and urged him to resolve the demands of the three banks. Cotton said the banks should agree among themselves about how payments should be received and security shared. Cotton thought he had similar talks with Westpac and the National Australia Bank that day.

Late that afternoon Cotton had a call from Marty Dougherty in Hawaii checking on how things were going. Cotton's evidence statement recorded his *cri de coeur*:

*Cotton:* Marty we are in a hell of a mess here. I have all the merchant banks threatening to take action or expressing concern in relation to the recovery of their funds. The National Australia Bank, Westpac and ANZ cannot reach agreement on how we will handle the Skase payments. The asset sale contracts were not proceeding and the ANZ are very nervous particularly about the effect on their cash flows and our ability to service the debt. Marty, I can't get hold of anybody, you are in Hawaii, Warwick is not around, Bert is in the States — where I don't know. I can't get Laurie. I can't get Aleco. Where are we going? Marty, it's all very well for you to ring up every

day and take ages wanting an update, which I am also doing
for Peter King and Warwick, but where are these people who
we are supposed to be paying to put this takeover together?
We need Laurie Connell here. I can't get him here. Will you
do something? We are paying them all this money and none
of them are here. They're the people who are supposed to
be putting this takeover together.
*Dougherty:* Ron, I realise you have a lot of pressure. I'll get
on to Laurie and make him aware of the situation. But look,
I must go now or my family will wonder where I am it being
Christmas Eve.

Friday was Christmas Day, starting the four-day holiday break
throughout Australia. Stutchbury from Westpac called Cotton and
Moore at Fairfax at 9.45 a.m. on Tuesday, 29 December and gave
them notice that the Bank was thinking of taking action under
Section 129. They did so later that day in the ACT Supreme Court.
That was the story Marty Dougherty tried unsuccessfully to
dissuade the *Sydney Morning Herald* editor, Max Prisk, from
running, questioning its validity and arguing that its publication
was not in the company's interests. Armbruster from the National
Australia Bank also called later that day saying that his bank was
thinking of starting proceedings under Section 129 of the Companies Act. And Cotton had a letter from the ANZ that shook him.
The ANZ warned that it was thinking of taking action under the
facility agreement to protect its position. The Bank wanted
detailed statements of the status of the asset sales by 5 January.
The next day Cotton unburdened his problems to Vrisakis over
lunch, emphasising that Connell was not returning his calls.
Vrisakis promised to contact Connell and see what he could do.
Still no calls from Connell. Vrisakis and Dougherty were becoming
concerned for Cotton's health.

The year ended on a low note for everyone. Cotton had another
letter from the ANZ, which he took to a meeting at Blake Dawson
Waldron with Vrisakis and Frecker. The ANZ wanted Tryart and John
Fairfax Ltd to give security under the facility for the benefit of
all lenders. The ANZ was still trying to resolve the dispute with
the other banks. It wanted the embarrassing Section 129
proceedings to be withdrawn as soon as possible. Vrisakis called

Connell. No reply. Armbruster of the National Australia Bank called that day to say his bank was taking action under Section 129. The National Mutual Royal Bank called with similar news. The First National Ltd, a subsidiary of the National Australia Bank, demanded, under its facility arrangement, repayment of the $13 million it had lent John Fairfax Ltd by 11 a.m. 7 January. None of the asset sale agreements with Packer, John B. Fairfax, Murdoch and Holmes a Court, which were to have brought in $700 million by the end of the year had been finalised. By 4 January Fairfax was looking for substitute purchasers if any of the agreements fell through.

Dougherty returned on 4 January, the day after the long New Year weekend. Warwick Fairfax also reappeared. The ANZ talked with those two alone about early finalisation of the asset sales and a proposal to put to the other banks. Marty was back on the job. That night he issued a statement which said that a proposal had been developed which the company believed would 'satisfactorily resolve the issue'. The statement continued:

John Fairfax Ltd's proprietor, Mr W. G. O. Fairfax, met senior ANZ bank officials in Sydney late today. Mr Fairfax is confident that the proposal will sensibly and satisfactorily protect the company's lenders. John Fairfax Ltd will put the proposal to the lending banks this week.

Warwick's statements were like the smile on the face of the Cheshire cat. His words were there but he wasn't. Dougherty, and, later, Peter King, continued to make statements saying 'Mr Fairfax thinks ...' or 'Mr Fairfax's view is ...'

Following that 4 January meeting the ANZ wanted written advice about the legality of reinvesting the retirement funds (Moore had warned Cotton about this problem six weeks previously), the current state of the asset sales and the Macquarie Network put option. They all apparently still thought that the Holmes a Court agreement would go through, with or without Macquarie. But the liquidity strains on the Holmes a Court companies were very evident. He had been liquidating assets and would have to liquidate more. The long-drawn negotiations about the difficult sale agreements for the *Australian Financial Review* and the *Times on Sunday* were looking increasingly like a filibuster.

The ANZ wrote to Warwick confirming the points made at the Monday meeting and outlining matters to be discussed at a meeting the next day, Wednesday 6 January. Cotton signed a long letter, which was hand-delivered to the bankers and merchant bankers seeking to reassure them about 'some uncertainties about the future directions of the group' and outlining the ANZ's proposals for an agreement that 'would provide the necessary levels of comfort for all lenders'. Broadly, this involved a six-month moratorium while the takeover settled down and the group's prospects could be reassessed. As the position became clearer during this period a 'club arrangement' would be established, the ANZ to hold first registered mortgages over all the group's assets as agent for the benefit of all present and future lenders to John Fairfax Ltd, not increasing above their present levels. The proceeds of asset sales would go proportionately to reducing the ANZ's privatisation support facility and the two $150 million loans from Westpac and the National Australia Bank. The supporting schedule of anticipated asset sales and other cash flows showed the retirement and long-service funds investing $220 million in Tryart. As the Westpac and National Australia Bank loans were repaid they would be replaced by an advance from the ANZ to Fairfax up to a limit of $300 million.

It was a very optimistic selling document. The banks did not buy it. They were sceptical about the company being able to achieve the scheduled asset sales. They were sceptical about the assumed $220 million reinvestment by the retirement funds. They were sceptical about Fairfax's continuing viability as an operating company. And they were being given some very hazy ideas about the fee due to Rothwells. The proposal seemed to confirm the ANZ's predicament. It had syndicated some of the $2.114 billion facility and was still within the Reserve Bank's prudential guidelines. But there might not be much room to increase the ANZ's exposure. Under the proposed formula, the ANZ's privatisation support facility would be repaid much more rapidly than the need for the Bank to top up the Westpac and National Australia Bank loans to Fairfax. The asset sales had failed to give it the quick reduction in the privatisation facility it had anticipated from the time Bert Reuter brought the proposal to the ANZ in August right through to the end of November.

The critical meeting set for 18 January in the Fairfax boardroom under the thrifty, prudent, Congregational eyes of the original John Fairfax and his sons, was attended by McConnell and Maisey of the ANZ and Warwick Fairfax, Dougherty, Connell and Cotton of Fairfax with their adviser Aleco Vrisakis — at least Warwick and Cotton thought Warwick was there, Connell and Dougherty thought not. The ANZ board had met the previous day. McConnell said they were concerned at the slow progress in reducing the debt but they remained committed to the Tryart privatisation. He emphasised the effect all the publicity about the Section 129 actions was having on the ANZ. It was starting to affect the price of the Bank's shares. Fairfax's image was suffering too. 'There is nothing that directors dislike more than being criticised publicly for the decisions and actions taken by the bank,' Cotton recalled him saying. 'The board indicated that collectively we have a big PR exercise to get through this.' McConnell wanted to know where Reuter was. Cotton gave the current count on the Section 129 actions, which had by then been lodged by Westpac, the National Australia Bank and National Mutual Royal Bank. Three other banks had asked Fairfax not to draw down any further on their lines. First National was demanding $13 million by 11 a.m. the next day. Connell said he was fixing things with Holmes a Court and Packer, should have them sorted out in the next few days and would talk to Skase. Cotton said Marty Dougherty had talked with Shearson Lehman in America (a William E. Simon connection) and they were waiting for a proposal that could help with the Westpac and National Australia Bank facilities. He also said Wardleys had asked if they could assist and were calling the next day. Connell, as deputy chairman, took charge of the Fairfax side, assigning tasks to Cotton and Dougherty and to himself. McConnell asked for daily reports on the asset sales and the Skase contract and the meeting broke up.

Malcolm Turnbull turned up by chance that afternoon, saw the opportunities for Whitlam Turnbull, offered to find the money to pay off First National and to help solve Fairfax's problems generally. Late that afternoon Cotton told Connell, who was by then back in Perth, about Malcolm Turnbull's approach. Connell dismissed the First National problem, saying that the ANZ would put up the $13 million if Fairfax took them to the brink. He favoured Wardleys before Whitlam Turnbull. Wardleys had orchestrated the $350 million rescue of Rothwells only two months previously. Wardleys were close to Connell's friend Alan Bond. They were all part of Perth's magic circle. Cotton recalled Connell saying, 'You mention talking to both Wardleys and Turnbull's. I think it would be better to deal with Wardleys, and perhaps you shouldn't finalise any arrangement without talking to me, for I would like us to enter into an arrangement with Wardleys.' But Malcolm Turnbull was the man on the spot. He turned up at Cotton's office the next morning just before 11 a.m. with a cheque for $13 million to take out First National and later in the day came back with Nick Whitlam to talk about the bigger financial issues. Whitlam Turnbull were in.

Wardleys made a proposal on 7 January about funding the Fairfax debt, which Cotton sent to McConnell in Melbourne. A few days later McConnell told Cotton that Wardley's proposal was not acceptable. The ANZ was not prepared to be subordinated to existing lenders. McConnell set up another meeting with Fairfax executives on 13 January. A week had passed since the last meeting. There was still no cash from the asset sales, no agreement with Westpac and the National Australia Bank, and the merchant banks were not responding favourably to the 5 January letter putting forward the 'Club Arrangement'. Moore, Dougherty and Cotton attended with Nick Whitlam for Fairfax, McConnell and Conn for the ANZ. The Packer contract had just been concluded, the John B. Fairfax contract was on its way, but there was still no sign of Connell delivering the Bell contracts. Whitlam Turnbull had been engaged to try and get a new arrangement for the $500 million owing to Westpac and the National Australia Bank and the merchant banks. In the next few days Westpac and the National Australia Bank formally rejected the 5 January proposal. Warwick Fairfax, Connell, Dougherty, Cotton and Peter King attended a Fairfax board meeting on 18 January, which discussed the banking situation and the Whitlam Turnbull mandate. Connell reassured them that the Bell contracts would go through and gave his view of how to cope with the banking crisis. Cotton recalled him saying, 'Ron, you have to learn to ride banks out. But at the end of the day they will still be there ... just ride them out.' Laurie loved horses. But horses did not have problems with Reserve Bank guidelines.

On Channel 10's first *Business Week* programme on Sunday, 10 January, Max Walsh had interviewed Bob Johnston, the governor of the Reserve Bank.

*Walsh:* How do you feel about a bank, like the ANZ, taking such a large position in a single takeover?
*Johnston:* In accordance with our rules and requests to banks, they had consulted us before they did it and I'm loath to get too far into the affairs of the banks, particularly individual customers, but we are aware of what the bank has done and we haven't offered any criticism of it.
*Walsh:* Is there a rule, a prudential requirement, that you are not allowed to lend more than a certain proportion of your paid up capital or your shareholders' funds?
*Johnston:* We haven't the power to make laws on the subject. What we have done is to ask the banks to consult with us in advance before they commit amounts of say, 30 per cent, of their capital to any particular party and to give us time to consider it and to comment on it.

This was all fairly discreet, as central bankers usually are, but perhaps the governor had something particular on his mind when he referred to 30 per cent of capital. It was the first time that ratio had been mentioned publicly. (The definition of a bank's capital was something else altogether.) Walsh's question reflected market concern with the ANZ's Fairfax commitment, which was telling on the Bank's share prices.

On 18 January Bert Reuter called Ron Cotton to say, 'I'm back. What's been happening?' Cotton filled him in. Reuter said he found the situation Cotton outlined hard to believe. Everything had been in place when he left. Cotton offered him an office in the Fairfax building. Reuter decided to operate from his Regent Hotel suite. But all the creative work was being done at Whitlam Turnbull's offices in the city. They had lined up a $500 million facility from Citibank to take out Westpac, the National Australia Bank and the merchant banks.

The ANZ wrote to approve the proposal for such a facility on 20 January. They also increased the fees on their own facility because of the extraordinary problems involved. Citibank wrote formally offering the $500 million on 27 January. If Whitlam Turnbull's arrival on 6 January had been like the relief of Mafeking, Citibank's offer was like the end of that phase of the war. The ANZ had the National Australia Bank and Westpac off its back, but at the cost of conceding Citibank security over Fairfax's prime assets: the *Sydney Morning Herald*, the *Age* and the *BRW* group. Those were the assets not for sale. The ANZ syndicate's exposure, after allowing for the proceeds of assets already sold, was down to about $1.5 billion. But that exposure still largely depended on the continued sale of assets already targeted. The proceeds of those sales would continue to go to the ANZ, but if any of the assets over which Citibank had security were sold, the proceeds would go equally to Citibank and the ANZ. The whole exercise required another advertisement of Section 129 notices giving creditors 21 days to object to the proposal. Westpac remained tough to the end, but by the end of February all the banks with pre-takeover debt agreed to roll over their loans for another month while the Citibank facility was formally put into place. By the end of March Fairfax was drawing down the $500 million to repay the banks.

These extraordinary events, involving a very public falling out between Australia's major trading banks, gave the US-owned Citibank a big break. In 22 years in Australia it had followed several leads with mixed results but until 1987–88 it had not been able to show its true paces as one of the world's most aggressive, innovative banks for corporate finance. It had come to Australia first, as the First National City Bank of New York, in the mid-1960s, taking a 50 per cent interest in Waltons Credit Corporation, the consumer finance subsidiary of Waltons Ltd, by then a major department store retailer but whose credit-based selling operations still reflected its pre-war origins as Cash Orders Amalgamated.

In the early 1970s First National broadened its Australian base by buying into Industrial Acceptance Corporation (IAC) Holdings, one of the country's oldest hire purchase financiers, with a solid base in the motor trade but without a trading bank as a major shareholder. Like other non-bank financiers throughout the world, particularly in countries like Australia and the UK with tightly controlled banking systems, IAC became deeply involved in booming property development finance. Many non-bank financiers in Australia and the UK and banks in North America were badly burned when that boom went bust in the 1970s. First National poured money and management resources into rescuing their investment in IAC. When the US company changed its name from First National City Bank to Citibank in 1976, its Australian investments included 51 per cent of IAC; 50 per cent of First National City Bank-Waltons, later sold to Barclays Bank; 44 per cent of an investment bank, Citinational Holdings, later sold to the National Mutual Life; and 50 per cent of a small Victorian building society, Arnotts First City. The next year Citibank bought out the outside shareholders in IAC.

In a review of Trevor Sykes's book *Two Centuries of Panic, a History of Corporate Collapse in Australia,* Professor Warren Hogan paid a generous tribute to Citibank:

> The story of the absorption of IAC by Citibank is more complicated than depicted. Platoons of Citibank men marched through IAC between 1974 and 1977 in response to the bad loan exposures and then to the responsibilities of majority ownership. By averting the collapse of IAC, Citibank propped up the entire finance company structure in Australia. In so doing it paid its dues well in advance of the banking authority that came its way a decade later.

Warren Hogan was Professor of Economics at the University of Sydney. He was also a director of Westpac. In resisting the ANZ's overtures in December and January for accommodation on the matter of its $150 million loan to Fairfax, Westpac, like the National Australia Bank, acted in its own immediate interests. In doing so the banks had given one of the biggest, most aggressive new banking competitors an opportunity to move centre stage in Australian banking. Citibank was not an institution to pass up the chance to shout about its achievements. Westpac and the National

Australia Bank had won that round with the ANZ. The tactical victory might also seem a strategic one by enhancing their reputation for sound banking. The ANZ was bleeding on the public relations front. But they had also given Citibank a gap that might later be regretted.

The ANZ was busy countering its knockers. At a press conference after its annual general meeting of shareholders on 18 January 1988, the chairman, Sir William Vines, and the managing director Will Bailey, spoke on a number of issues including the loans to Tryart. 'If you ask is Warwick viable, the answer is yes,' Bailey said. (That was hardly what Tryart would have wanted to hear in the subsequent court case when Tryart's counsel claimed the company was not commercially viable after the takeover and before 30 June.) Bailey said the repayment of the ANZ syndicate's loan had been discussed with Fairfax management and 'there was general understanding that they would be retired as they fell due. Some of the banks have decided that they want to be paid earlier. It's just a case of paying them out earlier rather than later'. That was certainly presenting a relaxed view of the tensions then existing between the ANZ, Westpac and the National Australia Bank. While the ANZ shareholders were meeting in Melbourne on 18 January, Laurie Connell in Sydney was telling the Fairfax board and Ron Cotton in particular that 'you have to learn to ride banks out ... just ride them out'. Sir William Vines said they were 'pretty comfortable' with 'the total indebtedness of Tryart and the resources available to meet those debts'. Rothwells would have been pretty comfortable with statements like that in the subsequent court case when Fairfax claimed the company was no longer commercially viable.

An article in *Australian Business* in April began:

The ANZ is attracting increasingly critical attention for its role in the struggles of Warwick Fairfax and Ariadne Australia. Concern is being expressed about the size and riskiness of loans to them and other entrepreneurial customers and about the bank policies that allowed such lending.

It quoted Will Bailey's rebuttal:

As far as being aggressive and chasing corporate business went, we were not. What we did was to respond to the needs of long-standing customers. Aggressively chasing lending implies that we were out chasing new companies; we were not. Every case went through the board. We want business but we don't want business at any price.

In June the ANZ sent to shareholders the first issue of a small publication called Shareholder Contact with a Question and Answer format dealing with some of the issues then concerning the market, including Third World debt.

*Q:* In view of recent mergers and takeovers in Australia, what is ANZ's position in regard to funding takeovers? Is there any adverse effect on ANZ's doubtful debt situation?
*A:* It is generally accepted that takeovers are a necessary and essential part of the free enterprise system. Industries have become more diversified through growth and takeovers, which have allowed them to operate competitively in domestic and international markets. Commitments by ANZ to fund takeovers are subject to prudent banking controls. They are undertaken only after long and careful evaluation of all fundamental credit considerations and bank exposure given the funding requirements. As a matter of policy we would not become involved in financing activities which we see as counterproductive and purely opportunistic.

The ANZ was not the only bank struggling to define its position in an aggressive takeover world in which transaction banking (opportunistic banking) was cutting across relationship banking (banking based on long-term client commitment). In a television interview at the end of 1987 as the ANZ was starting to feel the heat from its Tryart financing, the new managing director of Westpac, Stuart Fowler, said that his bank now preferred to finance mergers 'if they are friendly on both sides'. The emphasis was on 'preferred'. Most big Australian takeovers involved a possible conflict of interest for at least one of the four big Australian banks and confronted with such a situation Westpac, like the others, would do whatever it thought best suited its own interests. That might mean financing a hostile takeover bid as Westpac did in backing Kerry Packer's $700 million bid for the ANI engineering group in 1989. Westpac was one of ANI's bankers. But the Bank had kept a relatively low profile in the big corporate plays after feeling the heat in 1986 when it had backed Holmes a Court's Bell Resources in its bid for BHP. Westpac was not BHP's biggest banker but BHP quickly let the bank know that it could not serve both sides in that contest and that it could forget about doing business with BHP in future. The banks' involvement in the big takeover plays raised important policy issues for them. It took the Reserve Bank's prudential supervision into new territory too.

The Reserve Bank's governor, Bob Johnston, had told Max Walsh in his television interview, 'They [the ANZ] had consulted us before they did it ... we are aware of what the Bank has done and we haven't offered any criticism of it.' Presumably the ANZ had advised the Reserve of its proposed takeover financing late in August — a package of $1.7 billion, based on a $7.50 bid price, which could be increased with the Bank's consent, with details of its proposed syndication and assets sell-off. The ANZ might even have told the Reserve the name of the company involved. If not, it became obvious on 31 August. The takeover financing package rose to $2.1 billion over the next two months and presumably the Reserve was informed of the syndication progress. Once the bid was made on 31 August, however, the market took over. The takeover had a momentum of its own. The original package seen by the Reserve Bank, and not criticised by it, had become a very different package by the time the $2.1 billion facility was in place on 10 November. Presumably the Reserve relied on the bank to keep its commitment within the guidelines as the takeover price rose and to syndicate any excess. But what happened if the syndication proved difficult, or if, as a result of the stockmarket crash, the asset sales fell apart?

Having not criticised the ANZ on its original proposal, the Reserve could hardly criticise it, as others did, for what happened as a result of the market's crash. Prudential supervision in a boom market was not easy. But the Reserve Bank of Australia, unlike the Bank of England, seemed to come through without a major administrative failure, perhaps learning from London's mistakes.

The ANZ Bank had been rescued from its embarrassing confrontation with Westpac and the National Australia Bank early in 1988 by Citibank's action in taking over the $500 million of other bank loans to Fairfax. Although the asset sales that were finally achieved had reduced the ANZ syndicate's exposure to Fairfax to around $1 billion by the second half of 1988, Fairfax was still in critical financial condition. It still owed Citibank nearly $500 million. It was in default on its covenants to both banks. The company's assets might be worth about $1.8 billion. Its buoyant profits might support the interest payments on bank debt of about $1 billion. If the company was to survive it needed a heavy injection of funds that would not need servicing immediately. In the past those funds would have come from shareholders. But Warwick Fairfax had no money. Drexel Burnham Lambert filled the gap with junk bonds. In the decade of super-leveraged debt, junk bonds, the securities whose low security ranking was sweetened by high interest rates and often by the attachment of warrants to convert into shares, were taking the place of direct equity.

# CHAPTER 15

# THE MAN SAYS
# IT'S DO-ABLE

After their talks in London with Robert Maxwell, directors of the *Daily Telegraph* and others about the possible sale of the *Age* or other assets, Peter King and Warwick Fairfax went to North America to explore the prospects of financing their new long-term strategy of holding on to the *Age* and all the remaining NSW publishing assets. William E. Simon's investment company, WSGP International Inc, was waiting to hold their hands and open doors for them. WSGP had two strong personal contacts with Warwick Fairfax: William Simon himself and John W. Barber, the former Morgan Stanley man who had written the critical paper on the PIPs issue while staying at 'Harrington Park' in 1985. Both had been introduced into the 'Fairwater' Fairfax fold by Mary Fairfax. Simon, a former US Deputy Secretary and Secretary to the Treasury in the Nixon and Ford Administrations, had moved very successfully between business and government. He had had at least four careers. He had been in charge of bond trading and a senior partner at Salomon Bros when George Shultz, in 1973, picked him up to be his deputy Secretary of the Treasury. That put him into the Federal Energy Office and petrol rationing during the Arab oil embargo. He became Secretary of the Treasury from May 1974 to January 1977, which covered New York's fiscal crisis. He was an early adviser, with Shultz and Alan Greenspan, to Ronald Reagan in the run-up to Reagan's election as President in 1976 and thought he would return to the Treasury in Reagan's first Administration but was cut off by Reagan's closer advisers. He went back into private business, made some friends and enemies in the oil and gas business, did not pay much tax, built his wealth up to $35 million and met a tax accountant and nursing home financier, Ray Chambers. Together they formed an investment group, Wesray Corporation (Wesray: Simon's initials and Chambers's first name). Chambers was already into leveraged buyouts (LBOs).

They looked for lively operating divisions buried within large corporations and discovered Gibson Greeting Cards at Radio Corporation of America (RCA). Wesray bought Gibson Greetings for US$80 million on a $1 million deposit, of which Simon and Chambers put up $330 000 each. They borrowed the rest. They distributed some Gibson stock to the management and watched it go. In 1984 they floated Gibson to the public and came away with $70 million each. It was regarded as an early classic LBO exercise, which they repeated several times. Simon fine-tuned his techniques. He bought a large equity in Anchor Glass, charged the company a fee for taking it over, borrowed funds from the company to buy its real estate, which the company then leased back, and made a profit of over 450 per cent on his original investment when he floated the company. It was a performance to make even a West Australian adventurer envious. The LBO phase was very rewarding but became crowded. By 1986 Forbes Magazine listed his fortune at $200 million. He had houses at Nomis (Simon backwards) Hill, New Vernon, New Jersey and Nomis Dunes, East Hampton, an apartment at Beverly Hills and a yacht, 'Freedom', with equipment to produce the *Wall Street Journal* for him each morning. Simon summed up his business strategy as 'staying ahead of the power curve'.

In 1986 he turned his attention to the Pacific Basin and US savings and loans associations (commonly known as S and Ls or Thrifts — something like Australian building societies), which were in deep trouble due to bad loans, low fixed-rate loans and rising deposit rates. The US Government was coming to the rescue. Simon and some associates including Preston Martin, a former vice chairman of the Federal Reserve Board and former chairman of the Federal Home Loan Board, which regulated Thrifts, bought the Honolulu S and L, and Southern California and Western Federal S and Ls. In 1986 Simon met the New Zealander, Bruce Judge, whose Ariadne Australia Ltd was expanding at a breathtaking rate. Through Judge he met Mary Fairfax.

Simon and Judge were both athletic. Simon, a former surfer, was president of the US Olympic Committee. Judge, a top tennis player, had played hockey for New Zealand in the 1964 Tokyo Olympics. Judge had interests in Hong Kong and seemed to be well placed on the Pacific power curve. He was a potential buyer of exotic enterprises and put Ariadne into International Financial Services Inc with Simon and his partner Gerald Parsky, who had been Simon's assistant at the US Treasury. 'I told Bruce,' Simon said in a later interview, 'Why go for the broccoli and potatoes when you can have the steak and creamed spinach?' The partnership went into the S and Ls but it seemed that Ariadne was putting up the potatoes (capital), while Simon and Parsky were to get most of the steak (profits).

The S and L play turned out to be harder than was originally thought and Simon's Pacific Basin strategy looked a much longer term proposition than anything he had previously put together. Towards the end of 1987 he spoke of 'selling the whole thing to Bruce with me as vice chairman'. By that time Ariadne was in deep financial trouble and in the hands of its bankers. Simon spoke of the Ariadne connection as a 'very sad experience'.

The Fairfax link, however, had been made and thrived. William E. Simon had been a major benefactor of the University of Rochester's Graduate Business School. In recognition of this, in October 1986, the University renamed the school the William E. Simon Graduate School of Business Administration. Simon described Rochester as his type of university. It was regarded as second only to the University of Chicago for its emphasis on deregulation and monetarism.

At Camden, to the near west of Sydney, plans for the subdivision of part of Sir Warwick Fairfax's 800-hectare property, 'Harrington Park', had come to a standstill during Sir Warwick's final illness and after his death in January 1987. A year later, Mary Fairfax announced that she would donate 40 hectares of the property as the site for a privately funded university, which would start as a post-graduate school of business administration, a branch of the William E. Simon School at the University of Rochester.

The donation might not only have educational value, but, like the Bond University in Queensland, give a boost to adjacent land sub-divisions. It might even help overcome some of the continuing re-zoning problems at 'Harrington Park' where about half of the property, including possibly the 40 hectares, remained rural under a Government scenic protection order.

The capital requirements of the 'Harrington Park' project were still formidable. The NSW Government, under Liberal Premier Nick Greiner, agreed to allow the new school to be launched from temporary premises in the Sydney Harbour National Park and passed special legislation for it to be called the Australian William E. Simon University so that donations to it would be deductible for tax purposes. The temporary site was opposed, and its legal status challenged, by the local Woollahra Council and environmentalists. But in mid-1989 the university was inviting applications for enrolment in an MBA programme 'designed for fast-track, mid-career managers'. The university's interim council included Gerry Gleeson, the top public servant under Labor Premier Neville Wran, and Peter Dodd, an executive director of Whitlam Turnbull and Co., of which Wran was now chairman. Gleeson had become one of Mary's close advisers. Simon, or his group, was about to become one of John Fairfax Group's close advisers. The future of the Australian Simon University remained uncertain.

Simon and Gerald Parsky had formed WSGP International as an investment house to exploit their connections and talents. Simon had some strong critics but his business achievements impressed many others. And his Republican Party links were solid. He had been critical of the Reagan Administration's fiscal performance and had written two books, *A Time for Truth* (with forewords by Milton Friedman and F. A. von Hayek of the University of Chicago) and *Time for Action*, emphasising the traditional conservative Republican concerns for small government and balanced budgets. WSGP attracted the services of two bright young men, John W. Barber (a registered Democrat of Massachusetts) and Charles C. Berg, a lawyer who had worked with the Los Angeles law firm, Gibson, Drum and Crutcher, of which Parsky was senior partner. Barber and Berg became senior partners of WSGP in October 1987.

The Fairfax executives saw about 10 investment bankers, including Shearson Lehman and Bear Sterns in New York. Both showed some interest in, but not much enthusiasm for, the refinancing problems of the John Fairfax group. They were all after big kills in North America to try and match Drexel Burnham Lambert. Next stop: Los Angeles, high yield (junk bond) financing headquarters of Drexel Burnham Lambert who had revolutionised debt financing in North America. Fairfax and King saw the master himself, Michael Milken, head of the high-yield department, early in April 1988. Milken looked at the problem and said he would do it. That commitment, backed and taken over by Peter Ackerman, Milken's key man on buyouts, when Milken became increasingly involved in defending himself and Drexels against charges of breaching the US securities laws, held through the critical second half of 1988. Milken was the fountainhead. Whenever commitment flagged and doubts arose among those working on the Fairfax refinancing, they were sustained by, 'The Man (Milken) says it's Do-able'. The debt strategy was discussed at a Fairfax board meeting on 11 April.

Malcolm Turnbull, advising the board, continued to bring the full battery of his forensic skills to his basic argument that the company had to sell assets to Robert Maxwell. Only Maxwell talked about prices that would relieve the Fairfax debt. Warwick had paid too much for the company. Only somebody prepared to pay too much for some of the assets could get Warwick out of his hole. Retention of the *Age* and all other existing assets would require what Turnbull referred to as a 'quantum leap in earnings' to service the debt Warwick had placed around the company's neck.

The Fairfax board continued to listen to Turnbull but the strategy was swinging Drexel's way. Milken had estimated that Drexel could handle a refinancing package of around $A1.3 billion. Peter King was convinced that this was the way to go and that the William Simon-Gerald Parsky company, WSGP International, should be appointed to look after Fairfax's interests in the refinancing negotiations. Anderson in particular had severe doubts about Drexel. The Fairfax board was not prepared to make that final leap in the dark — yet. They were unwilling to abandon Maxwell until they had a firm commitment from Drexels. A week later it was decided that King would talk to Maxwell in London to try and hold him off without cutting off negotiations with him altogether, and to the Simon group in America on the latest from Drexels.

The critical meeting with Whitlam Turnbull took place on the afternoon of 18 April. They were told that King would ring Maxwell that night and tell him Fairfax would not accept less than $950 million for the *Age*. Whitlam and Turnbull counselled against this but were told the course had been settled. Turnbull could see the Fairfax strategy changing, moving away from Whitlam Turnbull, but the Fairfax board gave little away. Turnbull's notes of the meeting, later produced in the court case about payment of the $100 million fee to Rothwells, recorded his warnings to Warwick Fairfax about the grave risks he was taking, and Warwick's reply: 'When I decided to do this takeover, I knew all the risks and I assumed them. It was entirely my decision. I am not financially illiterate, I understand the situation and I will deal with it in my own way.' That remark was used against him in court in cross-examination by Turnbull's father-in-law, T. E. F. Hughes, QC.

From America, WSGP told Fairfax that they had a proposal from Drexel for a $1.2 billion refinancing. Fairfax formally decided to retain WSGP to represent and advise them. The first Drexel party, led by Bruce Raben, arrived at Fairfax's doorstep in Jones Street on Anzac Day, 25 April 1988. Talks with Anderson, Cotton and King were held in the 14th floor conference room in which Reuter had outlined Warwick's takeover bid to the old Fairfax board and their advisers eight months previously. The WSGP advisers, John Barber and Warren Schlichting, came in the next day. The Drexel people met Fairfax senior executives and the exhausting due diligence examination (inspection of the books and management systems — a super-audit of the company's housekeeping) began. The ANZ managers were becoming increasingly concerned about the future of their advances to Fairfax. Their current facility, under which interest on the Bank's loan was being capitalised, was due to expire on 30 June. After that, the interest would be due and payable, the Bank reminded Fairfax's financial executives. After a couple of days inside the company, feeling the weight of the products and the effectiveness of the management, from Anderson and Taylor down to major departmental heads, Raben of Drexel said the refinancing would be complex and difficult, but it was 'do-able'. The ANZ and Citibank were brought into the picture. They were, naturally enough, enthusiastic about the refinancing arrangements Drexel was proposing. Fairfax was in default, or in danger of default, to both banks. The refinancing would reduce their exposures. During this period, early in May, Laurie Connell and Marty Dougherty, who had both been sacked from the Fairfax board earlier in the year, approached King about a possible offer from Alan Bond for all or part of Fairfax. King saw them at the Intercontinental Hotel on 5 May. They said Bond was prepared to discuss an offer of $800 million for the *Age*. King said he would refer this to Warwick Fairfax. The Fairfax team wanted to keep open as many options as possible. King left for America on 7 May to join Warwick Fairfax and Ron Cotton for further talks with Drexel. The next day, Sunday, 8 May, Max Walsh reported on his *Business Week* television programme, that the three Fairfax men were in America to meet William Simon. Walsh said:

It appears that Bill Simon has lined up a junk bond financial package which will enable Fairfax to pay down its $2 billion plus debt to the ANZ Bank and Citibank. For the package to work would require something rather unorthodox by local standards involving probably a period of grace on debt payments and the issue of warrants.

Walsh said the refinancing would enable the Fairfax organisation to keep its major print assets — the *Age*, the *Sydney Morning Herald* and the *Financial Review*.

The newspapers followed up the story the next day. Chris Anderson, for Fairfax, said the Fairfax executives would be seeing a number of people in America. Simon was only one of them. 'Bill Simon, like Whitlam Turnbull, has been a financial adviser for some time,' he said. He was still trying to keep the field open for as long as possible. Whitlam Turnbull was still urging the company to sell the *Age*. But Anderson confirmed that refinancing of the company's debt would allow the company to retain the

*Age* and the *Australian Financial Review.* Anderson said the company's 'preferred option' had always been to keep the *Age.*

In America, Drexel started to talk about the need for equity in Fairfax to sweeten the bond issues it was proposing. But it reiterated its faith in the Fairfax executives' ability to 'drive the profits'. The new era in management and finance was developing a lexicon of its own. Management's job was not only to 'drive the profits' but to 'grow the company'. Managers of the Warwick Fairfax owned Fairfax company would certainly need to drive the profits hard for the next decade to get the bankers off the company's back. Warwick had not grown, but shrunk, the company.

The ANZ Bank welcomed the prospect of Drexel's bond raising, taking the strain off the Bank's commitment to Fairfax and allowing Fairfax to retain the *Age.* The ANZ might have had to take a good deal of the blame for the sale of the *Age* to some dreaded interloper. That would have embarrassed the Bank board in a parochial city like Melbourne. The Bank's loans to Fairfax allowed for a working capital overdraft of $50 million. By mid-May this was nudging the limit and rising. What, Bruce Maisey of the ANZ wanted to know, was Fairfax going to do about this? There was nothing it could do. Perhaps Laurie Connell was right after all: just ride the banks out. Fairfax turned again to the staff benefit funds. It had borrowed to the limit — $38 million — from the long-service and retirement funds. Cotton turned to the Fairfax Foundation and the Centenary Fund for $20 million to help Fairfax through this desperate phase. Fairfax were still waiting for Drexel's 'highly confident' letter to come through, a letter devised specially by Drexel to indicate that it was confident that the financing was 'do-able' but which fell short of an actual underwriting commitment.

Drexel continued to raise the prospect of some form of equity enhancer for the junk bonds it proposed issuing. It wanted the bonds to carry the right to equity capital in Fairfax at some future date. King was still trying to string Alan Bond's interest along just in case the Drexel financing fell apart. Everybody was intent on trying to keep as many balls as they could in the air at once. Marty Dougherty at mid-year was offering John Fairfax Ltd to Kerry

Packer for a suggested price of around $1.9 million. Marty was trying to put a deal together. Fairfax knew nothing about it.

Citibank was not a company to be over-awed by the drive and dexterity of Drexel Burnham Lambert and at the end of May was looking at the possibility of handling the refinancing itself with the ANZ. Deadlines were becoming urgent as the Citibank-ANZ facilities were due to expire in June. The Fairfax company by now was being clearly run by King and Anderson in Sydney and Taylor in Melbourne, King's outward confidence about the outcome of the Drexel financing being balanced, but never outweighed, by Anderson's reservations about Drexel. Much depended on the earnings projections being worked up by Drexel and Fairfax executives. Anderson remembered well the business recession of 1982, which continued into 1983–84, when he was editor of the *Sydney Morning Herald*. Saturday's issues were running at around 100 pages instead of the 200 plus being published five years later. He used the weight of those 1988 issues of the *Sydney Morning Herald* and the even bigger *Age* to thump on the table to impress the visiting bankers with their great earning capacity but remained sceptical about extrapolating their earnings too far and too fast. King's confidence carried the day.

On 12 July in Los Angeles Drexel's credit committee approved the Fairfax financing project. The next day, lawyers from O'Melveny and Myers, the old established Los Angeles law firm retained by Fairfax, arrived in Sydney to take the company through the stringent due diligence requirements of US laws. Drexel was committed, the ANZ was on side but worried, and Citibank was committed to Fairfax's survival in its present form but still looking for another way to finance it. The refinancing started to run into the big tax snags thrown up by Keating's 25 May statement and the need to restructure the Tryart-Rockwood-John Fairfax Ltd relationship. The structural problems could be overcome with Mary Fairfax's consent. But as her advisers pointed out: what's in it for her? Initially Mary Fairfax, or her advisers, wanted half of John Fairfax Ltd as the price of consent. Negotiations continued until 1 October when Mary signed for the Rockwood rearrangement (see Chapter 13) in the early hours of the morning. But the tax and structural problems caused all the bankers, particularly Drexel, to look again, more critically, at the refinancing plan.

Fairfax had one big factor going for it: earnings of its newspapers and magazines were charging ahead, easily outstripping the forecasts on which the bankers had been working since April. Contrary to Federal Treasury and Reserve Bank expectations, the Australian economy had been hit by four booms at once: in commodity exports, private investment, employment and consumption. The newspapers were fatter than ever with advertisements. Trading profits soared but still fell well short of servicing Warwick Fairfax's debt. Until the debt could be reorganised to give the company an interest holiday for a few years, interest was being capitalised and added to the Fairfax bank loans at the rate of about $4 million a week. Delays to the refinancing were very costly to the company. Peter Ackerman of Drexel thought the financing would be tight even with a heavy commitment of non-voting equity rights attached to the low ranking bonds. He was concerned about the attitude of the banks and the need for an agreed recession strategy.

The refinancing seemed to be losing momentum until Mary Fairfax was signed up. The tax problems still had to be resolved. Peter Ackerman appeared to solve the foreign exchange problem by committing Drexel to do the US issues in Australian dollars — the first issue in a foreign currency Drexel had ever handled. Initially it was assumed that Drexel or the US bondholders would carry the foreign exchange risks. The original Drexel plan had been for the Australian banks to put up $900 million in senior debt and Drexel to find $500 million, including a substantial amount in deferred interest bonds to give Fairfax time to get its earnings up to cover a full interest commitment. After testing the market it was found the deferred interest bonds in an unknown Australian company could not be sold and eventually the Australian banks took on the deferred interest element in the financing. Foreign exchange risks, for the company if the Drexel issues were in American dollars and for US investors if the issues were in Australian dollars, remained a problem, though Drexel was slow to admit it.

Drexel, the institution, and Milken and Simon personally, all had much bigger things on their minds than Fairfax's finance.

Drexel and Milken were facing charges of fraud and racketeering, which culminated late in December in Drexel agreeing to plead guilty to six felony counts and pay $760 million in fines and compensation. The settlement isolated Milken, who faced similar charges, leaving Ackerman to run the Los Angeles junk bond operation. At the same time the firm was marketing bonds for the biggest LBO ever, the US$25 billion buyout of R. J. Reynolds-Nabisco organised by the LBO leaders Kohlberg, Kravis, Roberts and Co. (KKR) for whom Drexel had raised billions in the past. William E. Simon still had political ambitions. After being Secretary to the Treasury under Nixon and Ford, he had been in business during the Reagan Administration. In the run up to the November 1988 presidential election, he was on the George Bush bandwagon. He could be up for a big job, perhaps Secretary of State, in the Bush Administration.

At Fairfax, Chris Anderson was keen to lock in the three principal financiers and keep them moving forward with a formal press statement publicly committing everyone to the refinancing. Once it was announced officially, he believed, the financiers' egos would make it difficult for them to back out. All the media reports so far had been speculative or based on on- or off-the-record statements by individual company executives. There had been no formal, official announcement from the company and the three financiers confirming that the refinancing was going ahead. This required some delicacy in negotiating the form of the announcement since none of the financiers could appear less important to the outcome than the others.

The statement, issued on 20 September, carefully negotiated these sensitivities. The first paragraph said:

John Fairfax Ltd announced today that the basic terms had been agreed for a long-term refinancing package to restructure its debt. The proposed refinancing package is to be provided by Citibank, ANZ and Drexel Burnham Lambert Incorporated, a leading US securities firm.

In the third paragraph:

The directors said the refinancing demonstrated a vote of confidence by one of the world's leading banks, Citibank, one of Australia's major banks, the ANZ and one of Wall Street's best known firms, Drexel Burnham Lambert — in Fairfax's world-quality products and in the company's staff and management.

The acknowledgements were nicely balanced. Citibank was significantly first as lead manager for the Australian bank loan. The statement gave no details of the refinancing.

The newspapers the following day of course took no notice of the statement's careful protocol and gave obviously well-sourced broad figures of the refinancing: Citibank and the ANZ would jointly share the $1.1 billion of Australian debt, while Drexel would put up $450 million in subordinated debentures ranking in security after the bank loans. The terms of the debentures, interest rates, and whatever enhancers would be needed to sell them to Drexel clients, would be set nearer the issue date. These funds would pay out the ANZ's debt of about $1 billion which remained from its original privatisation facility of $2 billion, and Citibank's initial loan of nearly $500 million. As was later disclosed, the $450 million was divided into $300 million in senior subordinated debentures carrying 18 per cent a year interest due in 2000, and $150 million in subordinated debentures carrying 18.5 per cent interest due in 2001.

The first enhancer to make the debenture more attractive consisted of Equity Appreciation Rights (EARs), which gave debenture holders and some others, including Drexel, WSGP and Fairfax executives rights to non-voting equity in the company during the 1990s. The second enhancer, Foreign Exchange Appreciation Rights (FEARs) came later and arose from Drexel's original commitment to break new ground by making the Fairfax issue in Australian dollars.

John Fairfax Group in effect ended up underwriting the foreign exchange risks for the US investors. From those investors' point of view they were FEARs. From the company's point of view they were foreign exchange depreciation liabilities (FEDLs). (Details of the debentures, EARs and FEARs are discussed in the End Notes to this chapter.)

The whole refinancing arrangement, however, still depended on restructuring John Fairfax Group (nee Tryart) so that it wholly owned John Fairfax Ltd by taking Mary Fairfax out of Acrux and

Rockwood, resolving the tax problems, and clearing up the loans from the smaller employee benefit funds.

Mary Fairfax was signed up on 1 October, but new problems were appearing. The company was about to engage in court action with Bond Media and Rothwells over payment of the $100 million fee Warwick Fairfax had agreed with Rothwells in the Tryart Agreement of 28 August 1987. Rothwells had assigned the fee to Bond Media, which was claiming payment. Fairfax claimed the fee had not been earned but Bond Media could be regarded as a creditor of Fairfax. If the refinancing again required Section 129 notices to be issued — the notices which had caused Westpac and the National Australia Bank to take action against the ANZ just after Christmas 1987 — would Alan Bond take action to stymie the plan?

Bond had waved his arms and made threatening noises in an interview published in the *Bulletin* magazine on 9 August (see Chapter 16) threatening to sabotage any Fairfax deal with Drexel. The possibility that he might take action under Section 129 was a risk that had to be taken. The Section 129 notices were published in the Fairfax papers on 10 October, seven days before the court case started. There was no response.

Drexel continued to be concerned about the potential tax liabilities, which had not been resolved. And there was the problem of the money, totalling $20 million, which had been borrowed from the Centenary Fund and the Fairfax Foundation. That money had been borrowed in haste to relieve the pressure on the ANZ's overdraft facilities. It had to be repaid or its status had to be legitimised. The trustees had not approved those advances to the company, nor had their capacity to do so under the trust deed been established.

The Centenary Fund and the Fairfax Foundation had both been established and totally funded by the company, to make grants to employees and their dependants in special need. Unlike the much bigger retirement and long-service funds, they had no specific commitments. But they had been shareholders in John Fairfax Ltd and the takeover had given them relatively big cash windfalls. If the trustees did approve loans to the company they could hardly do so with less security than the banks had. To legitimise the arrangement the company repaid the $20 million it had informally borrowed earlier in the year. The Fairfax Foundation trustees then resolved to lend $10 million to the company at 10 per cent for a maximum period of 12 years. It was a good deal for the company and provided the foundation with substantially higher income than it had been called on to use in recent years.

After 17 October, public attention focused on the court case and, after counsel's opening addresses, on Warwick Fairfax's appearance in the witness box. But while the court provided the public theatre, the real cliffhanger continued in private. The annual accounts of John Fairfax Group, as at 30 June 1988, had not been finalised and signed by the company's auditors, Touche Ross and Co. The auditors had a major problem: Fairfax Group was in breach of its loan commitments to the ANZ and Citibank. It could also have unspecified tax liabilities, which would add to its debt. Warwick's takeover, as it stood at 30 June 1988, had converted the Fairfax companies' shareholders' funds of $1.1 billion at 30 June 1987, to a deficiency of $276 million at 30 June 1988. Unless the auditor could be assured that the banks would continue to carry the company or that refinancing was in place to rectify the loan breaches and that the company could correct the deficiency, the auditors would be bound to advise that the company was insolvent.

Warwick Fairfax and his advisers had opted for Drexel junk bonds with their EAR warrants to provide the $450 million of finance his company needed to support the $1.1 billion of secured loans Citibank and the ANZ were providing. If it worked, Warwick would retain 100 per cent control of the company even though he and his mother might be entitled eventually to only 60 per cent of the profits — the other 40 per cent going to the holders of the EARs who could eventually have their EARs converted into non-voting C shares in John Fairfax group. An alternative, in those desperate months of 1988, would have been for Warwick to sell some of the equity immediately to an investor who would put up substantial loan funds to support the two banks. This would mean a loss of face for Warwick who had bought the company to secure it from outsiders, but it could mean a more secure and stable company for the future. It would also not require the exhaustive disclosures, including the latest audited accounts, required by the Securities and Exchange Commisssion for any securities issue in America. The AMP Society looked at the possibility of providing this basement support of loan funds plus equity. The AMP had been close to Fairfax, as shareholder and landlord, for many years. It had received about $160 million for the John Fairfax Ltd shares it had held in its various accounts as a result of Warwick's takeover. As Australia's biggest investor it could afford to take the long view needed for an equity investment in Warwick's reconstituted company. Anderson was close to Ray Greenshields and Leigh Hall of the AMP. He asked them to look at investing again. But the AMP was not interested in non-voting equity. As the takeover boom had mushroomed in the 1980s the Society had been forced to become active in using its voting strength in many companies to protect its own and, in most cases, other shareholders' interests. If the AMP was to invest in a Warwick-owned John Fairfax Group it would want a solid voting equity in the company. But Warwick and his advisers were not about to erode his total voting control now. The basement finance was coming from Drexels.

By mid-November the major roadblocks seemed to have been cleared. The new tax legislation foreshadowed by Keating on 25 May, adjusted slightly so as not to kneecap Fairfax or other companies accidentally caught by it, had been passed through the Senate on 8 November; and rulings had been received from the Tax Commissioner on the proposed restructuring. The refinancing could proceed and Touche Ross could sign the accounts with the important qualification that certain group companies were in breach of obligations imposed under secured borrowing covenants, but that arrangements were nearing completion for the refinancing of those borrowings on a long-term basis.

The accounts were finally signed on 23 December 'subject to any effect the non-completion of these arrangements may have on the group including the value of its assets'. But by mid-November the way had been cleared for Drexel to start selling the Fairfax debentures in America. King, Anderson, Greg Taylor, managing director of David Syme, Peter Gaunt and Jerry Austin (the Fairfax Group's chief accountant) went to Los Angeles to join Drexel's marketing roadshow.

The roadshow, or part of it, was to play in 14 cities in 19 days. Full dress rehearsal took place in the basement auditorium in Drexel's office in Beverly Hills before about 200 Drexel executives, bond salesmen and selected clients. The first performance was thought to be a bit slow. Ackerman ordered it to be tightened up, with bigger parts given to Anderson and Gaunt to emphasise their experience in publishing. The pace was quickened to fit the presentation into its allotted 28 minutes. Finely timed and tautly scripted, the 28-minute presentation would start with an opening spiel by Drexel executive Bruce Raben, who had led the first Drexel party to John Fairfax Ltd on 25 April. Raben gave a quick version of the Drexel gospel on junk bonds and the vital role they and Drexel had played in the reinvigoration of American corporations in the 1980s. This was Drexel's carefully designed counter to the mounting criticism of junk bond financing in America. Raben would then give a brief background on Australia and John Fairfax Ltd. Peter King followed with a video of the company and its operations, which Broadcom in Sydney had made for John Fairfax Ltd some months previously. It included a short segment with Warwick Fairfax talking about the company. Drexel insisted that this be edited out for the roadshow. This was hard sell, and whatever else Warwick was, he was not a salesman. Peter Gaunt was and he followed King's brief outline with the marketing pitch — print media's share of advertising revenue in Australia and the Fairfax products' unique reach into, and share of, that market. Gaunt had pitched to advertisers and agencies in Britain and Australia and had a lot of marketing runs on the board. This third act of the presentation was a smooth professional lead-up to the main pitch by Anderson on the company's strategy, its dominance of the quality press in Australia, its assets and projected earnings, the four-year gap before projected earnings would cover interest costs and the eventual growth in the equity value in Fairfax after that, all supported by slides showing pictures and diagrams.

All speakers searched for reference points that would be familiar and comfortable for investors being asked to put money into a strange company in a strange currency in a strange land. Raben could refer to the *Sydney Morning Herald*, the *Age* and the *Australian Financial Review* as being like the *New York Times*, the *Los Angeles Times* and the *Wall Street Journal* of Australia. Anderson could concentrate on the well-known American Rupert Murdoch's stated opinion that the *Age* and the *Sydney Morning Herald* were among the great newspapers of the world. He used the price-earnings multiples Murdoch had paid for the Herald and Weekly Times, and Tony O'Reilly, the Irish boss of the H. J. Heinz company, had paid for Provincial Newspapers (Queensland) to show how highly regarded media stocks were in Australia. Anderson dealt with the fundamentals, the underlying market and financial assumptions and projections on which this audacious financing was based. He was sometimes supported by Greg Taylor, the newsprint expert. They were the Australians in the presentation. Together they had been with Fairfax and Syme for over 50 years. Raben was the American bond salesman. King, a South African, had been with the company for less than a year. Gaunt, an Englishman, had been with the company for two relatively short periods of two or three years. Anderson and Taylor represented the continuity of management and commitment to the products which were so important to those earnings projections. Their experience was an additional selling point for wavering investors.

The roadshow criss-crossed the US making presentations to Drexel's clients in Los Angeles, Phoenix, San Francisco, New York, Minneapolis, Chicago, Boston, Miami, Houston, Kansas City, sometimes doubling up on individual cities. Clients were more important than geography. The roadshow opened in Los Angeles, flew to Phoenix, Arizona overnight, did a breakfast show in Phoenix, continued on to San Francisco for a luncheon presentation, to New York for an after-dinner show, then a late flight from New York to Chicago to present to mid-west clients the next day. The logistics management of Drexel's high-yield department was first class. Interspersed with this there were one-to-one presentations in which individual executives would meet individual clients. The programme would have tested the endurance and spirits of the most hardened stage trouper. Drexel said the show was playing well, very well, and kept the troup moving and morale up after the show's lowest point — a carefully prepared luncheon presentation at the Helmsley Palace hotel in New York on the day before Thanksgiving. Nobody turned up. Off they went to Boston in the afternoon for another presentation, then back to Los Angeles.

Was it all worthwhile? There was no way of knowing while the show was travelling. But it did help to identify some of the problems Drexel had assumed in making an Australian dollar issue. While the show was running in November the Australian dollar rose sharply to nearly 88 US cents from under 79 cents in September, then fell back to under 85 cents. The volatility unnerved US investors. In September their US dollars would have bought 10 per cent more bonds than they would in November. Two years previously the Australian dollar had been worth less than 65 cents and could be again. The US investor in Australian dollar securities in November-December 1988 was looking at some pretty heavy downside risks and it was clear that Drexel would have to find some way of underwriting them. Outside New York and Los Angeles Australia was virtually an unknown country. US investors who had put money into US dollar bond issues by Australian companies such as the Bond and Goldberg (Speedo) groups were critical of the lack of information they were getting about those groups' performances. The Fairfax presentation could score points with details of market dominance and the cash flows from the 'rivers of gold' — the *Age* and the *Sydney Morning Herald*. Big newspapers in America were losing some of their market gloss. The *Wall Street Journal* had run into a flat profit period and retail advertising in the big city dailies was being affected by takeovers and new marketing techniques in the industry. But Australia had been through that revolution in the past five years. It had been a big factor leading to Fairfax's decision to close the *Sun* in March 1988. Fairfax had adapted to the new trading patterns then affecting newspapers in America.

The roadshow had had one big vote of confidence in Los Angeles when Tom Spiegel of Columbia Savings and Loan, one of Drexel's biggest clients, rose after Anderson's closing spiel and said the issue would get 'not one cent' of his money unless the management got some of the action. Some of the EARs warrants were reserved for Fairfax executives.

Wherever they went the Fairfax team were asked one basic question: 'Who is War-wick [as in Dione War-wick] Fairfax?' In America the principals of big LBOs tended to be well up front, talking and selling hard, showing their teeth. Warwick Fairfax was not to be seen. But he was being heard, or read. Investors in Boston, Houston or Minneapolis could, and did, call up on the VDT screens reports of the court case in Sydney where Warwick was being cross-examined by T. E. F. Hughes, QC. They might have trouble finding Sydney on a map, but they knew about the case. They knew Warwick had just said the company's cash flows did not cover current interest payments and the company could not service its debt; that he had ditched his family and then his advisers; that reports of the hearing could make him appear dissembling, naive or ruthless, or all three. The roadshow focused their attention on revenues and market dominance — never mind the owner, feel the products.

In the middle of it all King and Anderson flew home from Pittsburgh for more talks with the AMP Society, which finally floundered, partly on the matter of voting equity. In any case, the Drexel arrangement was so far advanced that it could be very difficult and very expensive to break. King and Anderson flew back to America to rejoin the roadshow. After the US tour ended King and Gaunt went to London and Anderson to Hong Kong and Tokyo to continue selling, either for Drexel's debentures or for the syndication of Citibank's loan. In Australia the Westpac-owned leading stockbroking firm Ord Minnett, with Drexel's representatives, made presentations for the debentures to Australian institutions and funds. There were no takers. A year after the October 1987 stockmarket crash, Australian fund managers were still looking at their scars and taking no chances.

Drexel was under increasing pressure to nominate a completion date for the issue. The ANZ Bank, in particular, with $1 billion still advanced to Fairfax, was concerned to see Drexel's money. But the Fairfax matter was one of the lesser pressures on Drexel at that time. It had just agreed to plead guilty to six felony counts in America and pay over US$700 million in fines and penalties.

That was primarily a New York head office matter. The Los Angeles high yield office was torn between loyalty to Michael Milken, who was being cut adrift, and the firm's survival. Ackerman was the anchor. The Los Angeles office set 10 January 1989 as the target date for completion of the $450 million issues. On 5 January the target was put back to 17 January. Alan Bond's representatives suggested an offer of $2.1 billion for the Fairfax company on 4 January. Bond had bought heavily into the UK company, Lonrho, and Lonrho's founder and chairman, Roland (Tiny) Rowlands, had hit back with a propaganda assault on the Bond group, which proved devastating in its consequences for Bond. Lonrho called Bond Corporation a 'South Sea bubble of debt' and 'technically insolvent', enlarging on these themes in the following months. Rowlands's propaganda had helped unnerve most lenders. Bond's approach to Fairfax on 4 January was his last big throw for a while. Two weeks later he opened talks with Peter King for a settlement of the court case about the $100 million fee Bond Media had acquired from Rothwells.

Drexel's 17 January deadline came and went. Each postponement was being reported in the Fairfax and Murdoch newspapers. Drexel finally completed the issue on Australia Day, 26 January 1989, having started work on it on Anzac Day, 25 April 1988. An orgy of document signing took place in Canberra and Sydney on 27 January, mainly at Citibank's Sydney offices. Drexel's cheque for $450 million was banked that day. It was the ANZ Bank's turn to be relieved — again. Exactly one year previously Citibank had formally offered its $500 million solution to the ANZ's impasse with Westpac, the National Australia Bank and others.

The delays in Drexel's completion inevitably led to speculation and rumours that, for all the selling efforts in November and December, Drexel had been left holding most of the two debenture issues. The *Wall Street Journal* reported early in April that the debentures were still on Drexel's books. The report was taken up enthusiastically by the *Australian*, Rupert Murdoch's national flagship and later denied by Drexel and Fairfax executives. 'As far as the company is concerned we have the Drexel money in our tills,' Chris Anderson told the *Australian*. That was not the same as saying that Drexels had sold the debentures. Registration documents later filed with the Securities and Exchange Commission (SEC) in America revealed that all of the $300 million senior subordinated debentures and a good deal of the subordinated debentures appeared to have been sold. Drexel had been left with about $95 million of the latter. But in Drexel's networks it was difficult to know whether bonds had been bedded down permanently or were just spending the night. The firm's fee for handling the issue was over $33 million, plus some of the EARs warrants.

Drexel had plenty of enemies and competitors waiting to take advantage of the firm's confrontation with the US regulatory authorities. The adverse publicity about the Fairfax issue early in April 1989 came as Drexel's annual junk bond conference in Los Angeles was about to start. Fairfax executives were making a presentation at the conference, which Drexel hoped would help sell the $90 million of the Fairfax issues still held in the firm's books. After it was all over Drexel held a celebratory roast, rag or send-up of those involved in the issues on a boat that put out from Marina del Rey. It was attended by Warwick and Mary Fairfax and the roadshow team.

The Fairfax newspapers continued to prosper. For the year to 30 June 1989 the company earned $185 million before interest and tax, with an operating cash flow of $210 million compared with $136 million and $162 million shown in the estimates used in selling the debentures in December and January. Paul Keating's high interest rate brakes were taking a long time to slow down the economy. Soon after mid-1989, the John Fairfax Group board of directors, which until then had been Warwick Fairfax, Peter King and Chris Anderson, was built up with the appointment of William E. Simon in America; R. A. Johnston, recently retired governor of the Reserve Bank in Australia; and Bryan Kelman, former chief executive of Colonial Sugar Refineries (CSR) Ltd. Kelman became chairman. It was pointed out that he had accepted the appointment after commissioning a report on the company's prospects by the Macquarie Bank, of which he was a director. The new board would meet quarterly. The new appointments were clearly made to impress and reassure present and prospective bankers and other lenders. Operations of the company were in the hands of King, Anderson and Taylor. Warwick Fairfax lived in Chicago with his new wife. He went to work at the *Chicago Tribune*. There was no timetable for his return to Australia. Statements of his movements and intentions continued to be made by King. Simon's appointment did not last long. His resignation was announced early in October 1989 after the first quarterly board meeting in Sydney. John Fairfax Group, like most Australian companies paid for the insurance of its directors against claims of negligence. The premiums were rising as laws became tougher. Simon's great wealth and high public profile could increase his exposure to the possibility of negligence suits in America, particularly to do with securities issued by a company in Fairfax's condition, and the premium costs of his insurance were deemed too costly for the company to carry. Simon resigned.

Fairfax's newspaper operations had a lot going for them in 1988–89. Advertising revenues had soared with the expansion of the Australian economy. At the same time, newsprint, one of the main cost items involved in producing the fat newspapers carrying those ads, was costing less. In Fairfax's 10-year newsprint contract with Fletcher Challenge, arranged by Malcolm Turnbull early in 1988 when Fletcher Challenge bought Fairfax's interest in Australian Newsprint Mills, the purchase price was stated in US dollars, based on the New York posted price, a nominally agreed price between large producers and large consumers, converted to Australian dollars at exchange rates ruling at the end of each month. When the Australian dollar rose strongly against the US dollar in the last quarter of 1988, the company's newsprint costs were reduced. After February 1989, the Australian dollar fell back again, increasing Fairfax's newsprint costs. But the posted price was not reflecting the sharp fall in the spot market or discount price of newsprint as US newspaper sizes remained static or fell, while mill capacity increased. The Fairfax company would have gained more if the Fletcher Challenge contract had been tied to the New York discount price, rather than the official producers' price. Talks were opened with Fletcher Challenge to try and have prices reflect this market situation.

The future of the exchange rate was unpredictable. Substantial movements either way, through their impact on newsprint prices and, later in the 1990s, on the cost of the FEARs, could help make or break the company's financial strategy. Equally unpredictable, but even more vital for the financial strategy, was the future of interest rates. The Fairfax loan armoury supplied by the banks at the end of 1988 allowed some freedom of movement but was heavy and restrictive enough for the company to want to replace it with something lighter if the opportunity arose. The senior bank loan facility of $1.1 billion shared by Citibank and the ANZ was divided into two parts. The first, called a senior amortising facility, was a seven-year loan of $750 million, the principal of which would be repayable in varying quarterly amounts leaving a lump sum payment of $192.5 million at maturity in 1996. A swap agreement converted the floating interest rate on this loan to a fixed rate of 15.3425 per cent a year for the first five years. But the company would not have to pay this interest until after January 1994. The banks would in effect lend the company the accumulating interest which, at the end of the five years would total $703 million. That would be payable in January 1996 if not beforehand. The floating rate on this accreting facility would effectively be fixed at 16.8425 per cent by another interest rate swap. Interest on the senior amortising facility, after accumulating for the first five years would convert to a current pay basis for the last two years of its life by which time the principal would be substantially reduced by the quarterly staggered payments.

The second part of the $1.1 billion senior bank facility was a seven-year $350 million loan, known as a senior bullet facility, repayable in full in January 1996. Interest rate on this had been effectively fixed at 16.4367 per cent. Only $300 million of the bullet loan was to be drawn immediately. In addition the ANZ would provide $80 million for working capital if and when it was needed. That was called a revolver. Initially, at least, the company had the revolver and $50 million of the bullet up its sleeve. There were also the loans from the superannuation and provident funds. The net result of all this in a full year with the Australian loan armoury in place, say 1990, would be that the Australian loans, including those from the funds, would attract interest totalling $193 million. But only $57 million of this would be payable in that year. In addition, $82 million interest would be payable on the $450 million of debentures raised by Drexel. Earnings before interest in that year were forecast at $168 million and operating cash flow (earnings before interest plus depreciation) at $196 million. On that basis, allowing for $4 million for the company's investment income, the company would have operated at a loss of $90 million but with an operating cash flow surplus of $57 million. The surplus would be used to pay off, in the staggered instalments, the $750 million amortising facility.

The Australian bank loans were secured by all the assets of, and shares in, the John Fairfax group, except those of the US company set up to handle the debenture issues. The loan agreement subjected the company to covenants relating to any dividend payments, new borrowings, investments and capital expenditures, and committed the company to maintaining certain ratios and earning levels. The covenants effectively put the banks in charge if the company's performance slipped. The subordinated US debentures and EARs contain similar covenants on the sale of assets (including Mary Fairfax's assets, although she had greater leeway than Warwick or the company) and the maintenance of minimum cash flows. The covenants could inhibit the public flotation of John Fairfax Group, or any subsidiary, such as David Syme, in the 1990s.

Warwick Fairfax's takeover, at the end of 1987, had thus, at the beginning of 1989, delivered the company to the banks' control by exception. He needed the money, the banks needed security. To work its way out of this, his company, John Fairfax Group, would need substantial increases in cash flow from 1991 onwards and particularly after 1994 when interest would no longer be carried. It would hope for a continued, reasonably buoyant, though inevitably fluctuating, level of business in the first half of the 1990s. After 1991 it could refinance the senior bank debt without penalty if the market climate was right. The interest burden could be relieved by the introduction of new equity capital. That would depend on the company's operating performance and stockmarket conditions. No local investors would go in without voting rights and this could involve some tricky negotiations around the EARs covenants. The company would certainly look for substantially lower interest rates in 1994 and a rise in its own credit rating to allow it to refinance the $703 million of capitalised interest, then continued good trading conditions and reasonable interest rates in the second half of the 1990s: in 1996 when it could finance the repayment of the $350 million bullet facility and the remaining $192.5 million owing on the amortising facility at substantially lower rates than it had been paying for the previous seven years; and from 1999 onwards when it could pay out the subordinated debentures with funds costing much less than the 18 per cent and 18.5 per cent the company had been paying on those bonds. If this could be achieved with the Australian dollar at or above US88 cents so that the FEARs would not be a liability, then the company would pull off a remarkable treble: prosperous profits, low interest rates at the right time, and a high exchange rate against the US dollar at the right time. Continued inflation at a rate not likely to scare the central banks and not too far out of line with that of America would also help by reducing the real value of the debt. If all this happened, and the newspapers maintained their competitive position, Warwick Fairfax could greet the 21st century in sole control (assuming no new voting equity capital had been issued) of a prosperous, profitable company worth several billions of dollars. The odds about all three happening at the right time in the right place were very long indeed.

If all the EARs were paid out by the issue of C non-voting shares in John Fairfax Group, Warwick would own 45 per cent of the company's issued capital (all the Australian dollar A class full-voting shares), Mary Fairfax would own 15 per cent of the capital (all the Australian dollar B class non-voting shares) and ex-debenture holders and others would own 40 per cent of the capital (all the one cent C class non-voting shares).

Alternatively, Warwick could end up with very little, the banks having taken charge of the company due to continued breaches of its loan covenants. The banks may or may not have decided to sell assets to meet the company's debts. The ANZ and Citibank were very well secured. But as the disclosure documents filed with the SEC in America pointed out, 'mortgagees in possession or any receiver or manager appointed by the mortgagee have at law certain duties of fairness to a company in respect of the price realised upon the exercise of any power for sale'. Potential Australian buyers for the main newspapers at big prices would be few, as they were for the *Age* in 1988, and the banks could remain as lenders in possession, refinancing their loans into the never-never, waiting for buyers at the right price to turn up. The outcome could be somewhere between the ideal and the disaster. The company would be working for its bankers and advisers.

A possible complicating factor which could upset all predictions came out of the accounting profession in 1989. In order to keep some balance between shareholders' equity and rising debt, particularly when the capitalised interest came to be funded, and to rebuild equity during the early loss-making years, the company would be relying on revaluations of its assets, mainly its mast-heads. In this it would be following the same practice as another big borrower, Rupert Murdoch's News Corporation. This was essentially window dressing, building up public perception of the company's net worth. The accounting profession was becoming increasingly uneasy about masthead and brand name valuations in company accounts and later in 1989 proposals were put forward suggesting that companies should write those values off against profits over a suitable period, perhaps 20 years. The *Sydney Morning Herald* and the *Age* had built their valuations up over more than 150 years.

The proposed new accounting standards could decimate Fairfax's and News Corporation's profits and severely undermine their financial strategies.

At the end of 1989 business was still buoyant but slowing as the Government's high-interest rate regime put the brakes on the economy's too-rapid rate of expansion in 1988-89. The prospect was that interest rates would fall later in 1990 but that the business cycle would continue downwards before stabilising and moving up again. Business would continue to fluctuate at a reasonably high level but not, until late in the decade, on the strong growth pattern achieved in 1988-89. Prospects for interest rates and the exchange rate would depend partly on inflation, particularly compared to America, and the higher that was, the higher interest rates would be and the lower the exchange rate. On the experience of the unregulated markets of the 1980s, which were subject to heavy and unpredictable capital flows, it was unlikely that interest rates would be low and the exchange rate high at the same time in the 1990s, although the reverse could happen under high inflation. On these bases the company could get the first leg of the treble up, but probably only one of the other two.

Above these broad economic vistas there was a cloud somewhat bigger than a man's hand, in the shape of Rupert Murdoch. As the direct competitor with the *Age* and the *Sydney Morning Herald* in Melbourne and Sydney, Murdoch could attack their market shares in newspaper sales and advertising. His first assault was in Melbourne where he launched two Sunday newspapers, the *Sunday Herald* and the *Sunday Sun News-Pictorial*, forcing David Syme to launch the *Sunday Age*. All three hit the market on 20 August 1989. The Sunday *Age* had a lot to protect. Murdoch's long-term strategy would be to enlarge his newspapers' share of the total advertising market, particularly of the classified advertising market dominated by the *Age* and the *Sydney Morning Herald* in the two big capital cities. That could take a very long time. The Melbourne *Herald* had tried it before Murdoch took it over and the *Age* had fought back and won a total victory. In Sydney, Murdoch's *Daily* and *Sunday Telegraphs* had attacked the *Sydney Morning Herald*'s market position over many years and made some headway at times. But in the 1980s the *Sydney Morning Herald* had fought back strongly and increased its share. Debenture registration documents filed with the SEC in America showed that Fairfax had estimated a $7 million loss on the *Sunday Age* in the first year and continued losses for some years after that.

Murdoch had another punch coming in the 1990s. In Melbourne and Sydney he planned new newspaper printing plants with full colour presses, which would increase the competitive circulation and advertising pressures on Fairfax in both cities, particularly in Sydney where Fairfax's press lines had been designed to print many pages of editorial, display and classified advertising in black ink. To seasoned newspaper executives these were the continuing competitive challenges of an industry where gains were rarely quick or easily made. One quality needed in these long market battles was staying power, the qualities the pre-1987 Fairfax company had shown with the *Australian Financial Review* and the *National Times* and Murdoch had shown with the *Australian*. Warwick Fairfax had shown resilience at critical times in October 1987 and in the second half of 1988 but his long-term commitment and staying power were being increasingly questioned as 1989 turned into 1990. His bankers had had staying power thrust upon them, but could not be regarded as committed newspaper owners. Warwick paid a heavy price, through the terms he had to offer on the $450 million issue of subordinated debentures, to hold on to all the voting stock at the end of 1988. The EARs and FEARs were wild cards in all future plays about John Fairfax Group. Perhaps in 1988 Warwick felt that he could not part with some of his control so soon after the traumatic events he had been through to acquire it. He would have to reconsider this in the 1990s, as he looked for ways to ease the burden of the company's debt.

# CHAPTER 16

# THE FEE AS BIG AS THE RITZ

Early in the New Year of 1989 Nick Whitlam stood at the entrance of the house he had recently bought overlooking Whale Beach, an hour's drive north of Sydney, greeting his guests, 'Welcome to Wocka Waters.' He was acknowledging, in the Whitlam manner, the contribution Warwick (Wocka) Geoffrey Oswald Fairfax had made to Whitlam Turnbull's very successful first year in 1988. To John Fairfax Ltd, Whitlam Turnbull's arrival in January 1988 had been like Major Davies reaching Baden Powell at Mafeking. Fairfax had been relieved. As Warwick Fairfax explained when asked by T. E. F. Hughes, QC, in the fee case, whether he was surprised by the $2 million fee he said he understood Laurie Connell had paid Marty Dougherty for a couple of weeks public relations work during the rescue of Rothwells late in October 1987: 'Perhaps people tend to be grateful when they are saved from going under, and are more likely to be generous'.

Fairfax paid Whitlam Turnbull over $9 million in fees for their work early in 1988. A much bigger fee would have been earned if Whitlam Turnbull had sold all or part of David Syme Ltd. But the Fairfax board decided to keep Syme. When Warwick terminated Whitlam Turnbull's mandate to sell it at a meeting on 18 April, Nick Whitlam and Malcolm Turnbull withdrew from the room to talk. Turnbull recorded that, when they returned, he said, 'We consider an appropriate abort fee in the event of your deciding not to sell all of Syme is $3 million.' The Fairfax directors thought that would be all right but they would think about it first. The abort fee finally agreed and paid was $2 million. After a rewarding three months for both parties, relations between Fairfax and Whitlam Turnbull cooled rapidly after 18 April.

'Wocka Waters' was a relatively modest example of the way fees generated from mushrooming financial markets in the 1980s, fed the property boom in the central business districts and fashionable residential areas of the capital cities. In Sydney's Eastern suburbs merchant bankers and corporate jugglers, fire-eaters and trapeze artists from both sides of the Tasman Sea were pacesetters in the soaring residential market. In 1988 Nick Whitlam's partner Malcolm Turnbull paid $2.2 million for a Victorian villa in Paddington and in neighbouring Woollahra, Whitlam Turnbull's chairman Neville Wran, extended his house by buying and renovating the house next door. But Sydney's eastern suburbs could not match Perth for conspicuous fee-based property consumption. At the peak of his fortunes in 1987, as he looked forward to capitalising himself at $300 million on the stockmarket, before the National Companies and Securities Commission (NCSC) started moving in on him, Laurie Connell planned a $20 million house on the seven residential blocks he had bought and razed for the purpose. Laurie was the fee master.

The property markets were supercharged by fees. These included the time-based fees of the accountants and lawyers, the value based fees of the brokers and of the merchant bankers when they acted as brokers, and combinations of both, overlaid with the inspirational fees of the merchant bankers acting as advisers. Accounting firms, which 10 years previously had modestly shown a brass plate to the world, now occupied buildings bearing their names. Lawyers were slightly more reticent but were major occupiers of prime office space in the cities. The activities of both and merchant banking were overlapping as accountants and lawyers went after advisers' fees to help pay the rents. Excluding the $27 million Fairfax finally agreed to pay as full settlement of the $100 million Warwick Fairfax had initially agreed to pay Rothwells for organising his takeover of the company, Fairfax was up for around $80 million in fees in 1988–89, paid by being added to its bank loans. That helped pay some rents in Sydney and Melbourne and Los Angeles. The $80 million included fees to the bankers and the bankers' legal advisers as well as the company's own advisers.

Citibank was advised by Mallesons Stephen Jaques, normally Fairfax's lawyers too, but Mallesons could not act for both. Fairfax turned to Freehill, Hollingdale and Page. Drexel used Minter Ellison in Australia, the ANZ, Baker and McKenzie. In Los Angeles, Drexel was advised by Latham and Watkins and Fairfax by O'Melveny and Myers. The bills went to Fairfax. Fees were big all right. They substantially underwrote the property boom. But the $100 million Rothwells was to get from Fairfax for organising the takeover was the biggest of them all. (Rothwells did not get their $100 million and Fairfax was diminished by the takeover but the law firms kept growing. Rothwells, under a provisional liquidator, vacated their half floor of prime office space on the 12th floor at the AMP's 50 Bridge Street building on 31 December 1988. Baker and McKenzie moved in. The solicitors already occupied four floors of the building and needed more space. Further up, Mallesons occupied 10 floors and were also taking more. Baker and McKenzie's move brought them briefly closer to one of their clients, Spedley Securities, which occupied one of Sydney's most opulently furnished offices on the 10th floor. Closely associated with Rothwells, Spedley also went broke and moved out in April 1989. The Mitsui Bank moved in.)

Much of the work Whitlam Turnbull did for $9 million was highly critical of the work Rothwells had done for $100 million. That criticism helped Warwick Fairfax and his fellow Fairfax directors to decide not to pay the Rothwells fee. In the court case which followed, recollections differed about the origins of the fee. But on one matter all parties to the $100 million fee were agreed: it should remain secret for as long as possible. Warwick said he wanted to keep it secret because the media would not understand why it was so big and that could jeopardise the success of the takeover bid. Connell and Reuter went along with this. The $100 million fee formally agreed on 28 August 1987, was omitted from all financial estimates and projections supplied to the ANZ Bank by Bert Reuter and from all legal documents and other information supplied to Tryart's legal advisers, Blake Dawson Waldron. A Blake Dawson Waldron partner handling the takeover, David Frecker, said he did not know about the fee until November 1987.

The Rothwells fee for advice far exceeded the fees the ANZ Bank would earn by committing its funds to the takeover. The Bank's second offer of $1.75 billion was subject to a $5.47 million arrangement fee, of which $1.1 million was payable immediately on acceptance of the offer and $2.73 million on signing of documentation, plus a line fee based on the total amount payable monthly in advance irrespective of usage plus a utilisation fee when Tryart started drawing down the facility. Then there were stamp duties and other costs. Warwick had no money. He had to borrow $10 million from Rothwells to meet these upfront payments. That loan was secured by some of Rockwood's shares in John Fairfax Ltd. It was possibly the best-secured loan in Rothwells's loan book.

The Australian trading banks had come late to the big fee bonanza. Commitment and other fees had helped drive the US banks into their loans to Third World countries in the late 1970s and into other risky lending on property and inflated asset values, which caused a crisis in the US banking industry in the 1980s. Deregulation of Australian banking and foreign exchange markets in the 1980s let the Australian banks loose into new fee territory after years in the straightjacket of controls when they had had to rely wholly on the spread between borrowing and lending rates for their profits. The spread was still their bread and butter. Fees were, or could be, jam. Early enthusiasm for fees had lured some of them into the excesses of the Swiss loan switch they sold their customers into in 1984–85. That rebounded on them four years later when the customers queued to sue them for negligence or unfair practices.

The inevitable results of that early orgy had not curbed the banks' fee appetite. Big upfront corporate lending fees fed, and were fed by, the growth of such exploding stars as Ariadne, Equiticorp, Chase Corporation and the National Safety Council of Victoria. The lure of the fee and changes in prudential standards went hand in hand. The new emphasis on fees reflected the growing attraction and importance of transaction as against relationship banking, the shortening time frames in which finance-dominated enterprise was thinking, the emphasis on doing the deal, taking the fee, then looking for the next deal. That was the way markets worked and markets were always right.

The merchant banks had been perfecting the arts of advising and fee charging for over two hundred years. These arts had been developed in Europe and the City of London and adapted to the newer markets of America, Asia and Australasia. They had made fortunes for the Hambros, Rothschilds and Warburgs. At their peak Baring Bros had been described as the sixth power of a Europe dominated by England, France, Russia, Austria and Prussia. That was before Baring was caught by its own excessive enthusiasm for South American bonds and had to be rescued after the Gaucho banking scandal of 1890. The merchants had moved with the times. Instead of financing and advising on the wars and takeovers of sovereign states, they were into financing and advising on the wars and takeovers of commercial enterprises. But when it came to fee charging, the City's descendants in Australia were upstaged by the Little Steamroller, Laurie Connell.

Laurie, like his close friend Alan Bond, was a fee super-charger. He charged what the market would bear and the big bull market of the 1980s could bear a lot. Assuming legal and other costs of the takeover ran up to $10 million and Marty Dougherty got his $10 million, Connell and Reuter would get $40 million each for six months work. If they worked 12 hours a day for every day of that six months the fee would have been equal to nearly $20 000 an hour. When rumours started to spread in Australian financial markets in November 1987 about the size of Rothwells's fee for the Fairfax takeover it was generally assumed that Connell had set the figure and Warwick Fairfax, the novice, had gone along with it. But on evidence produced in the court case, which followed Fairfax's refusal to pay the $100 million, the initiative might equally have been Warwick's. William E. Simon, the US investment banker and Fairfax adviser, had said that Warwick knew the value of two dollars but did not know the value of $2 billion. Nobody was sure what Warwick's values were. He was certainly not impressed by a few more noughts in money figures. Bert Reuter recalled that when he told Warwick they would get less from the Skase contract than they had originally thought, Warwick

had said, 'That only means more junk finance doesn't it?' Laurie
Connell recalled that when they were closing the assets sale to
John B. Fairfax for $78 million he had suggested to Warwick that
another $10 million or $20 million could be got out of them.
But Warwick wanted to do the deal at $78 million — another
$10 or $20 million was neither here nor there.

The idea of a big fee payment for Connell to organise the Fairfax
takeover appeared to surface in June-July 1987. The original plan,
to make the bid through a joint venture between Laurie Connell
and Warwick Fairfax, faded when Warwick insisted on control. It
did not look too rewarding for Laurie either. He would have had
to put up $200 million for his share and $25 million for Warwick.
Somebody came up with an alternative. Laurie would do it for
a fee. Marty Dougherty said the idea was Warwick's, and that he
had a note made on the back of a babysitter's invoice to prove
it. He said that about 10 June he had a call at home in Sydney
from Warwick in America. Warwick was concerned for his control
of the takeover and of the company afterwards. According to Marty,
Warwick said, 'My inclination is that, instead of having a 50–50
partnership with Connell, at the eleventh hour I will tell him
I want 51 per cent of the venture with him to have 49 per cent,
or alternatively I will offer Connell a tremendous return for his
involvement, say, $100 million fee.' Marty said he scribbled notes
as they spoke on the back of a babysitter's bill, which happened
to be lying beside the telephone. The bill defined the date of
the conversation.

Warwick seemed to run hot and cold on Connell, but mainly
hot. He suggested to Dougherty that Reuter's work on the takeover
proposal had been so impressive that perhaps they should go
without Connell. Dougherty would not have that. He emphasised
that Warwick needed Connell. Dougherty went overseas in June,
then Connell went away in July. The takeover planning seemed
to languish. Then on about 22 July — a long time after 10 June
— Dougherty told Connell that Warwick had suggested a $100
million fee instead of the joint venture. Connell said he was happy
to change the position from that of joint venturer to adviser on
a fee basis. According to Marty he then rang Warwick and
said, 'I'm pretty sure that Laurie will do it for the $100 million

fee,' Warwick replied, 'That's terrific. You don't think he will change his mind?' Marty said, 'I don't think so.' Warwick finished, 'That's great.'

Warwick's story differed. He said he had raised the idea of a fee in May but Dougherty had said Connell would not be in it. Warwick claimed Marty later said to him, 'I have discussed it again with Laurie and he is willing to do it for a $100 million fee and not a joint venture. He says it is a take-it or leave-it fee, that he will do it for that and that is the price.' Warwick said he replied, 'That is a lot of money.' To that Marty said, 'It is a take-it or leave-it fee. Where else can we go?' Discussions followed. Warwick said he wanted to see a proposal before committing himself to the fee. Whichever story was correct Connell and Reuter quickly agreed on how the fee should be split.

On the morning of 22 July, the day or thereabouts that Marty as go-between said he had tentatively fixed the $100 million with Laurie Connell and Warwick Fairfax, Connell and Reuter agreed to split the fee between them after allowing Marty 10 per cent. But they also agreed that they would give Marty the impression that Reuter would only be getting 10 per cent, the same as Marty, and Connell would look after the rest — $80 million less certain expenses. They told Marty this at lunch. He was happy to think he would be getting the same as Reuter.

So at that stage this was the situation between Warwick and his key advisers: Warwick had agreed to pay $100 million, but the bank was not to know about it; Connell and Reuter knew how the fee was to be split; Dougherty thought he knew but was unaware that Reuter was to get as much as Connell; and Warwick, according to his later evidence, did not know Dougherty was to get anything at all from the fee. Dougherty denied this and claimed that a few days after the Perth meeting with Connell and Reuter, he had rung Warwick and said, 'Laurie has asked me to commit myself totally to the takeover process and to give up as far as I can the day to day work for my other clients. Laurie has instructed Reuter to prepare a plan based on the $100 million fee rather than the joint venture idea. He has locked Reuter into the deal by offering him 10 per cent of the fee. He has also offered me a bonus of up to 10 per cent of the fee, the same as he has offered Reuter.'

Marty said Warwick replied, 'That's fine by me.' Warwick denied the conversation ever took place. The only other people who knew about the fee appeared to be Warwick's and Mary's legal adviser, Carnegie Fieldhouse, and Peter King.

At various meetings in Fieldhouse's office during August the fee was discussed. Fieldhouse thought it was too high and should be negotiated down. On his brief visit in mid-August, Peter King, whom Warwick had approached about being his chief executive officer if he took over John Fairfax Ltd, also thought it was too high. Warwick was unfazed by these reservations. Connell had been pressing for the fee to be paid when Warwick got control of the Fairfax company, when he had 50.1 per cent of the shares (that is 36.15 per cent in addition to the shares he said he already controlled). This was impossible since Warwick had no money and he could not borrow it from the ANZ Bank since he did not want the Bank or anybody else outside the inner Tryart circle to know about it. At a meeting at Fieldhouse's office on 14 August it was agreed that the $100 million would have to be paid by John Fairfax Ltd, after Warwick had taken complete control of the company. About that time Connell decided that his share of the fee should go to Rothwells rather than direct to his own company, L. R. Connell and Associates. The fee payment was fixed at 180 days after Warwick's company obtained control of over 50.1 per cent of the shares. That should give Warwick, or Tryart, time to take control of John Fairfax Ltd's funds, from which the fee would be paid.

Friday, 28 August, was a big day in the history of the Fairfax takeover. On that day the ANZ Bank committed itself twice to finance the takeover: first for $1.3 billion, then for $1.7 billion (by 10 November it was $2.1 billion). Warwick acquired the two dollar company, Tryart Pty Ltd, as the takeover vehicle. And the Tryart agreement, which set out the terms of Rothwells's engagement, was signed. The agreement was between Rothwells, Tryart and The Rockwood Pastoral Co. Pty Ltd, the family company controlled by Warwick and his mother, Mary Fairfax. Warwick and Rockwood had one share each in Tryart. Mary Fairfax was overseas and Warwick had her power of attorney.

Fieldhouse continued to question the size of the fee and advised Warwick to negotiate it down. Warwick asked Marty

Dougherty what he thought. Warwick and Marty differed substantially in their versions of what happened next. According to Warwick, he, Marty and Fieldhouse left Connell and Reuter in Fieldhouse's office and caucused outside. According to Warwick, Marty said, 'We are being far too tough. We should not be so tough, otherwise Connell will walk away and if he does we've had it.' On the fee, according to Warwick, Dougherty said, 'The $100 million is cheap in comparison with the joint venture proposal.' Warwick claimed he replied, 'This is no notional buyout of Connell's interest in the joint venture. The question is whether the services provided during the takeover and restructuring are worth $100 million.'

Dougherty's version was that when Warwick asked for his opinion on negotiating the fee down, he, Dougherty, replied, 'It's up to you to decide whether you want to go ahead with the takeover or whether you don't want to go ahead with the takeover' to which Warwick replied, 'Well, clearly, I want to proceed.' Marty also recalled that when the meeting ended an exultant Warwick said to him as they left the office, 'Laurie doesn't know it but I would gladly have paid him $200 million to get control of the company in my own right.' Which version was correct, if either? Marty had 10 million reasons for pushing Warwick into a $100 million fee deal with Connell. But he claimed Warwick knew this. Warwick claimed he did not.

Warwick could not complain if Connell and Reuter appeared to be pushing him into the takeover, or at least not holding him back. He had agreed to a $100 million fee for Connell and knew Reuter would be getting some of it. They had cautioned him that the going could get pretty rough during the next few weeks but they were not cautioning him not to go ahead. Marty was a different matter. He was a family confidant of some years' standing. In neither version of the conversation on 28 August did he say, 'Look, I'm getting 10 per cent. Remember that when you ask me if the fee should be negotiated down.' One person might have quickly decided which of these versions of the conversation was correct — Carnegie Fieldhouse. Dougherty's solicitors, Gilbert and Tobin, explored the possibility of seeking a statement from Fieldhouse on the matter. But as a long-term legal adviser to the

Warwick and Mary Fairfax family, who was uninvolved with anyone else in the fee case, Fieldhouse could quite properly claim that such a statement would be a breach of professional privilege and none was asked for.

The Tryart agreement signed that day stated:

It is understood and agreed that Rothwells shall furnish its services under this agreement by and through:
(a) L. R. Connell and Bert Reuter; and
(b) such other consultants, solicitors and professional advisers as Rothwells may deem necessary subject always to obtaining the approval of the offeror in relation thereto.

Connell claimed Warwick insisted on this as, after Rothwells was named as the adviser, he wanted to be assured of the direct services of Connell and Reuter and not be left to rely on sub-ordinates. The wording could also justify Rothwells committing the fee to Connell and Reuter after meeting expenses. Dougherty was not mentioned. He witnessed Warwick's signature. Although Rothwells was to receive the $100 million under the agreement, Connell was only entitled to $45 million because of the secret 22 July agreement with Reuter and Dougherty, and this was all he could assign to Rothwells. As a result, Rothwells only raised $45 million in its own books as the fee due from Tryart. This had important consequences when the fee needed to be discounted in November.

For the next two months, Connell, Reuter and Dougherty were all busy earning the $100 million. On 27 October Tryart made its finally agreed offer of $8.50 a share. The next day Fairfax directors recommended that shareholders accept the offer and Warwick quickly had 50.1 per cent of the company. The $100 million would be payable at the end of April 1988. But Rothwells had been caught in the 19–20 October stockmarket crash and, despite a desperate injection of $300 million in a rescue operation over the weekend of 24–25 October, still needed all the ready money it could get. Connell and his legal adviser Aleco Vrisakis were preoccupied with Rothwells' rescue. On 29 October, Vrisakis had asked the NCSC to call off the investigations into Rothwells since they might jeopardise its rescue. The NCSC eventually agreed to do this if Rothwells surrendered its dealer's licence, Connell was replaced, the company no longer solicited funds from the public, and the company's practices be audited and overhauled. Vrisakis joined the Rothwells board. The objectives of the deal with the NCSC were never fulfilled. Vrisakis became the leading legal adviser to the Australian Securities Commission, which replaced the NCSC in 1990.

As the provisional liquidator of Rothwells, Ian Ferrier, later pointed out, the rescue of the company focused on the company's debts and not on the quality of its assets, which was very patchy indeed. Connell and Vrisakis, however, realised that the $100 million fee due from Warwick Fairfax could be one of the company's better assets and early in November 1987, set about discounting the fee for cash. The takeover had been exhausting but Warwick was on the verge of having 90 per cent of the shares and being able to acquire compulsorily any outstanding shares. The fee looked secure.

Warwick claimed that about this time Marty Dougherty told him that Connell had agreed to pay Marty $2 million for the public relations work Marty had done for Rothwells over those critical two weeks of late October, early November. He had been on a retainer of $10 000 a month from Rothwells to look after their public relations in the Eastern States. Marty was not yet in a position of editorial control at Fairfax, but Warwick had clearly won the company and he soon would be. He had no qualms, as Rothwells's consultant, about trying, unsuccessfully, to stop the Fairfax papers from reporting Rothwells's liquidity problems before and during the weekend of 24–25 October. Nevertheless, Marty was a very good media manipulator, as he had shown throughout the takeover, and Rothwells had a benign press immediately after the rescue. But $2 million for that? Marty's counsel, George Palmer, QC, argued in the fee case that Warwick had to invent some disclosure of a $2 million payment from Connell to Dougherty because he could not deny that he knew Dougherty was receiving $2 million from Connell well before he said he knew about Marty's split of the takeover fee. Warwick claimed throughout that the first he knew about that was after the litigation started at the beginning of July 1988.

In fact, many details of the fee had been published in an article headed 'The Mystery of the "Dynasty Corp" Success Fee', in the *Sydney Morning Herald* on 19 April 1988. The article, by Robert Whitehead, concluded, 'Mr Dougherty ... received both a large fee from Rothwells and a payout from Fairfax.' Warwick said he was not a regular reader of the *Sydney Morning Herald*, the newspaper he had just paid $2 billion to rescue. Sometimes his executives sent him cuttings from the papers. He could not remember Whitehead's article.

When it was decided to discount the $100 million Tryart fee, Rothwells turned to Whitlam Turnbull to help. Nick Whitlam had until recently been chief executive of the State Bank of NSW which was a possible discounter of the fee. Whitlam Turnbull would also have liked to establish a connection between Fairfax and the State Bank, which had become very active under Whitlam, widening and raising its client base.

The State Bank, as a matter of prudence, would not become involved in discounting the fee unless Warwick signed a document acknowledging that the fee was due and payable on the due date. This caused a problem. Acceptances of Warwick's takeover offer were pouring in, but the ANZ Bank had not yet formally committed itself to the $2.1 billion takeover facility, none of the asset sales agreements with John B. Fairfax, Murdoch, Packer or Holmes a Court had been consummated, and the refinancing of the ANZ debt was far from clear. If anything went wrong, the State Bank wanted to be assured that Warwick would still pay the $100 million. Warwick said he was being pushed by Vrisakis and Dougherty to sign the document for Laurie Connell who had done so much for him and who could fall over unless Warwick signed, and the last thing he wanted was for his merchant bank to fall over, wasn't it?

Warwick asked Bert Reuter what he thought. Reuter, after sleeping on it for a night, advised Warwick not to sign. Warwick also thought Reuter added, 'I think you should get another lawyer, other than Aleco, to look at this.' He consulted David Frecker of Blake, Dawson Waldron, who pointed to the hazards of signing. Warwick did not sign. He had come very close. Whitlam Turnbull later suggested to Laurie Connell that they should receive a kill fee of $1 million for the work they had done for Rothwells on attempts to discount the fee. Laurie understood fees. He also understood the condition of Rothwells. He agreed to the fee but only on condition that Whitlam Turnbull deposit the fee with Rothwells. In the Report on Rothwells's Affairs provided to the company's provisional liquidators in December 1988, Whitlam Turnbull was shown as an unsecured creditor for $1.01 million. Under the provisional liquidator's scheme the cut-off for repayment in full for unsecured creditors was $1 million. By late 1988, however, Whitlam Turnbull were advising the West Australian Government on its attempts to extricate itself from the Rothwells and associated affairs.

After the State Bank discounting effort failed, Whitlam Turnbull turned to Sir Peter Abeles and his international transport group, Thomas Nationwide Transport (TNT), though Connell had been keen to try and get Packer involved in the discounting deal. Abeles spoke to Warwick about it and an agreement was reached, which Warwick signed on 6 November. But that too fell through. Warwick said Marty Dougherty told him Connell had decided that the discount was too steep. That was timely. Connell's close friend Alan Bond had come up with a better idea for the fee. Details of this arrangement did not come out until Rothwells went into provisional liquidation, the litigation about the fee was settled in February 1989, and the managing director of Bond Media, Sam Chisholm, and the chairman, Warren Jones, were examined by the Australian Broadcasting Tribunal on the matter of Bond's fitness to hold a television broadcasting licence.

From these three sources it appeared that, when he learned Laurie Connell wanted to discount the fee, Alan Bond, or one of his advisers, saw an opportunity to give Bond Media's profits a much needed boost in 1987–88. Profits from television were nowhere near enough to justify the company's capitalisation. Bond, in Perth, called Warren Jones in Sydney and told him to get moving. Bond said there was an $18 million fee involved for Bond Media. The Bond Media plan for handling the fee seemed to go through several costume changes between 9 November and 19 November. In effect, Bond Media lent Rothwells $100 million. The fee was assigned to Bond Media in return for the loan, which was also guaranteed by Rothwells and Connell, personally. But Rothwells did not receive or keep the $100 million in cash. Connell's 45 per cent share only had been taken net into Rothwells's accounts. Rothwells may have been able to deal in the $100 million fee, but it was the beneficial owner of only 45 per cent of it. Reuter's and Dougherty's claims to the fee had to be acquired before it could be assigned to Bond Media.

Reuter was already very worried about what was happening to the fee. He, too, had been looking forward to 45 per cent of it. He knew about the attempts to discount or borrow against it with the State Bank on 5 November and TNT on 6 November. On Saturday, 7 November, he rang David Frecker. They met at Blake Dawson Waldron's office that morning. Reuter's relations with Vrisakis had cooled, as they had with Connell, over his advice to Warwick not to sign the State Bank agreement. He told Frecker about the arrangements made in July to split the fee. Reuter had made notes on a manila folder recording the way it was to be split, after costs had been met: 10 per cent to Dougherty for introducing the takeover project to Connell, the balance to be divided equally between Reuter and Connell. Frecker pointed out that he worked for Blake Dawson Waldron, advisers to Tryart, and Reuter should see someone else. (Blake Dawson were also advising Bond Media on the fee.) He referred Reuter to Robert Anderson of Sly and Russell (later Sly and Weigall).

This was one occasion when the need for independent advice for each individual party to these agreements was recognised. The lines between who was advising whom and whose interests they represented when giving that advice were becoming increasingly blurred. That was not unusual in 1987 and 1988 when the records of some companies, including Rothwells's, became one continuous blur. On 9 November, Sly and Russell, acting for Reuter, wrote to Warwick Fairfax and the directors of Tryart and The Rockwood Pastoral Co. Pty Ltd, referring to the payment of the $100 million fee agreed in August:

> As you know Rothwells is to receive that fee as trustee for certain parties including our client who has a substantial interest in it.

We understand that Rothwells is endeavouring to assign the benefits of the August agreement, which it holds in trust for the parties mentioned above.

We hereby request that you confirm to us that you will not consent to any such arrangement without first giving our client notice of the transaction in respect of which your consent has been requested, and further, that you will do all in your power to safeguard the interest of our client in the fee payable by your company to Rothwells pursuant to the August agreement.

Warwick did not respond to the letter. Reuter had been in touch with Connell in Perth about the fee over the weekend and Connell dispatched Dougherty to fix things up. Connell said they could have $10 million between them in full settlement of their claims. Connell knew his men. Reuter could see his prize shrinking. He knew he had a strong hand but he could use the money and realistically had to settle. Dougherty, who had thought he was entitled to half the $10 million, realised he had been hoodwinked in August into thinking he would be getting as much as Reuter. After some fairly tense discussions they agreed to settle and split the $10 million in about the ratio Reuter had originally agreed with Connell: Reuter took $8 million, Dougherty $2 million. In return they gave up their claims to the fee, signing a covenant with Bond Media to that effect on 19 November, the day Bond Media advanced the $100 million to Rothwells. Reuter and Dougherty were paid with cheques from Bond Media.

That was $10 million off the $100 million Bond Media lent Rothwells. Bond Media also took an $18 million fee for discounting the $100 million fee. So, of the $100 million loan, Rothwells received only about $72 million in cash. Of this $66 million came from the merchant bank, Indosuez Australia Ltd, secured against the fee and Rothwells's promise to pay up to $128 million to repay Bond Media's $100 million loan. Bond Corporation Finance also advanced Bond Media $16 million, which covered the payment to Reuter and Dougherty and most of the balance that went to Rothwells. The deal enabled Bond Media to claim its $18 million fee, less interest charges, as part of its profits for 1987–88. An added inducement for Warwick to sign this time was the extension of the due date for payment of the fee to 28 June 1988. This was still within Bond Media's financial year, which ended on 30 June.

In his opening address for Tryart in the fee case, Neil McPhee, QC, referred to Vrisakis as adviser to both Rothwells (where he also became a director) and Warwick Fairfax in November 1987, when assignment of the fee to the State Bank of NSW and then to TNT and Bond Media was being discussed. McPhee suggested that, at the time of the assignment of the fee to Bond Media it could be inferred that Vrisakis was acting for Bond and knew that Dougherty and Reuter, to whom Bond was paying $10 million for assignment of their interest in the fee, were directors of Tryart by whom the fee was payable. This led to a sharp exchange between McPhee and T. E. F. Hughes, QC, for Bond Media at the end of McPhee's opening address. Hughes wanted to know what McPhee meant by raising the matter of Vrisakis's role. It was not mentioned in Tryart's defence pleadings. Justice Giles asked McPhee whether he wanted to say whether or how he would rely upon 'acts or omissions' of Mr Vrisakis. McPhee said that all he had said was that Tryart might 'seek to rely on Mr Vrisakis's knowledge of certain matters'. The case was settled and the opportunity to do that was never tested.

In evidence before the Australian Broadcasting Tribunal on 28 February 1989, Sam Chisholm said that the fee deal was the only occasion when Bond Media had been used as a vehicle for 'other money-making enterprises outside broadcasting'. As a Bond Media director he had been present at the board meeting that approved the purchase of the fee from Rothwells. He said the board discussed the deal for 15 to 20 minutes before approving it after recommendation by Bond Media's chairman, Warren Jones. The directors had been given no documents to support the recommendation but Chisholm agreed that there had been careful analysis before deciding to acquire the fee. 'By whom?' asked Richard Burbidge, QC, assisting the Tribunal. Chisholm replied that it was assessed by Warren Jones or the chairman's advisers. 'He has his own advisers.' Chisholm did not say which chairman he was referring to. Alan Bond was commonly known as the Chairman in the Bond group. Chisholm said the board approved the deal because it looked like a chance to make a profit. On 29 February 1989, after the fee had been reduced from $100 million to $27 million, he said the 'final washup figure of the loss was $30 million'. The cross-examination in February 1989, suggested that Burbidge and Chisholm both thought that Rothwells had discounted the fee to Bond Media for '$60 million-odd'.

Warren Jones told the Broadcasting Tribunal on 1 May 1989, that he thought Bond rang him on Thursday 5 November 1987 to tell him about the fee discount opportunity. That was the day Warwick torpedoed the negotiations with the State Bank. Jones said he had never heard that the TNT discount fee was too steep. After talking to Alan Bond he had rung Connell who sent him a copy of the 28 August Tryart agreement. Bond Media then appointed Blake Dawson Waldron (represented by David Selig) to handle the legalities. Jones thought that the idea of obtaining a Memorandum of Understanding about Tryart's payment of the fee came from the 'Freehill's chap representing Indosuez' but could not be sure. 'It was a consultative type situation where everybody was pleased when it emerged,' he said. Jones said it had not occurred to him that Rothwells wanted to discount the fee because it had financial problems. He had also obtained personal guarantees about repayment of the loan to Rothwells from Laurie Connell. He thought he had probably asked Connell about his financial position before seeking his guarantee. The $10 million payment to Reuter and Dougherty was not explored at the Tribunal hearing.

Warwick Fairfax signed, on behalf of Tryart, the Memorandum of Understanding about the assignment of the fee to Bond Media on 9 November 1987. All moneys payable to Rothwells under the 28 August agreement would be payable to Bond Media. To make that effective they had to buy out Reuter's and Dougherty's claims to the fee. There was no suggestion then that the fee would not be paid but Warwick did not commit himself irrevocably to paying the fee as the State Bank had required. In the Memorandum, Tryart agreed that:

... so far as it is aware, Rothwells has complied with its obligations under the Tryart agreement (made on 28 August) and that it is not presently aware of anything which would entitle Tryart to refuse to pay a fee calculated in accordance with Clause 5 of the Tryart agreement at the end of the period.

The key words became 'so far as it is aware'.

In paragraph 100 of his evidence statement in the court case, Warwick said:

> At that time there was nothing to suggest to me that Rothwells had not performed their services properly. At that time we had the Packer, Holmes a Court, News Ltd and John B. Fairfax agreements signed and I was about to obtain control of John Fairfax Ltd. It was only later that the asset sale agreements started to collapse, that I found out that the Skase agreement was worth less than had been thought, that Tryart could not use the superannuation funds as planned, that the banks to which Fairfax was currently indebted objected to the ANZ Bank receiving priority of repayment from the asset sales, that there were pre-emptive rights which prevented the sale of the Australian Associated Press (AAP) and Australian Newsprint Mills (ANM) shares, and that the debt to the ANZ would not be serviceable, or able to be repaid. I had no forewarning of the many problems which were to arise in the restructuring. Nor did I foresee that when those problems arose I would get no assistance from Rothwells, Connell and Reuter.

Fairfax's decision not to pay the fee was linked to the decision early in 1988 to get rid of Connell off the Fairfax boards as soon as possible. Ron Cotton said that during December, January and February bankers had expressed surprise that Connell was on the Fairfax board. One remarked, 'He lacks credibility because of the Rothwells crash.' Another said that Connell's presence on the board created a problem for the company's credit applications before the bank's credit committee. They reinforced the reservations about appointing Connell to the Fairfax board Bert Reuter had expressed to Cotton in November and early December. Then, as Whitlam Turnbull went through the deals Connell had done in September and October, particularly the deal with Holmes a Court, they became highly critical of Rothwells's performance.

When King was briefly in Australia in mid-January, they had talked about not paying the fee because of all the problems coming out of the takeover. Marty Dougherty had defended Connell's performance. Later, when Marty was not present, Warwick, King and Cotton had talked about getting rid of Connell but decided that could wait until the financial crisis with the banks had passed. Apart from anything else, the fee made Connell, or Rothwells, a substantial creditor of Fairfax and as such he might have challenged the resolutions that the company had to pass to accommodate the financial arrangements then being made with Citibank, the ANZ, Westpac, the National Australia Bank and a number of merchant banks. So Connell attended a Fairfax board meeting on 18 January, and left, still a director.

King repeated his reservations about paying the $100 million fee when he returned to Australia on 14 February to start work as chief executive. Dougherty was forced out the next day and when Chris Anderson was asked to become group editorial director two days later, he said he would only do so if Connell left. King said that was under control. Towards the end of February they felt they could wait no longer. King reported that Malcolm Turnbull had told him that, unless they removed Connell from the board now, a court, in any future litigation, might think that Fairfax was satisfied with his services.

Fairfax was leaning heavily on Whitlam Turnbull at this time. Turnbull took them to Roderick Meagher, QC, who advised that Connell should be removed forthwith. Meagher said Warwick Fairfax should not meet Connell but should handle the matter by letter. Meagher drafted the letter, which Turnbull then put down on Fairfax letterhead. Warwick signed. The letter, dated 4 March, asked Connell to sign the enclosed Notice of Resignation or face dismissal. Connell replied on 9 March on L. R. Connell letterhead asking for a 'better and frank explanation' and reminded Warwick of all the complimentary things Warwick had said about Laurie at the victory dinner at 'Fairwater' on 8 December. Warwick replied on 11 March giving Connell until 2 p.m. on 14 March to resign or be dismissed. He resigned on 11 March.

Although there appeared to be no formal minute of a Fairfax board resolution not to pay the fee, this had apparently been agreed by May. Fairfax's legal advisers, Mallesons Stephen Jaques, briefed Murray Gleeson, QC, on the matter. The brief passed to Neil McPhee, QC, when Gleeson accepted appointment as Chief Justice of the NSW Supreme Court. The *Sydney Morning Herald* reported the appointment on 17 August 1988. He took office on 2 November.

Fairfax did not reveal its intentions and did not pay the $100 million to Bond Media by 29 June 1987. Five days later Bond Media and Rothwells started legal action against Tryart for payment of the fee. Six weeks later Tryart filed a claim against Bond Media and Rothwells seeking at least $160 million damages. Three weeks after that Tryart widened the action to include Marty Dougherty and Bert Reuter as co-defendants seeking from them damages of up to $68 million. By this time Tryart had changed its name to John Fairfax Group Ltd. Fairfax had discovered that Dougherty may have received some payment from Rothwells. After some preliminary hearings before Justice Rogers the action started in earnest before Justice Giles in the commercial division of the NSW Supreme Court on Monday, 17 October. Justice Rogers had withdrawn at the last minute. The hearing had initially been estimated to last three weeks. When it started before Justice Giles, it was estimated to last six weeks.

Six weeks later, on 1 December, the 28th day of proceedings, with only one witness, Warwick Fairfax, cross-examined, Justice Giles announced that he would hear the case until the court rose for the Christmas break on 16 December, or into the following week if necessary. The proceedings would then be stood over until 28 July 1989. 'What started as a three-week sprint has become a five-month marathon,' he said. The case had been given priority because of the unusually large sums of money involved and its significance beyond the immediate parties. However, he said it was 'unfair to other litigants' that the case should be allowed to take up 'one-quarter of the judicial resources of the division'. The message was clear: this case should be settled between the parties. Seven months should give them time to do so.

Justice Giles had, from the outset, established his control of the case and of the legal stars appearing before him. But his attempts to cut through the claims and counter-claims, to find the shortest distance between any two points, or even to establish what the key points at issue were, seemed to be frustrated by the confusion of evidence and possible issues which, if anything, increased as the hearing progressed. Warwick Fairfax set the pace for most of the first six weeks with long pauses between questions and answers, as he picked his way through the minefields being laid by opposing counsel, requests to T. E. F. Hughes, QC, to repeat his questions, exchanges with Hughes about the meaning of words, and his repeated use of the answer, 'I don't recall it, but I don't deny it.'

After a shaky start, during his six weeks in the witness box Warwick at times seemed to be sustained by the presence of members of his Christian fellowship. A week after the hearings started he was asked to leave the court while the implications of a question Hughes had asked were discussed by the Judge and counsel. When he returned his answer to Hughes's question was in fluent contrast to his previous slow responses. Warwick seemed to cover all the issues that had been raised during his absence. 'Did you talk to someone outside the Court?' Hughes asked sharply. 'Yes,' said Warwick, 'to a Mr Tom Tressider of the NSW Bible Society.' Mr Tressider was an acquaintance, not a lawyer. On another occasion Hughes put to Warwick that the family directors of the company before the takeover — James, John and Sir Vincent Fairfax — were proud men, 'proud in the good sense of the word'. Warwick: 'I'm not sure "proud" has a good sense.' Hughes: 'A man can be proud of his reputation — that's a good sense? A man can be proud of his commercial honour?' Warwick: 'There is a difference between desiring to have commercial honour and having it.'

Only Bruce Oslington, QC, for Bert Reuter, seemed able to set the pace of cross-examination, to elicit reasonably quick and unequivocal responses from Warwick, although Warwick had problems remembering when and where Tryart's directors' meetings were held. That was not surprising as the board meetings after 28 August were held at various times between 11 a.m. and 6.30 p.m., at 50 Bridge Street, 60 Martin Place, the Regent Hotel, the Intercontinental Hotel, and usually lasted five or ten minutes. One, on 18 December 1987, at 50 Bridge Street, started, according to the minutes, at 5 p.m. and concluded at 5 p.m. It was not until 19 November 1987, that a meeting was held to ratify Warwick's execution of the 28 August agreement with Rothwells. Bond Media needed that to be sure the $100 million fee it was being assigned for the $100 million it was lending Rothwells that day was a legally binding fee.

There were two versions of this minute. One included the words:

Pursuant to the terms of the [28 August] agreement, and in light of the circumstances prevailing at the date of this meeting, the company will be obliged to pay Rothwells a fee of $100 million.

These words had been crossed out. The other version, which Warwick signed, omitted these words altogether, and merely ratified the 28 August agreement. The first minute looked like a last-minute attempt to get Warwick to go beyond the 28 August agreement in committing Tryart to pay the $100 million. Cross-examined by George Palmer, QC, for Marty Dougherty, Warwick could not remember much about how the minute came into existence. Marty Dougherty was the other director said to be at the 19 November meeting. Neither version of the minute was in the Tryart minute book produced to the court.

While the case was being heard, the restructuring of Fairfax's $1.6 billion debt was taking place in Australia and America. Drexel Burnham Lambert and its clients were receiving reports on the court hearing from Sydney. On 27 October Hughes was thus able to bowl the unplayable googly at Warwick, 'Is the company viable?' If Warwick said yes it would prejudice his case against Rothwells and for not paying the fee to Bond Media. If he said no it would prejudice the US bond raising. Neil McPhee, QC, for Fairfax, suggested that the company was not commercially viable before 30 June, which left open the possibility that it could have become viable since then, or could be made viable at some time in the future. Or was it viable all the time since it was not in liquidation? The court considered these matters in closed sessions. If the company was viable, it would hardly have had to do that.

The concept of commercial viability was a bag of brown snakes. But it shaped as a key issue. Tryart (by then called John Fairfax Group) said it had not paid the $100 million because it had not been earned. But what had Rothwells been obliged to do? Rothwells said it had been obliged to deliver John Fairfax Ltd to Tryart and had done so. Warwick said no, it had been obliged to deliver John Fairfax Ltd in viable condition and the company was not viable at 30 June since it could not service its debt. Rothwells had two answers to that: Warwick always knew what he was getting into and he looked like refinancing his way out of his debt crises anyway. But as Warwick pointed out it might be years before they knew whether the company would survive and he was entitled to expect the company to be delivered to him in much better condition than that. He wasn't told by his advisers to expect a financial cripple.

Fairfax had expert witnesses to say Warwick should have been advised to call the whole thing off after 19 October. But Warwick himself had been most eager to go ahead. There was a myriad of issues, not least of which was the credit of key witnesses. Days could be spent on cross-examination aimed at damaging a witness's credibility.

There were several contradictory versions of how the fee had come into existence. Someone was lying or had a very unreliable memory. But the fact that the agreed fee was $100 million was not an issue. The main argument was about whether it had been earned or not. The case ended before Bond Media and Rothwells would or could produce expert witnesses to rebut Fairfax's expert witnesses in open court.

T. E. F. Hughes, QC, had said with rhetorical flourish in his opening address, 'Commercial honour is an issue in this case.' There could be a feast for both sides on that.

Then there was the enigma of Warwick himself. Hughes had called him a 'neophyte' (Warwick said he didn't know what that meant) when he criticised James and John as directors of the company. But Rothwells's case relied on Warwick being knowledgeable in financial affairs; that is, on being anything but a neophyte. Ron Cotton, for Fairfax, in cross-examination had suggested that Warwick was knowledgeable about financial affairs, then, on re-examination by Warwick's counsel, had to confirm that Warwick was, in fact, not knowledgeable — that he was in effect, a neophyte.

The remarkable thing was that the case had not been settled before it ever reached this stage, or before it came to court. But the possibility of such settlement was complicated by the assignment of the fee to Bond Media. Neither Rothwells and its associates nor Fairfax had any reason to look forward to lengthy exposure and cross-examination in court. Alan Bond was a different matter.

Bond fought with John Fairfax Ltd for years. Like the NSW Labor Government under Neville Wran in 1984, he had withdrawn his advertising, worth about $5 million a year, from the Fairfax group in December 1986, when he did not like what had been written about his companies. After negotiations between Bond and Fairfax the advertising was reinstated shortly afterwards. The Fairfax papers, particularly the *Sydney Morning Herald*, continued to devote a good deal of space to examining the activities of the Bond group. Bond's big television investment had not been very rewarding. The Australian Broadcasting Tribunal was a pain in the neck with its inquiries into his activities. Newspapers were not under such frustrating surveillance. And, as he knew when he acquired the *West Australian* from Robert Holmes a Court, newspapers could be very profitable. Entitlement to the $100 million fee gave him leverage to prise newspaper assets out of Fairfax.

Bond made three or four offers for the Fairfax company or parts of it between April 1988 and February 1989, first through Dougherty and Connell and then through other parties. His last offer for the company, for about $2 billion if it had been available in cash, would have enabled Warwick Fairfax to walk away with a $400 million profit on the Tryart exercise as well as 20 months rare experience. That Warwick refused seemed incredible to some market watchers, including Bond advisers and supporters. But whatever Warwick's values were, they did not include an overriding regard for very large and immediate sums of cash. And despite his lack of regard for the abilities and judgement of his relatives, could he really justify buying the company in order to save it from the alleged disastrous control of James and John Fairfax, Greg Gardiner and Max Suich, only to sell it to Alan Bond, or anyone else? Much remained to be explained about Warwick

Fairfax but he acted within his known character when he turned down the offers from Alan Bond.

A successful bid for the whole of John Fairfax Ltd would have caused Bond a problem with the cross-ownership rules the Hawke Government had introduced in November 1986, the rules that had helped precipitate Fairfax into this mess. Bond could not own a television station and a daily newspaper in one capital city. Ownership of the *West Australian* had forced him to sell Channel 9, Perth. If he bought Fairfax he could not keep the *Age* and the *Sydney Morning Herald* without selling down the holding in the two Channel 9 stations in Melbourne and Sydney he had bought from Kerry Packer for nearly $1 billion less than two years previously. In May 1988, he made a bid for the *Age*, or David Syme Ltd, which would nearly have matched the bid Robert Maxwell of London had made earlier that year. But by then Fairfax was committed to keeping its newspapers. The *Age* was not for sale. But if Fairfax had sold Bond the *Age* he could not have retained control of Channel 9, Melbourne.

Fairfax had one very desirable product that would have got him around the media cross-ownership provisions: the *Australian Financial Review*. In August he tried for that as settlement of the $100 million fee. The Bond camp appeared to be convinced that Fairfax would not pay the fee because they could not, that they did not have the money. That was an explanation the Bond crew could understand. So Bond proposed that Fairfax pay in assets, such as the *Financial Review*. Fairfax maintained that they would not pay because Rothwells had not earned the fee.

In August, after Bond Media sued for payment, Alan Bond turned up the heat by threatening to sabotage the refinancing of the Fairfax debt through Drexel Burnham Lambert. Bond was a Drexel client too. In an interview with the *Bulletin* magazine, published on 9 August, he put his position with customary force. He maintained that Laurie Connell and Warwick Fairfax had been joint venturers in the takeover and that he had Warwick's signature agreeing to this on two separate documents. 'The legal advice on the collection of that money is absolute. Two QCs in Sydney have advised us that if things go his way Laurie Connell will end up with 50 per cent of Fairfax,' Bond said. On the refinancing of the Fairfax debt he said:

> I know they can probably get the financing from Drexel in Los Angeles. But I know Drexel very well. I was with them last week and I told them they will not be allowed to go ahead with that proposal until this matter is settled because it relates to selling convertible equity. Fairfax won't be able to go ahead with their financing unless that money problem is solved … Laurie Connell's got him cold as far as I can see. I told Drexel that if they wanted to do the financing, we would have to be dealt with first.

Fairfax responded by counter-suing Bond Media and Rothwells.

Bond had another reason for spurning settlement. Theoretically he was on a winner to nothing. If Fairfax did not pay up, Rothwells or Connell would have to. What that would be worth in practice was doubtful, particularly after October 1987 and, although Bond Media was a secured creditor, became much more doubtful when Rothwells went into provisional liquidation in November 1988. On 17 October 1988, Rothwells had repaid Bond Media $25 million of the $100 million fee loan, but the Bond company was still a secured creditor for $80 million (which included $5 million interest) when the provisional liquidator was appointed.

Three days after the hearing started on 17 October, Judge Giles allowed a short adjournment while the main parties again discussed a possible settlement. But they were too far apart. They went back to court and stayed there, apart from a two-week break in November, until the court rose on 16 December, for a seven-month adjournment. By then the bargaining positions had changed. Fairfax may have started at the longer odds to win the case but the odds had shortened. The legal discovery process had turned up important evidence, particularly about the fee split arrangement between Connell and Reuter and then between them and Dougherty on 22 July 1987, and about the Bond Media purchase of the fee from Rothwells in November 1987. Connell's stature as a masterful merchant banker was diminishing daily as details of his intercompany transactions in Western Australia became public, culminating, for the time being, in the appointment of a provisional liquidator to Rothwells on 3 November. There was more to come from an NCSC report on the company in May 1989.

Alan Bond was being worked over by the Australian Broadcasting Tribunal in its various examinations of whether he or his substantially-owned company, Bond Media, was a fit and proper person to hold a television broadcasting licence. He was getting an even heavier working-over by Tiny Rowlands of Lonrho, in London. The critical public exposure he was getting could affect the resilience of even Alan Bond.

The Fairfax executives were not enjoying the court case either. On the bond-selling roadshow through the US organised by Drexel they were continually asked how Warwick Fairfax could have got himself into this mess. While they were there a long, damaging article about Warwick, titled 'Wocka the Terminator' had been published in Rupert Murdoch's *Sunday Times* colour magazine in London. Was he really as tricky, obtuse, or gullible as the article, the evidence and the cross-examination suggested? The cynical American advice to the Fairfax executives on how to handle such questions was: 'Trash the owner'. It might have been expedient but it was no way to run a reputable newspaper group. Only Judge Giles knew what he thought of Warwick's evidence after six weeks of cross-examination, but the Fairfax camp seemed confident that, particularly after their discovery windfalls, they could score more heavily on cross-examination of Connell and Dougherty than Hughes, Palmer and Oslington had scored against Warwick. But such cross-examination would not take place until after 28 July 1989, when the case was due to be resumed. And the legal costs for everyone were mounting. If the case went the distance they could easily total $15 million. The outcome no longer swung on whether Rothwells had earned the fee or not, but on the external forces pushing the parties towards a settlement. Fairfax's bankers, concerned for the company's credit status, favoured a settlement, even the ANZ Bank, which had originally been against paying Rothwells anything at all after the way the Bank had been deceived.

The forces favouring settlement on the other side were even stronger. Rothwells was in provisional liquidation. Connell's commercial reputation was suffering. Bond was getting a pasting in the market and in the media. About mid-January Peter King at Fairfax had a call from Alan Bond suggesting that they talk again about settling the case. They met at Bond's office at the State Bank building in Martin Place. King might be seen in that building without comment, but if Bond called at Jones Street the takeover rumour mills would have been working overtime.

The settlement negotiations over the next six weeks were handled directly between King and Bond, with briefings from their advisers between meetings. They settled in mid-February for a payment of $27 million from Fairfax in full settlement of the $100 million claimed by Bond Media and Rothwells. Bond had already agreed with the Rothwells provisional liquidator, Ian Ferrier, that Bond could keep the $25 million it received from Rothwells a couple of weeks before Ferrier was appointed, even though this could be regarded as a preferential payment and Bond could be forced to return it if Rothwells went into liquidation. In return Bond Media would give up its rights to appear as an unsecured creditor and receive a further sum from Rothwells depending on the outcome of the Fairfax case. If Fairfax settled for between $22 million and $30 million, Rothwells would pay Bond Media $20 million and if Rothwells's unsecured creditors then received 60 cents or more in the dollar, Bond Media would get a further $5 million.

Assuming the provisional liquidator's scheme of arrangement for Rothwells was accepted by Rothwells's creditors and the Queensland Supreme Court (Rothwells was registered in Queensland) Bond Media would end up with: the $25 million Rothwells paid it just before the provisional liquidator was appointed, $27 million from Fairfax, and a prospective further $20 million or $25 million from Rothwells — a total of $72 or $78 million. This meant a loss of $23 million or $28 million plus interest on the $66 million it had borrowed from Indosuez in November 1987 — about the $30 million Sam Chisholm had mentioned before the Australian Broadcasting Tribunal. That meant ignoring the $18 million fee as a paper transaction. If the provisional liquidator's scheme fell apart the sums might have to be done all over again. But the $27 million settlement was clear. Peter King said the settlement was a successful result for Fairfax. It coincided with completion of the group's refinancing and the company could concentrate its energies on being a publisher again. Parties close to Connell and Rothwells said they had been robbed of $73 million.

In 1921, two years before he wrote *The Great Gatsby,* F. Scott Fitzgerald wrote what is now generally regarded as his best short story, 'The Diamond as Big as the Ritz'. It is a fantasy about a diamond mine in the American West owned by the Washingtons, the richest family in the world. To protect its value the mine's existence has to be kept secret. This corrupts its ownership. The story satirises the American success ethic, which equates wealth with virtue and regards money as the only significant measure of value, and of what the philosopher William James called 'the bitch-goddess, Success.' Unlike Fitzgerald's diamond, the Rothwells's fee was not a fantasy. Nor did it have the Diamond's fatal consequences. But the fee, and the lesser fees that clustered around it and grew out of it, and the events which led up to it and flowed from it, seemed a fair reflection of ethics and values in Australian financial markets in the 1980s.

# EPILOGUE

## *SIMON SAYS* . . .

At the first quarterly meeting of the new board of John Fairfax Group held at the end of September 1989, senior executives outlined the company's position and prospects. It was the only board meeting attended by William E. Simon, who had recently been appointed a director but had to resign almost immediately — the company could not afford the million dollar premiums needed to insure him against possible negligence suits in the USA, where his high profile made him an exposed target. The executives' presentation focused on the company's bank debts and the US subordinated debentures — the junk bonds — with their exotic EARs and FEARs. Simon seemed to be less than well informed about the US securities and wanted the EARs and FEARs explained to him in detail. His firm, WSGP, had been Fairfax's advisers throughout the long refinancing negotiations with Drexel, Burnham, Lambert, the ANZ and Citibank. But the matter had been handled mainly by the younger executives, Barber and Schlichting, and by Simon's partner, Gerald Parsky. At the end of the presentation, Simon offered his diagnosis: 'Warwick, you are in deep shit.'

Wherever Warwick was, William E. Simon's company, WSGP, had helped him get there. Fairfax went cold on WSGP after that. The Fairfax retainer fee, said to be over $200 000 a month, no longer helped to pay the rent at 1800 Century Park East, Los Angeles. Simon was not popular, but he was not wrong. The enormity of the company's financial problems became increasingly apparent in the following months as asset markets in North America, Japan, the UK and Australia retreated from the excesses of the 1980s. The junk bond strategies of Drexel, Burnham, Lambert had always depended on the basic proposition that asset values would keep on rising. That would allow the junk to be scrapped and refinanced in a few years, then restructured and upgraded a few years after that, with everyone, particularly Drexel, enjoying a rake-off at each round. Whether they knew it or not, this was the basis of the strategy Fairfax had taken in 1988 when they decided to

389

keep the *Age* and go Drexel's way. By continuing to revalue and write up the value of the company's newspaper mastheads, they could keep dressing up the balance sheet to show that the assets were worth more than the liabilities. Bankers would be impressed and the company would carry on. The strategy fell apart as asset values fell under the impact of high interest rates, rising bank loan defaults and corporate collapses. Fairfax had taken on the restructured $1.6 billion debt in the second half of 1988 without a long-term plan to cope with it, other than hoping, or assuming, that time, an expanding economy and inflation would look after things. In the first half of 1990 time was running out; the economy, particularly the economy of media companies dependent on advertising revenues, was contracting; and asset values had collapsed.

At the end of June 1990, on a most optimistic assessment of John Fairfax Group's financial condition, it was barely afloat. It had just earned a trading profit of over $200 million for the year. But it owed $1.7 billion to its bankers and bond holders and that was rising with deferred interest. The great cash-generating power of its newspapers (which made them so attractive to Alan Bond in 1988 as he cast around for another last throw) was enabling it to meet its cash commitments and it had broken no banking covenants. Australian banks had worse cases on their books in 1990. Fairfax's assets, which were mainly its mastheads, may have been worth $1.7 billion. On that basis Warwick's voting equity and Mary's non-voting equity were worthless. The banks and debenture holders owned the company. Even if the equities were worth $100 million or $200 million, they were disappearing fast. The company was losing $6 million a month on a true accounting basis, that is, if it had been charged with all its interest commitments instead of having them capitalised or postponed. If Warwick's and Mary's equities were worth anything, they were shrinking rapidly as the losses accumulated. If they were worth nothing, the company was broke — its liabilities exceeded its assets — and it was becoming broker. The true accounting losses, if they continued while the masthead values continued to fall, or refused to rise, would be like a swarm of white ants: first they would eat, or had already eaten, the value of the shareholders' (Warwick's and Mary's) equity; then the value of the least secured tier of debt (in this case the holders of the $150 million junior debentures issued through Drexel, Burnham, Lambert); then the value of the next tier of debt (holders of the $350 million senior debentures); and finally they would get into the values of the most secure debt of all — that of the banks, if they suffered the company to continue as John Fairfax Group for so long. At mid-1990 the banks — Citibank and ANZ — remained supportive.

There was little else they could be. The ANZ Bank's loan of over $500 million (and rising) to John Fairfax Group in 1990 represented over 5 per cent of its total domestic, commercial and industrial loan portfolio. But it probably felt comfortable compared with the banks' total exposure to the Australian media and brewing industries, the cash flow darlings of the 1980s. There were no buyers in 1990 for media and brewing assets at the values the banks had lent on a few years previously. Kerry Packer, unable to extract his $200 million out of Bond Media (for the preference shares which should have been redeemed early in 1990), managed, in a complex share conversion deal, to take control of the company, thus resuming control of the Channel Nine television stations in Sydney and Melbourne that he had sold Bond in January 1987. But that was a one-off solution to the problems of a vastly overcapitalised industry. And it removed a potential buyer of Fairfax assets if the final crunch came. Under the Federal Government's media cross-ownership rules Packer could not own those stations and the *Age* or the *Sydney Morning Herald* as well. That would leave the *Australian Financial Review* if he was still interested. Packer had met William E. Simon in North America after Simon had left the Fairfax board. Packer was part of a takeover syndicate led by Sir James Goldsmith, who was friendly with Simon. Simon indicated that, if Packer was still interested in Fairfax, then he could forget about the company. It was worthless. Warwick's equity was an illusion. The implication was that Packer could afford to wait and pick off Fairfax's prize assets as they fell. But Packer's possible acquisitions were now limited by his television holdings.

To survive, John Fairfax Group had to reduce its debt, and minor asset sales would not do this. Major asset sales could be even worse since they might not even bring their book value in a market depressed by high interest rates. The collapse of the high yield bond market in the USA offered a glimmer of hope. In February 1990, Drexel, Burnham, Lambert filed for bankruptcy protection from its creditors. In April Michael Milken agreed to plead guilty to six felony charges and to pay fines of $US600 million in an out-of-court settlement with US criminal prosecutors and the Securities and Exchange Commission (SEC). He agreed to help the prosecutors and the SEC with further investigations in the US Savings and Loans (S and Ls) industry. The S and Ls were an important part of the market network Milken had created at Drexel for the sale of high yield bonds. The collapse of the high yield bond market in the USA opened up the possibility of buying back the bonds at a fraction of their issue price, thus cancelling a lot of the debt. If John Fairfax Group, or someone acting for it, could buy back the $450 million in debentures it had issued through Drexel in 1988–89 at less than half their issue price, it could cut say $250 million off its debt and replace the purchase price of $200 million with equity. Similar thoughts had occurred to other high-yield bond issuers, including the Bond Corporation in Australia.

And they were causing some familiar noises off-stage. In Perth, Robert Holmes a Court, his fortunes substantially restored after surviving the critical year after October 1987, continued to sweep global markets for investment opportunities. As the junk bond market fell apart, the Fairfax subordinated debentures became an obvious possibility to buy at a big discount. Inquiries at Drexel about whether there was a market in the bonds met little response. On 15 February, Holmes a Court's Perth office again called Drexel in Los Angeles to talk about the possibility of making an offer for the Fairfax bonds. There was no response. It was the day the company announced its bankruptcy petition. Holmes a Court may or may not have been serious about buying those bonds even if he could get them at the right price. But he always liked to know where a play might be opening up, where a bit of bamboozling could go a long way. Holmes a Court's interest was terminated by his sudden death by heart attack on 1 September 1990.

The buy-back strategy would only work if the bond holders were convinced that they might as well take some money now and cut their losses rather than wait and see their value disappear altogether. They would be unlikely to do this while the shareholders' equity had any value. So, in lightening the load on the Fairfax ship, Warwick and Mary would have to go overboard first. The bond holders might then be prepared to jump, at a price. Where would the money come from to buy the bond holders out? That was a problem for all those companies in financial difficulties, to which the possibility of buying back their junk bonds at a heavy discount seemed to offer a way out. Their financial condition would have to be so poor that the bond holders would be prepared to sell out. But it could not be so poor that no bank would finance the buy-back. In any event, there were big technical problems in a Fairfax buy-back. There were only 35 holders of the bonds. Many were in the hands of official managers, receivers, State or Federal regulatory authorities. Any attempt to buy back the debentures or swap them for shares in a restructured John Fairfax Group could run into a legal maze. But Fairfax's survival as a company appeared to depend on eliminating, or decimating, that $450 million of debenture debt. And that could only be done by first eliminating or decimating Warwick's and Mary's equity in the company. John Fairfax Group retained Goldman Sachs to advise them in New York. Warwick retained Lazard Frères to advise him.

This emphasised a growing division of opinion and interests on the board. Were the directors there primarily to look after the interests of the shareholders, Warwick and Mary Fairfax, or of the company and its long-term survival as a viable publishing group? Bryan Kelman said later that, when Warwick asked him to be chairman a year previously, Warwick made it clear that he wanted a policy designed to ensure the future of John Fairfax Group as an entity. Kelman said Warwick's own financial stake was to be regarded as subsidiary to this. Kelman, Johnston and Anderson then proceeded with a strategy aimed at recapitalising the company to maximise its chances of survival. In their view this meant Warwick and Mary would have to sacrifice most of their equity. Warwick had been unable to bring himself to do this in 1988, and the three directors overestimated his willingness to do it in 1990.

They also overestimated the banks' willingness to take action to protect their position. Citibank and the ANZ had firm security over John Fairfax Group's assets. And they had guarantees and indemnities from some of Mary's and Warwick's private companies. They saw no need to move in any way on John Fairfax Group until a monetary covenant was broken. That could be months away and the banks themselves could keep postponing it by continuing to meet the company's commitments, such as the interest due on the US debentures early in 1991. Laurie Connell's advice might hold good for many months — 'Just ride the banks out' — and thus keep Warwick in the saddle. At the end of 1989 the National Australia Bank (NAB) tried to appoint a receiver to Bond Corporation to protect its big loan to that group, but had its nose bloodied in the Victorian Supreme Court and had to withdraw the receiver. That stirred up Bond's US junk bond holders to assert their claims on Bond Corporation. The NAB had to watch a board in which it had no confidence continue to run Bond Corporation. Citibank and the ANZ had much stronger security over John Fairfax Group than the NAB had over Bond but the Bond case made all the banks careful to avoid taking precipitate action which might stir up a legal hornet's nest. The banks also would not be eager to change the status of the John Fairfax Group loans in their own books at a time when the Reserve Bank was increasing its interest in all the banks' non-performing loans and what impact they might have on the prudential standards that the Reserve required the banks to maintain. The ANZ, Westpac and NAB all balanced their books for the year on 30 September. The write-offs, provisions and disclosures on non-performing loans would be big and embarrassing enough without unnecessarily precipitating the possibility of more.

The three Fairfax directors had underestimated the stickiness of the system, what the great strategic theorist Clausewitz called 'frictions' — the impediments that appear from unexpected quarters to stand in the way of quickly achieving an apparently well-defined goal. The proliferation of advisers was another major friction in Fairfax affairs.

Warwick had returned with his wife to live in Australia as 1990 shaped as a critical year for his future in John Fairfax Group. As usual, they were not living at or near 'Fairwater' but with friends in an unpretentious, anonymous suburban brick house in the northern suburb of Chatswood. Relations with his mother seemed to be as complex as ever. Mary Fairfax was unwilling to admit that the Fairfax equity in the company had disappeared, or was disappearing fast, but was deeply concerned at her son's efforts to assert his control and preserve what he could of that equity.

These new developments were, as usual, proving a fee feast for advisers. As Mary Fairfax became increasingly concerned at reports that the company was worth less than $2 billion, and Warwick became concerned at losing his equity, they turned (as they had in February 1987, immediately after Sir Warwick's funeral, when they were planning how Warwick should move on John Fairfax Ltd) to Keith Halkerston, the former Potter Partners stockbroker, for advice. As Baring Bros Halkerston, he had advised Warwick in March 1987 against making a takeover bid for the company. That was too wimpish for Warwick. Halkerston had, with the knowledge of the Fairfax board, advised Warwick on Fairfax's capital-raising proposals at that time, which came to nothing. Halkerston retired from the Baring Bros partnership soon afterwards and, after severe illness, had gone to live in England. He had maintained an interest in the investment advice business by taking a share of a new firm, Beerworth & Partners. Bill Beerworth, a former partner in Fairfax's old law firm, Stephen, Jaques & Stephen, was one of the corporate lawyers who found the challenges and rewards of the high-fee merchant banking industry irresistible in the 1980s. In 1986 he joined Wardleys Australia Ltd, the merchant banking arm of the Hong Kong and Shanghai Bank. Wardleys, a pacemaker in the industry in the 1980s, saw some of its biggest clients, including Bond Corporation and Rothwells, fall apart at the end of the decade. Beerworth left and set up Beerworth & Partners with Halkerston's support. Now they were advising Warwick on restructuring the debt Warwick had imposed on the company because of the takeover Halkerston had advised him against three and a half years previously.

Peter King, the company's chief executive, who had spoken for Warwick for the past two and a half years, and held the company together during the first half of 1988, had become increasingly isolated from the top management. Anderson was running the company's operations and pushing the case for debt restructuring as a matter of urgency. King had been Warwick's man. Mary Fairfax had become increasingly suspicious of him. He was more relaxed about the debt problem than the other directors. He had a rich separation agreement and retired on 9 August 1990 with a payment of over $2 million. Warwick supported his retirement but questioned the separation payment, which was approved by the board. Anderson then became chief executive, thus fulfilling Sir Warwick Fairfax's policy that only a journalist should have the top executive position at John Fairfax Ltd. Sir Warwick had been the last journalist to hold that position. The *Sydney Morning Herald*'s page one story reporting these changes was headlined: 'Boardroom Coup: Warwick Fairfax's Dream Dissolves'. The report was premature. Two weeks later Warwick reversed the coup.

To Kelman, Johnston and Anderson (being legally advised on this matter by Jim Creer of Abbott, Tout, Russell, Kennedy), the need to restructure the company's capital and debt was based on inexorable logic. (The company itself was then being advised by the law firm Gadens.) It was given added urgency by the deterioration in the Group's trading position after the March quarter of 1990. There was no chance of repeating the $200 million-plus surplus achieved in 1989–90. The group would be lucky to earn two-thirds of that in 1990–91, even with the windfall help of a strong $A which rose to well over US80 cents in the wake of the confrontation between Iraq and the USA in the Middle East. Corporate collapses and financial crises (in Victoria in particular) cut the legs from under the *Age*'s advertising revenues. The *Sydney Morning Herald* was not hit as badly as the *Age* but its net revenues were down on the previous year and falling, as were those of the *Australian Financial Review*. The revenue losses were partly offset by lower newsprint prices due to the strength of the $A. The company was well run. Its share of the market had not suffered. In the three years since Rupert Murdoch had taken over the Herald & Weekly Times, his newspapers had made no inroads into the Fairfax Group's strongholds. But newspaper earnings were very sensitive to the Australian business cycle, focused as it usually was on property, housing and the building industry, and the Fairfax newspapers' big performance in 1989–90 was achieved largely by capitalising on all the work put into them over many years. As earnings declined in 1990 they had to support continuing losses in the *Age*'s new Sunday paper, which was locked into a defensive war with Murdoch's two new Sunday papers in Melbourne. That was developing into a war of attrition similar to that between the *Sun* and the *Daily Mirror* in Sydney. The previous Fairfax management was criticised for not ending that before 1987.

On all Fairfax fronts in 1990, strong long-term strategic and day-to-day management were needed for the company to survive. To most members of the board during the first eight months of the year, the strategies were dominated by the need to restructure the debt so that the company could get on with the job of staying on top of the Australian newspaper market. Around the end of September the company's auditors and directors were expected to sign the accounts as at 30 June 1990. If the company's assets did not cover its liabilities, they would have to be satisfied that financial arrangements were in place to allow the company to continue to meet its debts — the problem they faced during the refinancing negotiations in the second half of 1988. If directors failed to satisfy themselves about the adequacy of the financial arrangements, they could be personally liable for the company's subsequent debts. To Kelman, Johnston and Anderson, the case for urgent restructuring seemed watertight. They were unaware of how strongly Warwick thought, or was about to think, otherwise. Like the Fairfax board three years previously, they were about to be ambushed. Kelman had felt so confident after King's departure on 9 August that he referred publicly to the possibility that Warwick's equity might have to be reduced to as little as 5 per cent. It had, he said, all come about because, in 1987, 'essentially, Warwick paid too much money to get the other members of the family out'. There was also talk about placing some equity with the staff.

These events revived that old spectre at 'Fairwater' that had been haunting Mary Fairfax for the last thirty years and her son for the last ten: The Managers Were Taking Over. First it had been

Henderson and McLachlan; then Gardiner and James Fairfax; now Kelman and Anderson. Mary Fairfax had another reason for concern. A restructuring at John Fairfax Group might imperil the indexed annuity of $3 million a year the company was paying Mary Fairfax. Also, some of Mary's interests, through Tailer Investments as trustee for the Jones Trust, were involved in guaranteeing and indemnifying the banks' loans to John Fairfax Group. In 1989 she had tried to remove Tailer Investments as the Jones Trust trustee and have it replayed with one of her Darwin trustee companies, Achernar Pty Ltd. Citibank quickly stopped that. The guarantees could be triggered if John Fairfax Group stated that it could not pay its debts when they fell due.

The day after King resigned, Mary Fairfax issued a brief, formal statement through Australian Associated Press:

> Lady Fairfax wishes to go on record that the report in this morning's *Sydney Morning Herald* that Warwick Fairfax's takeover of John Fairfax Ltd was encouraged by Lady Fairfax is false. Lady Fairfax was totally opposed to the privatisation of John Fairfax Ltd.

If she was, she passed up an opportunity to stymie it at the outset by announcing that she would not be accepting Warwick's offer for the shares she owned or had a say in. Unlike Vincent, James and John Fairfax she was not a director of John Fairfax Ltd and had no responsibilities to the public shareholders. Instead Warwick was allowed to claim in the takeover documents filed before the stockmarket crash of 19–20 October 1987, that he beneficially owned or controlled all Mary's equity in the company. She was certainly against the takeover after 19–20 October. But her opposition had been negotiable and she was bought off with the annuity and the payment a year later of $30 million for her Fairfax shares. Mary had preserved a substantial private fortune largely invested in property and there were no signs of her throwing this behind Warwick to shore up their crumbling position in the company. That could be throwing 'Fairwater' and 'Harrington Park', the 2GB building and two floors of the Pierre Hotel in New York after the $500 million fortune (the original Rockwood and Kinghaven shares — 24 per cent of John Fairfax

Ltd) Warwick had already lost in the biggest takeover folly of the 1980s. But Mary still had a 25 per cent non-voting interest in John Fairfax Group and was becoming increasingly concerned at what she saw as the oppressive way in which Warwick was using his 75 per cent voting interest.

Kelman quickly denied after 9 August that the restructuring plan was a management buyout. But the damage had been done. On 14 August Warwick gave notice of a meeting on 28 August at which he proposed to remove Kelman and Johnston as directors. He had wanted to give shorter notice but Mary had objected and he had to apply the statutory fourteen days. He wanted Anderson to stay as chief executive. But Anderson had been deeply involved in developing plans for which Kelman and Johnston were now being sacked. If they went, he would go too.

These were developments the ANZ and Citibank could do without. But the company had broken none of its loan covenants and the banks remained passive. Compromises were sought: the existing board would stay, joined by Halkerston and Beerworth; or Halkerston and Beerworth would act as a separate refinancing board, with Anderson continuing as chief executive but independent of that board. No compromise was acceptable.

In North America the developments were being as closely monitored by Rupert Murdoch as they were by the banks and by Mary Fairfax and her advisers (Gerry Gleeson, the former top NSW public servant, Jim Momson of lawyers Minter Ellison, and Peter Done, of the accounting firm Peat Marwick). The Fairfax camp at Jones Street was alive with reports that Murdoch had rung Warwick, urging him to put down any upstart directors and managers, even offering to find him a manager should Anderson and others resign. Murdoch had a very special interest in whatever happened at Fairfax. He still regarded the *Age* and the *Sydney Morning Herald* as among the world's most desirable newspaper properties. He had nothing to match them in Australia. With his greatly enlarged Australian newspaper operations in the last three years he had hardly laid a glove on the Fairfax Group, except for engaging them in a debilitating Sunday war in Melbourne. He had his own debt problems. His most desirable scenario, assuming he could not buy the *Age* and the *Sydney Morning*

*Herald* himself, could be for John Fairfax Group to stay in the hands of Warwick. He would not be supporting Warwick if he thought that would harm News Corporation. He had a vested interest in the Australian Government's policy of keeping foreign ownership of media (except his own) limited to small minority holdings since this would, in particular, keep Robert Maxwell's hands off the Fairfax newspapers. In London, Maxwell's *Mirror* had been eating into the market lead of Murdoch's *Sun*. He would probably prefer the group to stay together under a financially crippled owner, rather than be broken up by its bankers. The newspapers independently, under new owners, might be unpredictable, unpragmatic, as the old John Fairfax Ltd had been.

Events were moving in a familiar cycle in the Fairfax family and company: a refinancing crisis at Jones Street; fears at 'Fairwater' that the managers were taking over; Warwick quietly planning a coup and hiring a new adviser to help him do it; Murdoch trying to ensure an outcome as favourable as possible to himself; Holmes a Court making smoke signals off-stage; Mary Fairfax becoming increasingly concerned about what Warwick's activities would mean for her financial security. By 23 August, Kelman, Johnston and Anderson had had enough. They quit. Warwick Fairfax announced that Keith Halkerston would become chairman and Bill Beerworth a director. Beerworth & Partners would co-ordinate the refinancing 'to which the board will now devote itself'. The board had been doing little else for the past nine months.

The next day Warwick moved into the big corner office on the fourteenth floor of the Fairfax building, the office his father and then his half-brother James had occupied as chairmen from the late 1950s until Warwick's takeover in December 1987. He had then installed Peter King in the room and was now moving in himself. As his father had done when, energised by his marriage to Mary, he took over as chairman and chief executive, exercising his powers as a board committee of one at the end of 1969, Warwick, on 24 August 1990, called the editors and managers to see him and told them that they would in future be reporting direct to him, that he had taken over the role of chief executive, or, as it was known in 1969, managing director. That was a role his father, after forty years' experience at the top of the John Fairfax company, had been unable to sustain during the years of economic and political turmoil in the first half of the 1970s. That led to his removal as chairman in 1976 and that, in turn, led to Warwick's takeover in 1987. But, at the beginning of the 1970s, the company had been financially strong and had a strong general manager to hold it together. In August 1990, the company again faced years of economic and political turmoil following the excesses of bank lending and the corporate orgies of the 1980s. But it was a financial cripple under the control of a chairman who showed no interest in management. Warwick showed no sign of having those vital qualities of energy and attention which Murdoch brought to News Corporation and which a succession of managing directors and general managers had provided at John Fairfax Ltd for several generations.

As Warwick and his new advisers moved into Jones Street during that second week of August, the Reserve Bank's annual report was tabled in Federal Parliament. The Reserve was outspokenly critical of bank-lending policies following deregulation of the industry in the 1980s. It was concerned about how the banks were identifying and planning to cope with their problem loans and cool about banks exchanging debt for equity in problem borrowers. The Fairfax loans were not classed as problems in Citibank's and the ANZ's books since they were performing in line with expectations that they could not perform — that is, the interest had to be capitalised until later in the 1990s. The future of the company depended on the two banks. They would not move until they were absolutely forced to. At the end of August 1990, the latest valuations of the company, as a going concern, by independent experts in the merchant banking industry, varied between $1.2 billion and $1.6 billion. Most were focused at the lower end of the scale. The $1.6 billion valuation depended on there being no statutory restraints on potential buyers, no foreign investment barriers to Robert Maxwell and others, no trade practices restraints on Rupert Murdoch and others, no cross-media ownership restraints on Kerry Packer and others. It was unrealistic — at least until after 1993 when a new government might relax the ownership rules. But even on that ideal basis, Warwick had blown his $500 million family inheritance. It had taken 150 years to build, three years to lose.

Warwick's last desperate efforts, with Beerworth and Halkerston, to salvage his equity in the company, ended on the second weekend in October, 1990. Lazard Freres in New York reported that they could not find investors to put money into the company on Warwick's terms. The company was then unable to supply the certificate necessary to renew about $800 million in bill finance then falling due to the banks. On Monday, 10 December, the ANZ and Citibank had receivers appointed to all the John Fairfax Group Australian companies. It was three years and three days since Warwick and his original advisers, led by Laurie Connell, had walked into the Fairfax boardroom to take charge of the company.

# END NOTES

## CHAPTER 1

Gavin Souter's book *Company of Heralds* (Melbourne University Press, 1981) is essential reading for any understanding of the Fairfax family and company. References to the family and company before 1960 in this and subsequent chapters rely heavily on Souter's book, supplemented by my own inquiries and research. For references after 1960 I have also relied on personal experience and observations as an employee of John Fairfax Ltd until 1986, conversations with most of the people involved in the events leading up to, during and after the takeover (but not with Mary and Warwick Fairfax) and, for company structures and share-holdings, available public documents. Mary Fairfax's views on life after the takeover have been published in News Ltd's *New Idea* magazine (10 and 17 July, 4 November 1989) and in an interview by Daphne Guinness published in the *Bulletin* (10 August 1989). *New Idea* also published an interview with Marty Dougherty ('They wanted a lynching to quieten the crowd! Far from being bitter or broken, the Fairfax "scapegoat" has hit the ground running') on 4 June 1988, which emphasised what Marty called the 'massive game of bluff' that Warwick and his advisers played during September 1987. The interview included Marty's line, 'Lady Fairfax is my only former friend'.

## CHAPTER 2

Warwick Fairfax's motives for making his takeover bid for John Fairfax Ltd were well explored in evidence and cross-examination during the court case about payment of the $100 million Rothwells fee in the last quarter of 1988. He made no attempt to hide his low regard for the abilities of his relatives on the company's board or for the management.

Four days after he announced his bid to take over the company, Warwick wrote, in his neat, tense, handwriting, to his distant cousin, John Brehmer Fairfax, who was then deputy chairman of the company. The letter reflected the confusion of business judgement, idealism and arrogance that appeared to motivate Warwick in making the bid.

14.9.87

Dear John

I am writing this letter to you to express some thoughts that I perhaps should have expressed some time ago. You have written some nice letters to me welcoming me home and on my future within the company.

John, I respect you a great deal. Your commitment to the company and family heritage is probably stronger than any of the rest of us in the family. You worked your way up in the company from a cadet reporter. You learnt the business from the ground up. I can tell you that in the three months I have been back, I have learnt that many people respect you in the company. They say that you are the only Fairfax that they have seen. They certainly do not think that you are a joke. I think what most people admire about you is that you don't talk down to them. You make them feel that you are their equal. No one doubts that you are a good man.

I know that you feel very hurt now. You had a vision of another Fairfax who cared about the business coming home. You wanted those two Fairfaxes to work side by side, as Geoffrey Fairfax and James Fairfax did before. Yet, no sooner did he come home, than he stabs you in the back and tramples on you. John, I understand how you feel. I am at a loss at how to get across that this was not an attack against you.

I have a vision that has been burning a hole in my heart for some time now. It has grown during the time that I have been away. It has come from reading many cases over the last two years about successful companies. It has come from working at Chase Manhattan Bank where I felt like a very small, unimportant cog in a big machine. It has come from working at the *Los Angeles Times* last year, where there was a tremendous feeling of loyalty and team spirit.

I want John Fairfax to be a company where there is a real sense of leadership and vision. I want people to be able to say that they know where the company is going for the next 10 years. I want them to know what our long-term strategy and mission is and how they fit into that mission. In the three months since I have been back I have found that the employees are very loyal to the company and that they would much prefer to work for us rather than Murdoch. But I want more than that. I want them to feel that senior management cares about their opinions and wishes to help each employee to be the best that they can be.

Your vision for the company is probably not that different. However, I am afraid I have not taken the time to learn about your vision. I would like this afternoon to sit down and really communicate and not let any suspicion hinder that.

Though we may differ on the business side at times, let us not let the decisions we make there impact on our relationship, which is far more important. What I did last Monday was for business reasons and I felt that despite the risks, that I had no choice.

John, I really appreciate your suggesting that we meet this afternoon at your home. I was actually in the middle of writing this letter when you called. I was planning to deliver it on the weekend. But I wanted you to know what was on my heart before we met this afternoon.

Regards

Warwick.

# CHAPTER 3

The Ownership and Control of Newspapers in Britain were subject to inquiry by Royal Commission in the late 1940s. Viscount Camrose wrote his own version while he waited for the commission to be set up: *British Newspapers and their Controllers* (Cassell, 1947). Many books have been written about the British Press Lords. Parts of this chapter have been influenced by:

*Beaverbrook* by A. J. P. Taylor (Hamish Hamilton, 1972); *Beaverbrook* by Tom Driberg (Weidenfeld and Nicolson, 1956); *The Fall of the House of Beaverbrook* by Lewis Chester and Jonathon Fenby (Andre Deutsch, 1979), an account of how the capital structure of voting and non-voting shares designed to protect the family's control was no defence when the family lacked will, and the financially-strained company was divided about who should rescue it: James Goldsmith, Rupert Murdoch, Tiny Rowland, Associated Newspapers or the company it finally went to, Trafalgar Holdings; *Northcliffe* by Reginald Pound and Geoffrey Harmsworth (Cassell, 1957); *The House of Northcliffe*, by Paul Ferris (World Publishing, 1972).

Several books have been written about Rupert Murdoch and the biographers are still queuing. The best written so far is *Rupert Murdoch, A Paper Prince* by George Munster (Viking, 1985), which brings out the extraordinary parallels in Rupert Murdoch's and his father Keith's abilities to deal with political leaders in Australia and Britain, which Rupert extended to America.

Among the books about the *New York Times*, the *Washington Post* and the *Los Angeles Times* one gives a short history of all three: *The Powers that Be* by David Halberstam (Alfred A. Knopf, 1979). *The Kingdom and the Power* by Gay Talese (Action Books, 1978) and *Without Fear or Favour* by Harrison Salisbury (Times Books, 1980) are insiders' accounts of power plays and commitments in a family owned newspaper company. The official history was *The Story of the New York Times* by Meyer Berger (Simon and Schuster, 1951). More recent books about family ownership of newspapers in North America include *The Binghams of Louisville* by David Leon Chandler (Crown Publications, 1987) and *Worldly Power, The Making of the Wall Street Journal* by Edward E. Scharff (Beaufort Books, 1986).

There are notable similarities in the way women came to assume direct control of the *Washington Post* and the *Wall Street Journal* and to exercise substantial influence at the *New York Times*. The owners of the three newspapers, Eugene Meyer, C. W. Barron and Adolph Ochs, had one child (a daughter) each. Katharine Meyer married Philip Graham, Jane Barron married Hugh Bancroft, Iphigene Ochs married Arthur Hays Sulzberger.

The three sons-in-law became chief executives, or publishers, of the three newspaper companies. Bancroft could not handle the pressure of the depression years and died in 1933, some thought by suicide. Philip Graham committed suicide in 1963 and his wife Katharine Graham took over as publisher of the *Washington Post* and *Newsweek*. Iphigene Sulzberger, representing the family ownership, was a major force at the *New York Times* with her husband as publisher. As Halberstam pointed out, of the four modern publishers of the *New York Times*, she was daughter of one, wife of another, mother-in-law of the third (Orvil Dryfoos) and mother of the fourth (Arthur Ochs Sulzberger).

Jane Bancroft was the least visible of the three women in their newspaper's affairs, but when her husband died in 1933 and she assumed the responsibilities of ownership and control, she committed herself to the survival of the *Journal* by foregoing dividends and appointing top executives to achieve her goals. When Jane Bancroft died in 1949, Joseph Kennedy tried to buy the Dow Jones Co. Her elder daughter, Jessie Cox, was said to have replied, 'Grandfather's company is not for sale to anybody — at any time, at any price.'

The three American newspaper owners were just as conservative as Warwick Fairfax was in 1961 in concerning themselves with male heirs, but their daughters showed the limitations of the men-only practice of business inheritance.

The division of Warwick Oswald Fairfax's shareholdings and the build-up of James Fairfax's holdings are based on the company's share register records. Changes in directorships and share structures of The Rockwood Pastoral Co. Pty Ltd and Tailer Investments Pty Ltd are taken from Corporate Affairs Commission records in Sydney and Canberra. The transformation of the Lorimer Dods Trust into the Guilford Bell Settlement was reported to the Sydney stock exchange and the company in August 1985, but passed without notice in the press. Activities of John Walker Wynyard and his associates in the tax avoidance industry were abundantly reported in Australian newspapers in the early 1980s.

This book is substantially about the Fourth Estate factor — the unique role newspapers and their owners and controllers can have, or be assumed to have, in national political affairs. The

Fourth Estate, as a description of the press, is generally attributed to T. B. Macaulay. In his essay on Hallam's *Constitutional History of England* (included in Everyman's Library No. 225), Macaulay praised the emancipation of the press from censorship soon after the Glorious Revolution (1688), the fact that 'the Government immediately fell under the censorship of the Press' and that, following the limitation of privileges of the House of Commons after the middle of the 18th century, particularly the privilege of secrecy, 'the gallery in which the reporters sit has become a fourth estate of the realm'. (To add to the other three: nobility, clergy and commons.) Macaulay noted in his essay:

> The conflict of the 17th century was maintained by the Parliament against the Crown. The conflict which commenced in the middle of the 18th century, which still remains undecided and in which our children and our grandchildren will probably be called to act or suffer, is between a large portion of the people on the one side, and the Crown and Parliament united on the other.

That conflict, with the Fourth Estate playing a leading role, had a good run in Queensland in the 1980s.

## CHAPTER 4

Books referred to in this chapter include: *The Unauthorised Biography of Wran* by Milton Cockburn and Mike Steketee (Allen and Unwin, 1986); *The Prince and the Premier* by David Hickie (Angus and Robertson, 1985); *Ascent to Power* by Brian Dale (Allen and Unwin, 1985); *Can of Worms* by Evan Whitton (The Fairfax Library, 1986); and *I Remember* by Jack Lang (Invincible Press) — in particular, Lang's article titled 'The Night the Press Nabob Wept'.

## CHAPTER 5

John Fairfax Ltd's purchase of shares in David Syme Ltd in 1979 and reactions to it, including the Norris Inquiry into Ownership of the Press in Victoria, are described in detail in *Paperchase* by

Les Carlyon (the Herald and Weekly Times, 1982). 'Fairfax Fund-Raising — the Mystery and the Drama' by Trevor Kennedy was published in the *Bulletin* issue dated 9 October 1984.

# CHAPTER 6

The Trade Practices Commission's report (August 1989) on its investigation into the disposal of the *Sun* and *Sunday Sun* in Brisbane and the *News* in Adelaide includes a background chronology of the Commission's involvement in the newspaper industry between December 1986 and October 1988. This has references to the November 1987 proposals by News Ltd to acquire the *Canberra Times* and the *Australian Financial Review* and by Consolidated Press to acquire *Business Review Weekly.*

The report also summarises a letter from the Commission's chairman, W. R. McComas, to Ken Cowley of News Ltd, dated 19 November 1987, giving the reasons for the Commission's view of News Ltd's *Canberra Times* and *Australian Financial Review* proposals. The summary includes, 'McComas indicates further discussions would be necessary before any arrangements are made for News Ltd to acquire the *West Australian* in light of changed circumstances in the newspaper market in Western Australia.' And concludes, 'McComas indicates the Commission's view that, as News Ltd now has such prominence in the publication of newspapers in Australia, any acquisition News Ltd might contemplate would need to be looked at very carefully before the Commission could be satisfied that it should not intervene.'

# CHAPTER 7

Aspects of the business and stockmarket boom of the 1960s were reported by John Brooks in the *New Yorker* at the time. The articles, with some additions, were published in *The Go-Go Years* (Weybright and Talley, 1973) and *Business Adventures* (Victor Gollancz, 1969). The same stockmarket boom and the 1970 bust were the subjects of two books by 'Adam Smith' (the alias of George J. W. Goodman): *The Money Game* and *Supermoney*

(Random House 1967 and 1972). The short, spectacular, highly-leveraged career of Goldman Sachs Trading Corporation is described in *The Great Crash* by J. K. Galbraith (Pelican Books, 1975). The Bank of England's problems in coping with deregulation are reported in *Portrait of an Old Lady* by Stephen Fay (Penguin Books, 1988). *In Whose Interest?* by Benjamin J. Cohen, a US Council on Foreign Relations Book (Yale University Press, 1986) deals with Third World debt. The Reserve Bank of Australia's Prudential Statements, addresses by the Bank's governor and deputy governor, and research papers by bank officers are published in the Bank's monthly bulletins.

# CHAPTER 8

Evan Whitton's report of Sir Warwick Fairfax's funeral, published in the *Sydney Morning Herald* on 31 January 1987, is a treat to read and the source for details of the service given in this Chapter. The origins of Mary Fairfax's shares have been traced through the share register. Soon after Warwick Oswald Fairfax's personal holdings were transferred to The Rockwood Co. Pty Ltd in 1972, Mary Fairfax's personal holdings were transferred to Oswald Pty Ltd and later to Acrux Holdings Pty Ltd, a Darwin registered company of which Warwick and Mary Fairfax were directors.

Acrux is a two dollar company, one share held by One Hundred and Thirty Seven Pty Ltd and one by Rectify Nominees (NSW) Pty Ltd, a nominee company of Peat, Marwick, Hungerfords. One Hundred and Thirty Seven Pty Ltd, which appears to be the ultimate holding company, has two ordinary shares held by Rectify Nominees, two held by Alsim Pty Ltd and 100 A class shares held by Dandaloo Pty Ltd. Alsim's two one dollar shares are held by Acrux and Rectify. Dandaloo's shareholders are Rectify and Acherson Pty Ltd, another Darwin company 'as trustee for the Warwick Geoffrey settlement'. The narrative of talks between Warwick Geoffrey Oswald Fairfax, Marty Dougherty, Carnegie Fieldhouse and Laurie Connell is based largely on evidence in the fee court case.

# Chapter 9

'The Incredible Fairfax Affair' by Lindsay Vincent was published in the *Observer*, London, on 10 July 1988; 'Wocka the Terminator — The Vanishing Empire' by Russell Meller in the *Sunday Times* magazine, London, on 20 November 1988, and 'Warwick Fairfax, the Man Behind the Mask' by John Lyons, in the *Australian* magazine, 12–13 November 1988. *Born Again* by Charles Colson (Hodder and Stoughton, 1976) gives a revealing account of how support systems can work in the fellowship movement. *Still Dancing* by Sir Lew Grade (Fontana/Collins, 1987) includes an account of his dealings with Robert Holmes a Court. Extracts from the profile of Carnegie Fieldhouse are published with the permission of the *Law Society Journal*. The original article was published in the *Law Society Journal*, vol. 21, 1983.

References to the NCSC's investigations into Rothwells and its associates are taken from the Commission's interim report to the Mnisterial Council for Companies and Securities and from the affidavit by R. J. Schoer, the NCSC's executive director, sworn on 17 January 1989.

# Chapter 10

Fairfax's property purchases and holdings in Hunter and Hamilton Streets are based on Sydney City Council records. Statements by Rupert Murdoch, Bert Reuter, Sir Peter Abeles, Robert Holmes a Court, Laurie Connell and Marty Dougherty during the course of takeover negotiations during September are taken from reports in the *Sydney Morning Herald* and the *Australian Financial Review*. This Chapter also relies on evidence in the fee court case and in conversations with various principals and their advisers and company executives. Details of whatever underwriting agreements existed had not been revealed when the fee case closed. John Law's broadcast on 2GB is based on transcripts by Media Monitors.

# CHAPTER 11

Reactions to the 19–20 October stockmarket crash are taken from newspaper reports at the time and reactions to Rothwells's crisis and its repercussions from newspaper reports and conversations with journalists and others involved.

# CHAPTER 12

The journalists' row with Marty Dougherty and their problems with the sale agreements with Packer and Holmes a Court were partly reported in the newspapers at the time. The journalists produced their own newspaper, *On Broadway,* to cover these events. Issues of *On Broadway* had much greater detail of negotiations with, and statements by, Dougherty. The Cotton-Dougherty concerns at the time are based on evidence in the fee case. Much of the material in this chapter, however, is based on talks with the people involved in this first crisis after the takeover.

# CHAPTER 13

Whitlam Turnbull's work for John Fairfax Ltd was broadly covered by documents produced in the fee case. The Trade Practices Commission's report on the disposal by News Ltd of the *Sun* and *Sunday Sun* in Brisbane and the *News* in Adelaide includes the chronology of its role in the proposed sale of Fairfax's ANM and AAP shares to News Ltd and the subsequent sales to Fletcher Challenge and Reuters. The tax problems that had to be coped with in mid-1988 can be traced through several sources: the Treasurer's 25 May Economic Statements (page 83, 'The Taxation of Certain Dividends Received by Private Companies'); the Tax Law Amendment Bill No. 4, 1988, particularly what became Section 53 (6) of Act No. 95 of 1988; and a substantial section of the May, 1989 Fairfax Debenture Registration document filed with the SEC. This section was headed 'Australian Tax Implications of the Debt Structure for the Fairfax Group'. The SEC filing also included some details of the restructuring of John Fairfax Group in October 1989. This has been supplemented by returns at the NSW Corporate Affairs Commission giving details of the new share capital structure.

Under the October 1988 agreement, John Fairfax Group agreed to buy Acrux's 3.3 million John Fairfax Ltd shares for $30.66 million (the October 1987 agreement had provided for the shares to be bought at $8.50, the original takeover price, adjusted for rises in the Consumer Price Index). The John Fairfax group also assumed the October 1987 obligation to pay Mary, for the rest of her life, $2.9 million annually, also adjusted for rises in the Consumer Price Index (but not for falls). Mary's consent enabled Rockwood to be acquired as on 30 September from the Jones and Oriolo trusts in exchange for 24 931 A shares in John Fairfax group to Oriolo (Warwick) and 24 931 B shares to Jones (Mary). The A shares carried voting rights in the John Fairfax group. The B shares carried none. In December Warwick received a further 50 136 A shares in John Fairfax group for the Kinghaven shares in John Fairfax Ltd. Mary's B shares carried certain rights to the first $150 million available to shareholders in the event of a winding up or capital return.

Two further elements in the Rockwood buyout were revealed in the debenture issues Registration document filed with the US SEC in May 1989. As part of the deal the John Fairfax group took over $38 million of indebtedness, presumably the loan, made first by Midland and then taken over by the ANZ Bank, to buy the 1.5 million John Fairfax Ltd shares in February 1987 plus interest. Separate from this, Note 2 to the Consolidated Financial Statement included in the filing revealed that, as part of the consideration in the buyouts, 'a loan to a director amounting to $26 960 000 was extinguished'. That presumably included the loan made to Warwick to buy the Kinghaven shares from his half-brother James Fairfax late in 1987. Details of the extinguished loan were not given.

At the end of all this restructuring, John Fairfax Group (nee Tryart) was established as the holding company for the group. It had a remarkable capital structure. Its authorised capital of $302 000 300 was divided into 200 million one dollar A class ordinary shares; 100 million one dollar B class ordinary shares; 100 million one cent C class ordinary shares; 100 million one cent redeemable C class preference shares and 30 000 one cent D class redeemable preference shares. In January 1989, Warwick's company (formerly James's) Serpentine Pty Ltd was issued with 25 207 of the D preference shares. Thus in May 1989 when the debenture registration documents were filed with the SEC, the issued capital was only 75 069 one dollar A shares (Warwick's), 24 931 one dollar B shares (Mary's) and 25 207 one cent D shares (Warwick's) — a total paid up capital of $100 292.07. But most of Warwick's A shares and Mary's B shares had been issued at a premium of over $5375 a share.

This included 45 123 A shares issued to Kinghaven Pty Ltd for the 33 994 116 John Fairfax Ltd shares James Fairfax agreed to transfer to Warwick on 9 October 1987, which had helped to make the takeover possible. They were the shares James had acquired from his father over the years since 1959. They had been partly, perhaps largely, responsible for the bitterness at 'Fairwater', which led to Warwick's takeover. Warwick had acquired them from James for $22.7 million. Two years later they were valued for the John Fairfax group restructuring at over $242 million — 45 123 A shares at a premium of over $5475 a share. At Warwick's takeover price of $8.50 a share in October 1987, they would have been worth nearly $300 million. A further 5013 A shares were issued to Kinghaven for cash, possibly as part of the liquidation of the unidentified $26 million loan. In all, the 100 000 A and B shares issued to Warwick and Mary Fairfax to bring the Kinghaven and Rockwood shares under John Fairfax Group ownership carried premiums totalling over $500 million. This enabled a major clean up in John Fairfax Group's balance sheet, eliminating the minority interests and converting the $276 million deficit in shareholders' equity at 30 June 1988, into a surplus of $173 million at 31 December 1988. The stockholders' funds of the John Fairfax group represented the John Fairfax Ltd shares Warwick claimed to have controlled or beneficially owned or had a relevant interest in before the takeover. The debt of the John Fairfax group represented the balance of the money he had borrowed to buy the rest of John Fairfax Ltd.

The very large, tiered, authorised capital was partly designed to cope with the Equity Appreciation Rights (EARs) attached to the debentures raised by Drexel Burnham in the US. Internally, the John Fairfax group owned all the Sydney-based newspaper and magazine assets. It also owned Rockwood and together they owned John Fairfax Ltd. John Fairfax Ltd, the old holding company, owned David Syme and all the other operating subsidiaries, including Newcastle Newspapers, the Illawarra *Mercury* and the community newspapers. It also owned John Fairfax Group Finance, which was set up to handle the bank financing, and John Fairfax Group (USA), set up to handle the US debenture raising.

After the shock of 25 May 1988, John Fairfax Ltd and other subsidiaries stopped passing funds up as loans to John Fairfax Group to service its ANZ Bank debt until the acquisition of the Acrux and Rockwood shares was complete and John Fairfax Ltd became a wholly owned subsidiary. Advances to John Fairfax Group were resumed after that. After the refinancing early in 1989 the group planned to continue to advance funds at no interest from the subsidiaries to John Fairfax Group which would in turn use those funds to service the new group borrower, John Fairfax Group Finance. To cope with the complex tax implications of all these arrangements John Fairfax Group obtained a number of rulings from the Tax Commissioner which were expected to carry it over the transitional refinancing period until 1 July 1990, when the structure and its tax implications would be simplified.

# CHAPTER 14

Most of the material concerning the ANZ Bank's takeover facility, Bert Reuter's financial workings and discussions between the banks and Fairfax about their competing claims on Fairfax's expected flow of funds comes from documents produced in the fee case. Professor Warren Hogan's review of *Two Centuries of Panic* appeared in the *Weekend Australian* of 27–28 August 1988. Remarks by Sir William Vines and Will Bailey after the ANZ Bank's annual meeting on 18 January 1988, were quoted in the *Financial Australian* the next day. The ANZ Bank seemed slow to question the capacity of the Fairfax retirement funds to reinvest in the company. In different circumstances the bank had a windfall from its own pension funds in April 1987. Its defined benefit superannuation scheme was replaced by a new accumulation-type scheme, resulting in an actuarial surplus from which $310 million was repaid to the Bank, giving an abnormal profit of $158 million after tax. This all went as a timely addition to its provision for bad and doubtful debts — mainly Third World debt the Australian holding company took over from its UK subsidiary.

# CHAPTER 15

A profile of William E. Simon published in the *New York Times* magazine on 27 December 1987 and an article in the *Wall Street Journal* of 26 August 1986 on the Simon group's problems with its Savings and Loans investments, plus shorter pieces in both newspapers on the renaming of the University of Rochester's graduate business school provided background material on Simon. Descriptions of the refinancing and the roadshow are based on interviews with some of the key players. Details of the Equity Appreciation Rights (EARs) and Foreign Exchange Appreciation Rights (FEARs) are gleaned from the SEC debenture registration documents.

*EARs:* These were added to debentures issued through Drexel Burnham Lambert to enhance their investment attractions. Holders of EARs could be entitled to share in John Fairfax Group's present and future equity. That is, they were given the possibility of a stake in John Fairfax Group's success in working its way out of its extreme debt burden. EARs, or warrants to acquire EARs, were also issued to Drexel Burnham Lambert, WSGP International and some executives at the John Fairfax group. Initially, on 27 January 1989, 25 000 EARs were issued. There were also warrants to acquire an additional 14 489 EARs. The EARs, like all John Fairfax Group shares, were mortgaged to the banks — Citibank and the ANZ — which own the EARs until the mortgage terminates. In the meantime the EARs are represented by Depositary Receipts issued by the Bankers Trust Company. The Depositary Receipts would be exchangeable for EARs when the banks' mortgages ended. Warrants for the purchase of 14 489 Depositary Receipts had an exercise price of $500 per Depositary Receipt. In all, the EARs represented the possibility of receiving about 40 per cent of John

Fairfax Group's fully diluted equity, every 1000 EARs representing the right to one per cent. The EARs could be exercised at either the company's call, or the holder's put option in staggered annual amounts between 30 January 1995 and 30 January 1998, or totally on the latter date. John Fairfax Group had the option of paying the EARs out in cash, by the issue of 10-year junior subordinated Australian dollar debentures, or by issuing C class ordinary shares. The method of payment must be approved by the banks.

Each EAR would entitle the holder to 1667 C shares, adjusted for capital changes at John Fairfax Group. That was based on John Fairfax Group's paid up ordinary share capital of $100 000 at 27 January 1989. The capital was made up of the 75 069 one dollar A shares owned by Warwick and 24 931 Australian dollar B shares owned by Mary Fairfax. (Warwick also had 25 207 one cent D class redeemable preference shares, which were irrelevant for equity calculations.) Fully diluted to allow for 40 per cent of the equity to be issued for the EARs, the ordinary capital would have been $166 666.67. Every 1000 EARs was worth one per cent of this $1666.67. Each EAR would be worth $1.667 in one cent shares.

The amount of cash or the face value of junior subordinated debentures payable in satisfaction of an EAR would be the fair market value of the C shares issuable at any time. The fair market value would be determined by two internationally recognised investment banking firms located in America and Australia, one chosen by the EARs agent and one by John Fairfax Group. If the two banks cannot agree within a certain time they select a third investment bank, which would make a conclusive valuation. The company has to be valued on an on-going basis. The EARs holders' put options could be triggered by a substantial sale of assets or public share flotation by Fairfax or one of its affiliates, and EARs holders would have to share in any distribution in cash or kind on John Fairfax Group's ordinary shares as if the EARs had been converted to C shares when the distribution was made. This would not apply to dividends on new equity securities totalling up to $300 million.

*FEARs:* Unlike EARs, which have a life of their own unattached to the debentures, FEARs were non-detachable. They went wherever the debentures went to preserve the original American dollar value of the debentures at maturity. The capital letters FEARs made a neat rhyming acronym to go with EARs but from the company's point of view the FEARs were Foreign Exchange Depreciation Liabilities (FEDLs). With FEARs, or FEDLs, the company underwrote, within limits, any losses a US debenture holder would incur if, at maturity, the Australian dollar was worth less against the American dollar than it was at the date of issue. This starting rate, in January 1989, was 88.186 US cents to the Australian dollar. That was around the highest level the Australian dollar had reached against the American dollar in four years. It had been as low as 57.10 US cents in July 1986 and around 80 cents between June and early October 1988 when Drexel's refinancing package was being put together. The foreign exchange risks for US investors in the Australian dollar securities were always evident. The delays in finalising the issue, which meant the base exchange rate was fixed at 88.186 US cents in January, rather than 80 cents or less in September or October, substantially increased the company's potential foreign exchange liability. The liability is limited to $A163 million for the senior subordinated debentures and $A67 million for the subordinated debentures.

The company's underwriting cuts out if and when the Australian dollar falls to 59 US cents. The underwriting thus covers the full range of the movement in the exchange rate between the two currencies over the four years before the issues. In addition, the company underwrote any fall in the American dollar equivalent of any subordinated debentures issued in satisfaction of interest payments on the original issue with a limit of 45 per cent of the principal amount of the additional debentures. Cash dividend payments are made in Australian dollars or in American dollars based on the exchange rate at the time the twice-yearly payments are made. Anything could happen to the exchange rate between the two currencies over the 12 years following the debenture issues. The senior debentures mature in 2000 and the debentures in 2001. But it was unfortunate for the company that the sub-ordinated debentures with the attached FEARs or FEDLs were issued when the Australian dollar was around its highest value against the American dollar in over four years.

# CHAPTER 16

'Wocka' is a natural familiar for Warwick and may have been applied before Owen Thompson, an ex-editor of the *Australian* and later managing director of Melbourne *Truth*, tagged Sir Warwick Fairfax Wocka in Bourke, western NSW, in the early 1970s. Thompson was staying at the Railway Hotel, gathering material for a substantial piece on the wool industry when Sir Warwick and young Warwick arrived on a motoring tour of western NSW. They sat at the table Thompson had been occupying by himself in the hotel dining room. Warwick Fairfax introduced himself and his son and spoke at some length on the Greek philosophers. The Fairfax drivers sat at another table. Thompson thought the conversation should be brought back to Bourke and called Sir Warwick Wocka, and referred to him, and introduced him as such, for the remainder of his stay.

This did not trouble Sir Warwick (as Hacca did Robert Holmes a Court). The story spread and Wocka was attached to the Fairfaxes, father and son, mainly by journalists and others telling stories about them but not, like Thompson, in their presence. Some years later, Sir Warwick and Owen Thompson sat next to each other at an official function and Sir Warwick accused Thompson of deceiving him by not revealing what he was doing in Bourke. But as Thompson pointed out to him, Wocka had not said that he controlled the *Sydney Morning Herald*, either.

The legal line-up before Justice Giles in the fee case which started on 17 October 1988 was:

(1) For Bond Media and Rothwells — T. E. F. Hughes, QC, assisted by Dyson Heydon, QC, and two senior juniors, Francis Douglas, who became a QC while the case was being heard, and Stephen Archer. They were instructed by Allen, Allen and Hemsley, whose partner coordinating the case was Paddy Jones, assisted by two junior solicitors, Michael Rose and Catherine Drayton.

(2) For John Fairfax Ltd: Neil McPhee, QC, assisted by W. W. Caldwell, QC, Stephen Rares and Michael Ellicott. They were instructed by Mallesons Stephen Jaques whose three partners

on the case were led by Richard Feetham. The others were
Gerald Raftesath and Belinda Gibson.

(3) For Martin Dougherty: George Palmer, QC, with Peter Gray
as junior. They were instructed by Danny Gilbert of Gilbert
and Tobin.

(4) For Bert Reuter: Bruce Oslington, QC, with John Graves as
junior. They were instructed by Tim Peken of Sly and Weigall
(of which Danny Gilbert and Tony Tobin had been former
partners).

# Chronology

**1959**    *June*    Warwick Oswald Fairfax sells half his Fairfax shareholding (the Kinghaven shares) to James Fairfax on extended payment terms.

       *3-4 July*    W. O. Fairfax marries Mary Symonds.

**1960**    *2 Dec.*    Warwick Geoffrey Oswald Fairfax born.

**1961**    *12 Jan.*    James Fairfax undertakes that control of the Kinghaven shares will eventually pass to W. G. O. Fairfax.

       *13 Jan.*    W. O. Fairfax resigns chairmanship of John Fairfax Ltd (JFL).

       *11 March*    W. O. Fairfax re-appointed chairman after settling Cedric Symonds's claims.

**1972**    *Feb.*    W. O. Fairfax acquires The Rockford Pastoral Co. Pty Ltd to hold his shares in JFL. Tailer Investments Pty Ltd established in Canberra to act as trustee. Jones and Oriolo trusts established.

**1976**    *1 May*    Wran-led Labor wins NSW elections.

       *21 Oct.*    W. O. Fairfax, following growing criticism by other directors, says he will retire as chairman in four months.

**1977**    *1 March*    James Fairfax appointed chairman.

**1979**    *20 Nov.*    Murdoch bids for the Herald & Weekly Times (HWT).

       *22 Nov.*    Murdoch sells out of the HWT; withdraws bid.

       *23 Nov.*    JFL acquires 14.9 per cent of the HWT.

**1980**    *1 Nov.*    G. J. Gardiner appointed general manager of JFL.

**1983**    *5 March*    Hawke-led Labor wins Federal elections.

**1984**    *Sept./Oct.*    JFL proposes issue of participating preference shares. W. O. Fairfax and family ('Fairwater') against issue. Proposal withdrawn.

| **1985** | *22 Aug.* | Guilford Bell Settlement — James Fairfax deeds control of the Kinghaven shares, on his death, to W. G. O. Fairfax. |
|---|---|---|
| **1986** | *March* | US prosecutors start investigating possible securities fraud at Drexel Burnham Lambert. |
| | *25 Nov.* | Labor Government changes TV station and cross-media ownership rules. |
| | *3 Dec.* | Murdoch bids for the HWT, starting a two-month takeover war. |
| **1987** | *14 Jan.* | W. O. Fairfax dies. |
| | *20 Jan.* | Bond buys Packer's TV and radio interests for $1050 million. |
| | *30 Jan.* | W. O. Fairfax's funeral. |
| | *7 Feb.* | Murdoch wins the HWT takeover war. JFL buys HSV7. |
| | *17 Feb.* | The Rockwood Pastoral Co. Pty Ltd, on W. G. O. Fairfax's instructions, buys 1 500 000 JFL shares for $30 million. |
| | *19 Feb.* | Bert Reuter leaves Bell group. |
| | *Feb.* | W. G. O. Fairfax (Warwick) asks Barings what he should do next. |
| | *March* | Baring Bros Halkerston suggests gradual build-up in Warwick's position in JFL. NCSC becomes interested in Rothwells and Vital Technology. |
| | *April* | Warwick rejects Baring's advice, talks to M. Dougherty. Dougherty talks to L. Connell. Connell engages Reuter to work on takeover project. |
| | *29 June* | Warwick joins marketing department of JFL. |
| | *11 July* | Labor Government returned in Federal election. |
| | *22 July* | Connell agrees to run the takeover for $100 million. Splits the fee with Reuter after Dougherty gets 10 per cent. |
| | *23 July* | JFL sells TV interests to Skase. |

**1987**   *3 Aug.*   Reuter joins board of Connell's company, Vital Technology.

*mid-Aug.*   NCSC interested in share dealings in Rothwells associates.

*18 Aug.*   Connell switches his fee to Rothwells.

*19 Aug.*   Reuter approaches ANZ Bank for takeover finance.

*28 Aug.*   Tryart set up. ANZ approves $1.7 billion finance. Tryart Agreement signed.

*30 Aug.*   Warwick calls on James and John B. Fairfax and G. J. Gardiner to tell them of next day's bid.

*31 Aug.*   Warwick, through Tryart, bids $7.50 a share for JFL.

*21-25 Sept.*   Takeover appears to come together at $8.50 a share with share swap alternatives and assets sales to J. B. Fairfax, K. Packer and R. Holmes a Court.

*Sept.*   NCSC intensifies Rothwells investigations.

*9 Oct.*   Formal agreements with James and John B. Fairfax for sale of their shares to Tryart and sale of James's Kinghaven interest to Warwick. Tryart files Part 'A' takeover statement with Corporate Affairs Commission (CAC) in Canberra.

*19-20 Oct.*   Stockmarket crashes. Heavy withdrawals start from Rothwells.

*20 Oct.*   Mary Fairfax at Regent Hotel wants Warwick to call off bid. Warwick won't see her.

*21 Oct.*   Warwick confirms bid will proceed. D. Syme share issue cancelled. JFL will sell Australian Newsprint Mills (ANM) and Australian Associated Press (AAP) shares instead.

*24 Oct.*   News Ltd agrees to buy ANM and AAP shares for $275 million.

*24 Oct. w/e*   Depositors rush Rothwells for withdrawals.

*25 Oct.*   Rescue organised by WA Inc. for Rothwells.

**1987**    *26 Oct.*    JFL board decide to recommend Tryart's offer.

*27 Oct.*    Tryart files its adjusted offer of $8.50 cash only. Date of first agreement with Mary Fairfax. Warwick agrees to pay her $2.9 million a year for life.

*28 Oct.*    JFL board files its statement recommending acceptance.

*29 Oct.*    Vrisakis negotiates with NCSC to call off Rothwells investigation.

*1 Nov.*    Rothwells seeks to discount the $100 million fee due from Warwick.

*8 Nov. w/e*    Fee to be discounted first by State Bank of NSW, then by Thomas Nationwide Transport (TNT). Warwick seeks Reuter's advice. Reuter seeks legal advice on his 45 per cent share. Alan Bond instructs Bond Media to discount the fee.

*9 Nov.*    Warwick agrees to assign payment of fee to Bond Media. Fee payment due 28 June 1988.

*10 Nov.*    Tryart claims ninety per cent of JFL shares. ANZ's $2.1 billion takeover facility signed.

*12 Nov.*    News Ltd seeks the reaction of Trade Practices Commission (TPC) to possible purchase of the *Australian Financial Review* and the *Canberra Times.*

*19 Nov.*    TPC indicates either purchase would contravene the Trade Practices Act. 'Further discussions' would be needed before News could acquire the *West Australian.* TPC also advises Packer that acquisition of *Business Review Weekly (BRW)* would contravene the Act. Rothwells-Bond Media fee deal settled. Bond Media lends Rothwells $100 million. Rothwells assigns fee to Bond Media.

*22 Nov.*    Rothwells loses its securities dealer's licence.

**1987**   *24 Nov.*   Problems with Skase payments for JFL's TV interests.

   *27 Nov.*   TPC freezes deal with News on ANM and AAP shares.

   *1 Dec.*   Problems with National Australia Bank (NAB) over repayment of loan.

   *3 Dec.*   Problems with Westpac over repayment of loan.

   *7 Dec.*   Warwick takes over. Old board leaves. Connell, Dougherty, Cotton, King appointed directors. Skase's first payment of $340 million doesn't arrive.

   *8 Dec.*   Victory dinner at 'Fairwater'.

   *9 Dec.*   Holmes a Court tells Bell annual general meeting in Perth he will put Macquarie Broadcasting back to JFL and of other problems with sale contract.

   *11 Dec.*   Packer's expected payment of $250 million doesn't arrive. John B. Fairfax's expected payment of $78 million doesn't arrive.

   *9-16 Dec.*   Problems with all the asset sales contracts and reinvestment of superannuation funds.

   *15 Dec.*   Holmes a Court's expected payment of $125 million doesn't arrive.

   *16 Dec.*   NCSC agrees, under certain conditions, not to pursue Rothwells and Connell.

   *21 Dec.*   News Ltd's expected payment of $275 million doesn't arrive. Purchase of ANM and AAP shares frozen by Federal Court. Dougherty and Reuter go overseas on holidays.

   *24 Dec.*   First scaled down payment of $282 million received from Skase.

   *29 Dec.*   Westpac takes action against JFL in ACT Supreme Court.

   *31 Dec.*   NAB takes action against JFL.

| **1988** | *4 Jan.* | Dougherty returns from holidays. |
| | *6 Jan.* | JFL board meets ANZ bankers. Where are the asset sales? Malcolm Turnbull arrives. |
| | *7 Jan.* | Whitlam Turnbull arrange $13 million to pay out First National. |
| | *8 Jan.* | Dougherty concludes revised deal with Packer for $211.6 million. |
| | *11 Jan.* | Packer's $211.6 million arrives. |
| | *13 Jan.* | Whitlam Turnbull arranging $500 million loan to pay out Westpac, NAB and merchant banks. |
| | *16 Jan.* | J. B. Fairfax's first payment of $48.5 million arrives. |
| | *18 Jan.* | JFL board meeting. Connell: 'Just ride the banks out.' Reuter returns from holidays. In Melbourne, ANZ chairman, Sir William Vines says the bank is 'pretty comfortable with Tryart'. Whitlam Turnbull lines up $500 million from Citibank to support ANZ. |
| | *27 Jan.* | Citibank formally offers $500 million to settle the other banks. |
| | *2 Feb.* | Asset sales to Holmes a Court cancelled. |
| | *8 Feb.* | Robert Maxwell's first 'outline of an offer' for JFL assets. |
| | *10 Feb.* | Journalists strike. Anderson and senior journalists resign. Cotton calls Warwick in Washington and King in South Africa. |
| | *12 Feb.* | Maxwell's second proposed offer. |
| | *13-14 Feb.* | Warwick and King arrive in Sydney. King raises doubts about paying $100 million fee. |
| | *15 Feb.* | Dougherty sacked — paid $3 million. |
| | *16 Feb.* | Anderson returns and joins JFL board. |
| | *19 Feb.* | J. B. Fairfax's final payment of $17 million arrives. Purchase of Macquarie Publications for $11 million cancelled. |

**1988**   *3 March*   Whitlam Turnbull for JFL makes counter offer to Maxwell.

*7 March*   JFL announces intention to keep the *Australian Financial Review*.

*8 March*   Maxwell suggests counter-counter offer.

*14 March*   Connell forced to resign. The *Sun* and *Times on Sunday* closed.

*21 March*   King and Turnbull talk to Maxwell in Paris.

*28 March*   Citibank loan drawn down. Other banks paid out.

*10 April*   Warwick and King meet Drexel Burnham Lambert in Los Angeles through William E. Simon's company, WSGP. Milken says, 'It's do-able.'

*11 April*   JFL considers debt strategy to keep the *Age*.

*April*   $222.5 million from Fletcher Challenge for ANM shares arrives.

*18 April*   JFL board decides to keep the *Age* and retain WSGP on US financing. Whitlam Turnbull connection fades.

*25 April*   Drexel's advance party arrives.

*26 April*   WSGP's advance party arrives.

*May*   $67.5 million plus interest from Reuters for AAP shares arrive.

*5 May*   Connell and Dougherty talk to King on possible offer by Alan Bond for all or part of JFL including $800 million for the *Age*.

*25 May*   Keating's economic statement puts possible tax liability of $500 million on JFL.

*28 June*   Tryart does not pay $100 million fee to Bond Media.

*4 July*   Bond Media and Rothwells start legal action to recover fee.

**1988**  *July–Aug.*  Citibank and ANZ advise John Fairfax Group
(JFG — formerly Tryart) it is in default on
their loans. Bank interest being capitalised
at $4 million a week.

*12 July*  Drexel credit committee approves Fairfax
financing project.

*Aug.*  Bond tries for the *Australian Financial Review*
as settlement for disputed fee.

*9 Aug.*  *Bulletin* article quotes Bond threat to JFG's
Drexel financing.

*14 Aug.*  JFG seeks damages of at least $160 million from
Rothwells and Bond Media.

*31 Aug.*  Amending tax legislation introduced to House
of Reps allowing JFG a way out of possible May
impost.

*9 Sept.*  Dougherty and Reuter joined in JFG's damages
claim.

*20 Sept.*  JFG to buy Mary Fairfax's Acrux shares in JFL for
$30.76 million and take on payment of her $2.9
million indexed annuity. JFG to buy Rockwood
by issuing shares to Jones and Oriolo trusts.

*Sept.*  US Securities and Exchange Commission
charges Drexel and Michael Milken with
insider trading and stock fraud.

*1 Oct.*  Mary Fairfax (second agreement) signs
Rockwood rearrangement about 4 a.m.

*17 Oct.*  Bond Media-JFG case starts before Justice Giles
in the NSW Supreme Court.

*19 Oct.*  Warwick enters witness box in fee case.
Amending tax legislation passes through House
of Representatives.

*27 Oct.*  T. E. F. Hughes, QC asks Warwick: 'Is the
company viable?' Court in closed sessions.

*3 Nov.*  Provisional liquidator appointed to Rothwells.

*8 Nov.*  Amending tax legislation passes through Senate.

**1988**  *Nov.*  JFG executives join Drexel's US roadshow selling JFG debentures. Talks with AMP Society on possible equity in JFG.

*21 Nov.*  Governor-General's assent to amending tax legislation.

*30 Nov.*  Warwick leaves witness box in fee case.

*1 Dec.*  Justice Giles says that after the Christmas break, the fee case will adjourn for seven months.

*16 Dec.*  Fee case adjourns until 28 July 1989.

*23 Dec.*  Drexel pleads guilty to six felony counts, agrees to pay $760 million in fines and compensation. Auditors Touche Ross sign JFG accounts.

**1989**  *4 Jan.*  Bond representatives suggest an offer of $2.1 billion for JFG.

*16 Jan.*  NCSC claims conditions of the 16 December 1987 agreement with Rothwells were never fulfilled.

*mid-Jan.*  Bond contacts King about settling the fee case.

*27 Jan.*  Refinancing through Citibank, ANZ and Drexel completed. Drexel's cheque for $450 million arrives.

*4 Feb.*  Fairfax and Bond agree on payment of $27
*w/e*  million in full settlement of $100 million fee.

*Feb.–*  Australian Broadcasting Tribunal inquiry into
*March*  Bond TV licences. Lonrho questions Bond Corp's viability.

*April*  Warwick and Mary Fairfax and executives attend Drexel's annual junk bond conference (Predators' Ball) in Los Angeles.

*July–Aug.*  New JFG directors appointed: B. Kelman (chairman), R. Johnston, W. E. Simon.

*20 Aug.*  Sunday newspapers start in Melbourne.

*30 Sept.*  JFG board meeting. Simon resigns, offers his opinion of JFG's position and prospects.

**1989**  *Oct.*  WSGP retainer terminated. Macquarie Bank appointed to look at future financing. Goldman Sachs for US advice. Warwick appoints Lazard Freres for his advice. He later appoints Beerworth and Partners for Australian advice.

*20 Nov.*  Skase companies in receivership.

**1990**  *14 Feb.*  Drexel Burnham Lambert files for bankruptcy.

*25 April*  Milken pleads guilty to felony charges, agrees to pay fines of $600 million and assist investigation of Savings and Loans institutions.

*July*  Packer acquires control of Bond Media.

*9 Aug.*  Peter King resigns from JFG. Company talks of urgent need for restructuring its capital.

*July–Aug.*  Newspaper reports suggest Warwick will have to surrender control in recapitalisation of the company.

*9 Aug.*  Peter King resigns. C. J. Anderson appointed chief executive. Warwick silent. Bryan Kelman says loss of Warwick's control is central to any debt restructuring.

*10 Aug.*  Mary Fairfax says she was totally opposed to the privatisation of John Fairfax Ltd.

*14 Aug.*  Warwick gives notice of meeting on 28 August to remove Kelman and Johnston as directors.

*16 Aug.*  Keith Halkerston and Bill Beerworth appear as Warwick's advisers.

*23 Aug.*  Kelman, Johnston, Anderson resign. Halkerston, Beerworth invited to join board.

*24 Aug.*  Warwick breaks twenty-one months' silence; announces the main task is to refinance; moves into chairman's office and assumes role of chief executive.

*10 Dec.*  Dee Nicholl of Deloitte Ross Tohmatsu appointed receiver to all John Fairfax Group Australian companies.

# THE FAIRFAX COMPANY
## BEFORE THE TAKEOVER

### THE 'FAIRWATER' FAIRFAXES
- The Rockwood Pastoral Co. Pty Ltd (Warwick and Mary), 12.8 per cent
- Acrux Holdings Pty Ltd (Mary), 1.1 per cent
- Other family, 0.6 per cent

### THE COMPANY (JONES STREET) FAIRFAXES
- James, 17.1 per cent
- Vincent, John B. and family, 14.5 per cent
- Other family, 4.1 per cent

## JOHN FAIRFAX LTD

### MAIN NEWSPAPERS

*Sydney Morning Herald*
*Sun*
*Sun-Herald*
*Australian Financial Review*
*Times on Sunday*
*Canberra Times*
*Newcastle Herald*
*Illawarra Mercury*
Sydney and Newcastle Community Newspapers

**David Syme**

*Age*
*Warrnambool Standard*
Syme Community Newspapers (Melbourne and Victorian country)

**Fourth Estate (NZ)**

*National Business Review*

### RADIO
**Macquarie Broadcasting**
2GB (Sydney)
2CA (Canberra)
2WL (Wollongong)
3AW (Melbourne)
4BH (Brisbane)
4RR (Townsville)
5DN (Adelaide)

### MAGAZINES
**Fairfax Magazines**

*Woman's Day*
*Cosmopolitan*
*Dolly*
*People*
*Smash Hits*
*Electronics Australia*
*Good Housekeeping*
*Harper's Bazaar*

**Syme Magazines**
Sports, motoring and lifestyle magazines

**Business Magazines**
*Business Review Weekly*
*Personal Investment*
*Australian Property News*

**Others**
*Good Weekend*
*Spectator* (UK)
*Time Australia* (50 per cent)
*Money Magazine* (UK)

### TELEVISION
ATN 7 (Sydney)
BTQ 7 (Brisbane)
HSV 7 (Melbourne)
(all sold in August 1987)

## INVESTMENTS
Australian Newsprint Mills, Rural Press, Macquarie Publications (Dubbo)
Australian Associated Press, Eastern Suburbs Newspapers

# THE FAIRFAX COMPANY
## AFTER THE TAKEOVER

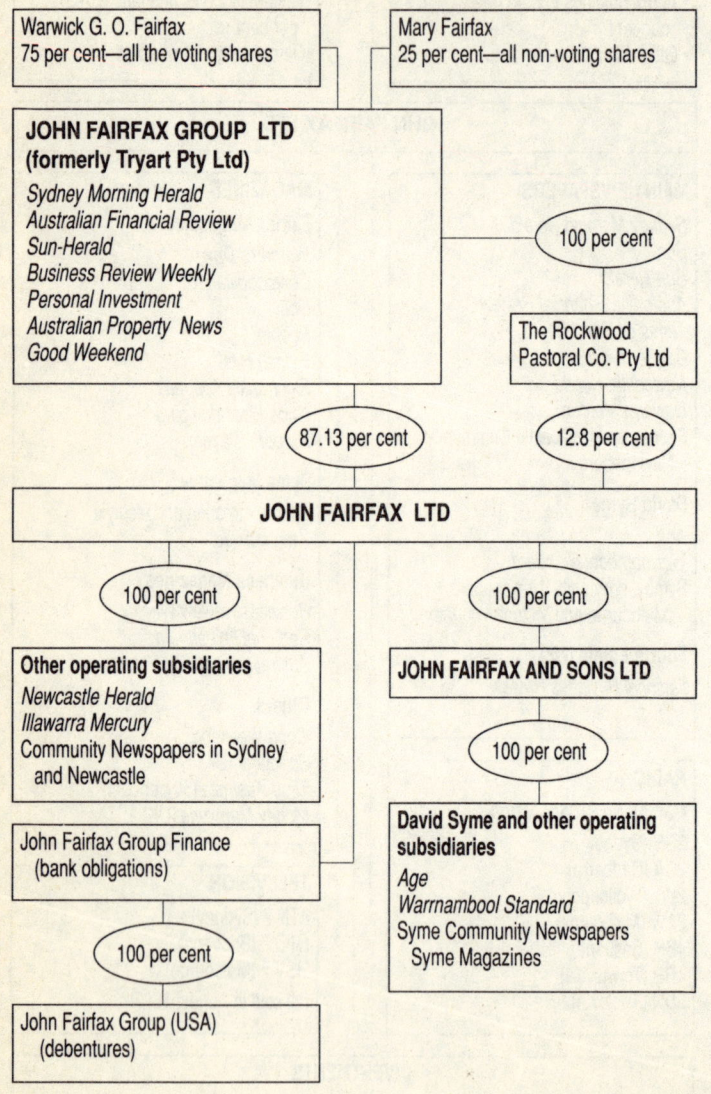

Warwick G. O. Fairfax
75 per cent—all the voting shares

Mary Fairfax
25 per cent—all non-voting shares

**JOHN FAIRFAX GROUP LTD**
**(formerly Tryart Pty Ltd)**

*Sydney Morning Herald*
*Australian Financial Review*
*Sun-Herald*
*Business Review Weekly*
*Personal Investment*
*Australian Property News*
*Good Weekend*

100 per cent

The Rockwood
Pastoral Co. Pty Ltd

87.13 per cent

12.8 per cent

**JOHN FAIRFAX LTD**

100 per cent

100 per cent

**Other operating subsidiaries**

*Newcastle Herald*
*Illawarra Mercury*
Community Newspapers in Sydney
   and Newcastle

**JOHN FAIRFAX AND SONS LTD**

100 per cent

John Fairfax Group Finance
   (bank obligations)

**David Syme and other operating**
**subsidiaries**

*Age*
*Warrnambool Standard*
Syme Community Newspapers
   Syme Magazines

100 per cent

John Fairfax Group (USA)
   (debentures)

# INDEX